DATE DUE

GAYLORD			PRINTED IN U.S.A.

LINCOLN AND THE COURT

LINCOLN AND THE COURT

Brian McGinty

HARVARD UNIVERSITY PRESS

Cambridge, Massachusetts · London, England — 2008

Library of Congress Cataloging-in-Publication Data
McGinty, Brian.
Lincoln and the Court / Brian McGinty.
p.   cm.
Includes bibliographical references and index.
ISBN-13: 978-0-674-02655-1 (alk. paper)
ISBN-10: 0-674-02655-1 (alk. paper)
1. United States. Supreme Court—History.   2. United States. Supreme Court—Biography.
3. Constitutional history—United States.   I. Title.
KF8742.M32   2008
347.73'2609—dc22   2007028163

To the memory of

SAMUEL WITT EATON,
chaplain, Seventh Wisconsin Volunteers (1862–1865),

and

MANASSEH BENJAMIN McGINTY,
second lieutenant, Phillips Legion Infantry,
Blackwell Volunteers, Georgia (1862–1865),

my great-great-grandfathers
in Blue and Gray

Contents

"A Gallery of Justices" follows page 144

Introduction

THE STORY OF Lincoln and the Supreme Court has been neglected for too long. Innumerable studies of the Civil War have almost wholly ignored Lincoln's relations with the Court and the role that it played in resolving the agonizing issues raised by the conflict. Lincoln's biographers, too, have slighted his role in appointing Supreme Court justices, and the effect his appointments had in shaping constitutional doctrine, both during the war and after. A recent study of Lincoln and Chief Justice Taney probed some of the issues that separated the wartime president from the Court's presiding justice, but it largely ignored the broader problems that the president confronted in his relations with the associate justices, and with the Court as an institution.[1]

On one level at least, this neglect is entirely understandable, for the military issues of the war were always more pressing than the legal issues, and they demanded more immediate attention. Men were dying on the nation's battlefields while lawyers and judges in Washington and elsewhere were debating the legality of secession, suspension of habeas corpus, imposition of martial law, legal tender, and the blockade of Southern ports. But not far beneath the surface of the battles and skirmishes, sieges and campaigns, the legal issues stirred uneasily.

The Civil War was, at its heart, a legal struggle between two competing theories of constitutional law. The first was that the United States was a league of sovereign states whose legal ties were severable at any time and for any reason, subject only to the political judgment of the severing states that the cause for the separation was sufficient. The second was that the United States was a permanent union of states, created by a sovereign "people of the United States" and tied together by a "supreme law" that created firm bonds of nationhood.[2] Whether secession was or was not permissible would be decided, in the first instance, by the armies and navies, the generals and admirals, the foot soldiers and sailors locked in deadly combat. Ultimately, however, the question would be argued by lawyers and judges, and submitted for judgment to the Supreme Court, in whose hands the power (and awesome responsibility) of interpreting the Constitution was entrusted. While the issues were being thrashed out in battle, they were also being contested in the courtroom of the Supreme Court in Washington.

Relations between Lincoln and the Supreme Court have a just claim on the attention of history. Lincoln was, more than any other chief executive in the nation's history, a "lawyerly" president. He was, of course, a veteran politician, steeped in the arts of persuasion and compromise, advancing proposals, building alliances, staking out positions, and ultimately counting votes. But he was also an experienced lawyer, the veteran of thousands of courtroom battles, where victories were won not by raw strength or superior numbers, but by appeals to reason and citations of precedent. For almost twenty-five years he made the law his occupation, representing clients, addressing juries, arguing appeals, drafting contracts, wills, and deeds. It was an honorable calling, and one that Lincoln found both financially and emotionally satisfying. But Lincoln's law practice was much more than a way for him to support himself and his family. It provided a framework for his outlook on life, a focus for his public and private energies, and a discipline for his political efforts, which continued through most of his adult life (although with wildly varying levels of success).

Many young men in nineteenth-century America became lawyers first and sought political office thereafter, often to gain notoriety and attract clients. Lincoln, in contrast, developed his interest in politics at about the same time that he became interested in the law. In the early 1830s, he began to read law books and to help his neighbors in New Salem, Illinois, draft legal documents and argue cases in the local justice court. At the same time, he made his first (unsuccessful) effort to win political office. He did not study law in a systematic way until he was elected to the Illinois legislature in 1834, although he had yearned to do so earlier.

His admission to the bar in 1837, and his growing involvement in the activities of the Whig political party, confirmed his belief in the importance of *law* and *order* in a self-governing society. Without order, a society would disintegrate into anarchy; without law, self-government would give way to tyranny and oppression. One of his first major public addresses, delivered to the Young Men's Lyceum of Springfield, Illinois, in 1838, was a plea for social order and respect for the law, in which he urged "reverence for the Constitution and laws" and exhorted "every American, every lover of liberty, every well wisher to his posterity" to swear "never to violate in the least particular, the laws of the country; and never to tolerate their violation by others."[3] As legal historian Mark E. Steiner has pointed out, the Whig Party "attracted lawyers because of the congruence between the Whig commitment to order and tradition and the lawyers' attachment to order and precedent."[4] In his Lyceum speech, Lincoln said that "reverence for the laws" should be "breathed by every American mother, . . . taught in schools, in seminaries, and in colleges. . . . In short," he proclaimed, "let it become the *political religion* of the nation."[5]

Practicing his profession in Illinois's Eighth Judicial Circuit, Lincoln became a skilled courtroom lawyer, able to speak to juries in words that common men could readily understand. But he also developed technical skills (he could, in the words of historian Robert V. Bruce, "split hairs as well as rails") and became a much sought after appellate attorney.[6] Of the several thousand cases he took, more than four hundred were appeals, which demanded extensive research and legal analysis. His most important appellate work was in the Illinois Supreme Court, but he also represented clients in several cases before the United States Supreme Court.[7]

As Lincoln's legal prowess grew through the 1840s and 1850s, he acquired a formidable reputation, first in Illinois, then more broadly in the Ohio River country. He was aware, of course, that many Americans had a low opinion of lawyers, regarding them as "hired guns" whose services were available to the highest bidders, without regard for the truth or justice of their positions. "There is a vague popular belief that lawyers are necessarily dishonest," he once wrote, but he quickly added: "I say vague, because when we consider to what extent confidence and honors are reposed in, and conferred upon lawyers by the people, it appears improbable that their impression of dishonesty is very distinct and vivid."[8] In a word of advice to young men contemplating a legal career, he wrote: "Let no young man choosing the law for a calling for a moment yield to the popular belief—resolve to be honest at all events; and if in your own judgment you cannot be an honest lawyer, resolve to be honest without being a lawyer."[9] Lincoln followed his own advice, earning the nickname "Honest Abe" in the courtroom and outside of it. It was a nickname that was to win him far greater rewards as a politician than as a lawyer.

Lincoln's emergence as a major player on the American political scene came in 1858, when he engaged in a series of widely publicized debates with Senator Stephen A. Douglas, the "Little Giant" of Illinois politics and the leading prospect for the Democratic presidential nomination in 1860. It was no accident that the principal subject of those debates was the great legal issue then racking the nation, whether the U.S. Supreme Court's controversial decision in *Dred Scott v. Sandford* had properly settled the issue of the expansion of slavery into the western territories.[10] Douglas was a former Illinois Supreme Court judge and current chairman of the Senate committee on territories, and thus well qualified to expound on the issue. Lincoln was a mere lawyer and a former one-term congressman, but in his debates with Douglas he showed an understanding of the constitutional principles underlying the slavery issue that attracted respect (if not agreement) all over the country. Douglas defended *Dred Scott,* while Lincoln deplored it.

Late in 1859, as the nation was beginning to consider candidates for the upcoming presidential campaign, Lincoln was invited to New York to speak on an important topic of the day. It was again no accident that the subject he chose to speak on was the great slavery issue then tormenting the country. Lincoln prepared assiduously for his speech, which was delivered in New York's Cooper Union in February 1860. He read accounts of the debates in the Constitutional Convention of 1787 and the state ratifying conventions that followed. He reviewed James Kent's *Commentaries on the Constitution,* one of the leading American legal texts of the first half of the nineteenth century. He searched the *Annals of Congress* and the *Congressional Globe* for early congressional debates and votes on the issue of slavery.[11] And the speech that he delivered in the Cooper Union read much as a legal brief might have read, for it was based on historical precedents, rigorously analyzed and woven together with logic and reason. Lincoln scholar Harold Holzer has described the speech as "a magnificent anomaly, both lawyerly and impassioned . . . ; almost mordantly legalistic and historical."[12] The speech was received in New York with great enthusiasm and, through verbatim texts printed in newspapers and pamphlets, was read all across the country. It spoke with authority and the persuasive power of a lawyer's closing argument to a jury, impressing political leaders that Abraham Lincoln, a little-known lawyer from the West, was a man who might carry the Republican banner in the upcoming presidential election—and, more important, do so successfully.

Lincoln's legal experience gave him insights into the slavery issue, and some definite opinions about what Congress could and could not do about it. He was, of course, personally opposed to slavery. "If slavery is not wrong," he once wrote to a newspaper editor, "nothing is wrong. I can not remember when I did not so think, and feel."[13] But his personal feelings were not embodied in the Constitution. Since the charter gave Congress no power to interfere with "domestic institutions" in the states, it was clear that the power to regulate slavery rested with the states. But the Constitution did give Congress the power to regulate slavery in the District of Columbia; and, despite the contrary holding in *Dred Scott*, Lincoln argued that it also gave Congress the power to exclude slavery from the western territories.[14] In addition, the Constitution's Fugitive Slave Clause, although not explicitly conferring any power on Congress, had traditionally been interpreted as giving the federal legislature the power to compel the return of runaway slaves to their masters.[15] Despite his own personal opposition to slavery, Lincoln was willing to recognize constitutional rules that sanctioned the institution, but firmly resolved not to extend them beyond the limits set by the Constitution. If slavery could not spread into the territories, Lincoln (and his fellow Republicans) believed that it would eventually shrivel and die. By halting its spread (and employing only those means prescribed by the Constitution to do so) they would put slavery on the road to "ultimate extinction."[16]

Lincoln's legal experience also gave him some strong ideas about secession. The intensity of the legal debate over secession is easy to forget, or at least to underestimate, one hundred fifty years after it was (for practical purposes, at least) resolved. It is not difficult to understand why Jefferson Davis argued that secession was a fundamental right, as firmly enshrined in the Constitution as the right of jury trial or the protection of private property.[17] Secession was the cornerstone upon which Davis and the Confederate States of America built their claim to join the community of nations. Many forget, however, that se-cession was also debated in the North, and that there was no unanimity of opinion on the subject.

While most legal authorities in loyal states undoubtedly believed that se-cession was unconstitutional, many argued that the federal government had no power to do anything to stop it. President James Buchanan, Lincoln's hapless predecessor in the White House, was one who argued that secession violated the Constitution, but that the Constitution conferred no power on the na-tional government to "coerce" a secessionist state from leaving the Union or, once having left, to compel it to return.[18] Buchanan's view was shared by the octogenarian chief justice of the Supreme Court, Roger Brooke Taney of Mary-land, the old Jacksonian who made a virtually identical argument and anx-iously awaited an opportunity to assert it in a Supreme Court opinion.[19] Taney, whose views of constitutional issues differed from Lincoln's in almost every im-portant particular, longed to confront the Civil War president with a judicial edict that would, in effect, have said: *The Southern states were wrong in seceding, but you, sir, are equally wrong in trying to bring them back into the Union.* But Taney died late in the fourth year of the war, before an opportunity arose for him to opine on this critical issue, an old man, sick and embittered by the fighting that was raging about him, convinced that it was all terribly, terribly wrong, and that Lincoln bore a lion's share of blame for the wrong.

Lincoln's Whiggish reverence for law and order continued unabated after he joined the new Republican Party in the mid-1850s. The Constitution was a "law," the "supreme law" of the land, and secession was rebellion, insurrection, and "disorder." By striking at the legal foundations of the supreme law, seces-sionists threatened to destroy the "order" that made the American promise a reality. In Lincoln's view, the Union was perpetual, and it could not unilater-ally be severed by any state or states.[20] As he made his way from Illinois to Washington in early 1861, prepared to take his place as president in one of the most critical times in the country's history, he repeatedly affirmed his loyalty to "the Union, the Constitution and the liberties of the people," concepts he re-garded as inseparable. In Lincoln's view, secession was wrong on political, eco-nomic, and moral grounds; but it was also wrong because it violated the Con-stitution.

Unlike Buchanan and Taney, Lincoln believed not only that the federal government had the right and the power under the Constitution to oppose the secessionist states but also that he, as "commander in chief of the Army and Navy of the United States, and of the militia of the several states, when called into the actual service of the United States," had the power, and the duty, to defend the Union.[21] He was, as he reminded those who witnessed his inauguration in 1861, sworn to "preserve, protect and defend the Constitution of the United States," at least to "the best of . . . [his] ability."[22] And so as he called militiamen to Washington, and declared a blockade of Southern ports, and authorized suspension of the writ of habeas corpus along the military line between Washington and Philadelphia, and appointed generals to lead military expeditions into the South, he crafted legal arguments that would sustain him in his efforts to preserve the Union and defend the Constitution.

Lincoln came to the presidency with some well-articulated views of the Supreme Court and its function in the American constitutional system. His respect for the Court, derived from his general reverence and regard for the law, was high. In his rivalry with Douglas, he had proclaimed that he believed as much as the senator "(perhaps more) in obedience to, and respect for the judicial department of the government." He thought that the Supreme Court's "decisions on Constitutional questions, when fully settled, should control, not only in the particular cases decided, but the general policy of the country, subject to be disturbed only by amendment of the Constitution as provided in that instrument itself." The rub, of course, was in the words "fully settled." He believed that the *Dred Scott* decision was "erroneous." But it *was* a decision of the Supreme Court. How could he oppose it? On what grounds could he argue against it? In a speech in his hometown of Springfield, he explained:

> If this important decision had been made by the unanimous concurrence of the judges, and without any apparent partisan bias, and in accordance with legal public expectation, and with the steady practice of the departments throughout our history, and had been in no part, based on assumed historical facts which are not really true; or, if wanting in some of these, it had been before the court more than once, and had there been affirmed and re-affirmed through a course of years, it

then might be, perhaps would be, factious, nay, even revolutionary to not acquiesce in it as a precedent.

But when, as it is true we find it wanting in all these claims to the public confidence, it is not resistance, it is not factious, it is not even disrespectful, to treat it as not having yet quite established a settled doctrine for the country.[23]

He made it clear that a Supreme Court decision, once made, was binding on the parties to the case and that it was improper for anyone to "resist" it. But if a decision was not "fully settled," those who believed it to be "erroneous" could properly criticize it, point out its deficiencies, and seek to have it changed. Again addressing *Dred Scott*, Lincoln said: "We know the court that made it, has often over-ruled its own decisions, and we shall do what we can to have it to over-rule this."[24]

Lincoln was not a constitutional scholar—nor did he ever claim to be one. His interest in the law was more practical than theoretical, directed more toward the solution of real problems than the exposition of theories. But he was far more than an "untutored country lawyer," as he has sometimes been portrayed. His biographer David Herbert Donald has noted that he was "an incredibly hardworking lawyer" and that he "took the law, and lawyers, very seriously."[25] And he often surprised those he met with his understanding of legal principles. When two English lawyers visited him one evening in 1864, expecting to encounter the unsophisticated "rail-splitter" they had read about in the newspapers, Lincoln turned the conversation, "unasked, into a forcibly drawn sketch of the constitution of the United States, and the material points of difference between the governments of the two countries." Informed that his visitors were lawyers, Lincoln began to talk "of the landed tenures of England" and explained that, when he was growing up in Kentucky, "they used to be troubled with the same mysterious relics of feudalism." Lincoln's commentary, one of the Englishmen later wrote, was "very lucid and intelligent."[26]

One of Lincoln's law partners once described him as a "case lawyer," a lawyer who studied the law that applied to the cases he was handling and showed little interest in broader or more general legal principles. But when faced with a "case," as another of his partners declared, he would "study out his case and make about as much of it as anybody."[27] Faced with the unprecedented legal problems presented by the Civil War, President Abraham Lincoln was determined to "study out his case" and "make about as much of it as anybody."

THE SUPREME COURT is a collegial institution. Its members are independent judges, chosen by successive presidents, belonging to competing political parties, varying in age, background, and judicial philosophy. Each judge has an equal voice in the Court's decisions. A decision can be made only by a majority vote, and only in a case that has been brought to the Court by litigants and attorneys.[28] The federal judiciary is an independent branch of the federal government, co-equal with the legislative and executive branches and substantially free of direct influence from either. The Supreme Court stands at the head of the federal judiciary, and its judges hold their positions "during good behavior" (that is, for life).[29] There is never any guarantee that the Supreme Court will support the other two branches of the government, endorse their measures, or affirm their decisions, even in times of war or under the duress of insurrection or rebellion. The Supreme Court exercises independent judgment, and hears cases and makes decisions based on the views of a majority of the judges.

During the Civil War, the Supreme Court could have defied Lincoln's intention to preserve the Union and thwarted his efforts to "defend" the Constitution. (If Taney had had his way, it would have done so.) It could have struck down the president's major war measures. It could have invalidated congressional enactments designed to support the president's prosecution of the war, declaring them unconstitutional and thus void. It could have effectively argued Jefferson Davis's cause in Washington, making it all but impossible for Lincoln to prosecute the war to a successful conclusion. But the Court chose not to do so. In a succession of important cases, some decided by a simple majority vote, the Court took substantially the same view that Lincoln took of his constitutional powers and duties, sustaining his and Congress's key efforts to put down the rebellion and bring the secessionist states back into the Union.

The view has sometimes been advanced that there is no "value" in judicial biography, and that those who write about the law would better spend their time "writing on other matters, cutting-edge issues which can have a significant impact on important questions of the day." According to this view, biographical information about judges "is irrelevant," for it makes no difference whether the author of a judicial opinion "came over on a boat in 1882 or whether the author's ancestors came over on a boat in 1620. Either way, the opinion has the same value."[30] This argument suggests that judges are automatons who mechanically apply legal rules to real-life controversies. This book rejects that argument for the view that the lives, backgrounds, experiences, temperaments, and characters of the judges who sat on the Supreme Court during the time that Lincoln was president—and in the years immediately following, when Lincoln's initiatives continued to come before the Court for review—are not only informative but also essential to understanding the decisions that the Court made and how the president and the Court interacted. To understand Taney's judicial views, for example, it is helpful to know that he was raised in the late eighteenth century on a tobacco plantation in southern Maryland, in the midst of a slave population; that he spent his early professional years as a lawyer in Frederick, Maryland, where slaves worked in his office and his home; that he rose to national prominence through the favor of President Andrew Jackson, also a slaveholder; and that, to the end of his long life, he sympathized with the South in its commercial, social, and political struggles with the North, growing bitter in the vague realization, as his biographer Carl Brent Swisher has written, that his views on the great issues dividing the nation were not shared by most Americans.[31]

The late Chief Justice William Rehnquist wrote about "the human factor that inevitably enters into even the most careful judicial decision."[32] This "human factor" recognizes that judges are not all alike; that they have feelings and emotions; that they experience disappointments and anxieties; that they have sympathies and sometimes resentments. Good judges strive to overcome their emotions, to apply the law dispassionately, and to make judgments that are firmly grounded in legal rules. Even the best judges, however, are unable to achieve this goal in all of their decisions. This book attempts to portray the Supreme Court justices of Lincoln's time as living and breathing human beings, buffeted by the exigencies of the time, attempting to live up to their judicial oaths, sometimes failing but mostly succeeding, shaped by their life experiences and the pressures of the war. They were not cogs in an impersonal machine but people—like generals and admirals and senators and congressmen, cabinet secretaries, and even the president himself. By coming to know them as people, we can better understand the arguments they advanced and the decisions they made.

This is a book about lawyers and laws, judges and courts, statutes and constitutional provisions. It is not, however, a "law book." It makes no effort to analyze the great legal issues of the Civil War to the point of exhaustion. It describes the legal controversies that arose during the fighting, and the lawyers and judges who participated in their resolution. It is a book that will, I hope, appeal to scholars and general readers, to lawyers, judges, and laymen, to those who are steeped in constitutional history and those who know little about it. It is a book of history—legal history, to be sure—but history first and foremost, and it tells how that history helped to affect the outcome of the war, and shape the future of the United States.

1   A Solemn Oath

MARCH 4, 1861, DAWNED dark and blustery in Washington, with clouds hovering low over the horizon, threatening to unleash a torrent of rain. A few drops of water fell before eight o'clock, but they were hardly enough to calm the dust that lay thick in the streets. A bracing wind soon swept in from the northwest, clearing the sky but also raising billows of dust that raced across Pennsylvania Avenue and its cross streets.

Abraham Lincoln had arisen at five o'clock in his bedroom in Willard's Hotel and begun preparations for the busy day ahead. After an early breakfast in his private parlor, the president-elect gathered his family around him and read aloud the inaugural address that he planned to deliver a few hours later at the Capitol. He conferred with Gideon Welles, his choice to be the new secretary of the navy, Edward Bates, his attorney general–designate, and Judge David Davis of Illinois, the man who had engineered his presidential nomination at the Republican convention the previous May. Retiring to his room, he dressed in a new black suit, with freshly shined boots, a stovepipe hat, and a gold-headed cane that had been given to him for use on this day, then awaited the arrival of the outgoing president, James Buchanan, who would transport him from the hotel to the Capitol in an open barouche.

The chamber of the United States Senate was crowded with spectators when Buchanan and Lincoln entered at a few minutes past one o'clock. The outgoing vice president, John C. Breckinridge of Kentucky, had already administered the oath of office to the new vice president, Hannibal Hamlin of Maine, and Hamlin now occupied the presiding officer's chair. The galleries were filled with hundreds of ladies, while the Senate floor was crowded with the important guests who, by tradition, would witness the departure of the old chief executive and the arrival of the new: the ministers and attachés of the diplomatic corps, the members of the Senate and House of Representatives, and the eight sitting judges of the Supreme Court.

Buchanan and Lincoln entered the chamber arm in arm, not to signify any political affinity (there was none), but to demonstrate the civil courtesies that should be exchanged when power passes from one president to another according to the dictates of the Constitution. Observing the two men, a reporter for the *New York Times* thought that Buchanan was "pale, sad, and nervous" and that Lincoln's face was "slightly flushed, with compressed lips." While an oath was administered to the newly elected Senator James Pearce of Maryland, Buchanan and Lincoln sat in front of Hamlin's marble desk. Buchanan "sighed audibly, and frequently," the *Times* reporter noted, while Lincoln was "grave and impassive as an Indian martyr."[1]

A line of procession now formed, with the marshal of the District of Columbia in the lead, followed by the judges of the Supreme Court, the sergeant at arms of the Senate, and the Senate committee on arrangements, headed up by Lincoln's old friend from Illinois, now senator of Oregon, Edward D. Baker. Then followed the president and the president-elect, the vice president, the secretary of the Senate, the senators and congressmen, and the other dignitaries. The procession passed through a corridor and out onto a large wooden platform that straddled the east-portico steps. Built specially for the inauguration, the platform was decorated with red, white, and blue bunting and guarded by fifty armed soldiers who stood silently beneath it. From two nearby artillery batteries, the army's aged general in chief, Winfield Scott, surveyed the portico, the platform, the unfinished dome of the Capitol (now being raised to a grander height), and the tens of thousands of guests who crowded the Capitol grounds.

Buchanan, Lincoln, the Supreme Court judges, and the members of the committee on arrangements seated themselves in plush chairs that had been removed from the Senate and placed beneath a small wooden canopy. Then Senator Baker stepped forward and announced, in the stentorian tones for which he was noted: "Fellow-Citizens: I introduce to you Abraham Lincoln, the President elect of the United States of America." Lincoln rose, walked to a table that had been placed beneath the canopy, and bowed low to acknowledge the applause of the crowd.[2]

Lincoln had come to the Capitol to take his oath of office as sixteenth president of the United States. The president's oath (the only one that the Constitution prescribes in precise terms) is set forth in Article II, Section 1, which provides (in relevant part): "Before he [the president] enter on the execution of his office, he shall take the following oath or affirmation:—'I do solemnly swear (or affirm) that I will faithfully execute the office of President of the United States, and will to the best of my ability, preserve, protect and defend the Constitution of the United States.'"

Long tradition dictated that the oath should be administered by the chief justice of the Supreme Court. Roger Taney was more experienced in carrying out this duty than any man in the history of the United States, for in the almost quarter-century he had occupied the chief justiceship he had administered the oath to six presidents (his first was Martin Van Buren in 1837). Now almost eighty-four years old, he was about to administer the oath to his seventh. Six feet tall, gaunt, with a flat chest, stooped shoulders, tobacco-stained teeth, and long hair that cascaded over his collar and drooped across his forehead, Taney was a living link with the history of the United States. Born in Maryland in 1777, he was more than thirty years older than the president-elect. He was, in fact, older than the Constitution, older than the Supreme Court, older than the Capitol before which he was now to perform a ceremonial duty of special solemnity and importance.

Although both the president-elect and the chief justice were tall, thin men, they contrasted in countless other ways. Taney was quiet, formal, and perpetually dignified, the president affable, casual, and habitually (some thought annoyingly) humorous. The customary expression on Taney's face was so dour that his severest critics professed to see a sinister look in it.[3] Originally a Federalist in the tradition of Alexander Hamilton, John Adams, and his venerated predecessor as chief justice, John Marshall, Taney came under the influence of Andrew Jackson late in the 1820s and soon became one of the Tennessean's most trusted lieutenants. In 1829, President Jackson made Taney his attorney general, and he filled the post with distinction until 1831, when he returned to his law practice in Baltimore. When Jackson embarked on a plan to dismantle the Second Bank of the United States (which he deemed a "monster") and when Secretary of the Treasury William J. Duane refused his order to withdraw federal deposits from the bank, Jackson fired Duane and named Taney as his successor. The promptness with which the Marylander carried out the president's order caused Jackson's opponents to condemn him as a lackey but persuaded the president that he was a man he could trust. In 1834, Jackson nominated Taney to be an associate justice of the Supreme Court but the Senate refused to confirm him. Then John Marshall died on July 6, 1835, ending a distinguished career of more than thirty-four years as head of the federal judiciary. Jackson took revenge on his enemies in the Senate by naming Taney to succeed Marshall as chief justice. Thanks to recent changes in the Senate, Taney's nomination was confirmed by a vote of twenty-nine to fifteen.[4]

Taney and Lincoln differed not only in appearance, demeanor, and experience but also in their views of the Constitution, and their conceptions of the role that the Supreme Court should play in settling the profound questions that now beset the nation. In his opinion in the *Dred Scott* case, Taney had publicly expressed confidence in the Supreme Court's authority to settle questions that gnawed at the heart of national policy—slavery in the territories, the status of free blacks, the future of the "peculiar institution" itself.[5]

Taney's public statements about slavery had been uniformly—and not surprisingly—supportive, for he was raised on a slave plantation and lived all of his life in Maryland and the District of Columbia, where slavery was a part of everyday life. In *Dred Scott*, he expressed harshly racist views of constitutional doctrine and history, making it clear that he believed that persons of African descent (whether slave or free) were ineligible to participate in the political life of the United States simply because of their race. After *Dred Scott* became a national cause célèbre, however, some of the chief justice's defenders claimed that he was "personally" opposed to slavery.[6] They reported the surprising fact that many years earlier, while arguing a case before a Maryland jury, he had described the institution as an "evil" and a "blot on our national character." It was in 1818, and Taney's client was a Methodist minister from Pennsylvania who had given an antislavery sermon in a camp meeting and thereafter been indicted for attempting to incite slaves to insurrection. Taney defended the minister on free-speech grounds but also told the jury that slavery "must be gradually wiped away." Around the same time, Taney was reported to have freed eight or more of his own slaves (though he kept a couple who were "too old to learn a living").

But after 1818 Taney cast no more aspersions on slavery, and in 1832, while serving as Andrew Jackson's attorney general, he made harshly racist statements that would have been very much at home in his *Dred Scott* opinion. In an official attorney general's opinion, he described Americans of African descent as "degraded" and "the only class of persons who can be held as mere property, as slaves." He charged that African Americans "were never regarded as a constituent portion of the sovereignty of any state." They were "not looked upon as citizens by the contracting parties who formed the Constitution" and were "evidently not supposed to be included by the term *citizens*."[7] If, in 1818, Taney had disparaged slavery in an effort to win a jury trial (he was successful in the effort), he staunchly defended slavery and denigrated African Americans during the rest of his long public life as both attorney general and chief justice.[8]

Taney's views about the secession crisis were expressed more privately. Like President Buchanan, he believed that secession was constitutionally impermissible but that the federal government had no authority to "coerce" a seceding state to remain in the Union. Buchanan's views on the subject had been expressed in his last annual message to Congress, delivered on December 3, 1860. The outgoing executive rejected the idea that the federal government was "a mere voluntary association of States, to be dissolved at pleasure by any one of the contracting parties." "If this be so," he argued, "the Confederacy is a rope of sand, to be penetrated and dissolved by the first adverse wave of public opinion in any of the States. . . . By this process a Union might be entirely broken into fragments in a few weeks which cost our forefathers many years of toil, privation, and blood to establish." But Buchanan searched the Constitution for any language that would give the president or Congress power to keep a state in the Union against its will and, "after much serious reflection," concluded that there was none.[9] Taney's own views on secession were expressed in an unpublished memorandum probably written in February 1861, about a month before he was to administer the presidential oath to Lincoln. In that memorandum, he said that the Confederate states were wrong to claim a constitutional right to secede. But, he wrote, federal laws could be enforced within a state only by its own citizens, and the federal military could enter a state only at the call of state officials. Thus it was impermissible for the federal government, against the will of a seceding state, to subject it to military action to prevent it from severing its ties with the Union.[10] It was thus wrong, in the view of both Buchanan and Taney, for a state to break the bonds that tied it to the other states, but also wrong for the federal government to attempt to stop it.

It was a cramped position that led Buchanan to a course of executive paralysis and Taney to a sense of impending doom. In a letter written late in 1860 to his son-in-law, the chief justice revealed that his thoughts had "been constantly turned to the fearful state of things in which we have been living for months past." He remembered the violent slave uprising that had swept over the Caribbean Island of Santo Domingo in the 1790s and harbored gloomy fears that similar bloodshed might be visited on the slaveholding states of the American South. He prayed that such a catastrophe could be averted and that his "fears may prove to be nothing more than the timidity of an old man."[11]

Taney *was* an old man (he was fond of reminding people of the fact, perhaps to gain their sympathy), but he had never been timid. He was as confident in his eighties of the rightness of his positions as he had been in his thirties and forties, and as forceful as ever in asserting them. When, in his *Dred Scott* opinion, he denied that African Americans were regarded by the framers of the Constitution as citizens of the United States, and asserted that Congress's effort in the Missouri Compromise of 1820 to restrict the spread of slavery into the western territories was unconstitutional (propositions that were as hotly contested in 1857 as they had been in 1820), he stated his positions with certainty. His propositions, he said, were "too plain for argument." He was interpreting the Constitution "according to its true intent and meaning," and "in a manner not to be mistaken."[12]

But Lincoln, and a host of other Americans, disagreed with Taney's positions—not just his notions about slavery and secession but also the constitutional principles that he asserted in *Dred Scott*. The latter had become a bone of contention in Lincoln's senatorial debates with Stephen Douglas in 1858. Now, as president, the Illinoisan would be called upon to make decisions that would almost certainly clash with the conclusions enunciated by the old chief justice in *Dred Scott*.

LINCOLN HAD BEEN in Washington only ten days when he took his seat on the inauguration platform, and he had been busy all of that time. He had been formally introduced to Taney and the associate justices of the Supreme Court eight days before, but he already knew much about them, for his legal practice had obliged him to study their opinions and occasionally represent clients who had cases before the Court. On March 7 and 8, 1849, just after his first (and only) term as a U.S. congressman came to an end, Lincoln appeared before Chief Justice Taney and the associate justices of the Supreme Court in Washington to argue the case of *Lewis v. Lewis*. This was an appeal from the U.S. Circuit Court for Illinois, where a suit had been filed in 1843 alleging the breach of a covenant in the sale of a parcel of real property. Lincoln represented the defendant and argued that the cause of action, which arose in 1819, was barred by the Illinois statute of limitations. The original statute, passed by the Illinois legislature in 1827, required that the suit be commenced within sixteen years but provided an exemption for persons who were outside Illinois. The plaintiff in *Lewis v. Lewis* was an Ohioan and thus outside Illinois. But in 1837 the statute was amended to repeal the exemption for persons outside the state. Lincoln argued that the statutory period should be measured from 1827, while the plaintiff's attorney argued that the sixteen-year clock did not start to run until 1837. It was a technical argument but an important one, both for the parties and for Illinois law. The Supreme Court's decision in *Ross v. Duval* (1839) appeared to support Lincoln's position.[13] But on March 13, 1849, Chief Justice Taney decided otherwise, ruling that the limitation period did not begin to run until 1837.[14] According to John P. Frank, a close student of Lincoln's legal career, Taney's decision was "utterly in conflict" with *Ross v. Duval* and "in all fairness . . . must be regarded as overruling the earlier case."[15] Associate Justice John McLean agreed and dissented from Taney's opinion, but the chief justice's view prevailed. Although the loss was difficult for Lincoln, it taught him some valuable lessons about Supreme Court decisions. Among them was one he would later remember when discussing the *Dred Scott* decision: No matter how clearly or emphatically it may be stated, a decision of the U.S. Supreme Court is not writ in stone. If members of the Court later decide to overrule (or merely disregard) it, an entirely different decision may be handed down.

Lincoln had been attorney of record in other cases before the United States Supreme Court, and he had participated in cases that were appealed to the Supreme Court by other lawyers. But his participation in these other cases was limited to trial work, writing briefs, or helping other lawyers prepare legal theories. *Lewis v. Lewis* was the only case in which he presented an oral argument.[16]

On Monday, February 25, 1861, the president-elect had made his first courtesy call on Chief Justice Taney and the associate justices of the Supreme Court. He met them in the reception room adjoining their new courtroom on the main floor of the Capitol, created out of the chamber vacated by the Senate when it moved into larger and grander quarters in the new north wing of the Capitol in January 1859. The Court had met for the first time in the new courtroom on December 4, 1860, when it opened the December term of that year. The new courtroom was a semicircular space, measuring forty-five feet across, with a domed ceiling, a large chandelier, a richly carpeted floor, and a marble colonnade in front of which the bench and the justices' chairs were laid out in a straight line. A gilded eagle, left over from the Senate days, looked down on the spectators from a perch above the chief justice's chair. Remodeled and furnished at a cost of $25,000, the new courtroom was a vast improvement over the damp, poorly lit basement room that had been the Court's headquarters from 1810 to 1860. When Justice John Catron of Tennessee first learned of plans for the new courtroom, he wrote the court clerk that the information was "truly gratifying to me, who has been greviously [sic] annoyed by the dampness, darkness, and want of venilation [sic], of the old basement room; into which, I have always supposed, the Sup. Court was thrust in a spirit of hostility to it, by the Political Department."[17]

Lincoln entered the justices' reception room at three o'clock in the afternoon, accompanied by Senator William H. Seward of New York, who was soon to become his secretary of state. Like Lincoln, Seward had been a critic of the *Dred Scott* decision, but he had gone much further than Lincoln, charging that, when the justices decided the case, they resembled the obsequious courtiers of the tyrannical King Charles I, and reminding his listeners that "judicial usurpation is more odious and intolerable than any other among the manifold practices of tyranny."[18] Seward's words had outraged Taney, who said privately that if the New Yorker had been nominated and elected president instead of Lincoln, he would have refused to administer the oath of office "to such a man."[19] If Taney still harbored personal enmity toward Seward when he and Lincoln came to the justices' reception room on February 25, no evidence of it has survived. In the biography that they later wrote about Lincoln, John G. Nicolay and John Hay, the new president's private secretaries, noted that when the president-elect went to the Capitol to meet members of Congress "he was enthusiastically welcomed by friends and somewhat sullenly greeted by foes." But when he went to the Supreme Court, the "venerable chief and associate justices extended to him an affable recognition as the lawful successor in constitutional rulership."[20]

As chief justice, Taney was the principal object of Lincoln's interest and attention. The old Marylander had a kind of charm that ingratiated him to new acquaintances, even those who did not share his views or admire his record. A man who knew him in Maryland said that he spoke with "so much sincerity . . . that it was next to impossible to believe he could be wrong." But another Marylander, alluding to Taney's Roman Catholic religion, complained of the judge's "infernal apostolic manner." He reminded many men of the Pope, speaking "ex cathedra, infallibly."[21]

Taney had never enjoyed robust health, and when he became chief justice he was already fifty-nine years old, so many people had expected him to serve a short term. Despite frequent absences from the bench due to sickness, he hung on to his position year after year, decade after decade, confounding those who thought he lacked staying power. In April 1860 he suffered a fall as he stepped from his carriage onto a marble pavement at the entrance to the Capitol and had to spend a long period away from the Court. This incident gave rise to reports that he was disabled, perhaps even near death. He relished the opportunity to deny them. "I see by the Baltimore Sun of yesterday," he wrote in May 1860, "that I am again put to death, with a very short reprieve. . . . I am fully sensible that in the course of nature, it cannot be long before my last hour may come, but it would seem that there are some political writers of letters, and some newspapers who think that the event has been delayed too long, and mean to kill me at least in public opinion, by the influence of the press."[22] Taney supported Breckinridge, the proslavery Democrat, in the presidential election of 1860, and after the Republicans won there were rumors that the chief justice would submit his resignation so that the Democratic president James Buchanan could name his successor. But Taney denied the rumors, writing in a letter to an admirer: "You are right in supposing that at such a time I should not think of resigning my place on the Bench of the Supreme Court. I am sensible that it would at this moment be highly injurious to the public, and subject me to the suspicion of acting from unworthy motives."[23]

When he took his position as successor to the great John Marshall in 1836, many thought Taney a poor choice. His critics said that he was too much of a politician to settle into the reflective habits of a jurist, and too closely associated with the combative style of Jackson's administration to be an impartial administrator of justice. But Jackson's critics would have considered any selection he made a poor choice. Those who venerated Marshall wanted Associate Justice Joseph Story to be named chief justice. One of the most scholarly judges ever to sit on the Court, Story had served as a loyal lieutenant to Marshall ever since his appointment by President Madison in 1811, helping Marshall craft a constitutional jurisprudence that accommodated national aspirations while it respected clearly defined limits of federal power. And while he served as an associate justice, Story built a reputation as a legal writer and educator of the first rank (he was Dane Professor of Law at Harvard and the author of a series of authoritative legal treatises). But Jackson had no affection for Marshall and little more for Story, and he chose instead to name one of his own loyalists. After Taney began his work as chief justice, Story came to admire him as a legal craftsman and a gentleman, but he never got over the loss of Chief Justice Marshall. "I miss the Chief Justice at every turn," Story admitted. "I am the last of the old race of Judges." Daniel Webster, one of the Supreme Court's great lawyers and a nationalist in the Marshall-Story mold, agreed. "Judge Story . . . thinks the Supreme Court is *gone* and I think so too."[24]

The Supreme Court was not gone, of course, but it *had* changed and would continue to change. And Andrew Jackson was responsible for much of that change, as Abraham Lincoln could perceive when he visited the judges on February 25. In fact, four of the eight sitting justices had been appointed directly by Jackson (Jackson nominated six justices in all, more than any other president up to that time except George Washington). The remaining four justices were appointees of presidents who were strongly influenced by Jackson, both in their political views and their judicial philosophies. "Old Hickory" had left the presidency twenty-four years before, but the mark he put on the Supreme Court was still very evident in February 1861.

The Supreme Court that Lincoln encountered was overwhelmingly Democratic. Only one of the justices, John McLean, was a Republican, and even he could trace his political roots to Andrew Jackson (McLean was Jackson's first Supreme Court appointment, in 1829). Four of the justices were from slaveholding states and supported slavery, both publicly and privately. Three were northern Democrats who supported slavery, or at least did not oppose it

(Democrats of this stripe were called doughfaces, because they could be easily twisted and shaped). Before May 31, 1860, the Court had had an even more Southern, proslavery, and Democratic tilt to it, but on that date Associate Justice Peter V. Daniel of Virginia died after eighteen years of Supreme Court service.

Daniel was a Southern aristocrat who vehemently defended states' rights and slavery and whose loyalty to the Democratic party was dependable. His appointment to the Supreme Court came from Martin Van Buren in 1841, but he had earlier been appointed to the federal district court by Jackson. While Daniel was on the bench, the Supreme Court had five justices from the South and only four from the North, eight who defended slavery and only one who opposed it, eight Democrats and only one Republican. Considering the population disparity between the two sections of the country (approximately 70 percent of the population lived in the North in 1860, only 30 percent in the South), the South's strong presence in the Supreme Court was remarkable. With characteristic indecisiveness, James Buchanan dithered over Daniel's successor for months. On February 5, 1861, with only a month left in his term, he nominated Jeremiah Sullivan Black of Pennsylvania, a doughface who had been Buchanan's attorney general from 1857 to 1860 and had briefly served as secretary of state. But Black's nomination to the Supreme Court was rejected by the Senate on February 21. A month earlier, Black had privately belittled Lincoln's abilities, dismissing him as being "very small potatoes and few in a hill" and writing: "He had no reputation even in the region where he belongs except what arose out of certain loose stump speeches consisting mainly in making comical faces and telling smutty anecdotes."[25] Now Lincoln would have the opportunity to appoint a Supreme Court justice to the seat Black had been denied.

John McLean was not the oldest justice in 1861, though he was the most senior, having served thirty-one years on the Court. Born in New Jersey in 1785, he had moved with his family through Virginia and Kentucky to Ohio, where he became a lawyer, a member of Congress, and a state supreme court judge before President James Monroe named him commissioner of the General Land Office in 1822. The following year Monroe promoted him to postmaster general, and he kept that position all through the presidency of John Quincy Adams. But in the next election he threw his support to Andrew Jackson, and

Jackson rewarded him with an appointment to the United States Supreme Court, where he took his oath of office in January 1830. A large man with a large head (in later years bald in front but covered on each side by long and somewhat disheveled hair), McLean was, as one historian put it, "a great man in body, and perhaps in mind." Edward Bates thought he had "great talents, with a mind able to comprehend the greatest subject," though future president Rutherford B. Hayes allowed that he could be "stiff as a crowbar."[26] McLean was less known for his judicial decisions than for the fact, as Daniel Webster put it, that he always had "his head turned too much by politics." During the whole of his career as a Supreme Court justice he had aspired to the presidency, first as a Jacksonian, later as a Whig, and finally as a Republican. McLean had his supporters, but they were never numerous enough to win him the nomination of any party. Though courteous in his relations with others, McLean often gave the impression of being cold and unfeeling. Salmon P. Chase, also an Ohioan, once commented of McLean: "It is a thousand pities that a man of such real benevolence of heart as the Judge possesses, should not allow more of it to flow out into his manners."[27]

Aside from his political ambition, McLean was best known for his steadfast opposition to slavery, an opposition that had its roots in the religious precepts of his Scotch-Irish forebears (Ulstermen who spelled their name "McClain" when they first came to America). In fact, McLean was the only justice still sitting on the Court in 1861 who had dissented from the pro-slavery *Dred Scott* decision of 1857. The dissent he filed in that case strongly challenged Chief Justice Taney's views about African Americans and the power of Congress to regulate slavery in the territories. Some thought, in fact, that McLean's views on those questions had precipitated Taney's extreme pronouncements on the same issues, for it was speculated that the chief justice would have refrained from addressing them if McLean had not insisted on doing so in his dissent. In *Dred Scott*, McLean argued from the Constitution and history but also from his conscience. It was a habit that went back to his days as a state court judge, when he often moralized from the bench. "On such occasions," his biographer said, "the Justice's role was approximating that of the Methodist lay preacher."[28]

Now seventy-five years old, McLean may still have had some presidential ambitions (as late as 1860 he received twelve votes at the Republican nominating convention in Chicago, and Lincoln himself spoke favorably about his candidacy), but nobody now expected him to attain that office.[29] It was McLean's duty as senior associate justice to preside over the Court during Taney's frequent absences, and he did this so expertly that the *New York Tribune* praised his efficiency, commenting in 1860: "During the recent illness of Judge Taney, he dispatched more business than was almost ever known before by the profession."[30]

Associate Justice James M. Wayne of Georgia was second in seniority to McLean. Nominated by Andrew Jackson in January 1835 and confirmed by the Senate just eight days later, Wayne was now seventy-one years old and beginning his twenty-seventh year on the Court. A one-time rice planter and slaveholder from Savannah, he had been a lawyer, a state court judge, mayor, and a Democratic congressman before he began his Supreme Court career. Wayne was a consistent supporter of slavery (in fact, he was the only associate justice who completely agreed with Taney's *Dred Scott* opinion in 1857). But his proslavery view was balanced by a nationalist outlook that led him to sustain federal power and rein in excessive claims of states' rights. A handsome man, and a favorite of the ladies when he was young, Wayne had matured over the years into a silver-haired gentleman of grace and impeccable manners. Though Lincoln's attorney general, Edward Bates, would soon declare him "habitually bland," he would allow that the septuagenarian from Georgian "never forgets that he, himself is a gentleman."[31]

Associate Justice John Catron of Tennessee was next in seniority to Wayne. Catron was cut from rougher cloth than the Georgian, though he shared many of the same political and judicial views, supporting slavery and following a constitutional jurisprudence that accommodated nationalist aspirations. Though it is uncertain where and exactly when Catron was born, it is believed he was born in Pennsylvania around the year 1786.[32] His parents were German immigrants who took him to Virginia and then to Kentucky while he was still a child. As an adult, he moved on to Tennessee, where he built his first home in the foothills of the Cumberland Mountains. In 1818, on the advice of Andrew Jackson (with whom he had served a brief stint as a soldier in the War of 1812), he moved to Nashville, where he became a successful lawyer.

Catron was more than six feet tall, with a large frame, black eyes, a big nose, and a prominent, almost combative jaw. As one of his biographers noted, his "manner attracted attention, and his supreme self-confidence begat the confidence of his clients."[33] After six years of legal practice, he was elected a justice of the Tennessee Court of Errors and Appeals, where he became chief judge in 1831. A loyal Jacksonian, Catron managed Martin Van Buren's presidential campaign in Tennessee in 1836, and on the very last day of Jackson's presidency, he was nominated to be an associate justice of the United States Supreme Court. The Senate confirmed the nomination five days later. Associate Justice John Archibald Campbell of Alabama commented that the Tennessee judge "had indomitable courage and practical ability" and was "always listened to with respect."[34] When Lincoln visited the justices in their new conference room, the seventy-five-year-old Catron was three months away from completing his twenty-fourth year of Supreme Court service.

Associate Justice Samuel Nelson of New York was sixty-eight years old and beginning his seventeenth year on the Supreme Court. Nominated by President John Tyler in February 1845 and confirmed by the Senate in the same month, Nelson was a doughface Democrat who had been a trial and appellate court judge in his home state before he joined the nation's highest court. Born in 1792, of Scotch-Irish ancestry, he spent his boyhood on a farm in upstate New York, then went away for three years of academy training and a rigorous course of study at Vermont's Middlebury College. After graduating in 1813, he returned to New York and embarked on a legal career that led him to choice political appointments, first as a local postmaster and later as a judge. Nelson's nomination to the United States Supreme Court was a kind of accident, made possible by the fact that President Tyler had been unsuccessful in his efforts to nominate a string of men before him. One of Tyler's nominees was denied confirmation by the Senate, another withdrew his name from consideration, and four or five potential nominees (including former President Martin Van Buren) either declined to be considered or were deemed so inappropriate that the president quickly dropped them. Nelson's name was offered and promptly confirmed by the Senate, in part to break the impasse.

In appearance, Nelson was a stern-looking man with a large head that was made to appear even larger by luxuriant hair and full side whiskers that drooped low across his collar. George Templeton Strong, a young lawyer who encountered him one day at a Columbia Law School commencement, described Nelson as looking "leonine and learned enough to represent Ellenborough and Kenyon and Mansfield and Marshall all in one."[35] Though a Northerner by birth and upbringing, Nelson was friendly to Southern interests, and his father was rumored to have financed his college education through the sale of a Negro slave girl, a fact that may have given the young man an early proslavery inclination.[36] Whether or not this was the case, his votes on the Supreme Court revealed a tendency to be, if not proslavery, at least "grimly anti-antislavery."[37]

Next in seniority after Nelson was Associate Justice Robert C. Grier of Pennsylvania. Like his New York colleague, the sixty-seven-year-old Grier was a doughface Democrat who supported the Supreme Court's proslavery positions while taking a generally centrist position on other issues. Born in Cumberland County, Pennsylvania in 1794, he had moved north to Lycoming County while he was still an infant. There his father supported his large family as a Presbyterian minister, farmer, and schoolmaster. Grier received his first lessons from his father, who was proficient in Greek and Latin. He later left for Dickinson College, the same school from which Chief Justice Taney had received his college education almost twenty years earlier. After graduating in 1812, Grier taught school for a while, and then in 1817 he embarked on a legal career that led him to the Allegheny County District Court at Pittsburgh in 1833. Grier's appointment to the Supreme Court, much like Nelson's, resulted from the inability of Presidents Tyler and Polk to fill a Supreme Court vacancy that first opened in 1844. After several unsuccessful attempts to find a suitable nominee (James Buchanan was twice offered the post but was unable to decide whether to accept it), Polk fixed on the almost unknown Grier, whose nomination was approved the day after it was submitted to the Senate.

Standing over six feet tall, with a rotund figure, a ruddy complexion, and blond hair, Grier was an imposing man with an explosive temper.[38] The *New York Tribune* described him as "impulsive and precipitate."[39] Edward Bates called him "a natural-born vulgarian, and, by long habit, coarse and harsh," though Justice Campbell praised his "vigorous thought" and "large mindedness."[40] His temperament aside, Grier was a man who commanded the respect of the other justices and the attorneys who argued their cases before the Supreme Court.

Associate Justice John Archibald Campbell of Alabama was the court's youngest member (only forty-nine years old on that day in 1861) but not the most junior in service. Born in Georgia in June 1811 to a successful attorney and plantation owner, Campbell had been a child prodigy and had entered Franklin College (later the University of Georgia) at the age of eleven, graduated at fourteen, and then accepted an appointment from Secretary of War John C. Calhoun to the U.S. Military Academy at West Point.[41] He had been at West Point for only three years when his father died and he had to return to Georgia to help support his family. Deciding to change his goal from a military to a legal career, he read law for a year and was admitted to the Georgia and Florida bars. In 1830 he moved to Montgomery, Alabama, where he married into a socially prominent family and began a successful law practice. After 1837 he continued his practice in Mobile.

A slaveholder in both Georgia and Alabama, Campbell was nonetheless reflective about the peculiar institution and its role in Southern life.[42] He wrote scholarly articles on the subject, arguing that slavery was an ancient institution that was both acceptable and useful. He pointed out that slavery in a particular state existed under the protection of that state's law and that neither the federal government nor any other state could interfere with it. Although admitting that the institution was disappearing around the world because it was no longer acceptable to modern societies, he believed that its final day was a long way off. Slaves had to be prepared for their freedom before they could be emancipated, he said, and white Southerners had to be constantly on guard against the kind of violence that had once swept Santo Domingo. Above all, Campbell argued, the South should never yield to "visionary and unreasonable fanatics" (that is, Northern abolitionists).[43]

Appointed to the Supreme Court by President Franklin Pierce in 1853, Campbell was nearing the end of his eighth year as an associate justice. Although he was admired for his intelligence and thoughtfulness, he was not widely loved, even in his home state of Alabama, where "to the general public he seemed cold."[44] He had a nervous habit of tugging on his bushy eyebrows when he was deep in thought (he was almost always deep in thought). Southerners suspected that he was not sufficiently loyal to slavery (though he took a strong proslavery stance in *Dred Scott*), and Northerners suspected that he was more devoted to his state and region than to the nation. The *New York Tribune* spoke for many Northerners in 1857 when it described Campbell as "more fanatical than the fanatics—more Southern than the extreme South from which he comes." Campbell, the *Tribune* said, was "a middle-aged, middle-sized man, bald, and possessed of middling talents."[45] Fair or not, the judgment summarized the feeling of many observers, both North and South.

Associate Justice Nathan Clifford of Maine was the junior member of the Supreme Court in 1861. Born in New Hampshire in 1803, he had begun his legal career in that state in 1827 but soon moved to Maine, where he served three terms in the legislature and was twice elected to the U.S. House of Representatives. President Polk named him U.S. attorney general in 1846, then in 1848 sent him to Mexico to negotiate a peace treaty with the southern republic. Once his work on the treaty was completed, he stayed on in Mexico as the American minister until the end of 1849.

A Democratic Party regular, Clifford sought election to the Senate in 1850 and again in 1853, but was unsuccessful both times. He was disappointed when President James Buchanan passed him over for a cabinet nomination in 1857, for he had been one of Buchanan's most loyal supporters, but was finally pleased when, after a predictable four months of hesitation, the president nominated him to succeed Associate Justice Benjamin R. Curtis of Massachusetts in 1858.[46] Like Buchanan, Clifford was a Northern man with Southern sympathies, and his nomination was controversial. The *New York Tribune* said that it confirmed Northern impressions that the Supreme Court had become "a mere party machine, to do the bidding of the dominant faction, and to supply places to reward party hacks." Despite stiff opposition in the Senate, the nomination was confirmed after thirty-four days by the thin margin of twenty-six to twenty-three.[47] In the three years that had passed since Clifford joined the Court, he had done nothing to change his image as a party hack.[48] A tall man who weighed upwards of three hundred pounds, Clifford seemed to wear a perpetually vacant expression on his face. Supreme Court historian Charles Fairman described him as "devoid of humor" and "the most prolix and most pedestrian member of the Court."[49]

AS THE LAST WORDS of Senator Baker's introduction boomed out from the inaugural platform, Abraham Lincoln rose and moved toward the speakers' table. The spectators' cheers were hesitant, for they could not see precisely what the president-elect was doing. Carrying both his top hat and his gold-headed cane, Lincoln paused for a moment, uncertain how to extract his speech from his pocket. Then Stephen Douglas extended his arm. "Permit me, sir," the Illinois senator said, taking the hat and holding it in his lap for the duration of Lincoln's speech. It was a gesture well calculated to show that, though the two men had clashed on many issues in the past, in the secession crisis that now faced the nation they stood together. Lincoln spread his text on the table, adjusted his reading glasses, and began to speak. His voice was high-pitched but calm, and it carried well over the crowd. A reporter for a Louisville newspaper who was sitting nearby thought that it sounded "as if he had been delivering inaugural addresses all his life."[50]

Lincoln began by reminding his "fellow citizens" that, in "compliance with a custom as old as the government itself," he was appearing before them "to take, in your presence, the oath prescribed by the Constitution of the United States, to be taken by the President 'before he enters on the execution of his office.'" He acknowledged that many people in the Southern states were apprehensive that the accession of a Republican president would endanger "their property, and their peace, and personal security," but he assured them that there had "never been any reasonable cause for such apprehension." He proceeded to address issues that he believed would calm Southern fears of the new administration. He repeated statements he had previously made in which he denied any intention of interfering with slavery in any state in which it then existed, and affirmed his intention to maintain "inviolate" the rights of the states, "especially the right of each State to order and control its own domestic institutions according to its own judgment exclusively." He pointedly denied an intention to invade any of the states that had just seceded from the Union, or to use force "against, or among the people anywhere." He would continue mail service in all parts of the country, he said, except where it was "repelled." He would hold and occupy "the property, and places belonging to the government," and collect federal duties and imposts. "In doing this," he said, "there needs to be no bloodshed or violence; and there shall be none, unless it is forced upon the national authority."

He spoke about the Fugitive Slave Law, which had occasioned so much controversy in both North and South, and quoted the precise language of Article IV, Section 2, of the Constitution, the Fugitive Slave Clause: "No person held to service or labor in one state, under the laws thereof, escaping into another, shall, in consequence of any law or regulation therein, be discharged from such service or labor, but shall be delivered up on claim of the party to whom such service or labor may be due."[51] He reiterated his intention to support this provision, although he allowed that there was "some difference of opinion" on whether it should be enforced by national or by state authority (the Constitution was silent on this point). But he said he thought that question was "not a very material one," for if "the slave is to be surrendered, it can be of but little consequence to him, or to others, by which authority it is done."

He next addressed the question of secession. He believed that the Union was perpetual and that it could not unilaterally be severed by any state or states. Perpetuity was "implied, if not expressed, in the fundamental law of all national governments," he said. It was also supported by the history of the United States, for the Articles of Confederation had expressly stated in 1778 that the Union was "perpetual," and the Constitution had been adopted in 1787 to establish "a more perfect Union." He all but pleaded with the states that had already joined the Confederacy to reconsider their positions, and with states that had not taken steps toward disunion to reflect "before entering upon so grave a matter as the destruction of our national fabric, with all its benefits, its memories, and its hopes." "Plainly," he declared, "the central idea of secession, is the essence of anarchy."

He then turned to a question of particular interest to Chief Justice Taney and the seven associate justices, who were listening to him speak. It was "the position assumed by some," he said, "that constitutional questions are to be decided by the Supreme Court." He was referring to the *Dred Scott* decision and the possibility that another such decision, made by the same justices (or perhaps a new group), would be advanced in an effort to decide, once and for all, the momentous issues that now faced the country. He did not deny that Supreme Court decisions "must be binding in any case, upon the parties to a suit as to the object of that suit," nor that those decisions "are also entitled to very high respect and consideration, in all parallel cases by all other departments of the government." But, he continued, "if the policy of the government, upon vital questions, affecting the whole people, is to be irrevocably fixed by decisions of the Supreme Court, the instant they are made, in ordinary litigation between parties, in personal actions, the people will have ceased, to be their own rulers, having, to that extent practically resigned their government, into the hands of that eminent tribunal."

He denied that the view he expressed represented an assault on the Supreme Court judges. It was their duty to decide cases properly brought before them, and it was "no fault of theirs, if others seek to turn their decisions to political purposes." But some issues were too big to be confided to any group of judges, however wise. "One section of our country believes slavery is *right*, and ought to be extended," he said, "while the other believes it is *wrong*, and ought not to be extended." He reminded his listeners that "this country, with its institutions, belongs to the people who inhabit it" and that, whenever they grew weary of the existing government, they could "exercise their *constitutional* right of amending it, or their *revolutionary* right to dismember, or overthrow it. I can not be ignorant of the fact that many worthy, and patriotic citizens are desirous of having the national constitution amended. While I make no recommendation of amendments, I fully recognize the rightful authority of the people over the whole subject." He said that he had a "patient confidence in the ultimate justice of the people" and asked: "Is there any better, or equal hope, in the world?"

Lincoln then proceeded to address the threat of impending military conflict—a threat that all felt, though few were willing to address head on. "In *your* hands, my dissatisfied fellow countrymen, and not in *mine*, is the momentous issue of civil war. The government will not assail *you*. You can have no conflict, without being yourself the aggressors. *You* have no oath registered in Heaven to destroy the government, while *I* shall have the most solemn one to 'preserve, protect and defend' it."

The president-elect closed his address with the affirmation that Americans, Northerners and Southerners alike, were "not enemies, but friends," saying almost imploringly: "We must not be enemies. Though passion may have strained, it must not break our bonds of affection. The mystic chords of memory, stretching from every battlefield, and patriot grave, to every living heart and hearthstone, all over this broad land, will yet swell the chorus of the Union, when again touched, as surely they will be, by the better angels of our nature."[52]

In all, Lincoln had spoken for thirty minutes. The *New York Times* reporter said that Chief Justice Taney "did not remove his eyes from Mr. Lincoln during the entire delivery." James Buchanan, in contrast, seemed "sleepy and tired," while Senator Douglas muttered from time to time during the presentation.

"Good," he said at one point. "That's so," at another. "No coercion," and "Good again."[53]

Now Chief Justice Taney stepped forward, holding out a Bible. In a low voice, he recited the prescribed words of the oath and asked Lincoln to repeat them. Speaking in a "firm but modest voice," the president proclaimed his oath: "I, Abraham Lincoln, do solemnly swear that I will faithfully execute the office of President of the United States, and will to the best of my ability, preserve, protect, and defend the Constitution of the United States."[54]

The chief justice was the first person who shook hands with the new president. Then came James Buchanan, Stephen A. Douglas, Salmon P. Chase, and a host of minor officials. After a brief delay, Lincoln and Buchanan, again arm in arm, retreated from the platform into the Senate chamber, while the Marine band outside played patriotic tunes, "Hail Columbia," "Yankee Doodle," and "The Star-Spangled Banner." In a little while another procession was formed outside the Capitol. Dignitaries once again took seats in their carriages, and the barouche with Abraham Lincoln and James Buchanan in it led the whole party to the White House.[55]

Lincoln now plunged into the work of the presidency. The day following his inauguration, he received an urgent message from Major Robert Anderson at Fort Sumter in South Carolina, advising him that it would take at least 20,000 men to reinforce the beleaguered fort in Charleston harbor, which state officials had demanded be turned over to them. The president conferred with General in Chief Winfield Scott, who agreed with Anderson's assessment. The Senate confirmed the president's cabinet nominations: William H. Seward of New York as secretary of state, Salmon P. Chase of Ohio as secretary of the treasury, Simon Cameron of Pennsylvania as secretary of war, Gideon Welles of Connecticut as secretary of the navy, Caleb B. Smith of Indiana as secretary of the interior, Montgomery Blair of Maryland as postmaster general, and Edward Bates of Missouri as attorney general. These seven men, representing different sections of the country and different factions of the Republican Party, had little more in common than a commitment to preservation of the Union and a desire to share in the spoils of Republican victory. Not surprisingly, however, five of the seven were lawyers by profession, like the president himself (Cameron was a printer and newspaper publisher, and Welles–originally a lawyer–was a journalist). Whatever their other abilities (or shortcomings), Lincoln's cabinet officers shared the new president's understanding of government as a legal process. Even the process of waging war—if a war there must be—would be conceived and carried out in the broad framework of legal rules and constitutional precepts.

WHILE THE PRESIDENT worked in the White House, the justices of the Supreme Court carried on their duties in the Capitol. They had memorialized the death of Associate Justice Peter V. Daniel of Virginia when they met for the first time in their new courtroom on December 4, 1860, then proceeded to consider the cases on their docket, listening patiently to the oral arguments of the lawyers (which sometimes seemed almost interminable), researching the controlling precedents, and retiring to their conference room to discuss the cases, assign the writing of opinions, and read the opinions in open court.[56] The docket for the December term of 1860 (most of which extended into 1861) contained a typical mix of cases, including land disputes, commercial disagreements, and real or imagined controversies between citizens of different states. Two cases, however, stood out from the rest, and decisions in both were announced on March 14, 1861.

Kentucky v. Dennison was one of many cases that had their origins in the desire of slaves to seek freedom, oftentimes by escaping into free states or, if brought by their masters into a free state while still in bondage, by running away. As human as this desire certainly was, it was firmly prohibited by the Fugitive Slave Clause. Although the clause did not explicitly authorize Congress to enact enforcing legislation, it was assumed from an early date that it had the power to do so, and Fugitive Slave Laws were enacted in 1793 and 1850, prescribing procedures under which slave owners could go into free states and demand the surrender of escaped slaves. When the constitutionality of the 1793 act was eventually challenged, it was upheld by the Supreme Court in *Prigg v. Pennsylvania* in 1842.[57] In that case, Justice Joseph Story sustained the federal law and condemned state "freedom laws" that attempted to interfere with it. Not surprisingly, Chief Justice Taney concurred in Story's 1842 opinion, while Justice McLean dissented from it.

In October 1859, a slave girl owned by a Kentuckian had run away from her master while he was traveling through Ohio on his way to Virginia. The girl, identified in the court records as Charlotte, was helped in her bid for freedom by an Ohio resident named Willis Lago, described in the same records as a "free man of color." Back in Kentucky an indictment was returned accusing Lago of the crime of "assisting a slave to escape." A copy of the indictment, certified and authenticated according to the Fugitive Slave Law of 1793, was presented to Governor William Dennison of Ohio, with a demand that Lago be turned over to the Kentucky authorities for trial. After conferring with his attorney general, Dennison determined that Lago was not subject to extradition, for Ohio law provided that a prisoner could be extradited only for treason or felony and, under Ohio law, Lago's alleged offense was neither. The Commonwealth of Kentucky then petitioned the Supreme Court in Washington to issue a writ of mandamus compelling Dennison to extradite Lago. Kentucky pointed out that the 1793 act provided that "it shall be the duty" of the governor to surrender a fugitive under the specified circumstances.[58]

The decision in *Kentucky v. Dennison* was announced on March 14 by Chief Justice Taney. He ruled that Kentucky's demand for Lago was plainly authorized by the act of 1793 and that the duty of Ohio's governor to surrender the man was clear. "The exception made to the validity of the indictment," he stated, "is altogether untenable." But Taney was more than usually sensitive to claims of state's rights. He knew that a writ of mandamus issuing from the Supreme Court to the governor of Ohio would signify that other states were also subject to the compulsion of federal law. In the nation's current secession crisis, a writ of mandamus would be taken as a precedent that the federal government could compel the states to act according to its dictates rather than theirs. It was a precedent that Taney was not willing to lay down. And so he examined the Fugitive Slave Law for any provision subjecting the governor of Ohio to a penalty for failing to do his duty. He found none. "It is true that Congress may authorize a particular State officer to perform a particular duty," Taney wrote, "but if he declines to do so, it does not follow that he may be coerced, or punished for his refusal." When the Constitution was framed, Taney said, "it was confidently believed that a sense of justice and of mutual interest would insure a faithful execution of this constitutional provision by the Executive of every State. . . . But if the Governor of Ohio refuses to discharge this duty, there is no power delegated to the General Government, either through the Judicial Department or any other department to use any coercive means to compel him." And upon that ground the Court overruled the motion for mandamus.[59] Charlotte had achieved her freedom, and Lago was not subject to the tender mercies of Kentucky justice.

The second case of special interest that was decided by the Supreme Court on March 14, 1861, drew a crowd of spectators to the tribunal's elegant new courtroom to hear Justice Wayne read the court's opinion. *Gaines v. Hennen* gave signs of signaling an end to one of the most celebrated (and protracted) legal struggles in American history. Usually referred to as the "Gaines case," the litigation involved the title to large tracts of land in New Orleans estimated to be worth as much as $15 million.

A woman who called herself Myra Clark had appeared in New Orleans in 1834 with a New York–born husband and a claim that she was the legitimate daughter of Daniel Clark, a wealthy Irishman who had died in New Orleans in 1813. After her birth, she said, her father had sent her off to be raised by a family in Delaware. He had visited her there from time to time but taken precautions to conceal his paternity (Myra's mother was an exotic New Orleans beauty who may or may not have been married to another man when she met Clark and conceived Myra). Myra and her husband had recently investigated the facts of Clark's marriage to her mother and convinced themselves not only that Myra was Clark's legitimate daughter but also that, shortly before his death, he had made a will leaving all of his New Orleans property to her. They said his business partners had suppressed the will and begun selling off parts of the property.

The legal wrangling over the Clark estate began in Louisiana state courts but soon found its way into the federal courts in New Orleans. At issue were the legitimacy of Myra Clark, the existence of Daniel Clark's will, the jurisdiction of the federal courts to become involved in the controversy, and the applicability of equity rules in federal courts. The case came before the United States Supreme Court more than a dozen times, where arguments were made by Chief Justice Taney's brother-in-law Francis Scott Key and by Taney's friend Reverdy Johnson. Even Daniel Webster, Henry Clay, and the future justice Campbell of Alabama, while still a practicing lawyer, became involved in the litigation. After the death of her first husband, Myra Clark married Major General Edmund P. Gaines, a hero of the War of 1812, who had the financial means to continue the litigation and who gave the case the name by which it would be remembered in the Supreme Court reports.

In this phase of her struggle, Mrs. Gaines, now represented by Caleb Cushing, a Massachusetts lawyer who was attorney general under President Franklin Pierce, was seeking to establish title to New Orleans land claimed by a man named Douglas Hennen. Although the Hennen tract was only part of the Clark estate, a newspaper reported that it covered "about two-thirds of the city of New Orleans." The Supreme Court case was argued in a crowded courtroom in mid-February 1861, and on March 14, in a long and detailed opinion, Justice Wayne sustained Mrs. Gaines's position.[60] If she was not technically legitimate, Wayne ruled, the evidence established that her father had married her mother in good faith, so for purposes of inheritance she would be regarded as legitimate and her claim to the Hennen property was valid. Justices McLean, Nelson, and Clifford concurred in Wayne's opinion. Chief Justice Taney and Justices Grier and Catron dissented. Because of his previous involvement in the case, Justice Campbell took no part in the decision. "Thus," Justice Wayne stated at the end of his opinion, "after a litigation of thirty years, has this Court adjudicated the principles applicable to [Mrs. Gaines's] rights in her father's estate. They are now finally settled. When, hereafter, some distinguished American shall retire from his practice to write the history of his country's jurisprudence, this case will be registered by him as the most remarkable in the records of its Courts."

Wayne was partly right and largely wrong. The legal principles established in the Gaines case were not especially noteworthy, although the case's fame proved to be long-lasting. But the decision rendered in 1861 did not finally settle the litigation. Mrs. Gaines went north after the decision, apprehensive that the victory she had won in Washington might be disregarded in the new Confederate State of Louisiana. Her apprehension was well founded, for her case was not finally settled until 1891, after the war that started in 1861 had been fought to a Confederate surrender and Louisiana and the other Confederate states had been subjected to the rigors of post-war reconstruction. But Mrs. Gaines had died at the age of eighty in 1885. By 1891 both she and Justice Wayne had long since been laid to rest in their graves.

FOLLOWING THE ANNOUNCEMENT of its decisions in *Kentucky v. Dennison* and *Gaines v. Hennen*, the Supreme Court adjourned. Their duties in Washington concluded, the judges left the capital city for their circuits, Justice McLean heading home to Ohio, Justice Clifford to Maine, Nelson to New York, and

Grier to Pennsylvania. It was more difficult for the Southern justices to determine exactly when they would leave Washington, or if they would leave at all. The federal courts were under siege in the states that had already seceded, and the status of the courts in the border states was uncertain. Justice Catron, determined to do his duty, announced that he was going home to Nashville. But Justice Wayne showed no interest in leaving for Savannah, and Justice Campbell decided to remain in Washington, at least for a while. Chief Justice Taney had, in the late 1850s, closed his house in Baltimore and settled into a rented house on Indiana Avenue in Washington. It was near enough to Baltimore that he could go there on short notice, if and when he was needed in the circuit court.

And so, ten days after Abraham Lincoln was inaugurated as sixteenth president of the United States, the Supreme Court found itself in a quandary. What were its duties in the looming sectional crisis, and how should those duties be discharged? On March 4, before tens of thousands of witnesses, the president had taken an "oath registered in Heaven" to "preserve, protect, and defend" the Constitution. The Supreme Court justices had also taken oaths to discharge their official duties "agreeably to the Constitution and laws of the United States."[61] Now each official—president and the Supreme Court justice—would have to decide how their oaths would govern their duties.

2   Dred Scott

A<small>NYONE IN WASHINGTON</small> in 1861 who doubted that the Supreme Court would be an important player in the great drama then unfolding in the nation had a very short memory. The Court, it is true, was a legal tribunal, a panel of jurists selected by presidents and senators for their knowledge of the Constitution and the laws, their familiarity with judicial precedents, and their ability to reflect soberly on conflicting claims of rights and privileges. The Founding Fathers had believed that the Supreme Court justices would be passive actors in the governmental process, unable to reach out into the body politic to impose their will but instead obliged to wait for issues to come to them for resolution. In the *Federalist Papers*, Alexander Hamilton had said that, of the three branches of government authorized by the Constitution, the judiciary would "always be the least dangerous to the political rights of the constitution; because it will be least in a capacity to annoy or injure them." While the executive, Hamilton noted, "holds the sword of the community," and the legislature "commands the purse" and "prescribes the rules by which the duties and rights of every citizen are to be regulated," the judiciary "may truly be said to have neither Force nor Will, but merely judgment; and must ultimately depend upon the aid of the executive arm even for the efficacy of its judgments."[1] In theory, of course, Hamilton was correct—but nations do not live by theory alone for, as Oliver Wendell Holmes, Jr., once noted, "The life of the law has not been logic, it has been experience."[2] Long before Abraham Lincoln took his oath to "preserve, protect, and defend" the Constitution, the American experience had shown that Congress, the president, and the Supreme Court all had the capacity to damage the nation through improvident decisions and foolish acts, or failures to act. Anyone who doubted that the high court could inflict wounds on the republic had to look no further than its decision in the case of *Dred Scott v. Sandford*, announced to an astonished courtroom and nation on March 6 and 7, 1857.

Dred Scott was the most highly publicized decision ever made by the Supreme Court, and one of its most ambitious. It was recognized throughout the country as a decision of great importance, though observers differed sharply as to whether it was incredibly wise or foolishly wrong. The verdict of history would eventually settle on the side of those who believed it wrong, but before that verdict was rendered, the social and economic life of the nation was disrupted, its political parties were rearranged, its elections were influenced, and a bloody war was fought. And all these consequences were attributable, at least in part, to the pronouncement of the Supreme Court justices in the case of *Dred Scott v. Sandford*. In the words of constitutional historian Paul Finkelman: "It would be an exaggeration to say that the *Dred Scott* decision *caused* the Civil War. But it certainly pushed the nation far closer to that war."[3]

THE LEGAL PROCEEDINGS that gave rise to *Dred Scott* began on April 6, 1846, when an obscure "man of color" appeared before a justice of the peace in St. Louis and swore to the truth of a petition filed that day in the St. Louis Circuit Court. The man, who bore the peculiar name of Dred Scott, was required to sign the petition at the same time that he swore to its truth. As a slave, however, he had never been taught to read or write, so the best he could do was make an X in the space provided for his signature. Scott's X would be repeated many times over in the dozen or so years that remained in his life, becoming a kind of symbol of one of the most sensational legal battles in the history of the United States. It would also reflect the deep scars that chattel slavery, and Dred Scott's effort to free himself from it, left on that history.

Dred Scott first saw the light of day in Virginia, on a plantation owned by a man named Peter Blow. No record of his birth was made, but historians estimate that it was around 1800, give or take five years. The slave boy grew up with the four sons and three daughters of Peter Blow. The Blows were his masters, but they also became his friends, and their friendship would later play an important role in his fight to become a free man.

Around 1818, Peter Blow left Virginia, taking his family and slaves with him. They went first to Alabama, where they remained for several years, and then to St. Louis, where Blow became the proprietor of the Jefferson Hotel. Blow died in 1832, and in the following year Dred Scott was sold, probably to raise funds to pay debts. His new master was an army surgeon named John Emerson, who had been ordered to report for duty at Fort Armstrong, about two hundred miles north of St. Louis.[4] While serving at his new post, Dr. Emerson acquired some adjoining land and built a log cabin on it. Dred Scott probably did much of the actual work of putting up the cabin, for Emerson himself was almost chronically sick. Fort Armstrong was located on Rock Island, near the confluence of the Rock River and the Mississippi. More important, it was in Illinois, which had been admitted to the Union in 1818 as a state in which slavery was prohibited both by the state constitution and by federal enactment.

Like all of the territory north and west of the Ohio River, Illinois had once been governed by the Northwest Ordinance, passed by Congress in 1787 under the old Articles of Confederation. This charter, which established the basic framework for the American territorial system, provided that there should be neither slavery nor involuntary servitude in that territory, "otherwise than in the punishment of crimes, whereof the party shall have been duly convicted." If either Dr. Emerson or Dred Scott was aware in 1832 that the law of Illinois forbade slavery, the record is silent on the point.

In 1836, Emerson was transferred to Fort Snelling, on the west bank of the Mississippi, near the place where St. Paul, Minnesota, was later built. Then part of Wisconsin Territory, Fort Snelling occupied land that had originally been part of the Louisiana Purchase and that had been governed since 1820 by the Missouri Compromise. Passed by Congress under the leadership of Kentucky's Henry Clay, the Missouri Compromise was the first major attempt to bridge the sectional differences that divided the Northern and the Southern states. It provided that Missouri would enter the Union as a slave state and Maine as a free state (thus preserving the North-South balance in Congress) and that slavery would be "forever prohibited" in the remaining Louisiana territory north of latitude 36° 30′ (the southern boundary of Missouri). At Fort Snelling, Scott met a slave girl named Harriet, the property of the resident Indian agent. With the agent himself performing the ceremony, Dred and Harriet were married. They proceeded to raise a family that eventually included two sons (later deceased) and two daughters, Eliza and Lizzie. Dred and

Harriet's marriage may have indicated that they were considered free blacks at Fort Snelling, for under the slave codes of the time, slaves were not permitted to marry.[5]

When Emerson was ordered back to Missouri in 1837, Dred and his new family remained at Fort Snelling, apparently unsupervised. But when the doctor received further orders to report to Fort Jesup in Louisiana, they came down the Mississippi to join him and his new bride, the former Irene Sanford. Emerson was miserable in the damp climate of Louisiana, however, and requested a transfer back to Fort Snelling. Once again, Dred and his family traveled north into land where slavery was forbidden. By 1840, the ever-restless Dr. Emerson had secured a new assignment, this time in Florida. His wife and slaves left Fort Snelling with him but stayed behind in St. Louis when he went on to Florida. Separated from the service in 1842, Emerson returned to St. Louis, then moved on to Iowa Territory, where he died in December 1843, leaving his widow, Irene, and his daughter, Henrietta, as his heirs.

For the next three years, Scott and his wife worked as hired slaves. Scott lived for a while with Mrs. Emerson's brother-in-law, an army captain named Henry Bainbridge, who took him to Texas. But he was back in St. Louis in 1846 and thinking about obtaining his freedom. He offered to buy his own and his family's freedom from Mrs. Emerson, but she refused. He then sought the assistance of an attorney named Francis B. Murdoch and, on April 6, 1846, filed suit in the St. Louis Circuit Court, reciting the facts of his residence in Illinois and the Wisconsin Territory and seeking a judgment establishing his and his family's status as free persons. Harriet Scott filed a petition alleging similar facts. After Mrs. Emerson filed her pleas of "not guilty," the attorneys began to prepare for the trial of the Scotts' lawsuit, which was set to be held at the St. Louis Courthouse in June 1847.

At first blush, the Scott case seemed eminently winnable. It was uncontested that both Dred and Harriet had been taken to reside on free soil—first in Illinois, later in Wisconsin Territory—and that they had lived on that soil for several years. The law of Missouri, established by the state's Supreme Court as early as 1824, was that residence in a free state like Illinois had the effect of emancipating a slave who was taken there.[6] This was also the law in Kentucky, Louisiana, and Mississippi.[7] The law was based on the principle, announced in 1772 in the English case of *Somerset v. Stewart*, that the status of a slave was "so odious, that nothing can be suffered to support it, but positive law."[8] Where there was no "positive [that is, statute] law" to support it, as in Illinois and the Wisconsin Territory, slaves reverted to their "natural status" as free persons. But the Scotts' attorneys (they now had two) had not adequately prepared for an essential part of their case, proving that Mrs. Emerson was holding Dred and Harriet Scott in slavery. The one witness who testified on the issue had to admit that he had no personal knowledge as to whether Irene Emerson did or did not claim to be the Scotts' owner. So when the case was submitted to the jury, a verdict was rendered in Mrs. Emerson's favor. The judge granted a motion for a new trial, but Mrs. Emerson appealed to the Missouri Supreme Court, which sent the case back with a reminder that an order granting a new trial was not subject to appeal. Meanwhile, valuable time had been lost.

It was January 1850 before the new trial got under way. This time the evidence of Mrs. Emerson's ownership was clear, and the jury's verdict was that Dred, Harriet, and their two daughters were free. But Mrs. Emerson appealed again. By 1852, when the case reached the Missouri Supreme Court for the second time, Missouri was in political turmoil, largely because slavery was becoming a more and more explosive issue both in the state and nationally. The state's veteran U.S. senator Thomas Hart Benton (a moderate on the issue of slavery) had been turned out of office, and two new judges (one a proslavery Democrat) had been elected to the three-member state Supreme Court. On March 22, 1852, the new proslavery judge, William Scott, joined forces with another proslavery judge and overturned long-standing Missouri precedents, deciding that, despite their long residences in Illinois and Wisconsin Territory, the Scotts were still slaves. Judge Scott said that the question of whether one state (such as Missouri) was obliged to recognize the laws of another state (such as Illinois) was to be answered according to principles of comity. "Every State has the right of determining how far, in a spirit of comity, it will respect the laws of other States," Scott said. "Those laws have no intrinsic right to be enforced beyond the limits of the State for which they were enacted." The judge admitted that his ruling upset established Missouri precedent, but he explained that "a dark and fell spirit in relation to slavery" had fallen across the country, forcing changes in the law governing the institution.[9] Dred Scott and his family might think they should be free; previous decisions of the Missouri Supreme Court might indicate that they deserved to be free; and the jury impaneled to hear their case in St. Louis might have decided that they were in fact free—but the Missouri Supreme Court, by a vote of two to one, decreed that they were still slaves.

The Scotts were disheartened by the decision but probably not surprised. They had already lived most of their lives as slaves, and slaves were used to disappointment. The whites who were now helping them prosecute their case—Dred Scott's boyhood chum, Taylor Blow, and other members of the Blow family—may have been more discomfited, for they were now paying the bills for the Scotts' attorneys, and thus far there was little to show for the money spent.

The Scotts' attorneys could have decided at this point to pursue an appeal from the Missouri Supreme Court to the United States Supreme Court. Section 25 of the Judiciary Act of 1789 gave the U.S. Supreme Court jurisdiction to review the decisions of state supreme courts under writs of error, but only in specified circumstances. Those circumstances generally required a showing that the state decision denied the validity of a federal statute or constitutional provision, or applied a state law in such a way as to deny the validity of a federal statute or constitutional provision.[10] But there was little in the record of the *Dred Scott* case that would support such a showing. Further, the U.S. Supreme Court had only the previous year decided a case that could be applied to deny any claim to freedom the Scotts might assert under the law of Illinois.

In that Supreme Court case, *Strader v. Graham* (1851), three slaves owned by a Kentuckian named Christopher Graham had escaped to freedom aboard an Ohio River steamboat owned by Jacob Strader. The slaves were musicians who had previously been permitted to travel in Ohio and Indiana to give performances. Under Kentucky law, if slaves escaped aboard a boat, the boat owner was liable to the slaveholder for the value of the slaves. When Graham sued Strader in a Kentucky court, Strader argued that the musicians were not slaves but free men, for Graham had previously allowed them to travel to Indiana and Ohio, parts of the old Northwest Territory, where slavery was prohibited. But the Kentucky courts sided with Graham, held that the musicians were still slaves, and entered judgment against Strader. The case was taken to the Kentucky Court of Appeals, where the judgment was affirmed, and then to the United States Supreme Court on a writ of error. Announcing a unanimous decision in the case, Chief Justice Taney had declared that "every State has an undoubted right to determine the *status* or domestic condition, of the persons domiciled within its territory." Thus Kentucky was fully within its rights in deciding that the three musicians were still slaves when they escaped on Strader's boat. Further, Taney asserted that the Northwest Ordinance no longer had any force and could not be used to free a slave. Even if it had been in force, he added, congressional legislation for a particular territory could have no power beyond the limits of that territory.[11] *Strader* was distinguishable in important particulars from Dred Scott's case (Graham's slaves had been in Ohio and Indiana only temporarily, while the Scotts had been in Illinois and the Wisconsin Territory as residents and for an extended time), but it was nonetheless a discouraging precedent.

In the meantime, the human landscape of the *Dred Scott* case changed dramatically. Mrs. Emerson moved to Massachusetts and married a man named Calvin Chaffee, and her brother, a St. Louis businessman named John F. A. Sanford, took control of the Scotts. Sanford, too, left Missouri for New York, leaving the Scotts behind in St. Louis, where they were hired out for work and their pay was collected by the sheriff to be turned over to the person or persons ultimately determined to be entitled to them (Dred and Harriet Scott if they were free, Irene Chaffee or John Sanford if they were still slaves). To add to the complications of the case, one of the attorneys who had been representing the Scotts died, another left the state, and a new attorney was retained. The new attorney was Roswell M. Field, a native of Vermont who had practiced law in St. Louis since 1839. Field was inexperienced in the intricacies of Missouri slave law (his specialty was land titles), and he was not an abolitionist. But he was opposed to slavery. More important, perhaps, he was concerned about the misapplication of Missouri law to Dred Scott's case.[12]

Field decided to file a new lawsuit, this time in the U.S. Circuit Court for the District of Missouri. His allegations, filed in St. Louis on November 2, 1853, were, first, that John Sanford was wrongfully holding Dred Scott, his wife, Harriet, and their daughters, Eliza and Lizzie, as slaves, to their damage in the sum of $9,000; and, second, that the Scotts were citizens of Missouri and that Sanford was a citizen of New York. The latter allegation, if true, would establish the federal court's jurisdiction to hear the case under Article III, Section 2, of the U.S. Constitution, which provides (in relevant part): "The judicial power [of the United States] shall extend . . . to controversies . . . between citizens of different states." Congress implemented this provision in the Judi-

ciary Act of 1789 by providing that "the circuit courts shall have original cognizance, concurrent with the courts of the several States, of all suits of a civil
nature at common law or in equity, where the matter in dispute exceeds, exclusive of costs, the sum or value of five hundred dollars, and . . . the suit is
between a citizen of the State where the suit is brought and a citizen of another
State."[13]

The constitutional provision is known as the Diversity Clause, and it is
customarily used to bring suits into the federal courts that might otherwise be
filed and tried in state courts. The statutory provision added the further requirement of a minimum amount in controversy (if the minimum amount was
not in controversy, the suit would be tried in a state court, even though it was
between citizens of different states). By claiming $9,000 damages, the Scotts
had met the requirement that the amount in controversy exceed five hundred
dollars. But Sanford was not prepared to concede that the circuit court had jurisdiction. His attorneys filed a plea in abatement, arguing that Dred Scott was
not a citizen of Missouri because his ancestors were "of pure African blood, and
were brought into this country and sold as negro slaves." If sustained, this plea
would remove the case from the operation of the Diversity Clause and require
the circuit court to dismiss the suit for lack of jurisdiction. The federal district
judge for Missouri was Robert W. Wells, a former Virginia slaveholder who had
long experience in the federal court in Missouri. After the Scotts' attorney filed
a demurrer to Sanford's plea in abatement, Wells ruled in favor of the Scotts,
saying that, for the purpose of bringing suit in federal court, citizenship meant
nothing more than residence in the designated state and the legal capacity to
own property. Wells did not determine that the Scotts were entitled to all of
the benefits of citizenship, merely that if, as they alleged, they were not slaves,
they were entitled to bring suit in the federal courts under the Diversity
Clause.

Judge Wells's ruling on the plea in abatement forced Sanford to reply to
the merits of the Scotts' lawsuit, and he did so, admitting that he had "restrained" the Scotts "of their liberty," but for good reason, for they were his
slaves. The case was submitted to a jury in May 1854, under instructions from
Judge Wells that the law "is with the defendant" (a recognition that the Missouri Supreme Court had already decided that the Scotts were still slaves).[14]
Since they were slaves, they were not "citizens" for purposes of diversity juris-

diction, even under Judge Wells's concept. At this point, the judge should have dismissed the case for lack of jurisdiction. But he did not, thus making it possible to take the case on to the United States Supreme Court.

It has been speculated that the federal suit was not filed for the purpose of obtaining relief in the circuit court in St. Louis, but to establish a record that could be submitted to the Supreme Court in Washington. The speculation seems plausible, although evidence supporting it is murky. Which side (the Scotts or Sanford) was most anxious to obtain a hearing in the Supreme Court? Did the Scotts ever have a realistic hope that the court presided over by Roger Taney would grant them relief? They must have known that the Supreme Court tilted heavily toward the South and that its recent opinion in *Strader v. Graham* did not favor them.

Missouri had already ruled that the Scotts were slaves under Missouri law. If that position had been affirmed in the United States Supreme Court, no one would have been surprised, and no explosion of public opinion could have been expected. At some point, however, the attorneys and parties realized that the case had broader implications than merely establishing the status of a single slave and his family. Congress was now involved in an angry debate over the Kansas-Nebraska Bill, which would repeal the part of the Missouri Compromise that prohibited slavery north of 36° 30′ and erect in its place the doctrine of "popular sovereignty." This would authorize the people of each territory to decide for themselves whether the territory would permit or prohibit slavery. Popular sovereignty was championed by the "Little Giant" of Illinois politics, Democratic Senator Stephen A. Douglas, who believed its passage would defuse tensions between the North and South and, in the process, further his own presidential ambitions. The Kansas-Nebraska Act became law on May 30, 1854, just days after Dred Scott's trial ended in the federal circuit court in St. Louis. But it did not calm the troubled waters. Agitation on the issue of slavery continued, though much of the force of the argument was now directed toward Kansas, where pro- and antislavery forces, energized by the promise of popular sovereignty, were jostling for control of the territorial government.

FOLLOWING THE FEDERAL circuit court's decision against them, Dred Scott's friends took steps to appeal the case to the United States Supreme

Court. On July 4, 1854, they published a pamphlet summarizing the history of the now eight-year-old litigation and voicing a personal plea from Scott that someone come forward to "speak for me at Washington, even without hope of other reward than the blessings of a poor black man and his family."[15] There had been no reply by Christmas, when Roswell Field wrote to a Washington attorney named Montgomery Blair, asking if he or some other lawyer in the capital city might serve "the cause of humanity" by taking up the case. Blair was one of Washington's best-known lawyers, but he also had strong ties to Missouri. His father was the Virginia-born Francis P. Blair, Sr., a close friend and adviser of President Andrew Jackson and a longtime publisher, first of the *Washington Globe* (1830–1854) and later of the *Congressional Globe* (1837–1872), predecessor of the *Congressional Record*. Montgomery Blair's younger brother, Francis P. (Frank) Blair, Jr., was also an attorney and one of the political leaders of Missouri.

Born in Kentucky in 1813, and educated at the U.S. Military Academy at West Point and at Kentucky's Transylvania College, Montgomery Blair moved in 1837 to Missouri, where he began his legal career. With the support of Senator Benton, he served as the U.S. district attorney for Missouri, mayor of St. Louis, and judge of the Court of Common Pleas. He moved to Washington in 1853 and took up residence in the family-owned Blair House, across the street from the White House. His wife was the daughter of Levi Woodbury of New Hampshire, an associate justice of the Supreme Court from 1845 to 1851. Once ardent Democrats, the Blairs were not strongly opposed to slavery, but they believed that the institution should not be extended into the western territories, and the violence that was now racking "Bleeding Kansas" was pushing them in the direction of the new Republican Party. Responding to Field's letter, Montgomery Blair agreed to take up the *Dred Scott* case in Washington, with Field preparing legal documents in St. Louis and Blair working on a Washington brief. Blair also agreed to present the oral argument in the Supreme Court.

Opposing Blair when the case finally reached the Supreme Court were two prominent attorneys in Washington: Henry S. Geyer, a proslavery Democrat recently elected to the United States Senate from Missouri, and Reverdy Johnson, a friend of Chief Justice Taney who had been a U.S. senator from Maryland from 1845 to 1849 and attorney general of the United States (appointed by Zachary Taylor) from 1849 to 1850. The eminence of the lawyers attested to the political significance that had attached to the case. Johnson, in particular, was a veteran of many important court battles, a supporter of slavery, and one of the ablest appellate attorneys in the country.

The Court heard oral arguments from February 11 through 14, 1856. Montgomery Blair led off by arguing that Judge Wells had correctly ruled that a person of African descent who was not a slave could be a citizen for purposes of commencing a lawsuit under the Diversity Clause, but in error when he instructed the jury that the Scotts' status had been finally determined by the Missouri Supreme Court. Geyer and Johnson argued that a person of African descent was never intended to be included within the term *citizen* as used in the Diversity Clause. Further, they advanced a new (and potentially explosive) argument: that the Missouri Compromise provision prohibiting slavery north of 36° 30′ was unconstitutional. They referred to Article IV, Section 3, of the Constitution, the so-called Territories Clause, which provides (in relevant part): "The Congress shall have power to dispose of and make all needful rules and regulations respecting the territory or other property belonging to the United States." This power, Geyer and Johnson argued, applied only to "land or other property" belonging to the United States. It did not include the power to make laws for the government of federal territories; certainly it did not include the power to prohibit slavery in the territories, or to prevent slaveholders from taking their slaves there from slaveholding states. Southern politicians had made similar arguments in Congress over a period of years, although never successfully, but they were now beginning to put this view forward with increasing vehemence.

The arguments concluded, the Court retired to confer on the case. The justices apparently were undecided as to exactly how to proceed, for they conferred a second time, then declared a month-long recess before returning for another series of conferences. Meanwhile, political arguments about slavery in the territories were becoming more and more heated. Violence was escalating in Kansas—evidence, many thought, that popular sovereignty was a poor answer to the great political issue that confronted the nation. And the political parties were gearing up for another presidential election in November. Recognizing that the issue was politically explosive, the Court decided on May 12 to put the whole matter over to the following term, ordering new arguments with special attention to the issue of whether a person of African descent could bring a lawsuit in federal court under the Diversity Clause.

The second round of arguments began on December 15, 1856, and continued again for four days. By this time, the lame-duck president Franklin Pierce, a doughface from New Hampshire, was preparing to turn over his executive power to the newly elected James Buchanan, a doughface from Pennsylvania who had just won election in a three-way race with the Know-Nothing candidate, Millard Fillmore, and the Republican nominee, John C. Frémont. Geyer and Johnson were on hand again to represent John F. A. Sanford (although it was increasingly clear that their real client was not Sanford but the slave-holding interests of the South). Montgomery Blair was there on behalf of Dred Scott and his family, but this time he was assisted by George T. Curtis of Massachusetts, who had agreed to present a short argument on Congress's power to exclude slavery from the western territories. Curtis was the brother of Associate Justice Benjamin R. Curtis of Massachusetts, one of the justices who would decide the Scotts' fate. Obviously, neither personal friendships (Taney's with Johnson) nor blood ties (Benjamin Curtis's with George Curtis) were considered sufficient grounds for the recusal of a Supreme Court justice in the middle of the nineteenth century.

Montgomery Blair spoke at length on the right of persons of African descent to be considered citizens under the Diversity Clause. He pointed out that the word *citizen* had been used in both state and federal laws over the years to mean "inhabitant" or "free inhabitant." A person who was a citizen for the purpose of bringing suit, he said, was not necessarily a citizen for other purposes, such as voting, holding office, or serving on a jury. Africans were relegated to a "caste in society," he said, by reason of "manners and customs" but not by law. Blair also argued that the Scotts' long residence in Illinois and the Wisconsin Territory had made them free persons. The Missouri Supreme Court's ruling to the contrary was not binding on the United States Supreme Court, he said, for freedom from slavery was a matter of general law, on which the opinion of the highest court of a state was not conclusive. Further, the Missouri decision had been made in defiance of a long line of Missouri precedents and for purely political reasons. Missouri had never before evidenced hostility to suits for freedom.

Geyer and Johnson repeated the arguments they had made the previous year, but this time they stressed Congress's lack of authority to legislate for the territories. The word *territory* as used in the Territories Clause meant nothing more than "land," they said; it could not be converted into general authority to legislate on the issue of slavery. What's more, the Missouri Compromise restriction on slavery north of 36° 30′ violated the spirit of the Constitution by disparaging the domestic institutions of some states and denying their citizens the right to move into the western territories with whatever property they might chose to bring there (such as slaves). Slavery, a defiant Reverdy Johnson declared, was an institution that would last "through all time."[16]

In reply, George T. Curtis argued that it was well within Congress's power under the Territories Clause to prohibit (or, if it chose, to permit) slavery in federal territories. Congress had done just this in the Missouri Compromise of 1820 and again in the Compromise of 1850. Even the Kansas-Nebraska Act, by authorizing voters in the western territories to exercise their "popular sovereignty" to decide whether they wished to permit or prohibit slavery, was evidence of this congressional power, although in the case of popular sovereignty, Congress's authority was not exercised directly but delegated to the voters.

By the conclusion of the argument, newspapers all over the country were reporting on the impending decision in *Dred Scott v. Sandford* (John Sanford's name was misspelled in the official reports of the case). It was increasingly clear that the issues before the Court corresponded closely with political questions then being debated in Congress, and that nine men in Washington could, if they chose, issue a pronouncement with broad implications for the nation. Alexander H. Stephens, a congressman from Georgia (later to be vice president of the Confederate States of America), had already referred to the litigation as a "great case." Even the president-elect, James Buchanan, was concerned about the upcoming pronouncement and what, if anything, he should say about it in the inaugural address he was to deliver on March 4, 1857. Buchanan had written Justice John Catron of Tennessee in February, asking how the justices were going to vote, and Catron had asked Buchanan to use his influence with Pennsylvania's Justice Robert Grier to urge him to join in an opinion declaring the Missouri Compromise invalid. Buchanan (quite improperly) did so, and Grier (equally improperly) responded to the pressure by assuring the president-elect that he would join with Taney and other justices to strike down the Compromise. On inauguration day, Buchanan appeared at the Capitol in Washington to take his oath of office from Taney and blandly inform the assembled spectators that a "difference of opinion" had arisen "in regard to the point of time when the people of a Territory" could exercise their right (under the doctrine of popular sovereignty) to decide whether to permit or prohibit slavery in the territory. Buchanan assured his listeners that the question was "of but little practical importance." It was "a judicial question," he said, "which legitimately belongs to the Supreme Court of the United States, before whom it is now pending, and will, it is understood, be speedily and finally settled." He further assured his listeners that he would "cheerfully submit" to the Court's decision "whatever this may be."[17]

On the inaugural platform, before the new president delivered his address, Buchanan was seen to exchange a few whispered words with Chief Justice Taney. They were probably only pleasantries, but they raised suspicions that the two men were discussing the *Dred Scott* decision. Of course Buchanan would "cheerfully submit" to a decision if the chief justice had told him in advance what it would be. But Buchanan did not need Taney to tell him what the Supreme Court would decide, for Justice Grier (and possibly other sources) had already done so.

ON MARCH 6, TWO DAYS after Buchanan's inauguration, the justices took their seats in a crowded courtroom in the Capitol and announced their decision. Chief Justice Taney was old and feeble (he would celebrate his eightieth birthday in just eleven days), but he seemed to be invigorated by the occasion. He spoke for two hours, reading from the draft of an "opinion of the Court." Taney might have avoided the thorny political issues of the case by simply deciding that Dred Scott was not a citizen for purposes of the Diversity Clause and thus not entitled to bring his suit in federal court. If that had been the decision, the federal courts would have had no jurisdiction to hear his appeal, and the whole case would have been dismissed. Alternatively, Taney might have decided that the issue of Scott's freedom was foreclosed by the Supreme Court's 1851 decision in *Strader v. Graham*, under which the status of a person domiciled within a state was to be determined by that state alone, without any interference from other states or the federal courts. Such a holding would have avoided the more explosive question of whether Congress had power under the Territories Clause to prohibit slavery in the western territories. But, as James Buchanan knew, Taney had already decided to meet that question head-on.

Taney announced his decision, first, that persons of African ancestry could not be citizens under the Constitution for, when the great charter was framed, the Founding Fathers did not intend to include them in the group denominated the "people of the United States"; nor did they intend to include them in the Declaration of Independence's soaring assertion that "all men are created equal." When the Declaration was signed and the Constitution was adopted, the chief justice said, persons of African descent were "considered as a subordinate and inferior class of beings, who had been subjugated by the dominant race, and, whether emancipated or not, yet remained subject to their authority." In fact, he said, Africans were then deemed "so far inferior that they had no rights which the white man was bound to respect."[18] Thus an African person, free or slave, could not maintain a suit in a federal court, and the circuit court in St. Louis was in error when it declined to dismiss Dred Scott's suit for want of jurisdiction.

Taney then proceeded to discuss the Missouri Compromise and its restriction on slavery north of 36° 30′. In a narrowly cramped reading of the Territories Clause, he said that the power given to Congress "to dispose of and make all needful rules and regulations respecting territory or other property belonging to the United States" referred only to "the territory which at that time belonged to, or was claimed by, the United States." Thus it applied only to the old Northwest Territory which, by 1857, had all been subdivided into self-governing states. He admitted that Congress had power, under Article IV, Section 3, to admit new states into the Union, and that, by implication from this power, it also had power to provide the initial government for a territory before it was admitted as a state. But if Congress actually governed a territory (or established rules under which the territory would be governed), he said, it would be maintaining "colonies bordering on the United States or at a distance to be ruled and governed at its own pleasure." Since Congress had no power to govern a territory, it had no power to exclude slavery from a territory. Further, Congress could not violate constitutional provisions guaranteeing personal rights, and one such provision was the Due Process Clause of the Fifth Amendment, which provides (in relevant part): "No person shall be . . . deprived of life, liberty, or property, without due process of law." Taney said that slaves were a form of property protected by the Fifth Amendment wherever their owner might take them.[19] Thus the provision of the Missouri Compromise that restricted slavery in the western territories was unconstitutional and void.

Justice Samuel Nelson of New York followed the chief justice, reading an opinion that concurred with Taney's result but offered a different rationale. In Nelson's opinion, the status of Dred Scott and his family was to be determined solely by the state of Missouri and solely under Missouri law. Nelson agreed that Congress had no power to prohibit slavery in any federal territory. But even if it did, he argued, a prohibition could not be given extraterritorial effect in a slaveholding state, for if Congress had the power to *prohibit* slavery in a territory, it would also have the power to *establish* slavery in a territory. Giving extraterritorial effect to a congressional enactment *establishing* slavery would require that an African who became a slave in a territory would have to be regarded as a slave in a free state.[20] Such a result would be absurd, Nelson said, and could not be tolerated in any free state.

Justice John Catron was next to read his opinion, which also concurred with the chief justice's result but stated different reasons. The Tennessean agreed that the Missouri Compromise provision restricting slavery was unconstitutional, but not because Congress lacked the power to govern the territories. In the exercise of his circuit court duties, Catron had for nearly twenty years been exercising jurisdiction from the western Missouri line to the Rocky Mountains (in some cases even imposing the death penalty) under the authority of legislation enacted by Congress. He thought it was "asking much" of a judge who had done this "to agree that he had been all the while acting in mistake, and as an usurper." But Catron maintained that the Missouri Compromise restriction on slavery violated the treaty with France under which the United States had acquired the Louisiana Territory. In that treaty, the United States agreed to protect the inhabitants of the territory "in the free enjoyment of their liberty, property, and the religion which they profess." Since the right to own slaves was guaranteed in French Louisiana, Catron said, Congress could not prohibit slavery in any part of that territory.[21]

On March 7, Justice John McLean and Justice Benjamin R. Curtis read their opinions, both of which dissented from Taney's. They vigorously disputed the chief justice's analysis of African American citizenship, insisting that there was no consensus among the founders that persons of African descent were disqualified from citizenship. In some states, free Africans were permitted to vote, to own property, and even to hold public office. It was a misreading of American history to conclude that they never had any rights under the Constitution. It has often been speculated that McLean's and Curtis's opinions were prepared before Taney prepared his, and that the chief justice was provoked into a discussion of the territorial question by the knowledge that McLean and Curtis would discuss that question in their opinions. The evidence on this question is not persuasive, however. McLean and Curtis were firm in their convictions that persons of African descent could be citizens under the Diversity Clause and that Congress had ample authority to deal with the question of slavery in the territories under the Territories Clause, and they were determined to state their views. And Roger Taney was firm in his contrary convictions, and equally determined to state them.

McLean's opposition to slavery was known throughout the country long before 1857. Benjamin Curtis's, in contrast, was not. A Whig from Massachusetts, Curtis had joined the Supreme Court in 1851 as an appointee of President Millard Fillmore. He was one of Boston's most respected lawyers, a graduate of Harvard College who had commenced his law studies under the revered Justice Joseph Story at Harvard Law School and had steadily built a reputation as a clear and forceful advocate. Conservative by nature and political inclination, he was a supporter of Daniel Webster (it was Webster who recommended that Fillmore nominate him to the Supreme Court) and a staunch defender of the Fugitive Slave Act, which he believed necessary to mollify the slaveholding states and maintain their loyalty to the Union. In 1836, in a case argued before the Supreme Judicial Court of Massachusetts, he had defended the right of a slaveholder to bring a slave into Massachusetts and then take the slave back home against his will. Though his argument in that case was not successful, it won Curtis the admiration of many New England lawyers, among them Webster.[22]

Curtis began his dissent by citing an opinion of the great Chief Justice John Marshall to the effect that "a citizen of the United States, residing in any state of the union, is a citizen of that state." Since it was admitted that Dred Scott was a resident of Missouri, Curtis argued that Missouri's law could not deprive him of his rights under the Constitution's Diversity Clause. The only question was whether he was ineligible for United States citizenship simply because he was of African descent. Curtis argued that United States citizenship antedated the adoption of the Constitution. The Constitution itself proved this, for in prescribing the qualifications of the president, Article II, Section 1, states that "no person except a natural born citizen, *or a citizen of the United States, at the time of the adoption of this Constitution*, shall be eligible to the office of President." Further, five states under the Articles of Confederation had recognized free Africans as citizens, and since the Constitution did not attempt to define citizenship, it did nothing to change the preexisting rule.[23] Thus, Curtis argued, Dred Scott had a right to file his suit in the federal court in St. Louis, and Judge Wells was correct in refusing to dismiss it.

Curtis also addressed the territories question, but merely for the purpose of demonstrating the error in Taney's opinion. Since the chief justice had decided that Dred Scott's African ancestry disqualified him from bringing suit, and that Judge Wells should have dismissed his suit for want of jurisdiction, the chief justice was wrong to inquire further into the merits of the case—wrong, most especially, in declaring the Missouri Compromise unconstitutional. Curtis did not "consider it to be within the scope of the judicial power of the majority of the court to pass upon any question respecting the plaintiff's citizenship in Missouri, save that raised by the plea to the jurisdiction." Further, Curtis said he did not "hold any opinion of this Court, or any court, binding, when expressed on a question not legitimately before it. . . . The judgment of this court is, that the case is to be dismissed for want of jurisdiction, because the plaintiff was not a citizen of Missouri. . . . Into that judgment, according to the settled course of this Court, nothing appearing after a plea to the merits can enter. A great question of constitutional law, deeply affecting the peace and welfare of the country, is not, in my opinion, a fit subject to be thus reached." But since Curtis believed that the circuit court did have jurisdiction of the case, he proceeded to discuss the judgment on the merits, arguing that Congress's power to legislate respecting the federal territories was fully and fairly expressed in the Territories Clause. In fact, Congress had passed legislation regulating territorial governments fourteen times since the Constitution came into force in 1789, and the legislation had been signed by seven presidents, beginning with George Washington himself. This "practical construction of the Constitution . . . by men intimately acquainted with its history" should, in Curtis's view, be entitled to "weight in the judicial mind."[24] If Taney was willing to concede that Congress had *implied power* to provide temporary government for a territory before it became a state (even in the absence of any provision in the Constitution to that effect), why was he unwilling to concede that Congress had the *express* power to provide government for a territory up to the time of its admission to the Union, when the Constitution contained an explicit provision to that effect?

The other justices—Wayne of Georgia, Grier of Pennsylvania, Daniel of Virginia, and Campbell of Alabama—filed their decisions with the clerk of the Supreme Court without reading them. All agreed with Taney's holding that Dred Scott was still a slave, but each expressed his own reasons for reaching that conclusion. There were so many opinions and so many reasons that observers expressed bewilderment as to what exactly the court had decided. Not surprisingly, however, most of the attention focused on Taney's "opinion of the Court" and Curtis's thirty-five-page dissent, which seemed to controvert the chief justice on almost every important point in the case.

AFTER ALL THE OPINIONS had been read, McLean and Curtis released their written opinions to the press. Taney, however, refused to release his. He said that he wanted to revise it. He had been outraged by some of the statements made by Curtis, and he thought McLean's and Curtis's eagerness to spread their views before the public indicated a desire to embarrass him. The conclusion is almost inevitable, too, that Taney recognized weaknesses in his arguments and thought (or at least hoped) that if he continued to work on his opinion he might make it more convincing. At the end of March, McLean wrote Montgomery Blair to ask about rumors that Taney's opinion had been "modified." "This, it appears to me, to be unusual, if not improper," McLean said.[25] When the rumors reached Curtis (by that time back in Boston), he wrote the clerk of the Court asking for a copy of Taney's opinion. But the chief justice had given orders that no one be permitted to see the opinion before it was published in the official reports. Curtis then wrote to Taney to ask if the order included other members of the Court, and the chief justice replied with a hostile letter in which he impugned Curtis's motives and asserted that he had no "right" to see his opinion. Privately Taney accused Curtis of adopting "the tone of a demagogue." After another unfriendly exchange of letters, Curtis decided that his relations with Taney had been so badly damaged that they could no longer work together, and, in September 1857, he submitted his resignation as an associate justice. Taney had won the argument—and the *Dred Scott* case—and Benjamin Curtis had lost his seat on the highest court in the United States.

It is not surprising that public reaction to the *Dred Scott* decision divided largely (although not entirely) along sectional lines. Horace Greeley's *New York Tribune* led the Northern antislavery voices, condemning the decision as "entitled to just so much moral weight as would be the judgment of a majority of those congregated in any Washington bar-room."[26] The *New York Independent* described it as a "horrible hand-book of tyranny" that reduced black men to "an ordinary article of merchandise."[27] And the *Chicago Tribune* branded it "one of those legal monstrosities which the Judicial tools of tyrants or the judicial confederates of parties have insanely perpetrated against right and justice."[28] But in the South, the *Richmond Enquirer* praised the decision as "definitive" and "authentic," and said that, by it, "the *nation* has achieved a triumph, *sectionalism* has been rebuked, and abolitionism has been staggered and stunned."[29] The *New Orleans Daily Picayune* congratulated the Supreme Court for dealing "a heavy blow to Black Republicanism and its allies."[30] And the *Charleston Mercury* said that the decision demonstrated that "in its most extreme demand the South contends only for its rights under the Constitution."[31]

Other voices saw ominous signs in the decision. The *New York Times* feared that the doctrine it promulgated would "sink deep into the public heart, and germinate there as the seed of discontent and contest and disaster hereafter."[32] And the *Charleston Mercury* doubted that the decision would settle the deep differences that still separated the North and the South. On the contrary, the *Mercury* predicted that it would accelerate "the final conflict between Slavery and Abolitionism." "The Abolitionists are not at all abashed or dismayed," the paper declared. "They know well enough that the Supreme Court is infallible only in a technical sense; and that even its decision may be reversed by the vote of a popular majority." "The Black Republican party will go into the canvass of 1860," the *Mercury* continued, "strengthened rather than discredited and weakened by the adverse judgment of the Supreme Court; and we might as well prepare for the struggle."[33]

If the South was not deluded by its "victory" in *Dred Scott v. Sandford*, the North was certainly not encouraged by its "loss." After the first flurry of condemnations and congratulations, it appeared to many sober observers that the Supreme Court's ruling had fundamentally changed the constitutional landscape of the country. If, as Chief Justice Taney had ruled, free blacks could never aspire to citizenship under the U.S. Constitution; if, as Taney had also ruled, Congress had no power to exclude slavery from the western territories; if, as he further ruled, the right to own slaves was a fundamental right, guaranteed by the Fifth Amendment to the Constitution, slavery had in a strange way become a national institution, protected by the most basic law of the land and no longer relegated to one section or a handful of states.

POLITICIANS BEGAN TO reflect on the consequences of the *Dred Scott* decision. In Illinois in 1858, the case became a major topic in the debates between the incumbent senator Stephen A. Douglas and his Republican challenger, Abraham Lincoln.

Lincoln had been slow to react to *Dred Scott*, in part because it included so many different opinions and was based on so many different rationales that it was difficult to know exactly what the Court had decided. The more he thought about the case, however, the more it troubled him. Chief Justice Taney's assertion that blacks were not included in the protections of the Constitution or the Declaration of Independence seemed to him particularly offensive, for he believed that the Declaration's promise of equality for all men was basic to the ideals of the founders. "In those days, our Declaration of Independence was held sacred by all," he said, "and thought to include all; but now, to aid in making the bondage of the negro universal and eternal, it is assailed, and sneered at, and construed, and hawked at, and torn, till, if its framers could rise from their graves, they could not at all recognize it."[34]

Douglas, in contrast, was quick to defend *Dred Scott*, arguing that "this Government was created on the white basis by white men for white men and their posterity forever, and should never be administered by any but white men."[35] Blacks, in Douglas's view, could be a species of property but not citizens. The senator seemed not to realize at the outset that Taney's decision threatened popular sovereignty as much as it threatened the Missouri Compromise. If, as Taney argued, Congress had no power to exclude slavery from the western territories, how could it authorize territorial voters to do that? A "nonexistent power" can hardly be delegated. Yet that in essence is what the Kansas-Nebraska Act purported to do, for by establishing the rule of popular sovereignty, Congress was authorizing the voters to make decisions about slavery that it could not itself make.[36]

On June 26, 1857, Lincoln made his first definitive statement on *Dred*

Scott. Speaking in his hometown of Springfield, he expressed his disagreement with the two basic rules of the case, that Negroes could not be citizens of the United States and that Congress could not prohibit slavery in the territories, and he backed up his disagreement with a discussion of the authority that Supreme Court decisions ought to command. In good legal fashion, he explained that judicial decisions "have two uses—first to absolutely determine the case decided, and secondly, to indicate to the public how other similar cases will be decided, when they arise. For the latter use, they are called 'precedents' and 'authorities.'" He acknowledged that a Supreme Court decision—any Supreme Court decision—was entitled to "respect." But the Court's decisions "should control, not only the particular cases decided, but the general policy of the country" only when "fully settled," and *Dred Scott,* he said, was not "fully settled." He reminded his listeners that the Supreme Court had in the past overruled some of its decisions when convinced that they were erroneous (had not Chief Justice Taney done that very thing when he ruled against Lincoln in the case of *Lewis v. Lewis* in 1849?), and he stated Republican intentions to do what they could to have *Dred Scott* overruled.[37] However, until that time arrived, he said, they would offer "no resistance" to it.[38]

In Chicago, on July 10, 1858, Lincoln restated his disagreement with the *Dred Scott* decision but again denied any intention of resisting it. "If I wanted to take Dred Scott from his master, I would be interfering with property. . . . But I am doing no such thing as that. . . . [A]ll that I am doing is refusing to obey it as a political rule. If I were in Congress, and a vote should come up on a question whether slavery should be prohibited in a new territory, in spite of that *Dred Scott* decision, I would vote that it should."[39]

In the Lincoln-Douglas debates of 1858, Lincoln continued to state his opposition to *Dred Scott,* while Douglas continued to support it. (Douglas even went so far as to declare that the decision was "pronounced by the highest judicial tribunal on earth" and that there was no appeal from it "this side of Heaven.")[40] Lincoln made it clear that his opposition to *Dred Scott* was based not only on what Chief Justice Taney had actually decided in the controversial ruling but also on what he (or some other like-minded judge) might decide in a future case. If in 1857 the Supreme Court had decided that slavery could not be excluded from a federal territory, the same tribunal might decide in 1858 or 1859 that slavery could not be excluded from a state, even a state that had banned slavery from its sovereign territory. "It needs only the formality of a sec-ond Dred Scott decision," Lincoln warned, ". . .to make slavery alike lawful in all the states, old as well as new."[41]

The 1858 election campaign in Illinois ended with Douglas's reelection to the United States Senate and Lincoln's return to his law practice in Spring-field, believing that he would "now sink out of view" and "be forgotten."[42] But political events were quickly moving beyond the control of men like Lincoln and Douglas, or judges like Taney and Benjamin Curtis. Kansas was still torn by bloody fighting between pro- and antislavery factions that were struggling for control of the territorial government. A farmer-turned-abolitionist named John Brown was leading a violent crusade against slavery in that territory, tell-ing his followers that freedom could be won only by the sword. And the Su-preme Court in Washington was going about its usual business, deciding land cases, settling commercial disputes, hearing appeals in contract and admiralty cases—and, inevitably, considering cases that involved the delicate question of slavery.

On March 7, 1859, Chief Justice Taney handed down the Court's decision in *Ableman v. Booth*, a highly publicized decision that, like *Dred Scott*, affirmed the authority of the United States Supreme Court to make definitive decisions regarding slavery. In this case, however, Taney was on firmer ground than he had been in *Dred Scott*, and his colleagues on the bench rallied much more closely around him. The case had arisen out of bitter differences in Wisconsin (now a state) over the operation of the Fugitive Slave Law of 1850. Sherman M. Booth was an abolitionist newspaper editor in Milwaukee who had helped a slave named Joshua Glover escape arrest under the federal law. Glover had been held in slavery in Missouri by a man named Benjamin Garland. After Glover escaped, Garland came to Milwaukee to recapture him. The Fugitive Slave Law was unpopular in Wisconsin, and after Glover was lodged in the Milwaukee jail, a Wisconsin state judge ordered his release on a writ of habeas corpus, asserting as his authority for doing so the alleged unconstitutionality of the Fugitive Slave Law. When the Wisconsin Supreme Court affirmed the state judge's order, the federal marshal in Milwaukee, a man named Stephen Ableman, appealed to the United States Supreme Court. In announcing the Supreme Court's unanimous decision in the case, Taney stressed that the recap-ture of fugitive slaves was a matter that the Constitution entrusted to federal law, not to the states, and that Wisconsin could not order the release of a man held under the authority of federal law. So long as the Constitution endured, Taney said, the Supreme Court "must exist with it, deciding in the peaceful forms of judicial proceeding the angry and irritating controversies between sovereignties, which in other countries have been determined by the arbitrament of force."[43]

Lincoln delivered his most forceful response to *Dred Scott* on February 27, 1860. Speaking before a large crowd in New York City's Cooper Union, he compared Taney's contention that Congress had no power to prohibit or restrict slavery in the federal territories with the opinions of the signers of the Constitution on that issue. With persuasive historical detail, he demonstrated that, of the thirty-nine men who actually signed the Constitution, at least twenty-three (a clear majority) had explicitly approved of prohibitions or restrictions on slavery in the territories, either by votes they cast in Congress or, in the case of George Washington, by signing an act of Congress approving the Northwest Ordinance and its prohibition of slavery in the Northwest Territories.[44] Lincoln also cited the expressed views of other signers of the Constitution (among them Benjamin Franklin and Alexander Hamilton) who strongly condemned slavery. Lincoln's research did not reveal even one signer who had ever expressed Taney's view that Congress had no power to restrict or prohibit slavery in the territories. Lincoln also attacked Taney's contention that the Fifth Amendment protected the right to own slaves, pointing out that the first ten amendments to the Constitution (the Bill of Rights) were approved by the same Congress that approved the antislavery provisions of the Northwest Ordinance. It was "impudently absurd," Lincoln said, to argue that these measures—the Northwest Ordinance, with its prohibition of slavery in federal territories, and the Fifth Amendment, with its guarantee that no person be deprived of "property, without due process of law"—were inconsistent with each other.[45]

Lincoln's Cooper Union speech was directed as much at Stephen Douglas as at Roger Taney, for Lincoln now sensed that he had a real chance to be nominated for president by the Republican Party and a further chance to meet the "Little Giant" in the presidential election of 1860. He attacked Douglas's doctrine of popular sovereignty with as much vigor as he attacked Taney's *Dred Scott* opinion, and on substantially the same grounds. His Cooper Union speech was a lawyerly disquisition on constitutional principles, carefully re-searched and eloquently delivered. Like a skilled courtroom advocate's plea to a jury, it rested on a careful recitation of facts tied together by logical analysis. And the cheers that greeted it in New York echoed around the country.

Eight months after Lincoln delivered his Cooper Union speech, a year and nine months after Taney delivered the Supreme Court's opinion in *Ableman v. Booth*, Lincoln was elected president of the United States. Historians have long pondered the peculiar set of circumstances that allowed this relatively in-experienced politician to triumph over a field of seasoned officeholders that in-cluded the powerful Senator Stephen Douglas (candidate of the regular Demo-crats), Vice President John C. Breckinridge of Kentucky (candidate of the Southern Democrats), and former senator and secretary of war John Bell of Tennessee (candidate of the newly organized Constitutional Union Party). They have also attempted to measure the effect the *Dred Scott* decision had on the election and the subsequent decisions of eleven Southern states to secede from the Union. There seems little doubt that *Dred Scott* contributed to a growing sense of crisis leading up to the 1860 election. It was a subject of al-most endless disagreement, discussion, and argument, in the government and elsewhere. One member of the U.S. House of Representatives during this pe-riod noted how often *Dred Scott* was debated in Congress by announcing one day that he had *not* risen to discuss *Dred Scott*. Another member suggested that the House might save time by setting aside one day each month for discus-sion of the decision; another concurred, urging that the day be called "black Friday."[46]

But *Dred Scott* was not decided in a vacuum. It was part of a continuum of events—the Kansas-Nebraska Act of 1854, the warfare in "Bleeding Kansas" from 1854 to 1859, the ultimate triumph of antislavery forces in Kansas in 1859, and the split in the Democratic Party between pro- and anti-Douglas forces in 1860—all of which contributed to the Republican victory and the in-auguration of Lincoln. As historian Don Fehrenbacher observed, "The *Dred Scott* decision by itself did not have a convulsive effect on sectional politics, but it became one of the elements in an explosive compound."[47] Fehrenbacher also believed that the 1860 division in the Democratic Party arose primarily out of a difference over the scope and application of the *Dred Scott* decision, with Southerners insisting that Taney's words absolutely prohibited any antislavery laws in the western territories and pro-Douglas Northerners arguing that territorial settlers still possessed "residual sovereignty" to vote on the question.[48] By 1860, the Southern struggle to extend slavery into the western territories had largely become an effort to defend the strict terms of the *Dred Scott* decision. That was a nearly impossible task, however, and the Republicans won the election. Thus in a roundabout way the Supreme Court's 1857 decision led to the election of one of *Dred Scott's* most determined critics. Supreme Court historian Charles Warren may have overstated the case when he wrote that "Chief Justice Taney elected Abraham Lincoln to the Presidency."[49] But there can be little doubt that Taney's 1857 decision made a substantial contribution to Lincoln's 1860 victory.

THE GRAND DRAMA that began when a slave named Dred Scott sued for his freedom in St. Louis in 1846 would not be complete without a word about the fate of the man who gave his name to the drama. Dred Scott, his wife Harriet, and their daughters Eliza and Lizzie were still living in St. Louis when the Supreme Court announced that, after all of their years of legal struggle, they were yet slaves. But the Scotts' friends had not exhausted all of their options. Taylor Blow, the white man who had been raised with Dred Scott in Virginia, managed to obtain ownership of the Scotts (whether by purchase from John F. A. Sanford or through some other stratagem, it is not clear).[50] And when he did, he manumitted his old friend and his family, giving them the freedom that the courts of Missouri and the United States had refused them.

A short while later a reporter for *Frank Leslie's Illustrated Newspaper* visited the Scotts in St. Louis. To support the family, Harriet Scott took in washing and ironing, which her husband delivered throughout the city. Dred Scott was described by the reporter as a "pure-blooded African, perhaps fifty years of age, with a shrewd, intelligent, good-natured face, of rather light frame, being not more than five feet six inches high." His wife was younger, probably in her thirties, a "smart, tidy-looking" woman whose manner and tone of voice clearly indicated that she was, as the reporter put it, "the legitimate owner of Dred."[51] The reporter had come to ask the Scotts to sit for daguerreotypes, and he also wanted to gather some information about them.

Dred Scott, he wrote, "is quite a humble but nevertheless a real hero, moving about the streets of St. Louis." He attracted a lot of attention from people who recognized him as the subject of the most famous Supreme Court case ever decided. He told the reporter that his legal proceedings had cost him "$500 in cash, besides labor to nearly the same amount." More important, he said, it had given him a "heap o' trouble," and if he had known that the lawsuit "was gwine to last so long," he would not have started it. The reporter was successful in getting Dred and Harriet Scott to sit for their portraits in Fitzgibbon's gallery, a local photographic studio, and then he went away.

Just a few months later, Dred Scott also went away. On September 17, 1858, the hero of *Dred Scott v. Sandford* died of tuberculosis in St. Louis and was buried in Wesleyan Cemetery there, thus bringing an inauspicious end to a long life of slavery and a few short months of freedom. But, as the newspaper reporter predicted, Dred Scott's name lived on as the symbol of a struggle, and one of the sparks that would ignite a great war.

3   First Blood

CHIEF JUSTICE TANEY WAS at home in his house on Indiana Avenue when a caller arrived at his door on Sunday, May 26, 1861. Rapping insistently, the caller was admitted to the house with a sheaf of papers for the judge's immediate attention.

It was not unusual for Supreme Court justices to be called on to perform official business in their private residences—most of their work was, in fact, done at home, where their law books were readily available and conditions were conducive to quiet study and reflection. But the man who arrived at the chief justice's Washington row house on that spring day carried tidings that were anything but usual. A petition had been hastily prepared by one of Baltimore's attorneys, George H. Williams, on behalf of a Marylander named John Merryman. It was an urgent request for a writ of habeas corpus, and it had been sworn to by Williams, before "the Holy Evangely of Almighty God," the day before in Baltimore. John Hanan, United States commissioner in Baltimore, had added his signature to Williams's to attest to the petition's truth and urgency.[1]

It is not known whether Williams himself carried the petition to Washington or he sent a messenger there with the document. In either case, Taney almost certainly recognized Merryman's name in the caption and quickly apprehended its importance. Merryman may have been a "personal friend" of the chief justice, as the *New York Times* reported, but even if he was not, he was the kind of man an old Baltimorean like Taney would have known something about.[2] Tall, handsome, and well-connected, the thirty-six-year-old Merryman was the owner of The Hayfields, a large farm just north of Baltimore, where he ran a herd of prize-winning cattle and kept a corps of black slaves. Merryman had been a vice president of the Maryland State Agricultural Society from 1852 to 1857, and was now its president. His father was an old acquaintance of the chief justice, for the senior Merryman had attended Dickinson College at the same time as Taney, more than sixty years before.[3]

In addition to knowing Merryman, it seems likely that the chief justice would have been aware of the circumstances that had prompted him to send his petition to Washington that day. Baltimore had been in almost constant tumult since the third week of April when, in response to Lincoln's call for 75,000 militiamen to suppress the rebellion in the South, Northern troops had attempted to cross through the city en route to Washington. The Twenty-fifth Pennsylvania Regiment was the first to arrive in Baltimore, on April 18. It was followed on April 19 by the Sixth Massachusetts Volunteer Regiment, 1,200 men hailing from Lexington and Concord. The Northern troops' progress through Baltimore was complicated by an 1831 ordinance (probably enacted to protect the jobs of teamsters) that forbade steam trains from operating in the heart of the city, so it was necessary for railroad cars carrying the regiments to stop at a station on the east side of the city and then be pulled by horses to a station on the west side. The route lay along Pratt Street, overlooking the city's harbor. Sentiments on the burning issues of the day—secession, slavery, and abolitionism—were sharply divided in Baltimore, with a large number of residents opposing secession and another large number favoring it. The slow, awkward transit of the Northern regiments through the center of Baltimore gave pro-secessionist residents an opportunity to confront the troops and impede their progress.

Soon after the regiments began crossing the city on April 19, demonstrators gathered along Pratt Street, waving Confederate flags and taunting the soldiers with insults. Quickly growing into a large crowd, they tore up some of the rails, heaped sand on the tracks, and hurled bricks and paving stones at the soldiers. Some even brandished guns. Fearful for their safety, some of the troops began to fire at the demonstrators, and the demonstrators fired back. Baltimore's mayor George W. Brown, antislavery and pro-Union but still friendly to the South, attempted to quell the unrest by marching with the Northern troops, but he soon gave up the effort. When the day closed, four soldiers had been killed, a dozen Baltimoreans lay dead, and an unknown number of soldiers and citizens had been wounded.[4] It was an ugly and, to many, frightening scene, properly remembered as the "first blood" of the great military conflict that was soon to engulf the nation. (The Southern assault on Fort Sumter had resulted in no deaths, though one soldier had lost his life when a cannon accidentally exploded during the ceremonial surrender of the installation.)

News of the conflict in Baltimore was swiftly telegraphed throughout the country. Confederate sympathizers began to speak of the events of April 19 as the "Battle of Baltimore," while Northerners labeled it "the Lexington of 1861" and vowed that, in the future, federal volunteers would "go through Baltimore or die." Mayor Brown ordered railroad bridges north of the city to be burned so no more Northern troops could pass over them.[5] More Marylanders began taking sides in the conflict, some insisting that the state must remain loyal to the federal government, while others argued that it should join its Southern brothers in secession. Yet another group, impatient with the legislature's failure to decide whether Maryland should or should not secede, formed volunteer militia units to aid the Southern cause.

Faced with the turmoil in Maryland, Lincoln quickly decided that he would have to send militiamen around Baltimore rather than through it. Maryland's loss to the Confederate cause would be disastrous for the Union, and to continue marching troops through the city would provoke more anti-Union protests. Virginia had seceded on April 17, sealing off all approaches to Washington from the south; if Maryland followed, the capital would be surrounded by rebels and virtually indefensible. United States senators and representatives might even be blocked from attending a session of Congress.

The president was besieged with advice about how to handle the crisis. Illinois senator Lyman Trumbull wrote him from Springfield that the people there were "greatly excited" over events in Maryland and that he should "take possession of Baltimore at once."[6] Orville Hickman Browning, one of Lincoln's old Illinois friends (soon to succeed Stephen Douglas in the Senate), wrote the president that it was essential to keep communications to Washington open and that "Baltimore must not stand in the way."[7] In late April, Lincoln was informed that the Maryland legislature was about to meet in Annapolis and that it would probably vote to "arm the people of that State against the United

States." But he resisted suggestions that he order General in Chief Scott to arrest the legislators. Maryland's elected representatives had a legal right to meet, the president said, and it was impossible to know in advance that their actions would not be "lawful and peaceful." If, however, they should actually vote to raise arms against the government, he would authorize Scott to "adopt the most prompt and efficient means to counteract it [their action], even, if necessary to the bombardment of their cities—and in the extreme necessity, *the suspension of the writ of habeas corpus.*"[8]

Lincoln's letter to Scott seems to have been his first written reference to a possible suspension of habeas corpus. He probably knew that suspensions of habeas corpus had been rare in American history—in fact almost nonexistent. In 1814 General Andrew Jackson had suspended habeas corpus in New Orleans. When the federal district judge in the city defied the suspension, he had the judge arrested, and when the United States district attorney procured a writ of habeas corpus for the judge, Jackson jailed him too. Fined $1,000 for contempt of court, Jackson defiantly paid the fine with his own funds but still kept the judge in prison.[9]

Habeas corpus had also been suspended in Rhode Island in 1842, when the elected government of the state was challenged by an insurgent government led by Thomas Dorr. The suspension was ordered by the Rhode Island legislature. The legality of the suspension in what came to be known as Dorr's Rebellion was tested a few years later in the United States Supreme Court, where Chief Justice Taney sustained it. Writing in the case of *Luther v. Borden* (1849), Taney affirmed the right of a state to "use its military power to put down an armed insurrection, too strong to be controlled by the civil authority." The power to do this, he declared, "is essential to the existence of every government, essential to the preservation of order and free institutions, and . . . as necessary to the States of this Union as to any other government."[10]

Beyond the examples provided by Jackson in New Orleans and Dorr in Rhode Island, however, the United States had had virtually no experience with the suspension of habeas corpus. It was a history waiting to be written.

THE WRIT OF HABEAS corpus was in 1861, as it is now, one of the keystones of Anglo-American law, a special judicial proceeding that evolved in the common-law courts of England to protect innocent persons from illegal arrest and imprisonment. By its terms, the custodian of the detained person was ordered to "have the body" (habeas corpus) of the detainee in court, where the reasons for the detention could be examined. Because it was used so often to protect British subjects from tyrannical monarchs, it came to be referred to as the Great Writ and to be accorded special respect. It came to the British colonies in North America with other provisions of English law and, after the adoption of the U.S. Constitution, was revered as one of the bulwarks of American liberty. One of the first statutes adopted by Congress under the new Constitution was the Judiciary Act of 1789, which, among other things, granted federal courts and judges jurisdiction to issue writs of habeas corpus.[11]

Lincoln believed that authorizing Scott to suspend habeas corpus would help his troops subdue pro-secessionist lawbreakers in Maryland, for it would give Scott authority "to arrest, and detain, without resort to the ordinary processes and forms of law, such individuals as he might deem dangerous to the public safety."[12] He sensed that if he authorized a suspension of the writ he would be condemned for trampling on individual rights. But he also believed that if persons arrested by federal troops could be freed almost overnight by pro-Southern judges, it would be difficult for the army to secure its supply lines and guard against attack. If habeas corpus was not suspended, federal judges could release dangerous persons as quickly as the army could arrest and detain them.

The Constitution itself contains only a cursory reference to habeas corpus—a single sentence in Article I, Section 9, that provides: "The privilege of the writ of habeas corpus shall not be suspended, unless when in cases of rebellion or invasion the public safety may require it." Although this provision (commonly referred to as the Suspension Clause) does not specify who may suspend habeas corpus, the fact that it is located in Article I lends support to the argument that the suspension must be by Congress, for Article I is the section of the Constitution that defines and limits the powers of Congress. Lincoln, however, believed that other provisions of the Constitution were relevant to the question. Article II, Section 2, for example, provides (in relevant part): "The President shall be commander in chief of the Army and Navy of the United States, and of the militia of the several states, when called into the actual service of the United States." And Article II, Section 1, provides that, before the president enters on the execution of his office, he must take the fol-

lowing oath or affirmation: "I do solemnly swear (or affirm) that I will faithfully
execute the office of President of the United States, and will to the best of my
ability, preserve, protect, and defend the Constitution of the United States."

Did Lincoln's constitutional authority as "commander in chief of the
Army and Navy of the United States" give him the power to authorize the general in chief of the army to suspend habeas corpus? Did his constitutional duty
to "preserve, protect, and defend the Constitution" confer on him the necessary power to do those things? Few would deny the commander in chief's authority to take necessary military action in Maryland, even to the extent of
"bombarding" the state's cities if he and his generals deemed it necessary to do
so, and many Americans sincerely believed, as did Lincoln, that secession
threatened the Constitution. Yet the president's letter to Scott revealed that he
suspected it might be more acceptable to "bombard" cities than to suspend habeas corpus.[13] As Lincoln biographer James G. Randall has written, "Few measures of the Lincoln administration were adopted with more reluctance than
this suspension of the citizen's safeguard against arbitrary arrest."[14]

Seward remembered years later that Lincoln pondered the question at
some length. "There were two points in the administration," Seward said,
". . . upon which all subsequent events hinged. One was the suspension of
the Habeas Corpus Act. . . . The Habeas Corpus Act had not been suspended
because of Mr. Lincoln's extreme reluctance at that period to assume such a
responsibility. Those to whom he looked for advice, almost to a man, opposed
this action." But one morning (Seward recalled it was a Sunday) the secretary
of state went to the White House alone and told Lincoln "that this step could
no longer be delayed." The president still argued against it. Seward continued:
"I told him emphatically that perdition was the sure penalty of further hesitation. He sat for some time in silence, then took up his pen and said: 'It shall
be so!'"[15]

On April 27 Lincoln addressed a letter to General Scott in which he
wrote:

> You are engaged in repressing an insurrection against the laws of the
> United States. If at any point on or in the vicinity of the military line,
> which is now used between the City of Philadelphia and the City of
> Washington, via Ferryville, Annapolis City, and Annapolis Junction,

you find resistance which renders it necessary to suspend the writ of
Habeas Corpus for the public safety, you, personally or through the officer in command at the point where the resistance occurs, are authorized to suspend that writ.[16]

Lincoln's suspension of habeas corpus was not immediately publicized, but
it soon became known that he had taken that step. On May 2 the U.S. district
judge in Baltimore, William F. Giles, issued a writ of habeas corpus for a young
Marylander named John Mullen, who had enlisted in the federal forces and
whose father now sought his release from the service on the ground that he was
a minor. When the writ was presented to Major W. W. Morris of the Union
army, he handed it back with the statement that he "would see the court and
the marshal damned before delivering up one of his men." Judge Giles ordered
Morris to appear in court and to show cause why an attachment should not be
issued against him for disobeying the writ. Morris replied on May 6 with a
scathing denunciation of the violence in Baltimore and a charge that, in the
hands of an unfriendly power, the writ of habeas corpus could be used to "de-
populate" Fort McHenry, the federal fort that guarded Baltimore and its harbor.
Giles shot back that the power to suspend habeas corpus was "a power which in
my opinion belongs to Congress alone," thus suggesting that he had already
heard of Lincoln's order of suspension (for Morris himself had not raised it in
his defense). Giles reluctantly concluded that he could not enforce any order
that Morris chose to resist and merely sent the papers in the Mullen case to the
U.S. district attorney in Baltimore, with the suggestion that they be forwarded
to Washington.[17]

In the meantime, a regiment of federal volunteers arrived in Baltimore under the command of the Massachusetts lawyer-turned-general Benjamin F. Butler. When he learned of the riots in Baltimore, Butler had commandeered a
steamboat at the head of Chesapeake Bay and used it to ferry his troops to
Annapolis; then he led them overland by train to Baltimore, repairing sabotaged portions of the tracks along the way. On May 13, Butler led his regiment
into the heart of the city and threw up a makeshift bastion atop Federal Hill.
Almost at once the Massachusetts troops began to make arrests in the city.[18]

Chastened by the federal force in their midst, Baltimoreans grew quiet.
Judge Giles refrained from issuing any more writs of habeas corpus, at least for

the moment. Within days, however, Lincoln's suspension of habeas corpus was to come under attack from a higher authority than Judge Giles.

JOHN MERRYMAN HAD been arrested at his home north of Baltimore at two o'clock on Saturday morning, May 25, by soldiers who whisked him away to Fort McHenry. Though formal charges were not laid against him, the military authorities alleged that Merryman was guilty of "acts of treason," that he was a lieutenant in a "company having in their possession arms belonging to the United States," and that he had "made open and unreserved declarations" of his "readiness to co-operate with those engaged in the present rebellion against the government of the United States."[19] Newspaper reports were more explicit, asserting that Merryman "held a commission as Lieutenant in the rebel forces," that he "was active in inciting the revolt which resulted in the murder of the Massachusetts soldiers in the streets of Baltimore," and that he was "the principal agent in the destruction of the bridges between Baltimore and Washington, which cut off communication between those two cities."[20]

George H. Williams went to Fort McHenry to inquire about Merryman's arrest and personally met with Brevet Major General George Cadwalader, commander of the military district that included Baltimore. Cadwalader refused to release Merryman or even to let Williams see the papers under which he was detained.[21] Almost immediately, the lawyer took steps to obtain a writ of habeas corpus from the chief justice of the United States Supreme Court.

Taney later wrote that Merryman's petition was "presented to me, at Washington, under the impression that I would order the prisoner to be brought before me there." But as Merryman was confined in Baltimore, and as Baltimore was in Taney's Fourth Circuit, the chief justice decided to hear the case there. This would also excuse Cadwalader of the necessity of leaving "the limits of his military command." Taking up his pen, the chief justice issued the following order:

In the matter of the petition of John Merryman, for a writ of habeas corpus: Ordered, this 26th day of May, A.D. 1861, that the writ of habeas corpus issue in this case, as prayed, and that the same be directed to General George Cadwalader, and be issued in the usual form, by Thomas Spicer, clerk of the circuit court of the United States in and for the district of Maryland, and that the said writ of habeas corpus be returnable at eleven o'clock, on Monday, the 27th of May 1861, at the circuit court room, in the Masonic Hall, in the city of Baltimore, before me, chief justice of the Supreme Court of the United States. R. B. Taney.[22]

Taney lost no time in leaving Washington for Baltimore. The chief justice was always welcome in the Baltimore house of his daughter Anne and her husband, the attorney J. Mason Campbell; it was his own home away from home whenever he was on circuit-court duty in Baltimore. It may well be that Taney left for the Campbell home that same Sunday, for he was escorted into his Baltimore courtroom the following morning by his seventeen-year-old grandson, Roger B. Taney Campbell. Seemingly energized by the historic confrontation he was now to preside over, the old chief justice was seated behind the bench in his courtroom in the Masonic Hall promptly at eleven o'clock on Monday, May 27. Merryman was represented by two lawyers, George H. Williams and George M. Gill, and the government by the U.S. district attorney William Meade Addison.[23] District Judge Giles was also present, but conspicuously silent. Following Taney's previous order, the clerk had issued a writ commanding Cadwalader to appear in the United States courtroom at the appointed time. The writ further instructed Cadwalader to "have with you the body of John Merryman, of Baltimore county, and now in your custody, and that you certify and make known the day and cause of the capture and detention of the said John Merryman, and that you then and there, do, submit to, and receive whatsoever the said chief justice shall determine upon concerning you on this behalf, according to law, and have you then and there this writ."

The writ was served on General Cadwalader by Washington Bonifant, the United States marshal. A few minutes after the chief justice took his seat in the hall, a Colonel Lee, resplendent in red sash and military sword, appeared with a written "return" from Cadwalader. The general himself was nowhere to be seen, nor was John Merryman. Dated at Fort McHenry on May 26, Cadwalader's return explained that Merryman had been arrested and brought to McHenry on May 20, "charged with various acts of treason" against the government of the United States. The general had been "duly authorized by the President of the United States in such cases to suspend the writ of habeas corpus, for the public safety." It was a "high and delicate trust," Cadwalader admitted, that "should be executed with judgment and discretion," but he had been instructed "that in times of civil strife, errors, if any, should be on the side of the safety of the country." He "most respectfully" asked Taney to postpone further action in the case until he could "receive instructions from the President of the United States, when you shall hear further from him."[24]

It was a courteous statement and, in view of the unusual circumstances of the case, a reasonable request for postponement. Cadwalader himself was a lawyer, a veteran of many years of practice in Philadelphia, where his brother, John Cadwalader, was the United States district judge. The Cadwaladers were upstanding public officials and well known to the chief justice, and, as historian Harold Hyman has noted, "Legal custom was that officials deserve from judges a presumption of rectitude."[25] But Taney was disinclined to honor any presumption in favor of a general, even a lawyer-general such as Cadwalader. He asked Colonel Lee if he had brought the body of John Merryman to court. When Lee replied that he had no instructions but to deliver the commanding general's response, the chief justice announced sternly: "General Cadwalader was commanded to produce the body of Mr. Merryman before me this morning, that the case might be heard, and the petitioner be either remanded to custody, or set at liberty, if held on insufficient grounds; but he has acted in disobedience to the writ, and I therefore direct that an attachment be at once issued against him, returnable before me here, at twelve o'clock tomorrow."

The courtroom cleared. Taney made his way out of the building and back to the Campbell home, as word of the growing confrontation spread through Baltimore.

The following morning, a crowd of two thousand gathered on St. Paul's Street in front of the federal court. As he left his son-in-law's house, Taney remarked that "it was likely he should be imprisoned in Fort McHenry before night; but that he was going to Court to do his duty."[26] When he arrived at the Masonic Hall, he was leaning on the arm of his grandson. Mayor Brown reported that, as the judge made his way slowly through the crowd, they "silently and with lifted hats opened the way for him to pass."[27]

In the courtroom, Taney once again took his seat on the bench. Colonel Lee was present, as were Marshal Bonifant and the attorneys for Merryman and the government. Judge Giles was absent, as were Cadwalader and Merryman. Bonifant reported that he had gone to Fort McHenry with the writ of attachment, but he had not been admitted and Merryman had not been produced. Taney replied that the marshal could have summoned a posse to help him obtain the prisoner, but that the attempt would obviously have been futile, for "the power refusing obedience was so notoriously superior to any the marshal could command." He excused the marshal from further duty in the matter, then proceeded to read a statement. He said he had ordered the attachment against Cadwalader because, "upon the face of the return," Merryman's detention at Fort McHenry was unlawful. He stated that the president, "under the constitution of the United States, cannot suspend the privilege of the writ of habeas corpus, nor authorize a military officer to do so." He said that a military officer had no right to arrest or detain "a person not subject to the rules and articles of war, for an offence against the laws of the United States, except in aid of the judicial authority, and subject to its control." If such a person was arrested by the military, it was the duty of the officer "to deliver him over immediately to the civil authority, to be dealt with according to law." To underline his position, Taney said it was "very clear" that Merryman was entitled to be "discharged immediately from imprisonment." In the previous day's hearing, he had declined to state the reasons for his decision, lest they be misunderstood. Now, however, he would put his opinion in writing "and file it in the office of the clerk of the circuit court, in the course of the week."[28]

The chief justice's decision created what one of the reporters in the courtroom called "a sensation."[29] The highest judicial officer of the United States had publicly challenged the highest executive officer, and the challenge struck at the foundations of the executive's authority to deal with the growing rebellion. It was a confrontation not merely between two men, or two officials, but between two sharply contrasting views of governmental power, and the proper means for exercising that power under the Constitution.

Reactions in the courtroom to Taney's decision were enthusiastic and favorable. The *Baltimore Daily Republican* reported that the decision met "with heartfelt exclamations of approbation, such as 'Thank God for such a man,' 'God grant that he may live many years to protect us,'" and similar remarks.[30] After the court adjourned, Mayor Brown went up to the bench and thanked Taney for "upholding, in its integrity, the writ of *habeas corpus*."

"Mr. Brown," the chief justice replied, "I am an old man, a very old man, but perhaps I was preserved for this occasion."

"Sir," Brown replied, "I thank God that you were."[31]

Reactions outside Baltimore were not as positive. The *New York Tribune* condemned Taney as "a hoary apologist for crime" and Merryman as a "traitor." The *New York Evening Post* noted that newly selected federal officeholders were required to take an oath of loyalty to the United States and that it might be well to require the chief justice to take the same oath. The *New York Herald* thought that the chief justice had unknowingly made himself a tool of Maryland secessionists, while the *New York Times* denounced him for issuing what it called a "libel" upon "free government everywhere." "It is melancholy enough to see young men impelled by the ardor of youth, the impulsiveness of inexperience, and actuated by false ideas of patriotism, plunge into rebellion," the *Times* continued, "but it is a thousand times more melancholy to see an octogenarian turning back from the grave, on the verge of which he was standing, to strike one last though impotent blow at the existence of a Government he has repeatedly sworn to support. This is precisely what Roger B. Taney is doing now."[32]

When Mayor Brown spoke with him, Taney imparted an ominous bit of information. He said "that his own imprisonment had been a matter of consultation, but that the danger had passed, and he warned me, from information he had received, that my time would come."[33] The clear suggestion was that someone in the military chain of command (perhaps the commander in chief himself) had threatened the chief justice with incarceration. Some years later, Lincoln's friend Ward Hill Lamon left an unpublished manuscript that lent some support to Taney's charge. According to Lamon, "After due consideration the administration determined upon the arrest of the Chief justice." Lincoln issued a "presidential arrest warrant" for Taney, Lamon wrote, but could not decide who should arrest him or where he should be imprisoned. He finally gave the warrant to Lamon, who was the United States Marshal for the District of Columbia, telling him to "use his own discretion about making the arrest unless he should receive further orders." Lamon decided not to arrest the chief justice.[34] If Lamon's account is true, Lincoln's plan to arrest Taney would have been both reckless and inflammatory, for it would have dramatically escalated the confrontation between the executive and judicial branches of the government and excited public opinion all over the country. But Lamon's story was never confirmed by Lincoln's principal biographers, and it stretches credulity to believe that Lincoln would approve such a grand provocation or, if he did, that he would let a minor official like Lamon decide whether or not to carry it out.[35] Lamon's published *Recollections of Abraham Lincoln* contains no hint of the plan to arrest the chief justice. In fact, Taney was never molested by any official of the federal government, though Lamon (and virtually every other federal official in both Baltimore and Washington) knew at all times which city he was in and where they could lay their hands on him.

Taney was not daunted by talk of his threatened imprisonment, nor intimidated by Northern criticism of his decision. Without any hesitation, he promptly began to prepare the "opinion in writing" he had promised at the conclusion of the *Merryman* hearing. He was always a skillful writer, though his poor eyesight and general weakness had slowed him in recent years. He wrote out his opinion by hand, labeling it "Before the Chief Justice of the Supreme Court of the United States at chambers." If any of the observers in Baltimore had failed to notice that the rebuke he had delivered to Lincoln emanated from the highest judicial officer in the United States, his written opinion would make that abundantly clear.[36]

He began by reviewing the procedural history of the *Merryman* case. He noted that the president had given no official notice that he claimed the power to suspend habeas corpus and said that he had listened to the claim "with some surprise, for I had supposed it to be one of those points of constitutional law upon which there was no difference of opinion, and that it was admitted on all hands, that the privilege of the writ could not be suspended, except by act of Congress." (Taney was careful here to distinguish between a suspension of the writ and a suspension of the "privilege" of the writ, which is the precise language used in the Constitution. When habeas corpus is suspended, it is not the writ itself but the right of a confined person to win freedom through its exercise—the "privilege" of the writ—that is suspended.[37] It is a fine distinction, but one that a careful judge like Taney would certainly make.)

Taney recalled that the conspiracy headed up by Aaron Burr, which greatly excited the nation in 1807, had suggested to President Jefferson the necessity for a suspension of habeas corpus, but that Jefferson never supposed he had the right to suspend it; rather he called on Congress to do so. (Congress, however, was unable to act, for the Senate favored suspension and the House opposed it.[38]) Taney therefore "regarded the question as too plain and too well settled to be open to dispute." But since Lincoln obviously disputed it, the chief justice now undertook to prove him wrong.

He reviewed some of the history of habeas corpus in the common law of England. He referred to Blackstone's *Commentaries* and Hallam's *Constitutional History* to show that restriction of the writ had been a legislative and not an executive function. He quoted from the *Commentaries* of Joseph Story (before his death in 1845, a highly esteemed colleague of Taney on the Supreme Court) that "it would seem, as the power is given to Congress to suspend the writ of habeas corpus, in cases of rebellion or invasion, that the right to judge whether the exigency had arisen must exclusively belong to that body." He also quoted a statement made by Chief Justice John Marshall in the case of *Ex parte Bollman* (1807): "If at any time the public safety should require the suspension of the powers vested by this act [the Judiciary Act of 1789] in the courts of the United States, it is for the legislature to say so. That question depends on political considerations, on which the legislature is to decide; until the legislative will be expressed, this court can only see its duty, and must obey the laws."[39]

Taney was emphatic in concluding that the president of the United States had no power to suspend the writ of habeas corpus. If the Constitution gave him that authority, the chief justice said, it would have given him "more regal and absolute power over the liberty of the citizen than the people of England have thought it safe to intrust to the Crown." But Taney went a step further and stated that, even if Congress had suspended the writ, the president had no power to hold Merryman under his military authority. At the time Merryman was arrested, Taney declared, state and federal judges were exercising their authority in Baltimore, only a few miles from Merryman's home, and there had never been "the slightest resistance or obstruction to the process of any court or judicial officer" in the state, "except by the military authority." If a military officer or any other person had reason to believe that Merryman had committed an offense against the laws of the United States, Taney said, "it was his duty to give information of the fact and the evidence to support it to the district attorney, and it would then have become the duty of that officer to bring the matter before the district judge or commissioner." None of this had been done in Merryman's case. In Taney's view, there was no place for martial law, for military arrests, for military detentions or military trials in places like Maryland. Since the courts were open and functioning, all violations of the criminal law had to be dealt with in the usual way before the usual courts. All those arrested in Maryland during the tumult of April and May 1861 were entitled to the full panoply of procedural and substantive rights that applied in Maryland in 1801 or New York in 1851, and not one jot or tittle less. Those rights included the right to due process of law as guaranteed by the Fifth Amendment to the Constitution and the right to jury trial as guaranteed by the Sixth Amendment.[40]

Having enunciated the law as he saw it, the chief justice now added a rhetorical flourish to what he must certainly have realized would be a widely quoted and discussed opinion:

> In such a case my duty was too plain to be mistaken. I have exercised all the power which the Constitution and laws confer on me but that power has been resisted by a force too strong for me to overcome. It is possible that the officer who has incurred this grave responsibility may have misunderstood his instructions and exceeded the authority intended to be given him. I shall therefore order all the proceedings in this case with my opinion to be filed and recorded in the circuit court of the United States for the district of Maryland and direct the clerk to transmit a copy under seal to the President of the United States. It will then remain for that high officer in fulfillment of his constitutional obligation to "take care that the laws be faithfully executed" to determine what measures he will take to cause the civil process of the United States to be respected and enforced.[41]

Taney's opinion was filed with the clerk of the circuit court in Baltimore on June 1, after which a copy was sent to Lincoln.[42] At the same time, copies were distributed to reporters, who saw to it that it was reprinted in newspapers all over the country. Pamphleteers also picked up the opinion and reprinted Taney's text with their comments—some congratulatory, others bitterly condemnatory.

Horace Binney, a Philadelphia lawyer once mentioned as a possible justice of the United States Supreme Court, published one of the sharpest attacks on Taney's opinion.[43] He argued at some length that the military arrest and detention of civilians was justified in specific circumstances and fully authorized by the Constitution. Binney's pamphlet was widely read by judges and members of Congress. Supreme Court Justice Robert Grier liked it so much that he lent his copy to friends and eventually lost it, and when Justices Catron and Wayne asked to see it, he sent away to Philadelphia for a dozen additional copies.[44] On the other side, former Justice Benjamin Curtis, who had dissented from Taney's opinion in the *Dred Scott* case, published another pamphlet in which he agreed with Taney's conclusions and roundly condemned Lincoln's assumption of the power to order military arrests and detentions.[45]

Press reactions to Taney's written opinion were as passionate as reactions had been in the courtroom when he announced his decision from the bench. Northern papers condemned the chief justice as a tool of secessionists and a coddler of traitors, while in the South he was praised as a defender of liberty. The *Baltimore Sun*'s praise was typical of comments in the border states:

> Long after this terrible conflict shall have been brought to an end; when the fanaticism and commercial aggrandizement it is waged to serve shall have subsided; when the peace of desolation or of prosperity shall brood over the land, the grand, true, cogent, resistless influence of this document from the mind of Roger B. Taney will live, at once a vindication of the principles of the republic, and of the fundamental rights of the people, and an overwhelming protest against the action of those who have so rudely assailed them.[46]

It has often been charged that Lincoln "ignored" Taney's *Merryman* decision.[47] But the allegation suggests a kind of executive disdain that was foreign to Lincoln's character and is frankly false. Although the president's initial reaction to the decision has not been documented, it is clear that he reflected on it at some length and eventually expressed some cogent thoughts on the issues it raised. The *New York Herald* reported in early June that he wrote a personal letter to the chief justice, but the letter was not made public and no copy of it has survived.[48] On May 30 he asked Attorney General Bates to prepare an "argument for the suspension of the Habeas Corpus,"[49] and on July 4 he delivered a long message to the special session of Congress he had called to address issues raised by the war. In the message, he discussed his order authorizing General Scott to suspend habeas corpus, noting that the authority had been exercised "very sparingly." "Nevertheless," he said, "the legality and propriety of what has been done under it, are questioned; and the attention of the country has been called to the proposition that one who is sworn to 'take care that the laws be faithfully executed,' should not himself violate them." (In the original handwritten draft of the message Lincoln noted that the question had come from a "high quarter"—that is, from the chief justice of the United States, though he omitted that reference in the final draft. Lincoln scholar Douglas L. Wilson has suggested that the omission was designed to make his differences with Taney "less personal.")[50] "Of course." Lincoln continued, "some consideration was given to the questions of power, and propriety, before this matter was acted upon." Then he added:

> The whole of the laws which were required to be faithfully executed, were being resisted, and failing of execution, in nearly one-third of the States. Must they be allowed to finally fail of execution, even had it been perfectly clear, that by the use of the means necessary to their execution, some single law, made in such extreme tenderness of the citizen's liberty, that practically, it relieves more of the guilty, than of the innocent, should, to a very limited extent, be violated? To state the question more directly, are all the laws, *but one*, to go unexecuted, and the government itself go to pieces, lest that one be violated? Even in such a case, would not the official oath be broken, if the government should be overthrown, when it was believed that disregarding the single law, would tend to preserve it?[51]

In all, Lincoln devoted four pages of his handwritten draft to the sensitive issue of habeas corpus.

Some thought that Lincoln's defense of his suspension rested on a "rule of necessity," according to which the Constitution does not apply (or may be violated) when observance of its requirements would open the country up to an even greater calamity. The editors of the *New York Times* expressed such a view on May 29 when they wrote that "the majesty of the law must, in all cases, succumb to the necessities of war."[52] But this was not Lincoln's view. As Hyman has written: "Lincoln never believed that the Constitution was unworkable, and so never needed to descend to the argument of necessity."[53] According to his biographer David Herbert Donald, Lincoln "saw the emergency powers he assumed during the war years as a fulfillment, not an abandonment, of the rule of law."[54] In his message to Congress, the president denied that "any law was violated" by his suspension of habeas corpus and explained:

> The provision of the Constitution that "The privilege of the writ of habeas corpus, shall not be suspended unless when, in cases of rebellion or invasion, the public safety may require it," is equivalent to a provision—is a provision—that such privilege may be suspended when, in cases of rebellion, or invasion, the public safety *does* require it. It was decided that we have a case of rebellion, and that the public safety does require the qualified suspension of the privilege of the writ which was authorized to be made.

It was a point that Taney had avoided entirely in his *Merryman* opinion. But allowing that the circumstances for suspension had arisen does not answer the chief justice's question of who has the authority to order the suspension. Taney insisted that the power resided exclusively with Congress. Lincoln disagreed: "But the Constitution itself, is silent as to which, or who, is to exercise the power; and as the provision was plainly made for a dangerous emergency, it cannot be believed the framers of the instrument intended, that in every case, the danger should run its course, until Congress could be called together; the very assembling of which might be prevented, as was intended in this case, by the rebellion."

Lincoln was arguing that, as commander in chief of the armed forces of the United States, and as the only federal official charged with a constitutional duty to "preserve, protect, and defend the Constitution," he was as fully empowered by the Constitution as Congress was, to decide if and when the "public safety" required a suspension of habeas corpus. But he was not anxious to overstate his argument. He knew that contrary arguments could be made and that a final resolution of the question might depend on future events. Legal historian Mark E. Steiner has written that, when Lincoln was "pressed by necessity, he was a sophisticated user of the available sources of legal information."[55] In this particular case, Lincoln was "pressed by necessity" as never before, and more in need of a practical solution than he had ever been in a courtroom. He had asked the attorney general to render a formal opinion on the issue, and he recognized that Congress might also be heard on the question. Any legislation that might be enacted on the subject would, he said, be "submitted entirely to the better judgment of Congress."[56]

On July 5 Attorney General Bates rendered the opinion requested by the president.[57] Bates was an old lawyer with a wealth of political and legal experience. He had been a delegate to the convention that drafted Missouri's first constitution in 1820, a member of the Missouri state legislature, a congressman, a United States district attorney, and a judge of the St. Louis Land Court. But his instincts for legal analysis were less sure than Lincoln's, and he had none of the president's genius for explaining complicated legal propositions in words that ordinary men and women could understand. Bates pointed out that the Constitution itself required the president to "preserve, protect, and defend" it, while it required that other officers of the government (including federal judges) simply "support" it.[58] The phrase "preserve, protect, and defend," he argued, gave the president the duty to suppress the rebellion and also, by implication, the power to do so. And because the means of suppression were not prescribed in the Constitution, the president had discretion to choose them. On this point, the attorney general's argument was persuasive. But his further argument—that because the executive, legislative, and judicial branches of the federal government are coequal and independent, the Supreme Court had no right to impose its will on the president—was less so. In 1803, in the landmark case of *Marbury v. Madison,* Marshall had stated that it is "emphatically the province and duty of the judicial department to say what the law is," and in the almost half-century since then, the proposition had not been seriously challenged.[59] Bates thought suspension of habeas corpus was a "political" rather than a "judicial" question and thus not subject to judicial supervision. His words were serious and his conclusion—that the president had ample constitutional power to suspend the privilege of the writ of habeas corpus—was emphatic. But his reasoning did not carry a fraction of the persuasive power that Lincoln had imparted in the simple question he put to Congress: "Are all the laws, *but one,* to go unexecuted, and the government itself go to pieces, lest that one be violated?"

IF TANEY WAS RIGHT that the power of suspending habeas corpus rested solely with Congress, the federal legislature could have expressed its opinion on the subject at any time after Lincoln called it into special session in July

1861. Efforts were repeatedly made in the Senate and the House to address the habeas corpus issue head on, but they were repeatedly frustrated, not so much because senators and representatives were unwilling to take a stand on the issue as because they could not agree on what stand to take. If Taney thought that only Congress could suspend habeas corpus, he gave no consideration to the need for prompt or expeditious suspension. More than a month after it began its special session, Congress approved an act ratifying and approving the president's previous war measures. The actual language was "that all the acts, proclamations and orders of the President . . . [after March 4, 1861] respecting the army and navy of the United States, and calling out or relating to the militia or volunteers from the States, are hereby approved and in all respects legalized and made valid . . . as if they had been issued and done under the previous express authority and direction of the Congress of the United States."[60] This language did not explicitly refer to the president's order suspending habeas corpus, though it was broad enough to apply to it. Thus, less than two months after it was filed in the circuit court in Baltimore, Taney's opinion seemed to have become moot. But the important constitutional points made in it clearly had not, for Congress's action did not settle the basic question of whether Congress or the president had power under the Constitution to suspend the precious writ. Difficult questions still were unanswered: What would have been the effect of Lincoln's suspension if Congress had not ratified it? Does the president have authority to act when Congress cannot (because, for example, it is not in session, or it is prevented from assembling by interrupted transportation lines to Washington or hostile military action around the capital)? Is the government paralyzed when legislative action is impossible?

Conceding the importance of Taney's *Merryman* opinion, it is nevertheless appropriate to point out some of its weaknesses. The chief justice's assertion that Congress, and only Congress, has constitutional authority to suspend habeas corpus assumes that proposition without proving it. The suspension clause does not state that only Congress may suspend habeas corpus, and it is by no means certain that, because the clause is located in Article I, this is what it must have meant. In fact, records of the debates in the Constitutional Convention of 1787 show that the framers at one time proposed to include the suspension clause in the article governing the federal judiciary, and that the Committee on Style moved it at the last minute to the article governing the legislature, without offering any explanation for the move.[61] Taney correctly quoted Marshall's comments about habeas corpus, but the quotation was misleading, for Marshall's comments—made in *Ex parte Bollman* (1807)—were obiter dicta (statements unnecessary to the decision of the case and not binding precedent in future cases). In that case, Marshall decided that the Supreme Court could issue writs of habeas corpus in aid of its appellate jurisdiction. He did not decide whether Congress or the president could suspend the writ when "the public safety may require it," as the case did not raise that question.[62]

Taney should also be faulted for failing to describe the tumult that prompted Lincoln to suspend the writ in the first place. For all that appears from the chief justice's opinion, Baltimore was a peaceful city in April 1861, its residents were duly respectful of their obligations to obey the law, and "the public safety" required no extraordinary measures. Taney did not discuss the rebellion then facing the federal government or the threats posed to federal troops. Nor did he note that saboteurs and bombers in Maryland in 1861 could be dealt with under the civil law only in the United States courts in Maryland, and that the only law that could be applied in those courts was woefully inadequate to the task.

In fact, federal law then on the books was excruciatingly thin. There were few federal crimes, and the prescribed penalties were either so lenient as to be almost inconsequential, or draconian in their severity. Hyman has pointed out that disloyalty itself was not a crime in 1861.[63] Almost the only federal law that could be applied to the conditions in Maryland in 1861 was the 1790 statute prescribing death as the penalty for treason.[64] This statute was enacted pursuant to the definition of treason set forth in Article III, Section 3, of the Constitution: "Treason against the United States, shall consist only in levying war against them, or in adhering to their enemies, giving them aid and comfort. No person shall be convicted of treason unless on the testimony of two witnesses to the same overt act, or on confession in open court." Merryman and others like him may well have been guilty of treason under the constitutional definition, but it was wildly unrealistic to suppose that juries composed of Marylanders would convict them of any crime for which they could be hanged. Even assuming that enough federal judges, district attorneys, and jurors could be assembled to hear charges against all of the disloyal residents of Maryland, and further assuming that two witnesses could be produced to testify to each "overt act" charged in all the indictments that would have to be filed, the notion that the slow and cumbersome processes of the federal courts could make Maryland safe for troops marching through the state on their way to the national capital, free of saboteurs and attackers along the way, was frankly unsupportable. Taney did not mention these troubling realities in his opinion.

Taney also ignored his own opinion in *Luther v. Borden* (1849), in which he had decided that the federal courts had no authority to second-guess executive and legislative officials who had acted to put down the Dorr Rebellion in Rhode Island. As part of their response to that emergency, state officials had asked President John Tyler to give them military assistance. They argued that the federal power to help them suppress the insurgency derived from Article IV, Section 4, of the federal Constitution, which provides: "The United States shall guarantee to every state in this union a republican form of government, and shall protect each of them against invasion; and on application of the legislature, or of the executive (when the legislature cannot be convened) against domestic violence." But the rebels claimed that they, and not the existing state officials, were the legitimate government of Rhode Island, and thus the existing officials had no authority to call for federal intervention. In his opinion siding with the existing state officials, Taney observed that the power to determine whether the federal government should help to put down a state rebellion rested initially with Congress; but, by statute, Congress had delegated the power to the president.[65] It was therefore a "political decision" and not one that the courts should interfere with. He wrote: "After the President has acted and called out the militia, is a Circuit Court of the United States authorized to inquire whether his decision was right? . . . If the judicial power extends so far, the guarantee contained in the Constitution of the United States is a guarantee of anarchy, and not of order."[66]

As Hyman has observed, Taney's pronouncement that Lincoln could not suspend the writ of habeas corpus in 1861 to put down a national rebellion is difficult to reconcile with his earlier pronouncement that John Tyler could call out federal troops in 1842 to put down a state rebellion.[67] In Maryland, Lincoln acted under the Constitution's habeas corpus clause; in Rhode Island, Tyler was asked to act under the Constitution's republican form of government clause. Both presidents were called upon to exercise discretion. But Taney found Tyler fully empowered to exercise his discretion and Lincoln powerless to do so. As constitutional historian Daniel Farber has observed, Taney "failed to realize the relevance . . . of his own opinion in *Luther v. Borden*."[68]

Further, Taney never discussed Lincoln's constitutional duty to "preserve, protect, and defend" the Constitution, which he seemed to regard as irrelevant to the whole question of resisting an insurrection. And his assertion that the question of who has power to suspend habeas was "one of those points of constitutional law upon which there was no difference of opinion," and that it was "too plain and too well settled to be open to dispute," was simply false. The question was, as lawyers say, a case of "first impression," for neither the president nor Congress had ever previously suspended habeas, or asserted the power to do so.[69] The constitutional question had never previously been asked of a federal court, and it was presumptuous for Taney to claim that a question that had not even been asked had been definitively answered.

Finally, Taney failed to recognize the unique opportunities Merryman's case afforded him to exhort lawbreakers in Maryland to obey the law. As chief justice of the United States, he was invested not just with legal power, but also with moral authority. Yet he made no effort in his *Merryman* opinion to call for calm in Maryland, to warn disloyal Marylanders to refrain from attacking federal troops and stop blowing up bridges. As Bernard Steiner, one of Taney's early biographers, stated: "The occasion offered Taney a magnificent opportunity to give men a clarion call to patriotic fulfilment of their Constitutional duties and to personal service to secure the preservation of the Union." Yet Taney showed "no appreciation of the facts that the life of the country was at stake."[70]

Aside from the constitutional argument he made in his message to Congress on July 4, 1861, and apart from the formal opinion that he asked Attorney General Bates to prepare, what did Lincoln actually do about *Ex parte Merryman* after Taney rendered his opinion? The answer is that he declined to comply with it. He did not concede Taney's point about the power to suspend habeas corpus, and he did not formally "obey" the ruling. In fact, the military continued to make arrests throughout most of the war; habeas corpus was suspended again, and in other parts of the country; trials were held before military commissions, and punishments were imposed, for Lincoln continued to assert the constitutional power to do all these things. But John Merryman himself did not suffer unduly because of this. When Secretary of War Simon Cameron visited Fort

McHenry on July 4, the day Lincoln delivered his message to Congress, he promised Merryman a parole, and on July 13, forty-nine days after his arrest, the Marylander was delivered to the custody of the United States marshal to be dealt with in the U.S. district court. Indirectly, he was now being accorded the procedural and substantive rights that Taney said he was entitled to. An indictment was handed down charging that Merryman "did intend to levy war and carry on war, insurrection, and rebellion against the United States of America," but he was admitted to bail and never brought to trial. The case was postponed and ultimately dropped. Merryman was a free man once again, and he had no doubt who was responsible for his freedom.[71] When his next son was born, on December 5, 1864, Merryman paid tribute to the old judge who had presided over the habeas corpus hearing in Baltimore by naming the child Roger Brooke Taney Merryman.[72]

In a book-length study of civil liberties in wartime, the late Chief Justice William Rehnquist raised the question of why Taney's decision in Ex parte Merryman was not appealed to the full Supreme Court.[73] Although Taney himself said that his decision was made in his capacity as "Chief Justice of the Supreme Court of the United States at chambers," Rehnquist believed that it was made in his capacity as a circuit judge. The original writ, after all, was issued by the clerk of the circuit court in Baltimore; the hearing was held in the courtroom of the circuit court; the opinion was filed with the circuit clerk; and the opinion was eventually printed in Federal Cases, a set of volumes devoted to decisions of the district and circuit courts, but was never published in United States Reports, the official repository of Supreme Court decisions. And in Federal Cases, the case was identified as a decision of the Circuit Court for the District of Maryland.[74]

If the decision was in fact a circuit court decision, Taney could have arranged to have it reviewed in the Supreme Court by persuading Judge Giles to join him in the Merryman hearing and then issuing a certificate of division. The certificate of division, authorized by Congress in 1802, was frequently used by district and circuit court judges to bring cases before the Supreme Court. It was even used when their opinions did not actually differ but they considered the case, or the issues raised by it, important enough to be reviewed by the full Supreme Court.[75] Giles was deferential to Taney and would not have objected to this procedure. But the certificate of division applied only to circuit court decisions, and no other statute permitted appeals to the full court from decisions of individual Supreme Court justices.

Although the precise capacity in which the decision was made is not entirely clear, the better view seems to agree with Taney that it was a decision of the chief justice "in chambers."[76] Since the Supreme Court's inception in 1789, both the full Court and its individual justices have had jurisdiction, pursuant to statute, to grant writs of habeas corpus.[77] But the full Court's habeas power can be exercised only as part of its appellate jurisdiction (that is, when a decision of an inferior court is being reviewed), and not when a habeas corpus petition is presented to it as an "original" matter, for the Constitution specifies that the Supreme Court's "original jurisdiction" extends only to "cases affecting ambassadors, other public ministers and consuls, and those in which a state shall be a party." In all other cases (that is, in nearly all the cases that come before it), the Court has only appellate jurisdiction, "with such exceptions, and under such regulations as the Congress shall make."[78] But individual justices are not subject to this same limitation on their "original" jurisdiction and can issue writs of habeas corpus (and other writs as well) as original matters. They may do so only when the full court is not assembled, however; that is, they may do this only when they are on circuit or acting "in chambers."[79] When Taney issued the writ in *Ex parte Merryman*, the full Supreme Court was not in session, and he explicitly stated that he was acting in chambers. Interestingly, Judge Giles's absence during the *Merryman* hearing is explainable if the decision was an in-chambers decision of the chief justice. If it had been a circuit court decision, Giles would have had every right to participate, and would normally have done so. If it was an in-chambers decision, however, he had no right to participate.

As an in-chambers decision, Taney's ruling in *Merryman* was unreviewable, and Lincoln could not have appealed it to the Supreme Court. He (or Attorney General Bates acting for him) might have steered a case presenting the same question to the high court, but neither Bates nor Lincoln was confident that the Supreme Court would sustain their position, for the court in 1861 was still dominated by justices with strong Southern sympathies. As late as January 1863, Bates advised Secretary of War Edwin Stanton not to appeal a decision of the Wisconsin Supreme Court that held that the president could not suspend the writ of habeas corpus in that state.[80] The attorney general feared that the Supreme Court would sustain the Wisconsin ruling and that this would "do more to paralyze the Executive arm and to animate the enemies of the Union than the worse defeat our armies have yet sustained."[81] And so Taney's decision in *Merryman* stood unchallenged by any contrary rulings.

Regardless of the capacity in which it was made, it is clear that Taney's decision was made in haste and without first hearing both sides of the question. Rehnquist thought that Taney's "refusal to countenance any delay at all for the purpose of allowing the government to present its case" did not "speak well for either his judgment or his impartiality." (If General Cadwalader's request for a postponement so he could consult the president had been granted, he might have shed further light upon the important constitutional question before the court.)[82] Taney's eagerness to take a public stand on the habeas corpus issue suggests that he approached it with the zeal of a partisan, not the impartiality of a judge, and his final opinion reads more like an attorney's brief than a jurist's reasoned conclusion. Lincoln biographer Phillip Shaw Paludan has described the opinion as a "blistering lecture to the president and the American people."[83] Hyman has described it as "a sermon on the Constitution."[84] With its publication, it became apparent, if it had not been before, that the chief justice had taken sides in the sectional struggle that threatened to destroy the Union, casting his lot with the South against the North.

But Taney's strong, pro-Southern response did not answer all of the troubling questions raised by Lincoln's suspension of habeas corpus. When all is said and done, the chief justice may have been more right than wrong about habeas corpus. Perhaps Congress is the only federal authority that has power under the Constitution to suspend the writ.[85] Perhaps Lincoln's action was in fact in excess of his constitutional powers as president. If it was, however, Taney's decision in *Merryman* did not settle the question in a convincing and authoritative way. His opinion was not published in the reports of the Supreme Court, and the views expressed in it, at least insofar as the issue of habeas corpus was concerned, were never endorsed by a subsequent Supreme Court decision.[86] Whether the president has power under the Constitution to suspend habeas corpus is, so far as the federal courts are concerned, a question that still remains unanswered.[87]

This is not to say that Taney's opinion in *Merryman* was meaningless. Far from it. It represented an early and serious challenge to Lincoln's prosecution of the war. It aroused passions in all sections of the country. It raised fears in the North that the federal judiciary might wage war on the administration even as the administration waged war on the South, and it raised hopes in the Confederate states that the federal government would falter in its purpose and ultimately abandon its effort to "coerce" its Southern brethren. Carl Brent Swisher wrote that Taney's *Merryman* opinion "had the impact of a military victory for the South."[88] But as the chief justice soon learned, one battle does not make a war. The first victory went to Taney, but there were battles yet to be waged, and victories and defeats yet to be tallied up.

4   Judges and Circuits

ONE SEAT ON THE Supreme Court was vacant when Lincoln took his oath of office on March 4, and two more were teetering on the brink of vacancy. The seat of Justice Peter V. Daniel of Virginia still remained unfilled nine months after his death, thanks in large part to James Buchanan's chronic indecisiveness. Justice John Archibald Campbell of Alabama was making noises about leaving the Court for his home state, for which he felt a strong but (as he would soon discover) unreciprocated affection. And with every appearance in or about the Capitol, Chief Justice Taney aroused hope in Unionists and fear in secessionists that his advanced years and decrepitude would finally force his departure from the bench—through resignation or death it seemed not to matter much.

Rumors had been rife in the final months of Buchanan's administration that Taney would step down. In the summer of 1860, a U.S. district judge in Wisconsin had suggested that American lawyers should raise private funds to replace the salary the chief justice would lose by resigning, but nobody had enough nerve to approach Taney with the proposal.[1] (He *was* dependent on his judicial salary for his living expenses, but was far too proud to be reminded of the fact.) Taney's frequent absences from the bench due to illness caused many Democrats in the last months of Buchanan's administration to speculate about a possible successor. Benjamin F. Butler, a lawyer-politician in Massachusetts, went so far as to ask the Boston bar to petition Buchanan to name Caleb Cushing as the next chief justice. Cushing was a loyal Democrat who had been attorney general under Franklin Pierce, and he probably would have been confirmed if Taney had cooperated. But he did not.

Shortly after Lincoln was elected president, it was rumored that Taney had at last resigned, but the rumors were quickly denied. Former Chief Justice Ellis Lewis of the Pennsylvania Supreme Court wrote Taney that his departure at that critical juncture in the nation's history "would be dangerous, and might furnish grounds for comments which your friends might not desire to hear." Taney concurred and assured Lewis that he intended to stay on.[2] But he was so old and frail that the rumors of his impending departure refused to die.

While Campbell was much younger than Taney (only forty-nine when Lincoln was inaugurated), he shared many of the chief justice's views. He had earned a reputation as a brilliant lawyer after he moved from his native Georgia to Alabama in 1830. Between 1849 and 1852, he argued eleven cases in the United States Supreme Court, making such a favorable impression on the justices that, when a vacancy opened in 1852, they unanimously petitioned President Franklin Pierce to name him to fill it. Pierce acquiesced, and Campbell joined the Court in 1853 at the age of only forty-one.[3]

Campbell had some nuanced ideas about slavery, admitting that it hampered the South economically and socially but insisting that it was both constitutional and moral. He personally continued to buy and sell slaves while serving on the Supreme Court and, in 1857 in the *Dred Scott* case, he joined Taney in declaring the Missouri Compromise restrictions on slavery in the western territories unconstitutional.[4] He thought Lincoln's election in 1860 was "a calamity to the country" but denied that it was sufficient cause for secession. Although he believed that secession was sanctioned by the Constitution, he thought such a draconian measure should be reserved for evils that were "imminent and beyond reach of regular and constitutional modes of redress."[5] When it became clear that sentiment for secession was approaching a climax, he proposed measures that he thought would persuade the South to remain in the Union: amending the Constitution to protect slavery forever, and making the amendment itself unamendable.[6] After attending Lincoln's inauguration, he condemned the president's inaugural address as "a *stump* speech" that was "wanting in statesmanship . . . and of dignity and decorum."[7] And after Lincoln was sworn in, he and Associate Justice Samuel Nelson of New York tried to work out a compromise that would avert war. Campbell met with Secretary of

State William Seward to urge that Lincoln confer with a trio of peace commissioners sent to Washington by Jefferson Davis, and he asked Seward for assurances that Lincoln would order the evacuation of Fort Sumter. Without Lincoln's knowledge or authority, Seward gave him the assurances; but when days and then weeks passed, and it became apparent that the South Carolina fort was not to be evacuated—but was in fact to be resupplied—Campbell concluded that Seward had deceived him.

When Confederate batteries began shelling Sumter on April 12, Campbell decided to resign his seat on the Supreme Court. One of his biographers has suggested that his decision to resign flowed naturally from his belief that he was a citizen not of the United States but of Alabama, and that, unless he wanted to become a citizen of another state, he was obliged to follow Alabama out of the Union.[8] Another of Campbell's biographer's has written that he wanted to retain his position but could not do so while Alabama was at war with the United States, because for him "everything of any true meaning or value was in Alabama."[9] He sent a resignation letter to Lincoln on April 26, and officially left the Court on May 1. The celebrated diarist Mary Boykin Chesnut, herself the wife of a resigned United States senator from South Carolina, observed sadly: "A resigned judge of the Supreme Court of the United States!! Resigned–and for a cause that he is hardly more than half in sympathy with. His is one of the hardest cases."[10]

Campbell returned to his home in Mobile, Alabama, where he made it known that he was willing to serve his state in any capacity his fellow Alabamians might deem appropriate. But they were not as committed to him as he was to them. Secessionists resented his moderate statements on the Confederate cause, and his neighbors treated him and his family with what he described as "coldness, aversion, or contumely." So he moved to New Orleans, where he attempted to establish a new law practice. When, in the spring of 1862, New Orleans was occupied by Union troops, Campbell felt obliged to move on again, this time to the new Confederate capital of Richmond, Virginia.

Even before Campbell resigned his Supreme Court seat, another vacancy was created by the death of Associate Justice John McLean of Ohio. McLean had served so long and so vigorously that his admirers found it hard to believe that illness and old age had finally overtaken him. He was seventy-six years old and suffering from a severe cold when he left Washington on March 22 for his home in the hills above Cincinnati where, on April 4, he succumbed to pneumonia.[11] McLean had opposed slavery and supported the Union, so it was natural that Northerners regretted his loss. Taney had little sympathy with the Ohioan's judicial views, though he felt genuine sorrow over his passing. In a memorial statement, the chief justice paid tribute to McLean's "firm, frank, and vigorous" mind, and affirmed that "his best eulogy will be found in the reports of the decisions of this court."[12]

There was no lack of aspirants for the vacant judicial seats–there were now three—or for any of the other positions subject to presidential appointment, for patronage still played a large role in American politics. With hundreds of federal offices ready to be surrendered and thousands of would-be clerks, postmasters, marshals, district attorneys, army and navy officers, and judges turning their eyes toward the White House, Lincoln found it necessary to spend long hours every day listening to personal pleas for appointments, or answering letters from political supporters who sought positions for their friends. This was one of the burdens of the presidency. It was also one of Lincoln's obligations as the leader of a new political party, for Republicans had never previously controlled the government, and the president and his supporters owed political debts to all who had helped them win the election.

Only one day after Lincoln was inaugurated, Secretary of State Seward had asked the outgoing attorney general, Edwin M. Stanton, to draw up papers nominating John J. Crittenden of Kentucky to fill Justice Daniel's vacant Supreme Court seat. Seward had assumed that he would act as a kind of prime minister to the inexperienced president (an assumption Lincoln soon disabused him of) and that his authority included the right to pick judicial candidates. At seventy-four, Crittenden was too old to begin a strenuous new career on the high court, but he was a respected politician with a wealth of legal experience. Like Lincoln, he had once been a Whig and an admirer of Henry Clay. Unlike Lincoln, he had become a Democrat after the Whigs foundered in the mid-1850s on the issue of the expansion of slavery into the territories. He had been governor of Kentucky, United States senator from that state, and attorney general of the United States under Presidents William Henry Harrison and Millard Fillmore. More important, he was an influential Unionist from a border state that had not yet taken a stand on secession. Lincoln had some personal experience with Crittenden, for the Kentuckian had intervened in the Illinois

Senate contest in 1858, writing a series of letters that urged former Whigs to support Stephen Douglas over Lincoln. Some of Lincoln's supporters blamed his loss to Douglas on Crittenden's "meddling" in an election that did not concern him. But Lincoln wrote Crittenden to assure him that he did not blame him for the loss and did not "for a moment suspect you of anything dishonorable."[13]

During the last weeks of Buchanan's administration, while Crittenden was still serving Kentucky in the Senate, he sponsored the so-called Crittenden Compromise, a last-minute effort to bridge differences between North and South and stem the tide of war. When reports that Crittenden would be appointed to the Supreme Court reached the newspapers, they were hailed in Northern and border states. The *New York Times* told its readers that no other act would "so much reassure Conservative Southern men,"[14] while Governor Thomas H. Hicks of Maryland wrote Lincoln that, "if it could only be true, that he or some such man shall be appointed by you, it would be hailed by the unionists throughout the South."[15] Stanton drafted a nomination for Crittenden and submitted it to Lincoln for his signature.[16] But the president did not sign it. The Crittenden Compromise went down to defeat, and Seward's effort to elevate him to the Supreme Court withered before the opposition of Northerners such as Senator Lyman Trumbull of Illinois and the new secretary of the treasury, Salmon P. Chase.[17]

Joseph Holt, secretary of war in the last weeks of Buchanan's administration, was also mentioned as a possible Supreme Court nominee. Holt was another Kentuckian and, like Crittenden, an accomplished lawyer. Both Crittenden and Holt were Unionists, and Confederates grumbled about their coziness with the Republican administration. Rose O'Neal Greenhow, a Washington socialite and Confederate spy, believed that both Kentuckians had been "bribed with the same bait–a seat on the Supreme Court bench."[18] But if the Supreme Court was bait, it was nothing more—for neither Crittenden nor Holt was nominated.

Other names were soon being discussed as possible nominees. The new attorney general, Edward Bates, was one. A respected lawyer and long-time officeholder in Missouri, Bates had risen to political prominence as a staunch foe of secession and an equally strong champion of the Republican Party. At the Chicago convention in 1860, he was one of Lincoln's chief rivals for the presidential nomination, but after the nod went to Lincoln, Bates worked diligently for his election. Secretary Chase was also discussed as a potential Supreme Court justice, particularly after reports were leaked that he and Bates had been involved in a cabinet altercation.[19] But both men realized that it would be unseemly for members of the cabinet to leave the administration so soon, and that Southerners would see the departure of either man as a sign of discord. So neither pursued the matter with Lincoln.

Two days after the president was inaugurated, Henry Winter Davis of Maryland wrote the president to urge that his cousin, Judge David Davis of Bloomington, Illinois, be nominated to the Supreme Court. Henry Winter Davis was a former congressman and a leader of the Republican Party in Maryland. David Davis was, of course, well known to Lincoln, as the president had practiced law in his Eighth Illinois Circuit Court for years. What's more, Lincoln owed an enormous political debt to the judge, for Davis had managed Lincoln's campaign for the presidential nomination at the 1860 convention in Chicago. Henry Winter Davis argued that his cousin was qualified by "experience, learning, judicial habits, & judicial cast of mind" to serve on the Supreme Court. He also believed that the president should abandon the usual custom of appointing a Southerner to the position (Justice Daniel had lived in Virginia but had circuit court responsibilities for Mississippi and Arkansas), since the slave states already had sufficient representation on the Court.[20]

THE FEDERAL CIRCUIT SYSTEM was key to the organization of the federal judiciary, and one of the chief obstacles that Lincoln faced in his efforts to fill vacant judgeships. Article III, Section 1 of the Constitution provides simply: "The judicial power of the United States, shall be vested in one Supreme Court, and in such inferior courts as the Congress may from time to time ordain and establish."

In the Judiciary Act of 1789, Congress had divided the country into districts and circuits, with one district judge in each state (eventually more in the larger states) and the districts aggregated into circuits.[21] There were originally three circuits, but the number was increased to seven in 1807 and nine in 1837. From 1802 on, one Supreme Court justice was assigned to each circuit. It was the duty of the district judges to preside over the district courts and to join with the Supreme Court justices to hear cases in the circuit courts. When a Supreme Court justice was not present, the district judge held the circuit court alone.[22]

The circuit court system required that the justices attend the circuit courts ("ride circuit") at least twice a year. When they did that, they bore the title of circuit judge. Because the circuits lay at the heart of the federal judicial system, it was customary for the president to select Supreme Court judges from the respective circuits. Thus geographical representation loomed as large as professional qualifications and judicial temperament in choosing judges. This made legal as well as geographical sense, for litigation in the federal courts consisted mostly of "diversity cases" (suits between citizens of different states).[23] Diversity cases were largely governed by the laws of the states involved, and a judge who lived in or near such a state would naturally be more familiar with its laws than a judge from a distant part of the country.[24]

Justice McLean had served the Seventh Circuit (Ohio, Indiana, Illinois, and Michigan). His death provoked a host of entreaties for his judgeship. David Davis immediately expressed interest in the position, though he feared that others would have superior claims to it, among them U.S. District Judge Thomas Drummond of Chicago, former Illinois Circuit Judge Stephen T. Logan of Springfield (Lincoln's second law partner), and Secretary Chase. Noah H. Swayne, a prominent attorney in Columbus, Ohio, was also considered a likely candidate, for he was a friend of Justice McLean, and McLean had expressed the hope that Swayne would succeed him.[25] Swayne opposed slavery and had good ties to the business community, in both Ohio and New York. And, as evidence of his eagerness for the position, he had written Chase on the day of McLean's death soliciting his support for his candidacy.[26]

Orville Hickman Browning, one of Lincoln's oldest and most trusted friends, also expressed interest in the Seventh Circuit appointment. Only five days after McLean's death, Browning wrote Lincoln to ask that he be appointed to the position. He told the president that "there is nothing in your power to do for me which would gratify me so much as this. It is an office peculiarly adapted to my tastes, and the faithful and honest performance of the duties of which would be my highest pride and ambition."[27] But Browning was concerned that, if Lincoln rejected his application, he not subject him to the "mortification of letting it be known that I personally solicited the office and was refused."[28] After Stephen A. Douglas's death on June 3, 1861, Illinois governor Richard

Yates appointed Browning to serve out Douglas's unexpired term in the Senate. But the appointment did not take Browning out of consideration for the Supreme Court, for he let it be known that his interest in the Senate was only temporary and that his real ambition was to serve on the high court.[29]

The Supreme Court vacancies were not the only judicial concerns that Lincoln faced in the summer of 1861. Many federal judges in the Southern states were resigning their positions and announcing their allegiance to the Confederate government. Others were walking away from their courts without the formality of resigning. In the border states of Kentucky and Missouri, federal judges were under pressure from Confederate sympathizers to give up their positions, or at least to refrain from making decisions that would weaken the secessionist cause. And some who remained on the bench were suspected of disloyalty to the Union or, worse, pro-Southern partisanship. Justice Grier went to Kentucky in the summer to visit his daughter and her husband, Thomas B. Monroe, Jr., Kentucky's secretary of state. Monroe's father, Thomas B. Monroe, Sr., was a long-time U.S. district judge with strong Southern sympathies. Grier found the Monroe family awash in secessionist sentiment. In a letter to Justice Clifford, he wrote that his son-in-law was "a secessionist, as insane as the others." The rout of the Union Army at Bull Run on July 21 had convinced Grier that the war would be long, but he was equally convinced that it had to be won. "We must conquer this rebellion or declare our republican government a failure," Grier told Clifford.[30]

In the District of Columbia, Judge William Merrick became the object of Unionist criticism after he issued a writ of habeas corpus in the case of a Union solider whose father claimed he was under age when he enlisted and thus entitled to be discharged from the service. Merrick belonged to a well-connected Maryland family and was suspected of pro-Confederate sympathies. When Seward heard about Merrick's action, he condemned it as judicial interference with military enlistments and ordered the provost marshal, General Andrew Porter, to post a guard at Merrick's residence. Porter asked if this meant that Merrick was under house arrest. Seward answered that he was not, explaining: "Indeed it may be sufficient to make him understand that at a juncture like this when the public enemy is as it were at the gates of the capital the public safety is deemed to require that his correspondence and proceedings should be observed."[31] Merrick's fellow judges rallied around him, ordering Porter to show cause why he should not be held in contempt of court. But the deputy marshal refused to serve the order on the ground that Lincoln had suspended habeas corpus. Meanwhile, Senator Henry Wilson of Massachusetts charged that Merrick's heart was "sweltering with treason" and that his home was a "resort where sympathizers with disloyal men have held councils."[32]

After the Supreme Court adjourned on March 24, Associate Justice John Catron returned to his Eighth Circuit (Kentucky, Tennessee, and Missouri) and, as he later told District Judge Samuel Treat, found it engulfed in a "tempest of passion and folly and crime."[33] Though Kentucky was teetering on the edge of secession, Catron managed to hold court in one of his posts there. He then continued on to Tennessee, which had seceded and begun to raise a pro-Confederate army. Judge West H. Humphreys had abandoned his U.S. district court in Nashville to take up the duties of a Confederate district judge there. In his new capacity, Humphreys converted the three federal district courts in Tennessee into Confederate courts and presided over proceedings in which Tennessee's loyalist United States Senator Andrew Johnson was declared an alien enemy and his property was confiscated.[34] Meanwhile, Thomas B. Monroe, Sr., resigned his federal judgeship in Kentucky and came to Nashville to swear his allegiance to the Confederate government before Judge Humphreys.[35]

Despite all the secessionist activity in his home state, Catron remained firm in his loyalty to the United States government. He announced that he would hold court in Nashville, but relented when the marshal refused to prepare the courtroom for his use. He then went to St. Louis, where Judge Treat and Judge Robert W. Wells asked him to help with their upcoming court sessions. Treat and Wells worried that Missouri was about to follow Tennessee out of the Union and wanted to deliver a grand jury charge that would discourage such an eventuality. With Catron's concurrence, they prepared constitutional and legal definitions of treason and delivered a strong statement condemning all those who would help the secessionist cause.[36] By the middle of July, news of the St. Louis statement had reached New York, where Horace Greeley's *Tribune* hailed it as a "Light out of Darkness" and praised Catron as "an upright judge among rebels."[37] But Missouri's lieutenant governor Thomas C. Reynolds had a different opinion. He wrote Catron, ominously warning the judge against any attempt to punish rebels as traitors. And residents of Nashville were so upset by Catron's St. Louis charge that they demanded that he resign his Supreme Court seat and give his support to the Confederacy.

Catron returned to Nashville, where a friend announced that he had come back because of the ill health of a friend and had no intention of holding court. But the secessionists pressed their demands. A group of Nashvilleans called on Catron and informed him that he had twenty-four hours to leave the city.[38] He quickly departed for Louisville, leaving his ailing wife behind. Within two weeks, however, Mrs. Catron was also evicted from Nashville, having been forced to abandon all of the family's possessions except their clothing.[39]

Although Associate Justice James M. Wayne of Georgia was as loyal to the Union as Catron, he did not suffer the indignities of his Tennessee colleague. This was not because Georgians were more tolerant of Unionists, but because he made no attempt to return to his home in the Sixth Circuit (North Carolina, South Carolina, and Georgia) after the Supreme Court adjourned in March 1861. There is no doubt that Wayne's loyalty was to the Union and not to his region or state, though he seems never to have explained why.[40] He was a native and long-time civic leader of Savannah, where he had served in important public offices for more than forty years. He was a firm supporter of slavery and an equally firm opponent of the Bank of the United States (a fact that undoubtedly persuaded Andrew Jackson to name him to the Supreme Court in 1835).[41] But he did not share the enthusiasm of many Southern judges for inflated claims of states' rights. He opposed the doctrine of nullification when John C. Calhoun urged it in 1832–1833, supported exclusive federal regulation of interstate commerce, and argued for an expanded view of the federal admiralty power.[42] Wayne's constitutional jurisprudence, however, was more practical than theoretical—he once said the constitution should not be interpreted by the "logic of ifs and syllogisms." Perhaps it was his practical side—and his advanced age—that persuaded him to stay in Washington after the war broke out. He was comfortable in the federal city, where he had a home and was widely admired for his social graces. He was seventy years of age, too old to be establishing a new career under a new government and a new set of laws (Justice Campbell was a full twenty years younger).[43] He knew that the people of Georgia would not be friendly to a Unionist in their midst. And, as he told his son shortly after the war broke out, "To break up the Court would be to the injury of many private rights, involving much money, before it." "I expect to be misunderstood and misjudged," Wayne added, "but I shall leave posterity to do me justice."[44]

Before posterity could pass judgment on Justice Wayne, however, his fellow Georgians claimed the right to do so. Early in 1862, a grand jury assembled in Savannah to declare the justice an "alien enemy" and order that his property—real estate, stocks, and even some slaves—all be confiscated. The property was transferred to his son, Henry Wayne, who had resigned his commission as a major in the United States Army to become adjutant and inspector general of Georgia.[45] Northern newspapers congratulated Justice Wayne on his loyalty to the Union. The *New York Tribune* commended "the firmness of this distinguished jurist" and saluted him with the words: "All honor to Judge Wayne!"[46] And the *New York Herald* said that Wayne's loyalty was "a living rebuke to the small souled political tricksters whose mad ambition have brought us to the horrors of civil war."[47] But in Wayne's home state the newspapers were less complimentary. The *Southern Confederacy* of Atlanta informed its readers in August that "Judge Wayne is not a citizen of Georgia. He once was; but his residence has been in Washington for a number of years past and he has not even been in his native State for a great while. Georgia does not claim him, and he is no more of us."[48]

LINCOLN WAS AS ANXIOUS as any of his predecessors to appoint judges to the Supreme Court, but in doing so he was faced with circumstances that none of his predecessors had encountered. Although secession had rent the judicial as well as the political fabric of the nation, the president insisted that the states that rallied under the Confederate flag had not actually left the Union—they were merely in "rebellion" against the federal government. When the Southern states rejoined their Northern sisters (as they eventually would) they would need to have representatives on the Supreme Court, for the circuit duties of the Supreme Court judges still constituted a large part of their official responsibilities. Lincoln was also acutely conscious that any preference he might show the North in appointing judges could be interpreted as a slight to border states and tip their sentiments dangerously southward.[49] The fact that both the Court and Congress were out of session for most of his first year as president was another consideration. Any Supreme Court justice he might nominate could not be confirmed until the Senate reconvened in regular session, and a successful nominee would not be called upon to sit with the other judges until the Court commenced its term in December 1861. These considerations were certainly political, but not unduly partisan. Lincoln sought, first, competent men to fill the Court vacancies. Next, he sought men who would support the Union in its great struggle with the South. If possible, he would also like to find men who could represent the diverse geographic regions of the country. He naturally looked to his Republican supporters for candidates they could suggest. But he was not bound to one party, and he was in no rush to pick names.

His search for nominees was further complicated by population changes that had taken place since 1837, when the federal circuit system was last reorganized. In those twenty-four years, the population of the North had grown more rapidly than that of the South. In Justice McLean's Seventh Circuit alone, the population had more than doubled, so that by 1860 it had more than six million residents, representing one out of every five Americans. There had also been substantial population growth in Wisconsin, Minnesota, Iowa, and Kansas, in Florida and Texas, and in California and Oregon, states that were wholly unrepresented on the Supreme Court. In California, the gold rush had caused an unprecedented population explosion, prompting Congress to create a separate circuit court there.[50] Thus, from 1855 on, a former Georgian named Matthew Hall McAllister presided over the new U.S. circuit court in San Francisco. McAllister's position in the federal judicial system was unique, for he was the only judge in the nation who presided over a federal circuit without also having a seat on the Supreme Court in Washington.[51]

In his annual message to Congress on December 3, 1861, Lincoln summarized the difficulties that he faced in filling Supreme Court vacancies and suggested three possibilities for overcoming them. He noted that large sections of the country had never been represented on the high court and that it would be impossible to provide such representation without reorganizing the circuits. Simply adding additional justices would, he said, "create a court altogether too numerous for a judicial body of any sort," adding: "Circuit courts are useful, or they are not useful. If useful, no State should be denied them; if not useful, no State should have them. Let them be provided for all, or abolished as to all."[52]

The problem, he said, could be remedied by dividing the whole country (North and South, East and West) into circuits "of convenient size," with Supreme Court justices appointed in some and independent circuit judges in the rest. Alternatively, the Supreme Court judges could be relieved of their circuit duties and separate circuit judges provided for all of the circuits. A third possibility would be to dispense with circuit courts altogether and organize the federal judiciary around district courts and an independent Supreme Court. He left it up to Congress to decide which of these solutions was most suitable.[53]

Well before the president delivered his annual message, Northern newspapers had issued strident calls for reform of the federal judiciary. The *Chicago Tribune*, dismissing the Supreme Court as a "bench-full of Southern lawyers, which gentlemen of a political temperament call an 'August tribunal,'" urged that it be reconstituted by "the dropping off of a few of its members and the appointment of better men in their places."[54] The *New York Tribune* proposed that the Court be increased to thirteen members, so the Republican president could immediately appoint seven new justices.[55] And the day after Lincoln delivered his annual message, Republican senator John P. Hale of New Hampshire astounded his colleagues by proposing that the entire Supreme Court be abolished and a new one created in its place.[56] Defending his proposal against charges that it flagrantly violated the Constitution, Hale pointed out that the charter confided the federal judicial power in "one Supreme Court, and in such inferior courts as the Congress may from time to time ordain and establish."[57] He demanded that senators "look this thing right in the face, right in the eye, and march up to their duty and establish a Supreme Court as the Constitution requires them to do 'from time to time;' yes, sir, 'from time to time.' . . . My idea is that the time has come; that this is one of the very times the framers of the Constitution contemplated."[58]

Hale's tortured reading of the constitutional language received some support out of Congress, but little within. New York attorney John Jay, grandson of the first chief justice, wrote the senator to express general agreement with his call for radical judicial reform, complaining that the present Supreme Court could not be depended upon to overrule the habeas corpus views expressed by Taney in *Ex parte Merryman* and to sustain the government's war measures.[59] But Republican senator Lafayette Foster of Connecticut denied that Congress had any authority to abolish the Supreme Court, and pointed out that, even if it did, a new Court would be nominated by a "fallible President" and confirmed or rejected by a "fallible Senate," with a result that might not be any better than what they already had.[60] Republican senator Jacob Collamer of Vermont also opposed Hale's proposal, saying he could "hardly conceive of anything more radical." Hale attempted to keep his proposal alive by explaining that it only called for an "inquiry" into abolition of the Supreme Court, and that such an inquiry was "simple, harmless, eminently necessary." But the new senator from Illinois, Orville Browning, retorted that it "might be just as appropriate to inquire into the expediency of repealing the Constitution."[61]

While senators wrangled about Hale's proposal, the new senator from Ohio, John Sherman, made a much more modest proposal. Ignoring arguments that the Supreme Court be abolished, or greatly enlarged, Sherman suggested simply that the federal circuits be reorganized so as to equalize the population served by each. Sherman's Ohio colleague, Senator Benjamin F. Wade, objected to this proposal, but Senator Trumbull supported it. "The Supreme Court has but six judges on the bench," Trumbull reminded his colleagues. "The other three ought to be appointed, but I presume they will not be appointed until some bill passes on the subject, and I think it would be best to act upon it as early as we conveniently can."[62]

Though no plan for reorganization had yet been agreed on, Lincoln was under continuing pressure to make a Supreme Court appointment, particularly after the Court opened its new term on December 2, 1861, with three conspicuously empty seats. Swayne, Browning, Davis, Drummond, and Chase were still in the running for nominations, and Secretary of the Interior Caleb B. Smith had recently been added to the list. But the president still delayed, hoping that Congress could reorganize the federal circuits before he made any Supreme Court appointments. While he waited for Congress to act, he considered potential nominees.

It has been speculated that Lincoln's interest in Browning as a Supreme Court judge cooled during this period, in part because his old friend had taken issue with the government's military policies in Missouri.[63] At the end of August, Major General John C. Frémont, commander of the St. Louis–based Department of the West, had proclaimed martial law in Missouri, announcing that civilians bearing arms would be tried by court-martial, and shot if convicted, and that all slaves owned by Confederate activists would immediately be freed. Frémont issued his order without consulting Lincoln (or any of his military superiors), and it violated the president's promise not to interfere with slavery in the states. Further, it went well beyond the terms of the Confiscation Act just passed by Congress, which provided that property (including slaves) owned by persons engaged in insurrection against the government would be confiscated, but only if actually used in the insurrection.[64] Lincoln asked Frémont to modify his order, arguing that a policy of shooting civilians would inevitably lead to retaliation against Union soldiers, and that indiscriminate confiscation of property and liberation of slaves would "alarm our Southern Union friends, and turn them against us—perhaps ruin our rather fair prospect for Kentucky."[65] But Frémont refused to modify his proclamation without a public order to do so and sent Mrs. Frémont to Washington to argue the issue with the president. After a short interval, Lincoln removed Frémont from his command.

Browning took Frémont's side in the Missouri controversy, writing Lincoln a sharply worded letter in which he insisted that the general's order was "necessary, and will do good," and that it had "the full approval of all loyal citizens of the west and North West."[66] Lincoln replied that he did not object to a general's seizing rebel property, even slaves, when needed for military purposes, but seizure could be justified only by "military necessity." Since Frémont's proclamation was not justified by necessity, it was "purely political"—an act of "dictatorship." "Can it be pretended," Lincoln asked Browning, "that it is any longer the government of the U.S.—any government of Constitution and laws,—wherein a General, or a President, may make permanent rules of property by proclamation?"[67]

If Lincoln's inclination to appoint Browning was cooling because of the Frémont affair, his interest in Noah Swayne was warming. Ohio's senators Wade and Sherman joined the state's governor, William Dennison, in urging that Swayne be nominated.[68] Swayne himself was active in soliciting an appointment, writing letters to the president and prominent politicians in other states. He also sought the support of Salmon P. Chase, though he suspected that Chase himself was angling for a nomination. But Lincoln did not need much persuasion to conclude that Swayne would be a good nominee, for he was a loyal supporter of the president's war policies, and his views on slavery were similar to Lincoln's. Born to a Quaker family in Virginia in 1804, Swayne had first studied medicine but switched to law when he was still a young man. He could have had a successful legal career in Virginia, but his opposition to slavery was so great that he resolved to move to Ohio. A Democrat in his early years, Swayne supported President Andrew Jackson and was rewarded in 1829 with an appointment as U.S. district attorney for Ohio. While serving in that position, he was elected to the state legislature, and he also found time to build

up a lucrative private legal practice. His marriage in 1832 to a Virginia woman brought several slaves into his family, but he and his wife promptly freed
them. In the 1850s, the crisis over the extension of slavery into the territories
prompted Swayne to leave the party of Jackson and become a Republican. By
this time, he had won a reputation as one of the best trial lawyers in the nation
and built up a clientele that included influential banks, railroad companies,
and other corporations. This spoke well for him in Lincoln's mind, for the president believed that business support would do much to help the North win the
war. Swayne was a large man, both in height and in girth, with a massive head,
a ruddy complexion, and dark hair that tended in later years to baldness. His
photographs reveal a handsome face, deeply lined as he grew older, a high forehead, and a curious habit of tilting his head to the right. Lincoln nominated
Swayne to the Supreme Court on January 21, 1862, and the nomination was
confirmed by the Senate on January 24 by a vote of thirty-eight to one. Three
days later, Swayne took his oath of office.[69]

The *New York Evening Post* reported that Lincoln's intention to wait until
the federal circuits had been reorganized before making an appointment had
given way to the entreaties of Governor Dennison, Senators Wade and
Sherman, and other prominent Ohioans, that "the business of the Supreme
Court could not go on" without new judges, for the work of the Court was
hampered not only by the existing vacancies but also by the fact that Justices
Taney and Catron were frequently ill and unable to attend court. The Ohioans
"represented the needs of the country to be so urgent in this respect," according to the *Post*, "that the President, unexpectedly, sent into the Senate the
nomination of Swayne."[70] Although the *Chicago Tribune* expressed surprise that
Lincoln had made the nomination before the circuit reorganization was complete, its editors said they believed that Swayne was a good appointee. The *National Intelligencer* in Washington congratulated the president on choosing a
nominee of "great legal training and eminence in the walks of his profession,"
while the *Washington Evening Star* emphasized Swayne's Southern birth and the
part he had played in giving Ohio "its material eminence."[71]

As Swayne began his Supreme Court work, Congress was still arguing
about the circuits. The large populations of Ohio and Illinois virtually guaranteed that those states would be the linchpins of separate circuits, but there was
no agreement about how to allocate Michigan, Wisconsin, Minnesota, and

Iowa. Senator Joseph A. Wright of Indiana argued that his state should be joined with Ohio, while Senator James W. Grimes and Congressman James F. Wilson of Iowa argued that Missouri, Iowa, Kansas, and Minnesota should have a separate circuit, for their legal traditions were rooted in the old Louisiana Territory and not in the common-law traditions that prevailed east of the Mississippi. And there was the thorny problem of what to do with Kentucky, a border state that had traditionally been linked with Virginia and Tennessee but that many Northerners wanted to coax into cooperation with Ohio, Indiana, and Illinois. By late spring of 1862, there was still no reorganization bill. Awaiting congressional action, Lincoln withheld any further nominations. But advocates of judicial reform were beginning to lose patience.

Congress at last completed passage of the Judicial Reorganization Act of 1862 on July 12, and it became law when Lincoln signed it three days later. In their final forms, the new Fourth Circuit included Maryland, Delaware, Virginia, and North Carolina; the Fifth, South Carolina, Georgia, Alabama, Mississippi, and Florida; the Sixth, Louisiana, Texas, Arkansas, Kentucky, and Tennessee. The circuit arrangement in the upper Middle West satisfied the demands of the Iowans, with a new Seventh Circuit consisting of Ohio and Indiana; a new Eighth that included Michigan, Wisconsin, and Illinois; and a Ninth Circuit that embraced Missouri, Iowa, Kansas, and Minnesota.[72] Illinois and Iowa were, as the Iowans had insisted, allocated to different circuits. Oregon and California, the latter served by Judge McAllister's circuit, were still outside the system.

Even before passage of the Reorganization Act, it had become apparent that the real reason for the Iowans' stubbornness on the reorganization issue was that they were backing their own Supreme Court candidate and wanted to ensure that a circuit would be open for him. The candidate's name was Samuel Freeman Miller, and he was at once a highly qualified and a thoroughly improbable prospect for a Supreme Court nomination.

Miller was born in Kentucky in 1816 and raised on a farm in the central part of the state. Six feet tall, with a large head and a square jaw, he was both physically powerful and intellectually restless. He had no liking for farm life and, while still a teenager, began to work in a local drugstore. There he had access to medical texts, which absorbed his mental energy. He went to medical school in Lexington and, upon graduation, began to practice medicine in a small town in the foothills of the Appalachians. He acquired ownership of a handful of slaves through a gift from his father-in-law but never became a robust supporter of slavery. By the late 1840s he had become convinced that slavery was impeding Kentucky's economic development and lent his support to a movement to bring about gradual emancipation in the state. At the same time, he decided that the life of a small-town doctor would do little to serve his ambitions and began to study law. Soon he was well established in a legal practice. When Kentucky's voters decisively rejected gradual emancipation, Miller left for the free state of Iowa, where he settled in the river town of Keokuk, a busy transportation and shipping center that he believed might one day rival Chicago and St. Louis as an important city.

Originally a Whig, Miller joined the Republican Party in the wake of the Kansas-Nebraska controversy of the mid-1850s. He was an enthusiastic advocate of economic development and an eloquent opponent of slavery. But, like the Republican Party itself, he rejected the "radical" doctrine of abolitionism. Running up to the presidential election of 1860, he also became Iowa's most dedicated campaigner for Lincoln. Miller's success as a lawyer and his ability as a public speaker earned him the respect of political leaders up and down the Mississippi River. Though his own political career was lackluster (he ran for elective office only once and was defeated), prominent politicians inside and outside Iowa began to tout his qualifications for the United States Supreme Court.[73]

A campaign to promote Miller's candidacy started as soon as Congress began its debate on circuit reorganization. Lawyers and judges wrote Lincoln, extolling Miller's character, intelligence, and record of Republican service. Senator Grimes circulated a petition urging Miller's nomination that received the signatures of 28 of the 32 senators then in Congress, while Congressman Wilson obtained 120 signatures on a similar petition in the House of Representatives.[74] At Miller's request, John Kasson of Des Moines, Lincoln's assistant postmaster general, made a personal visit to the president. Lincoln listened politely as Kasson praised the Keokuk lawyer, but it soon became evident that the president did not know who Miller was, for he confused him with former Iowa congressman Daniel F. Miller. When Iowa's governor, Samuel Kirkwood, made a personal visit to the White House, in company with Senator James Harlan and several congressmen, Lincoln was not aware that they had come in Miller's behalf. He had heard so many pleas for office seekers that he decided to play a joke on them. When they finished speaking, he put pen to paper and, as if he were about to make out an appointment, asked, "What is the office and whom do you wish to be placed in it?" An astounded Harlan replied that the office was the Supreme Court and that they wished Samuel F. Miller to be appointed to it. "Well, well," the president answered, putting his pen down and pushing back his paper, "that is a very important position and I will have to give it serious consideration. I had supposed you wanted me to make some one a Brigadier General for you." The Iowans left with no assurances from the president.[75]

On July 16, one day after he signed the Judicial Reorganization Act, Lincoln did nominate Miller to the Supreme Court, with circuit-court duties in the new Ninth Circuit. The Senate unanimously confirmed the nomination within a half hour, and the Iowan received his commission on July 19. On July 21, Miller took his oath of office before Chief Justice Taney.[76]

WITH ONE SUPREME COURT seat remaining unfilled, Lincoln now had to weigh the merits of the Illinois candidates. Orville Browning, David Davis, and Thomas Drummond each held out hope that the president would tap him for this final seat, although none had much confidence that he would be the ultimate choice. Lincoln was content to reflect on the matter while he gave his immediate attention to more pressing concerns.

On July 22, the president read a preliminary draft of an Emancipation Proclamation to his cabinet, announcing that, as of January 1, 1863, "all persons held as slaves within any state or states, wherein the constitutional authority of the United States shall not then be practically recognized, submitted to, and maintained," would "then, thenceforward, and forever, be free." The proclamation was to be made by the president under his constitutional authority as commander in chief of the army and navy of the United States.[77] Increasingly over the course of the war, Lincoln had agonized over the awful suffering the military struggle was causing and the persistence of Confederate resistance to the Union armies, and by little steps he had come to believe that the emancipation of all slaves in the rebellious states and territories was justified by military necessity—the same military necessity he had found wanting in Frémont's Missouri proclamation a year earlier. His personal and moral opposition to slavery was well known to his political friends as well as his enemies, but as president he had focused on preservation of the Union and the restoration of law and order throughout the United States. He had made it clear in his First Inaugural Address that he did not intend to interfere with slavery in any state—indeed, that the Constitution gave him no power to do so. As the war progressed, however, it became more and more evident that the Confederacy was making extensive use of slaves in all of its war efforts, using them to dig trenches, build roads and bridges, carry supplies, drive wagons, haul arms and ammunition. Behind the battle lines, Southern slaves were laboring mightily in the fields, producing cotton, raising corn and wheat and rice and sugar, all to feed and clothe Confederate soldiers. Slaves had thus become instruments of war, much like rifles or cannons or horses or wagons. To take those slaves away from the enemy would weaken the Confederacy's armies, and freeing slaves to join Northern forces would strengthen the Union's own efforts.

Lincoln now saw a military necessity, and thus a military *justification*, in emancipation. The fighting had gone on so long, and the rebels were inflicting such severe losses on the Union armies, that the government could no longer, in the president's words, "play a game in which it stakes all, and its enemies stake nothing." As he wrote the New York financier August Belmont, the government's enemies "must understand that they cannot experiment for ten years trying to destroy the government, and if they fail still come back into the Union unhurt."[78] But the president deferred public announcement of the proclamation until the Union armies achieved a battlefield victory, for he wanted emancipation to be perceived as the purposeful strategy of a victor and not (as Seward warned it might be without a victory) "the last measure of an exhausted government, a cry for help."[79]

Late in August, the president was horrified by news from the military front. Major General Henry W. Halleck, newly named to the position of general in chief of the army, had consolidated federal forces in northern Virginia under Major General John Pope, hoping to mount an attack on the Confederate capital at Richmond. But on August 29 and 30, at the Second Battle of Bull Run, Pope's army was met by Confederate forces under Major General Thomas J. ("Stonewall") Jackson and General Robert E. Lee. The resulting Union defeat inflicted severe losses on federal troops (16,000 casualties out of a total of 75,000 troops) and forced them to retreat toward Washington. In a few hours, the battle erased all of the military advantage the North had won in the first year of fighting and relieved Richmond from the threat of imminent attack. It also opened the way for Confederate advances toward the North.

Lee pressed his advantage by crossing the Potomac into Maryland. But on September 17, near the town of Sharpsburg on Antietam Creek, Lee and 40,000 men of his Army of Northern Virginia were met by 75,000 men of the Army of the Potomac under Major General George B. McClellan. In the ensuing battle, 2,100 Union soldiers were killed, 9,550 wounded, and 750 reported as missing or captured, while the Confederates suffered 1,550 killed, 7,750 wounded, and 1,020 captured or wounded. This, the bloodiest single day of the entire war, was put down as a Union victory. "At last our Generals in the field seem to have risen to the grandeur of the National crisis," the *New York Times* proclaimed.[80] The victory was diminished by McClellan's failure to follow Lee's army as it retreated back across the Potomac, but it was good enough for Lincoln to publicly announce his preliminary Emancipation Proclamation on September 22, making known to all the world that the termination of slavery had now become the official policy of his government.

Burdened as he was by the military struggle, the president continued to think about the Supreme Court vacancy. Chicago's Judge Drummond had some influential supporters. Lincoln himself was personally acquainted with Drummond, for he had practiced in his Chicago court, and he thought highly of him. But Browning had not been ruled out of consideration. As a United States senator, Browning had frequent and easy access to the president, and the two men still felt the ties of their old friendship. In February, after Lincoln's eleven-year-old son Willie died in the White House (probably of typhoid fever), Mr. and Mrs. Browning came to the White House to console the grieving president and his wife. Browning helped Lincoln's secretary, John G. Nicolay, arrange the boy's funeral, and the Brownings stayed with the Lincolns for about a week. Lincoln was frank with Browning about his workload and the toll it was taking on him. He said that he found his job exhausting and that he often suffered from headaches. Browning was able to cheer the president up by spending time with him, discussing books and reading poetry.[81]

Browning also had admirers outside the White House. Attorney General Bates pronounced him "a proper man" for the Court, and Chief Justice Taney wrote Justice Clifford that "the appointment of Mr. Browning to the vacant circuit, although probable was not certain."[82] Lincoln himself was reported as saying: "I do not know what I may do when the time comes, but there has never been a day when if I had to act I should not have appointed Browning."[83] But the president had not forgotten his once-loyal friend's disappointing behavior during the Frémont controversy. And he had also learned that Browning had some vocal enemies in Illinois. One was Joseph Medill, a prominent Republican and editor of the *Chicago Tribune*, who wrote Senator Trumbull that Browning represented only the "secesh" (secessionists) of Illinois and that the Republicans in that state "detest and despise him." Medill added that Browning's "elevation to the Supreme Bench will be the most unpopular act of Mr. Lincoln's life and he ought to be informed of it, before he does the deed."[84]

David Davis was another prospective Supreme Court judge. Born on Maryland's Eastern Shore in 1815, Davis was descended on his mother's side from a wealthy plantation family. But his father died before he was born, and for most of the first two decades of his life he was shunted from one house to another, living for a time with his uncle, an Episcopal rector who served a brief term as president of St. John's College in Annapolis, and for a time with his mother and stepfather. In 1828, Davis enrolled at Ohio's fledgling Kenyon College, founded by Salmon P. Chase's uncle, the Episcopal bishop Philander Chase. After graduating in 1832, he went to Lenox, Massachusetts, where he read law in an attorney's office, and then to Connecticut's New Haven Law School, where he took a few classes. He moved west in 1835, bringing with him a mixture of Southern tradition and Yankee virtue that was to serve him well in his legal career on the Illinois prairies. Settling in Bloomington, northeast of Lincoln's hometown of Springfield, Davis became a successful—though not a brilliant—lawyer, whose practice consisted mostly of collection cases.[85]

In 1848, at the age of thirty-three, Davis was elected judge of the Eighth Illinois Circuit Court. Twice a year, in the spring and the fall, it was his duty to travel from county to county through his circuit, with a retinue of lawyers in tow, holding court in county seats, sleeping and eating in frontier taverns, listening to the pleas of plaintiffs and defendants, presiding over juries, and deciding the fates of criminal defendants. Though there were many skilled lawyers in Davis's group, Lincoln stood out from all the rest. He was the only man besides the judge and the state's attorney who regularly made the circuit of all of the counties, a trek that kept him away from home for several months each year. More significant, he was a lawyer's lawyer who impressed all who watched him with his intelligence, fairness, and inexhaustible store of good humor. After court hours, when the judge and the lawyers gathered in local taverns, Lincoln regaled them with funny and often bawdy stories.

President Lincoln called on Judge Davis to help clean up the mess left in Missouri after Frémont was relieved of duty there, appointing him to a three-member commission to examine and settle several million dollars in unpaid claims against the army and the government. But he did not consult him on major appointments, or seek his advice on important issues. Davis hoped that he might be considered for a judicial appointment, but he was not certain in his own mind that he was qualified for the Supreme Court. He had years of experience as a judge, but only at the trial-court level. He had never argued an appeal, even in the Illinois Supreme Court (Lincoln had argued many cases there). "I often doubt," Davis wrote a friend in January 1862, "whether I could sustain myself on the Supreme Bench. It may be that I am not self confident enough. I certainly could not without hard study. I have but little legal learning, and whether study would suit me now may be very doubtful."[86] Thinking that Judge Drummond might be nominated to the Supreme Court, Davis expressed some interest in taking Drummond's place in Chicago. Lincoln knew Davis as well as any of his legal and political friends and probably shared some of the judge's own doubts about his qualifications for the Supreme Court. Whatever limits there were to Davis's learning, however, the president knew that he was an honorable man, attentive to his duties and dependably collegial.

Still Lincoln did not tip his hand. In May 1862, John P. Usher, an Indiana lawyer who had become assistant to Secretary of the Interior Caleb Smith, wrote Davis that Orville Browning had become very friendly with the Lincolns. Browning would probably be appointed to the Supreme Court, Usher said, and Davis might want a seat on the U.S. Court of Claims. In reply, Davis wrote Usher a letter that he believed (quite reasonably) would be shown to the president:

> I feel that the President should be left free from the suggestions of personal friendship, to select those who can most assist him in his great work. . . . I cannot by any act of my own add to the weight of his embarrassment. The President and myself have been associated in most intimate and pleasant relations for the greater part of our lives.

Any representations made to him, however partial or however unjust, could hardly change the judgment he may have formed of me. He knows me well, and the character of service, if any, I could render my country. If he should desire me to act in any capacity, . . . I should not feel at liberty to decline, but I cannot, either directly or indirectly, or through my friends, importune him for any position, whether humble or exalted.[87]

Davis had many friends, but he also had enemies. Among the most determined were the abolitionists, and former Democrats in the Republican Party, who believed that Lincoln should take an aggressive stance against slavery. Like Lincoln, Davis believed that it was no business of the federal government to interfere with slavery in the states where it already existed, although it should firmly oppose the extension of slavery into the territories. Congressman Elihu B. Washburne of northern Illinois was one of Davis's opponents. He told Lincoln that Davis's appointment would not only be bad on policy grounds but would also pose a danger to the Chicago clerkship of William H. Bradley, who was one of Lincoln's Illinois friends.[88]

Mrs. Lincoln, however, was well-disposed to Davis and urged that her husband appoint him. Although the Brownings had been attentive to her after Willie's death, she was apparently turning against them. When Leonard Swett, one of Lincoln's old Illinois friends, came to Washington, she told him that Browning had become "distressingly loving." In June, another friend wrote Davis from Washington: "Mrs. Lincoln is your warm friend and . . . presses your claims upon the President seeking every opportunity to put in a good word and . . . is unceasing in her endeavours for your appointment."[89] At the end of July Swett left Washington for New York, where he wrote his wife that Lincoln had decided to appoint Davis to the Supreme Court. "A few nights before I left I called upon Mrs. Lincoln," Swett wrote. "She told me she had been fighting Davis's battles, that Browning had gone home, & she was glad of it. . . . When I left, she told me again at the door to tell Judge Davis his matter was all right."[90]

On August 27, Lincoln wrote Davis: "My mind is made up to appoint you Supreme Judge; but I am so anxious that Mr. Bradley, present Clerk at Chicago shall be retained, that I think it no dishonor for me to ask, and for you to tell me, that you will not remove him. Please answer."[91]

On September 1, Davis answered:

> I cannot, in words, sufficiently express, my thankfulness and grati-
> tude, for this distinguished mark of your confidence & favor.
> While I shall assume the responsibilities of this office, with great
> distrust in my abilities, yet, I hope by labor and application, to dis-
> charge its duties, satisfactorily.
> I should not in any event think of displacing Mr. Bradley, as I know,
> with you, his fitness for the position he holds; but especially as you re-
> quest it, I shall take great pleasure in retaining him.[92]

Lincoln did not immediately announce his decision to appoint Davis.
Congress had gone into recess on July 17 and was not due to reconvene until
December 1, so a Davis nomination could not be taken up before then. But the
fall congressional elections were approaching, and Lincoln was sensitive to the
political infighting in Illinois. Leonard Swett was running for Congress in the
president's old central Illinois district, against Lincoln's first law partner, John
T. Stuart. Swett was the Republican nominee and Stuart the Democrat, and
Davis was active in Swett's campaign. According to Davis's biographer, many
of Davis's friends in central Illinois "resented Lincoln's failure to give him an
important post" and believed that it "would help Swett to defeat Stuart if
this feeling could be removed."[93] So the president asked Attorney General
Bates if he could give Davis a recess appointment, pursuant to Article II, Section 2 of the Constitution, which provides (in relevant part): "The President
shall have power to fill up all vacancies that may happen during the recess of
the Senate, by granting commissions which shall expire at the end of their
next session."

Recess appointments of Supreme Court justices were not unusual. In fact,
there had been eight such appointments before Lincoln took office: two by
George Washington and one each by John Adams, Thomas Jefferson, James
Monroe, Martin Van Buren, James K. Polk, and Millard Fillmore.[94] More interesting, perhaps, was the question of whether the vacancy had to have been created (or to have "happened") during the last recess of the Senate, or whether,
as in the case of Davis, a recess appointment could be made for a vacancy that
predated the last recess. Attorney General Bates researched the question and
replied with a formal opinion on October 15. "If the question were new, and

now, for the first time, to be considered," Bates told Lincoln, "I might have serious doubts of your constitutional power to fill up the vacancy. . . . But the question is not new. It is settled, in favor of the power, as far, at least, as a constitutional question can be settled by the continued practice of your predecessors, and the reiterated opinions of mine, and sanctioned, as far as I know or believe by the unbroken acquiescence of the Senate."[95]

Accordingly, Lincoln made out a commission for Davis on October 17. News of the appointment came out shortly before the election but did little to help Swett in his contest with Stuart, for Swett was soundly defeated in the election of November 4.[96] Democrats scored substantial gains not only in Illinois but also in Wisconsin, Indiana, Ohio, and Pennsylvania.

On December 1, Lincoln sent the Senate a formal notice nominating David Davis to be a justice of the Supreme Court. On December 8, Davis was confirmed by the full Senate in a voice vote.

Two of Lincoln's new justices, Noah Swayne and Samuel Miller, were on hand when the Supreme Court opened its term on December 1. Justices Wayne, Grier, and Clifford also took their seats on the bench that day, but Catron, Nelson, and Taney were indisposed and unable to appear.

His confirmation complete, David Davis was on hand for the Court's session on December 10, taking his seat in the junior justice's chair on the far left side of the bench. Taney was well enough to take his place in the center of the courtroom that day and administer the oath of office to the new justice from Illinois.

For the first time in more than two years, the bench of the Supreme Court was full.

5   The Prizes

EARLY IN JULY 1861, a sailing ship struggled through heavy seas off the coast of Virginia. It was the brig *Amy Warwick*, a merchant ship with tall masts and billowing sails designed to catch the stiff winds necessary to carry it on long voyages across the ocean. The ship had begun its voyage in Rio de Janeiro, where longshoremen speaking in Portuguese and English and a half-dozen other languages had filled its creaking hull with more than five thousand bags of Brazilian coffee. The coffee was bound for Hampton Roads, Virginia, gateway to the James River and the city of Richmond, newly proclaimed capital of the Confederate States of America. Although the cargo had no military importance, it was of considerable commercial value for, war or no, Virginians still liked to drink coffee, and soldiers manning the picket lines that guarded Richmond from the threat of Yankee attack liked to hoist tin cups of steaming black java as they surveyed the horizon for signs of enemy patrols. The *Amy Warwick* had left Rio on May 29, in time to know that the president of the United States had proclaimed a blockade of the Southern coast and that, if it were to reach its destination, it would have to run the blockade.

On April 19 Lincoln had publicly announced his intention "to set on foot a blockade" of the ports of South Carolina, Georgia, Florida, Alabama, Mississippi, Louisiana, and Texas, states then in secession from the United States.[1] He had given as reasons for the blockade the existence of "an insurrection against the Government of the United States" in the secessionist states and the fact that revenue laws in those states could not be enforced "conformably to that provision of the Constitution which requires duties to be uniform throughout the United States."[2] He also noted that "a combination of persons" engaged in the insurrection had "threatened to grant pretended letters of marque to authorize the bearers thereof to commit assaults on the lives, vessels, and property of good citizens of the country lawfully engaged in commerce on the high seas, and in waters of the United States."[3] On April 27, after North Carolina and Virginia joined the other states in breaking away from the Union, the president extended the blockade to cover their ports as well.[4] With this final action, he proclaimed his government's intention of blockading the entire Southern coastline, from the entrance to Chesapeake Bay in Virginia; past Wilmington, North Carolina; Charleston, South Carolina; and Savannah; around the peninsula of Florida and its keys; past the Gulf Coast ports of Mobile, Alabama; Biloxi, Mississippi; New Orleans; and Galveston, Texas; to the mouth of the Rio Grande below Brownsville, Texas. It was an astounding distance and an astounding coastline—more than 3,500 miles of capes, headlands, bays, sounds, inlets, rivers, reefs, coves, and islands, all under the claimed jurisdiction of the government headed up by Jefferson Davis. And the task of patrolling this coastline seemed equally astounding, for the United States Navy in 1861 had only ninety ships in its fleet, and barely half were fit for blockade duty. Some were hopelessly antiquated, others were in disrepair, and yet others were guarding American naval interests in distant parts of the globe—the Mediterranean, the coast of Africa, and the Orient.

THE U.S.S. QUAKER CITY was one of the ships Secretary of the Navy Gideon Welles had ordered to blockade duty off the Virginia coast. Equipped with sails and a powerful steam engine, the 1,600-ton side-wheeler carried a crew of 129 and was armed with four guns. Though commissioned as a navy vessel, it was a private ship, owned by investors in New York, and had been chartered for blockade duty as part of Welles's hasty effort to strengthen his fleet. While taking the first steps to establish a long-term shipbuilding program, the secretary had also searched for private vessels that could quickly be converted into navy ships, acquiring some by purchase and others, like the *Quaker City*, by charter. When vessels were chartered, it was the responsibility of the private owners to equip them, provide their crews, and maintain them in good repair, while the navy put officers aboard to command their operations. The *Quaker City* was initially chartered for only thirty days, because Welles, like most other government officials, had thought the war would be short. The term was extended, however, as it became clear that hostilities would continue for months, perhaps even years. The *Quaker City* was sent south from New York with orders to guard the shipping lanes at the mouth of Chesapeake Bay, the most important waterway on the Atlantic coast of the Confederacy.

The *Quaker City* sailed under Commander Overton Carr of the U.S. Navy, who reported to Flag Officer Silas H. Stringham. Stringham gave his orders from the *U.S.S. Minnesota*, flagship of the Atlantic Blockading Squadron. The "squadron" designation was impressive but somewhat misleading, for Stringham's command included only a handful of ships and support boats.

It is difficult to determine precisely when and with whom the idea of the blockade originated, though it is clear that Secretary of State Seward and General in Chief Scott were both early proponents. And it is equally clear that Jefferson Davis's decision to issue letters of marque to any ships that would attack American vessels added to the logic of a blockade. Davis's decision signified his belief that naval warfare would play an important part in the coming conflict. The Confederate president's proclamation was issued on April 17, just two days before Lincoln's blockade proclamation. Since Lincoln refused to recognize the legality of the Confederate States, he regarded Davis's decision to issue letters of marque as an invitation to piracy, which was a capital offense under United States law.[5]

Even before Davis's proclamation, however, there was talk in the North of blockading the Southern coast. As early as 1860, General Scott had suggested that Southern secession—if it came—might be dealt with, at least in part, by a blockade. He later developed a more comprehensive plan for dealing with secession that included a complete blockade of the Southern coast and the establishment of a military cordon along the Mississippi River, supported by gunboats and tens of thousands of soldiers. Though loyal to the Union, the Virginia-born general in chief was loath to propose a military invasion of the South, for, as he said, "the destruction of life and property, on the other side, would be frightful." Better, he thought, to envelope the seceding states, cut them off from trade by land and water, and let them die by starvation. Half derisively, half admiringly, newspaper writers called Scott's proposal the "Anaconda Plan," or "Scott's Anaconda," for its resemblance to the great snake that wraps itself around its prey and slowly squeezes the life out of it. Seward was as impressed by Scott's proposals as he was by the general's flattering (but mistaken) suggestion that he was to be the "chief" of Lincoln's cabinet.[6]

Interdicting Southern trade was an idea that made both commercial and military sense. The South, much more than the North, was dependent on ocean commerce for its economic well-being, for the Southern states were agricultural producers and required foreign markets to thrive. Their principal crops—tobacco, rice, sugar, and, most important of all, raw cotton—were immensely valuable. Since the South itself had only a rudimentary textile industry, approximately 95 percent of its cotton production was exported (70 percent to Europe and 25 percent to the Northern states).[7] Great Britain, which had an enormous textile industry, depended heavily on shipments of cotton from the South.

As important as agriculture was to the Southern economy, industrial production was correspondingly unimportant. The South had few factories or shipyards. Its most important cities were all seaports, which depended on the coming and going of ships for their prosperity. Even railroads in the South were primitive. Though a third of the nation's total tracks were in the South in 1861, railroads traced a confusing web across the Southern countryside, with differing rail widths and unconnected lines. When Jefferson Davis left his plantation near Vicksburg, Mississippi, in February 1861, for his inauguration in Montgomery, Alabama, two hundred miles away, he first had to take a train to Jackson, Mississippi, then make a 700-mile detour north into Tennessee and east to Atlanta before turning south to reach Montgomery, for, as Civil War historian William C. Davis points out, there was no rail connection that was more direct.[8] Industrially weak, the South depended on the same ocean commerce that supported its agricultural production for the basic manufactured goods of modern life—cloth, buttons, boots, shoes, wagons, carts, agricultural implements, guns, and even ships and railroad supplies. The Confederate States had virtually no shipbuilding industry in 1861 and next to no capacity for manufacturing munitions. To mount a serious war effort, they would have to import almost all of their manufactures from their European trading partners, and those same partners would have to supply them with the financial wherewithal to pay for their imports. If the North could interdict the sea traffic into and out of the South, or even seriously curtail it, its natural military advantage would be enormous.

Like Seward and Scott, Gideon Welles realized the military importance of interdicting Southern trade, but he disagreed as to the propriety of blockading Southern ports. When two nations were at war, he argued, they were regarded by all the world as belligerents and accorded the right of blockading each other's ports. But the secessionist states were in rebellion; they were not a separate nation and they did not have the rights of belligerents. A blockade "was not a domestic but an international question—legitimate and proper as between two distinct nations" but wholly improper in a domestic conflict. In Welles's view, a blockade would constitute "a concession to the Confederate organization virtually admitting it to be a quasi government—giving to that organization a position among nations that we would not and could not recognize or sanction, and which would inevitably lead to embarrassments."[9] Simply closing the Southern ports would not entail any such embarrassments, for it was well within the authority of a sovereign nation to provide by law which of its ports were open to trade and which were closed; and any foreigners who violated such a law would be smugglers—common criminals subject to the penalties provided by law.

Like Welles (and virtually every other federal officer loyal to the Union), Lincoln refused to recognize the Confederacy as a legitimate government. He had argued in his inaugural address that no state or combination of states could, on their own motion, "lawfully get out of the Union," and that resolutions and ordinances purporting to do that were "legally void." Following this logic, acts of violence in support of secession were "insurrectionary or revolutionary, according to circumstances."[10] In his first blockade proclamation, the president described the Confederates as "a combination of persons" engaged in "an insurrection against the Government of the United States."[11] They were not a government, and certainly not a nation entitled to recognition as a "belligerent power" under international law.

Seward agreed with Lincoln (and with Welles) on all these points, but he had different ideas about the blockade. He had been in contact with the British minister in Washington, Lord Lyons, and, through him, the British foreign secretary, Lord Russell, and they had made it clear to him that, if Lincoln was determined to restrict Southern trade, a blockade would be preferable to any effort to close the ports. One of the key points of blockade law was the requirement that a blockade be "effectual," that is, that it be accompanied by the "actual presence of a maritime force, stationed at the entrance of the port, sufficiently near to prevent communication."[12] A blockade that was not effectual was a mere "paper blockade" and, in legal contemplation, a nullity. The United States Navy was small and would be hard put to patrol all 3,500 miles of the Southern coastline, and British shippers would do whatever they could to get in and out of Southern ports. As Russell himself admitted, Englishmen would, "if money were to be made by it, send supplies even to hell at the risk of burning their sails."[13] But if a blockade were imposed, Britain would be entitled to exercise the rights of a neutral nation, allied neither with the North nor the South. It would have freedom of navigation between neutral ports, an immensely valuable maritime right in time of war. If, however, an effort were made to close Southern ports, British shippers would run the risk of arrest and imprisonment for common smuggling. The British government felt so strongly about this issue that it hinted that it might resort to force, if necessary, to prevent what British leaders regarded as flagrant violations of their subjects' shipping rights. As Lord Lyons expressed it in a letter to Russell, a "paper blockade" would "justify Great Britain and France in recognizing the Southern Confederacy and sending their fleets to force the U.S. to treat British and French vessels as neutrals in conforming with the law of nations."[14]

Taking the British at their word, Seward urged Lincoln to proclaim a blockade and not try to close secessionist ports. The president understood the gravity of the issue, and met with his cabinet in marathon sessions, some extending into the small hours of the night, to discuss the alternatives. Secretary of War Simon Cameron and Secretary of the Interior Caleb Smith joined Seward in recommending a blockade, while the others sided with Welles in urging a port closure. Lincoln listened carefully to their respective arguments, pondered them for five days, and then issued his blockade proclamation.

Even then, however, his mind was not closed on the subject. When Congress assembled on July 4 for the special session he had called, it passed a flurry of measures designed to deal with the Southern insurrection. One was an act approving and ratifying all of the acts, proclamations, and orders made by the president after March 4, 1861, respecting the army and navy and the calling out of the militia.[15] Another was an act authorizing (although not requiring) the president to close any Southern port if, in his judgment, federal duties there could not be effectually collected "by the ordinary means or in the ordinary way."[16] The latter statute gave Gideon Welles a second opportunity to press his case against the blockade. To do so, he prepared a long and carefully worded brief in which he renewed his argument that closing Southern ports would preserve the "integrity and independence" of the United States, while a blockade would elevate the secessionists "to the dignity of nationality."[17] Lincoln once again considered his navy secretary's arguments and once again decided, with Seward, that the blockade would remain in force. It was a difficult decision, presenting momentous questions with no clear answers, but Lincoln was, by the summer of 1861, accustomed to making such decisions.

This did not immunize him from criticism, however. Thaddeus Stevens, an abolitionist congressman from Pennsylvania, regarded the president's decision as "a great blunder and absurdity" and personally went to the White House to tell him that the blockade was a "stultification" of the government's position in relation to the Confederate states; that, instead of being blockaded, the Southern ports "should have been closed, and a sufficient number of armed revenue vessels sent out on the seas to prevent smuggling." Some years later, Stevens recalled that Lincoln answered, "Well, that's a fact. I see the point now, but I don't know anything about the law of nations, and I thought it was alright."

"As a lawyer, Mr. Lincoln," Stevens chided, "I should have supposed you would have seen the difficulty at once."

"Oh, well," the president replied, "I'm a good enough lawyer in a Western law court, I suppose, but we don't practice the law of nations up there, and I supposed Seward knew all about it, and I left it to him. But it's done now and can't be helped so we must get along as well as we can."[18]

If Stevens's recollection of his conversation with the president was accurate, Lincoln may have been assuming a mask of false modesty to avoid an argument with the assertive congressman from Pennsylvania, for he was far more than "a good enough lawyer in a Western law court" and had given more attention to the blockade issue than merely "supposing" that Seward knew all about it. Orville Browning had shared a midday meal with the Lincolns at the White House one Sunday in July 1861, and he spent an hour or two alone with the president talking about the war. Lincoln made it clear to Browning that he understood the issues raised by the blockade quite well. Browning asked the president if there was "any danger of becoming involved in difficulties with foreign powers." Lincoln said there was, that the British "were determined to have the cotton crop as soon as it matured—that our coast was so extensive that we could not make the blockade of all the Ports effectual—and that England was now assuming the ground that a nation had no right, whilst a portion of its citizens were in revolt to close its port or any of them against foreign Nations." Lincoln told Browning that he did not intend to use the act recently passed by Congress giving him discretion to close the ports, for if he tried to close the ports, he said, "he had no doubt it would result in a foreign war, and that under the circumstances we had better increase the navy as fast as we could and blockade such ports as our force would enable us to, and say nothing about the rest."[19]

Welles expressed Lincoln's thought more tersely when he recorded his recollections of the president's decision. The possibility of an armed conflict with Great Britain was, according to Welles, the deciding factor. "The President said we could not afford to have two wars on our hands at once."[20]

Thus before either Stevens or Browning talked with Lincoln about the blockade, the argument had been practically settled, for the British government had cast its vote on the question—and in the minds of both Lincoln and Seward, the great maritime power's vote on this issue was the one that really counted. On May 6, a little more than a week after Lincoln extended the blockade to North Carolina and Virginia, Lord Russell announced in Parliament that his government had decided to recognize the Confederate States as belligerents, but not as a nation. Then, on May 13, the British government issued a formal proclamation of neutrality, according both sides in the North American struggle the rights of belligerents but warning British subjects against assisting either side.[21] France quickly issued a similar declaration. For good or ill, the blockade controversy had been decided.

It still remained, however, for American courts to deal with the blockade—and for the United States Supreme Court, in particular, to decide whether Lincoln's decision accorded with his constitutional responsibilities and powers.

ON JULY 10, IN THE sea off Cape Henry, the point of land that guards the mouth of Chesapeake Bay at its southern end, the *Amy Warwick* and the *Quaker City* encountered each other. The next day, Flag Officer Stringham wrote Secretary Welles from his flagship in nearby Hampton Roads that the *Amy Warwick* had left Rio de Janeiro "loaded with coffee," that it was "owned in Richmond, Va.," and that he had "ordered her to Boston . . . in charge of Acting Master J. B. Gordon."[22]

Stringham's letter is disappointingly terse. When and how did the ships first catch sight of each other? Did the *Amy Warwick* stop when first asked to, or was it necessary for the *Quaker City* to fire shots across its bow and stern? Was there a chase? The rights and obligations of vessels under a blockade had been established over decades, even centuries, but in particular cases they were not always observed. When approached by a blockading ship, it was the responsibility of the other vessel to stop and allow officers of the blockading ship to board. If the ship did not stop, the blockading vessel could give chase and, if necessary, use force to overpower it. The boarding officers were then entitled to examine the ship's papers, inspect its cargo, and make a preliminary determination as to whether it was violating (or attempting to violate) the blockade. If all seemed innocent, the ship and cargo would be sent on their way. If, however, the ship or its cargo was determined to be enemy property (that is, owned by persons subject to or resident in the enemy territory), the ship became a prize of war and the blockading officers would take possession of it, remove its officers, and put a prize master and crew aboard. Then the captured vessel would be sent to a port of the blockading power, to be dealt with in a prize court.

The papers found aboard the *Amy Warwick* told an interesting story. The ship was owned by three partners who lived and did business in Richmond, Virginia. In March 1861, they chartered the ship to a Richmond firm for a voyage to Rio and back, but paid the master and crew out of their own pockets and retained ownership of the vessel during the voyage. The Richmond firm put a cargo on board that was consigned to an English firm with offices in New York and Liverpool. When the cargo arrived in Rio and was sold, the English firm took the proceeds, added some money of its own, and purchased 4,700 bags of coffee, which they put on board the *Amy Warwick* for the return voyage to Virginia. An additional 400 bags of coffee were purchased for the benefit of another firm doing business in Richmond. Thus, fully loaded, the ship carried 5,100 bags of coffee, all bound for Richmond.

Under the federal system, United States district courts had jurisdiction in prize cases.[23] The principal prize courts in Union hands in 1861 were in Boston, Providence, New York, Philadelphia, Baltimore, Washington, and Key

West, Florida.[24] Boston was a favorite destination for captured blockade runners, not just because it was one of the busiest seaports on the Atlantic Coast but also because court officials there were particularly efficient in handling prize cases.[25] Stringham's letter to Welles indicates that the navy lost no time in sending the *Amy Warwick* to Boston, where Peleg Sprague was the U.S. district judge and Richard Henry Dana, Jr., the U.S. district attorney.

A former congressman and senator from Maine, the sixty-eight-year-old Sprague was a veteran of the federal bench and one of the country's experts on admiralty law. Dana was a scion of one of Boston's most aristocratic families, a graduate of Harvard Law School, and a highly respected admiralty lawyer. He also happened to be one of the most popular writers in the United States, author of the perennial favorite *Two Years Before the Mast* (1840), a thrilling tale of life at sea, and *The Seaman's Friend* (1841), a guide to sailors' legal rights. On April 12, 1861, on the recommendation of Senator Charles Sumner, Lincoln had appointed Dana to the important position of U.S. district attorney for Massachusetts.

After the *Amy Warwick* was brought into Boston harbor, Dana began legal proceedings by filing a libel (the first pleading in an admiralty case) that asked the court to condemn the ship and its cargo as prizes of war. Representatives of the ship and cargo owners were given opportunities to file claims and present evidence. It was admitted that the vessel and 400 bags of the coffee on board belonged to permanent residents of Richmond. Dana asked Sprague to condemn both of these on the ground that they were "enemy property" and thus subject to capture and condemnation. Sidney Bartlett and Edward Bangs, attorneys for the owners of the rest of the cargo, appeared before the judge and argued that, as there was no proof that their clients actually supported secession, their property could not be condemned as "enemy property." It was unjust, they argued, to condemn the property of all who lived or did business in Virginia without any proof that they had aided the Confederate cause. The attorneys also argued that the laws of war did not apply to the capture of the *Amy Warwick*, because Congress had never declared war against the seceding states. Article I, Section 8, clause 11, clearly gives Congress the power "to declare war." In the absence of such a declaration, Bangs and Bartlett averred, there was no war and the president of the United States could not exercise war powers.

Judge Sprague was unpersuaded by these arguments. It was clear that, in time of war, a belligerent had the right to seize and confiscate all of the property of its enemy, and that this right extended to property found at sea. When property was found at sea, the judge ruled, its character was determined by the permanent residence of its owners, regardless of whether they were personally hostile or friendly to the belligerent government. "Property captured at sea and owned by persons resident in an enemy's country is deemed hostile and subject to condemnation," Sprague said, "without any evidence as to the individual opinions or predilections of the owner," for his residence "in the enemy's country impresses upon his property engaged in commerce and found upon the ocean a hostile character, and subjects it to condemnation."[26] Nor did the fact that Congress had not declared war exempt the property of Richmond residents from the onus of being "enemy property." The conflict between the United States and the secessionist states was clearly "a war." Sprague said that it began when a "traitorous confederation, comprising several organized States," seized several forts and custom houses, attacked a United States fort garrisoned with soldiers, and, "under the sanctity of its flag, and by superior military force compelled those soldiers to surrender." This was "war," Sprague said, "open, flagrant, flagitious war; and it has never ceased to be waged by the same confederates with their utmost ability." The Constitution declares that the president is commander in chief of the army and navy of the United States.[27] When the United States is attacked by an armed force that threatens to overthrow the government, invade its soil, and menace its capital, the president is bound to resist the attacking force. "And he may do so," Sprague declared, "in the manner, and by the measures, usual in modern civilized warfare; one of the most familiar of which is the capture of enemy's property, public and private, on the ocean."[28]

Since the Amy Warwick and 400 bags of the coffee were owned by permanent residents of Virginia, a state that was in insurrection against the United States, Judge Sprague had no difficulty in deciding that the ship and those 400 bags were all enemy property. But the result was somewhat different for the remaining 4,700 bags of coffee. Although the principal owners of those bags were admitted to be Richmond residents, a British firm also claimed an interest in them, since it had advanced part of the money for their purchase. British subjects were, as their government had declared, neutrals in the struggle between the North and South, and under blockade law the property of neutrals was not subject to condemnation. The British firm's attorneys thus asked Judge Sprague to release all 4,700 bags to them, on their posting a bond for their value. The judge refused to do this, instead ordering that the entire cargo be sold at public auction and the proceeds held in the court's registry until he could finally determine who was entitled to them. After the sale was completed, Sprague heard evidence on the British firm's claim and determined that the value of its interest in the cargo was $10,793.63. Accordingly, that amount was paid to the British claimants, leaving $145,393.04 as the balance of the sale's proceeds.[29] Half of that amount was distributed to the government and half to the officers and crew of the *Quaker City*, with the shares of each proportional to his normal pay.[30] The fact that a capture at sea could profit individual sailors added a distinctive dimension to the proceedings in a prize court. As Attorney General Edward Bates explained in a legal opinion he delivered to Lincoln: "The part given by law to individual captors, is, avowedly, a bounty, designed to stimulate the zeal and courage of our naval men; and the part reserved to the nation, is transferred by law, to the Navy Pension Fund, which is only another form of a bounty to the same meritorious class."[31] The ship and its cargo were thus "prizes" in a double sense.

Boston was a busy venue for prize cases. The law allowed Dana to pocket as much as $6,000 a year in prize fees in addition to his government salary of $6,000; and by May 1863 he and Judge Sprague were able to advise Gideon Welles that they had processed a total of sixteen prize cases in their court.[32] Other seaports were also busy processing prize cases and, in the process, establishing the groundwork for an eventual Supreme Court review of the whole issue of the blockade.

New York, not surprisingly, handled a large share of the prize cases. Samuel R. Betts, the U.S. district judge in New York, was seventy-four years old in 1861 and in his thirty-ninth year as a federal judge. By the beginning of August 1861, Betts's prize court was so busy that he had a lineup of ten cases to decide—the fates of ten vessels captured in the blockade. Because many of the issues presented in the cases were identical, he agreed to hear lengthy arguments in three of them and to base his rulings in the others on the same legal principles. Betts presided over nine days of hearings and six days of argument before he committed his decisions to writing.[33]

The three cases Betts heard arose out of the captures of the barks *Hiawatha* and *Pioneer* and the schooner *Crenshaw,* merchant vessels that were brought into New York from Virginia in the first days of the blockade. The *Hiawatha* was captured on May 20 in Hampton Roads by the *U.S.S. Minnesota.* It had just completed a voyage from Liverpool with a cargo of salt that it had unloaded in Richmond, and at the time of its capture it was attempting to leave Richmond with tobacco and cotton, for a return voyage to Liverpool. The vessel's owners were British, a fact that might have exempted their ship from capture but for the U.S. district attorney's allegation that the ship had knowingly violated the blockade and was subject to condemnation on that ground. Attorneys for the owners argued that they had no knowledge that the blockade was in force at the time the *Hiawatha* began its return voyage. Lincoln's proclamation of April 19 had merely announced his intention "to set on foot a blockade" of the Southern ports, and it was up to naval officers to proclaim actual blockades of each port. Commodore Garrett Pendergrast had done this with respect to Richmond on April 30, announcing that an actual blockade of the port would begin fifteen days later. The *Hiawatha* had loaded its outward-bound cargo on May 14 and 15 and proceeded down the James River toward Hampton Roads on May 16. On May 20, it was stopped, boarded, and seized by the *Minnesota.* Betts found ample evidence that the master and crew of the ship knew that Richmond was to be blockaded and that they had only fifteen days after April 30 (or until May 15) to clear the port. Having failed to do so within the specified time, they were in violation of the blockade and their ship was properly condemned as a prize.[34]

The bark *Pioneer* was captured on May 20 by the *U.S.S. Quaker City.* The capture was on the high seas outside Chesapeake Bay, and the vessel was taken to New York as a prize. Attorneys for the owners presented the same arguments that had been advanced in the case of the *Amy Warwick* in Boston, denying that there was any war between the United States and the secessionist states, denying that Lincoln had any authority to declare a blockade, and denying that property owned by residents of Richmond could be deemed enemy property merely because of their residence. All of these arguments were denied by Judge Betts.[35]

The schooner *Crenshaw* was captured by the *Minnesota* on May 17 in Hampton Roads and taken to New York. Like the *Pioneer,* the *Crenshaw* was owned by residents of Richmond and subject to condemnation as enemy property. But attorneys for the owners raised the special argument that, since Virginians were citizens of the United States, they could not be deemed "enemies" of the federal government. Judge Betts overruled that argument on the ground that the organization of the Confederate States, its military mobilization against the federal government, and the fact that it claimed the right to control Virginia, made all of the residents of that state "enemies" for purposes of prize law. Betts also rejected the argument that, since part of the cargo was owned by investors who resided in New York, their part of the cargo could not be deemed "enemy property." Since the tobacco and cotton carried by the *Crenshaw* had originated in territory claimed by the Confederacy, all of it was enemy property, even though some of its owners lived in New York. The blockade was intended to interdict trade between the North and the South as well as between foreign countries and the states in secession.

A claim to part of the *Crenshaw's* cargo was filed on behalf of the firm of Laurie, Son & Company, who proved that they were residents of Scotland and, as such, entitled to the protection of the British declaration of neutrality. Since that firm had received no direct notice of the blockade, and no connection with the owners of the ship could be shown, Betts ruled that their part of the cargo was exempt from condemnation.

Another active prize court was in Key West, which was in Union control throughout the war and where a loyal U.S. district judge continued to hold court. Key West was a convenient destination for ships that were captured trying to run the blockades of Mobile, Biloxi, and New Orleans. William Marvin was the federal judge in Key West. A New York native who had moved south in the 1830s and received an appointment as U.S. district judge from Andrew Jackson, Marvin supported slavery but opposed secession. The only sitting federal judge south of Washington, he was an expert in maritime law and the author of a respected legal treatise on the law of wreck and salvage, published in Boston in 1858.[36]

The most important prize ship brought into Key West in the early days of the blockade was the *Brilliante*, a schooner from Campeche, Mexico. Owned by a Mexican citizen and a naturalized American, the schooner was bound for New Orleans with a cargo of Mexican flour when it tried to enter the mouth of the Mississippi but was warned away by the U.S. warship *Brooklyn*. One of the owners was on board the *Brilliante* and told the *Brooklyn's* captain that he had a son attending college near Mobile and wanted to go there to pick him up. The captain obligingly gave him a letter to the captain of the *U.S.S. Niagara*, then blockading Mobile, granting him permission to sail into Mobile for this limited purpose. The *Brilliante* then headed toward Mobile, but when safely out of sight of the *Brooklyn* it turned north into Lake Pontchartrain, proceeded to a wharf on the lake side of New Orleans, and discharged its cargo. It then took on another cargo and headed back into the Gulf of Mexico. On June 23, while anchored at Biloxi Bay, it was met by the *U.S.S. Massachusetts*, captured, and sent to the U.S. district court in Key West. Judge Marvin followed the lead of the judges in Boston and New York in upholding the legality of the blockade. Although Mexico was a neutral nation and the *Brilliante* was not enemy property, the ship had flagrantly run the blockade when it entered Lake Pontchartrain. Accordingly, Marvin entered an order against both the ship and its cargo, condemning them as prizes.

Appeals from prize court decisions in the district courts were taken to the U.S. circuit courts. In New York, Supreme Court Justice Samuel Nelson, in his capacity as a judge of the Second Circuit, devoted a full week to the difficult issues presented by the New York cases. He had serious doubts about the constitutionality of the district court decisions but was reluctant to stand in the way of the blockade, so he affirmed Betts's rulings, not because he agreed with them but because he wanted the whole issue to be taken up by the Supreme Court. Attorneys for the ship owners pressed for an early Supreme Court hearing, but the cases could be advanced on the calendar only at the request of the government, and Attorney General Bates believed he had no clear grounds for making such a request. William M. Evarts, an attorney who had helped present the government's cases before Betts, reinforced Bates's reluctance to advance the cases by reminding him that the high court still had three vacancies and that five of the six sitting justices had sided with Chief Justice Taney in the now-infamous *Dred Scott* decision. Under these circumstances, Evarts argued, the government could not confidently rely on the Supreme Court to sustain the blockade.[37] Thus, with Bates's acquiescence, the cases were put over to the Court's next term, scheduled to begin in December.

The government was encouraged in the summer of 1862 when Justice Robert Grier, sitting as a circuit judge in Pennsylvania, upheld the blockade on an appeal from the district court in Philadelphia. Grier was no special friend of the Lincoln administration, but he was a fervent defender of the Union. "Judge Grier's opinion is the more important," the *Philadelphia Public Ledger* declared, "from the fact that it is the first given by a member of the Supreme Court."[38] The government was discouraged, however, when Justice Nathan Clifford announced his decision in a blockade case in November of that year. Clifford had been sitting as a circuit judge in an appeal from Judge Sprague's Boston court. Clifford had never been successful in concealing his Southern sympathies, yet he was not willing to stand alone in opposition to the blockade. In his opinion in the case, the New Englander expressed the hope that the Supreme Court would soon take up the question and added, "My mind is open to conviction on this great question, if it shall come before me, as one of the judges of the Supreme Court."[39]

Clifford's admirers and detractors alike could agree that the prize cases presented a "great question," but they would be hard put to agree how the Supreme Court should answer it, for opinions on the issue varied widely. Opponents of the blockade argued that Lincoln exceeded his constitutional powers when he proclaimed the blockade and that all of the ships condemned as prizes of the war were wrongly taken from their owners. The president's chief legal officer, Attorney General Bates, was concerned that the blockade might be struck down, for he, like all administration officers, realized the enormous consequences that could flow from an unfavorable Supreme Court ruling. It was not merely the blockade that would be at stake but potentially all of the decisions Lincoln had made as commander in chief. If the president had no authority under the Constitution to blockade the Confederate States, what authority did he have to call up the militia in the first days of the rebellion? To suspend the privilege of the writ of habeas corpus when federal troops were assaulted on their passage through Maryland? Or to emancipate the slaves in states or parts of states in rebellion against the government? If the commander in chief's hands were tied, the war effort could be crippled, and immeasurable damage could be inflicted on the nation's standing in the world community. As the *Washington Republican* editorialized: "How deeply these questions touch the powers of our Government, at this interesting period, can at once be seen; and the decision of the Supreme Court upon them cannot fail to be one of the most grave duties of their session."[40]

THE COURT HAD REACHED full strength by the second week of February 1863, when it met to hear arguments in four prize cases appealed from the district courts. Noah Swayne, Samuel Miller, and David Davis were all on hand, as were the old judges from the *Dred Scott* days—Taney, Wayne, Catron, Nelson, Grier, and Clifford—to hear a panel of what one contemporary called "the ablest lawyers of the country" argue the merits and weaknesses of the blockade.[41] There were nominally four cases—*The Amy Warwick,* on appeal from Judge Sprague's court in Boston, *The Hiawatha* and *The Crenshaw,* from Judge Betts's New York court, and *The Brilliante,* from Judge Marvin's district court in Key West. But the cases had been consolidated for argument under the overall title of the *Prize Cases.*

Attorney General Bates was the principal attorney for the United States, although—bowing to the realities of the litigation and the difficult legal questions involved—he delegated the arguments to Charles Eames, William M. Evarts, Richard Henry Dana, Jr., and Charles B. Sedgwick. Eames was a Harvard graduate who had worked for the Navy Department in Washington, edited a Washington newspaper, and served as U.S. minister to Venezuela before becoming one of the busiest attorneys in the wartime capital. He often represented the Navy Department on important business and had earned Secretary Welles's accolade as "the most correct admiralty lawyer in the country."[42] Evarts was a grandson of Roger Sherman (a signer of both the Declaration of Independence and the Constitution), a friend and political supporter of Secretary of State Seward, and one of the most admired courtroom lawyers in New York. He played a leading role in the prosecution of prize cases that came before Judge Betts, but his practice in both New York and Washington was wide and broad. Sedgwick was a lawyer and Republican congressman from Syracuse, New York, who was just completing a term as chairman of the House Committee on Naval Affairs. Appearing on behalf of the claimants in *The Amy Warwick* was Edward Bangs, one of the Boston attorneys who had argued the case before Judge Sprague. The claimants in *The Hiawatha* and *The Crenshaw* were represented by Daniel Lord, a veteran of appellate litigation, assisted by Charles Edwards and Charles Donohue. James M. Carlisle, a close friend of Chief Justice Taney, represented the claimants in *The Brilliante.*

The Supreme Court's Capitol chamber was crowded with spectators as the justices took their seats on Tuesday, February 10, to hear the opening arguments in the case. For twelve days, they listened patiently as the attorneys articulated their positions.

On behalf of the *Brilliante's* owners, Carlisle led off with a vigorous attack on the power of the president to blockade the Southern coast. The chief executive had no such power, he said, because a blockade was a war measure and the Constitution gave Congress, not the president, the power to declare war. The Constitution makes the president the commander in chief, but that designation merely gives him the power to command the armed forces. It does not give him power to make laws, to change laws, or in any other way to exercise the powers of Congress. "He is to act as Commander-in-Chief," Carlisle asserted, "not as legislator or Emperor. To say that he can 'declare war,' because in the event of war he commands the Army, Navy and Militia in service, when war is declared, under the Constitution, is absurd."[43] At least three of the justices were delighted with Carlisle's argument; immediately after the hearing, Justice Catron wrote the attorney a congratulatory letter in which he said that he, Nelson, and Clifford were anxious to have the argument printed verbatim in the Court's reports.[44]

Charles Eames followed with an argument on behalf of the government. The substance of Eames's argument has been lost because it was not printed in the Court's reports, though the suspicion is strong that he badly overstated the government's position, for several of the justices later expressed dissatisfaction with his presentation. Justice Swayne felt so strongly about Eames's argument that he called on Bates after the hearing was over and complained that Eames's "speech" was "no argument at all," that he had acted "like a harlequin" and turned the solemn proceedings "into a farce." Swayne told Bates that Taney had made a cutting remark about Eames's argument. Alluding to the recent court-martial of Union brigadier general Fitz John Porter, in which Eames had unsuccessfully attempted to defend the general against charges of misconduct at the Second Battle of Bull Run, Taney said he no longer wondered at Porter's conviction (he was cashiered from the army in January 1863), adding, "He deserved to be convicted for trusting his case to such a counsel!" Bates thought all of this criticism "very unjust" and believed that it showed "a degree of passion and prejudice not very creditable to that high court."[45] But it also indicated that at least some of the justices were likely to rule against the government's position.

William Evarts's argument was much more effective than that of Eames. He argued that the rebellion in the Southern states was both a war and an insurrection and that, in meeting it, the government was not compelled to choose one theory or another. A state of war was a question of fact and did not depend on a declaration by Congress. When the insurrection began in the South, Evarts said, the president was confronted with a war, and it was his duty to respond to it.[46]

Dana's argument was thought by many observers to be the most effective of all. He reiterated many of the same points as Evarts but expanded on the issue of "enemy property." It was a vexing legal question and one that the judges did not all agree on. The capture of ships at sea, Dana said, was "the most mild and humane form of war," for it amounted to taking the enemy's property rather than his life. A blockade interfered with the enemy's ability to conduct profitable business at sea, and that was always preferable to killing the enemy on land. Charles Francis Adams, Jr., son of Lincoln's minister to Great Britain, was in the courtroom during Dana's argument. He later called it a "luminous and exquisite presentation." "Dry legal questions were lifted into the higher regions of international discussion," Adams said, "and the philosophy of the barbaric right of capture of private property at sea was for the first time in the hearing of most of the judges then on the bench applied to the pending situation with a power of reasoning and a wealth of illustration and felicity of style that swept all before them."[47] After Dana finished, Adams encountered Justice Grier in the corridor behind the bench. Grier had enjoyed the presentation and, in a burst of what Adams called "unjudicial enthusiasm," said to him: "Well, your little 'Two Years Before the Mast' has settled that question; there is nothing more to say about it!"[48]

Dana wrote to the assistant U.S. district attorney in Boston, Thornton K. Lothrop, saying that he had "won Judge Grier's heart. He pats me on the shoulder and says I have cleared up all his doubts, and that it is the best argument he has heard for five years, etc. The Attorney-general seems quite overcome with his emotions on the subject, and cannot say enough. Seward is flattering, and others."[49]

The court heard the last arguments in the *Prize Cases* on February 25, then took the case under submission. Despite all the compliments he received, Dana was not sure that his side would prevail. He was in a reflective mood when he wrote Minister Adams in London:

These causes present our Constitution in a new and peculiar light. In all States but ours, now existing or that have ever existed, the function of the judiciary is to interpret the acts of the government. In ours, it is to decide upon their legality. The government is carrying on a war. It is exerting all the powers of war. Yet the claimants of the captured vessels not only seek to save their vessels by denying that they are liable to capture, but deny the right of the government to exercise war powers,—deny that this can be, in point of law, a war. So the judiciary is actually, after a war of twenty-three months' duration, to decide whether the government has the legal capacity to exert these war powers. This is the result of a written Constitution, as a supreme law, under which there is no sovereign power, but only coordinate departments.[50]

Dana correctly identified the question that the *Prize Cases* presented. It was whether the president of the United States had acted within his constitutional power as commander in chief when he proclaimed a blockade of Confederate ports. Now the Supreme Court of the United States was to decide whether the president had acted legally. It was, as Dana asserted, a question that could not be asked in any other nation in the world in 1863, for no other nation was subject to the same constitutional strictures as the United States, and the acts of no other government were subject to the same judicial review as those of the government headed by Abraham Lincoln. But it is difficult to agree with Dana's conclusion that this system, based on a "written" constitution, reflected weakness rather than strength. In his letter to Minister Adams, he continued:

> Contemplate, my dear sir, the possibility of a Supreme Court deciding that this blockade is illegal! What a position it would put us in before the world whose commerce we have been illegally prohibiting, whom we have unlawfully subjected to a cotton famine and domestic dangers and distress for two years! It would end the war, and where it would leave us with neutral powers it is fearful to contemplate! . . . The bare contemplation of such a possibility makes us pause in our boastful assertion that our written Constitution is clearly the best adapted to all exigencies, the last, best gift to man.[51]

Dana may have been more encouraged about the American constitutional system when the Supreme Court assembled on March 10 to announce its decision in the *Prize Cases*. The courtroom was thronged once again, not merely because the justices were to hand down a definitive pronouncement on the blockade, but also because their long-awaited decision in the case of *Castillero v. United States* was to be announced. That litigation involved conflicting claims to the ownership of the New Almaden quicksilver mine in California, an incredibly valuable property that represented an important financial resource for the Union war effort (quicksilver was used in refining gold and silver, and gold and silver from Western mines were mainstays of the Union's war economy). Justice Clifford spent three hours reading his opinion in the *Castillero* case.[52] Justice Grier took somewhat less time to read his opinion in the *Prize Cases*, but there was no lack of interest in his words. The minutes of the Court reveal that Chief Justice Taney was "prevented by indisposition from attending" ("indisposition" had long since become a habit with the now-eighty-six-year-old justice), though he had authorized his colleagues to say that he concurred in Clifford's opinion and dissented from Grier's.

Grier began by identifying the two key questions in the case:

1st. Had the President a right to institute a blockade of ports in possession of persons in armed rebellion against the Government, on the principles of international law, as known and acknowledged among civilized States?
2d. Was the property of persons domiciled or residing within those States a proper subject of capture on the sea as "enemies' property?"

He acknowledged that the law of blockade had its origins in the *jus belli*, or law of war, and that a blockade could be justified only if there was an actual war. But he rejected the argument that, because the secessionist states were in insurrection, there was no war and the government could not treat the insurrectionists as enemies. He also rejected the argument that, because Lincoln regarded the Confederacy as a mere "combination" of rebels, and because Congress had never declared war against the Confederate States, the government could not regard the secessionists as "belligerents." He wrote:

It is not necessary to constitute war, that both parties should be acknowledged as independent nations or sovereign States. A war may exist where one of the belligerents, claims sovereign rights as against the other.

Insurrection against a government may or may not culminate in an organized rebellion, but a civil war always begins by insurrection against the lawful authority of the Government. A civil war is never solemnly declared; it becomes such by its accidents—the number, power, and organization of the persons who originate and carry it on. When the party in rebellion occupy and hold in a hostile manner a certain portion of territory; have declared their independence; have cast off their allegiance; have organized armies; have commenced hostilities against their former sovereign, the world acknowledges them as belligerents, and the contest a *war*.[53]

Grier acknowledged that, under the Constitution, Congress alone has the power to declare war. But he noted that the Constitution gives the president "the whole Executive power" of the government. It commands him to "take care that the laws be faithfully executed," and it makes him "Commander-in-Chief of the Army and Navy of the United States, and of the military of the several States when called into the actual service of the United States." Grier continued:

This greatest of civil wars was not gradually developed by popular commotion, tumultuous assemblies, or local unorganized insurrections. However long may have been its previous conception, it nevertheless sprung forth suddenly from the parent brain, a Minerva in the full panoply of war. The President was bound to meet it in the shape it presented itself, without waiting for Congress to baptize it with a name; and no name given to it by him or them could change the fact.

It would be anomalous, Grier said, to require that the government declare that "insurgents who have risen in rebellion against their sovereign, expelled her Courts, established a revolutionary government, organized armies, and commenced hostilities" are not *enemies* because they are *traitors*, or to argue that "a war levied on the Government by traitors, in order to dismember and destroy it" was not a *war* because it was an *insurrection*. Whether the president, in fulfilling his duties as commander in chief, regarded the hostile resistance to the government as serious enough to treat the insurrectionists as belligerents was, Grier said, "a question to be decided by *him*" and not the Court. "He must determine what degree of force the crisis demands."[54]

Even if the president had no authority to meet the insurrection with a blockade, Grier pointed out that Congress had approved and ratified all of his acts and orders "as if they had been done under the previous express authority and direction of the Congress." "Without admitting that such an act was necessary under the circumstances," Grier said, "it is plain that if the President had in any manner assumed powers which it was necessary should have the authority or sanction of Congress, . . . this ratification has operated to perfectly cure the defect."[55]

Grier's opinion was strong and emphatic, but not strong or emphatic enough to convince more than five members of the Court. Justice Nelson filed (but did not read) a dissent in which he stated that the president could not be invested with the power to wage war until Congress acted to either declare war or "recognize its existence." Nelson said that Congress did not finally "recognize" the existence of the war between the North and South until July 13, 1861, when it authorized the president to take decisive action against the insurgents. Before that, he wrote, the chief executive "had no power to set on foot a blockade under the law of nations." Accordingly, all of the ships that were captured before July 13 were illegally captured and should be restored to their owners.

Grier's opinion was concurred in by Justices Swayne, Miller, and Davis. The only other justice from the old *Dred Scott* coalition who sided with it was James Wayne, the courtly Georgian who was steadfastly loyal to the Union throughout the war. Nelson's dissent was, not surprisingly, supported by the "indisposed" chief justice. It was also supported by Justices Catron and Clifford, though it is difficult to determine with what enthusiasm. According to newspaper reports, Catron left the bench before the reading was concluded (he had apparently joined Taney in "indisposition"), and Clifford decided only at the last minute to join in the dissent. Thus the opinion upholding Lincoln and the blockade was sustained by the narrowest of margins, only five to four. Without the support of the three Lincoln justices, it would have faced certain defeat.

Although four judges joined in the dissent, Nelson's opinion was narrowly tailored. He did not broadly condemn the administration's prosecution of the war; he merely found the authority for it lacking before Congress "recognized" the war on July 13, 1861. After that date, the war was prosecuted with the full authority of Congress and met the requirements of the Constitution. If Nelson's opinion had commanded the support of a majority of the justices, the Union's war effort would undoubtedly have suffered a major setback. The liability claims of those whose ships had been captured and condemned would have been enormous, and the anger expressed by foreign powers such as Great Britain and France, whose shipping had been "illegally" disrupted, would have been, to adopt Dana's words, "fearful to contemplate." But it is hard to imagine that Lincoln could not have recovered from the setback. Northerners would have protested another Supreme Court decision (*Dred Scott* was the first) that arrayed the federal judiciary against their region and raged at yet more evidence of the pro-Southern tilt of the high bench. It was unnecessary to contemplate that unhappy consequence, however, because five members of the Supreme Court sided with the administration.

Newspaper editors in the North recognized the importance of the decision in the *Prize Cases,* even if they did not all endorse it. The *New York Times* thought the decision had crushed the hope of the Copperheads "to cast a vast burden upon the Treasury by annulling the blockade," and predicted that the Supreme Court would now "indorse the constitutional validity of every important act of the Executive or of Congress thus far in the rebellion."[56] But the *New York World* disagreed, arguing that the "reasoning of the minority seems to be decidedly the stronger, and more accordant with the spirit as well as letter of the Constitution."[57]

Some years later Thornton K. Lothrop, a Boston attorney who knew Richard Henry Dana, Jr., well, reflected on the *Prize Cases* and their significance in the prosecution of the war. He recognized that the decision had resolved a great doubt that was hanging over the administration's war effort and immensely strengthened the hand of those who were struggling to preserve the Union. And he gave much of the credit for the successful outcome to Dana. He said that Dana's argument before the high tribunal had provided the justices with the legal grounding they needed to sustain the blockade. It had, in Lothrop's words, "rescued them from their apprehended peril. It satisfied the court that the government could at the same time treat the South both as rebels and belligerents, without giving the owners of neutral vessels violating the blockade, or their governments, any just cause of complaint." And, Lothrop said, Judge Grier's opinion closely followed Dana's argument in the case. "His work in these causes was Mr. Dana's great contribution to the successful prosecution of the war, and its importance at that time can hardly be overestimated."[58]

The Supreme Court's decision in the *Prize Cases* was, as Charles Francis Adams wrote, "a great issue before a great tribunal."[59] It was the most important decision rendered by the high tribunal during the war. Had Justice Nelson's dissenting views commanded a majority of the justices, the result could have been disastrous. That Grier's views prevailed, however, indicated to the nation and the world that a majority of the justices were prepared to sustain the government's war efforts. There is no reason to suggest that they would ever have sustained a clearly unconstitutional grab for power by either the executive or the legislative branch of the government. They were, however, prepared to "stretch" constitutional doctrine to meet the extraordinary exigencies of the crisis, to see issues in a light in which they had never previously seen them, and to judge challenges to government action by standards they had never previously applied. In the words of the Supreme Court historian Charles Warren, the *Prize Cases* "were far more momentous in the issue involved than any other war case; and their final determination favorable to the Government's contention was almost a necessary factor in the suppression of the war."[60]

THOUGH RICHARD HENRY DANA, JR., had made a powerful argument in support of one of Lincoln's most controversial war measures, and though he owed his appointment as U.S. district attorney in Boston to Lincoln, he never really warmed to the wartime president. Letters he wrote during the war, and even after, reveal a patronizing, sometimes dismissive attitude toward the chief executive. He acknowledged that Lincoln had "a kind of shrewdness and commonsense," and what he called a "slipshod, low levelled honesty, that made him a good western jury lawyer." But, in Dana's view, Lincoln was an "unutterable calamity" as president.[61] A year after the *Prize Cases* were decided, Dana went to the White House and spent a half hour with Mrs. Lincoln and, after that, a half hour with the president. After the visit, he wrote his impressions:

I cannot describe the President; it is impossible. He was sobered in his talk, told no extreme stories, said some good things and some helplessly natural and naive things. You can't help feeling an interest in him, a sympathy and a kind of pity; feeling, too, that he has some qualities of great value, yet fearing that his weak points may wreck him or wreck something. His life seems a series of wise, sound conclusions, slowly reached, oddly worked out, on great questions, with constant failures in administration of details and dealings with individuals.[62]

At this same meeting, Lincoln and the Boston attorney talked about the *Prize Cases*. Dana's argument had by this time been published in pamphlet form. The president had read the pamphlet, and he complimented him on it. He said that "it had cleared up his mind on the subject entirely; that it reasoned out and put into scientific statement what he had all along felt in his bones must be the truth of the matter, and was not able to find anywhere in the books, or to reason out satisfactorily to himself."[63]

Thus ended the last recorded meeting between the president of the United States and a brilliant lawyer from Boston—the one "a good western jury lawyer," the other an expert in admiralty law and the victor in a great Supreme Court case; the one a humble Illinoisan, the other a Northeastern patrician and the author of best-selling books; the one a man of enormous responsibility and humanity who was willing to credit the other with a job well done. In one there was a generous spirit, in the other condescension. But one was to lead a great nation to a new birth of freedom; the other was to retire to a study in Boston to edit a treatise on international law.[64] Through such little stories of men caught up in a fearful conflict was the great history of a great struggle to be truly remembered.

A Gallery of Justices

The Old Supreme Court Chamber in the U.S. Capitol (1860–1935).

JOHN McLEAN

John McLean of Ohio was a large man, both physically and intellectually, with a handsome face, a high forehead, and a presence and manner that reminded many of George Washington. The first of Andrew Jackson's four appointments to the Supreme Court (he began his service in 1829), McLean was seventy-five years old and in his thirty-second year as a justice when Lincoln became president in March 1861. Despite his judicial longevity, McLean was less known for his judicial decisions than for the fact, as Daniel Webster put it, that he had always had "his head turned too much by politics." From Jackson's time through Buchanan's administration, McLean had almost continuously aspired to the presidency, first as a Democrat, later as a Whig and a Free-Soiler, and finally as a Republican. Lincoln was an admirer of McLean, who was one of only two dissenters from the notorious *Dred Scott* decision of 1857. Formal and courteous, McLean often gave the impression of being cold and unfeeling. Salmon Chase, also an Ohioan, once commented of McLean: "It is a thousand pities that a man of such real benevolence of heart as the Judge possesses, should not allow more of it to flow out into his manners." Though in generally good health, McLean was suffering from a severe cold when he left Washington on March 22, 1861, for his home in the hills above Cincinnati where, on April 4, he succumbed to pneumonia. A contemporary noted that there was always about McLean "a suggestion of greatness never quite attained."

(Photo credit: Collection of the Supreme Court of the United States.)

JAMES M. WAYNE

James M. Wayne of Georgia was one of two Southern justices (Tennessee's John Catron was the other) who refused to resign their Supreme Court seats during the war. Born in Savannah in 1790, educated at the College of New Jersey at Princeton, Wayne was a veteran of Georgia politics, having served successively as a state legislator, mayor of Savannah, judge of the city's Court of Common Pleas, and judge of the Superior Court for the Eastern District. He was a member of the federal House of Representatives from 1829 until President Jackson appointed him to the Supreme Court in 1835. Standing about five feet ten inches tall, with a ruddy complexion, brown, wavy hair, and regular features, Wayne was much admired by the ladies, especially as a young man. Fond of good food, good whiskey, and well-aged Madeira wine, he was likened during Buchanan's administration to "a portrait of St. Jerome by the tender pencil of Guido." Though a defender of slavery, Wayne was a loyal defender of the Union during the war. His vote to sustain the blockade in the *Prize Cases* (1863) made the difference between victory and a crushing defeat for the administration. Wayne was in his seventy-seventh year of life when he died in Washington on July 5, 1867, having completed thirty-two years, five months, and twenty-one days of Supreme Court service, a record exceeded up to that time only by the great Chief Justice John Marshall.

(Photo credit: Matthew Brady, Collection of the Supreme Court of the United States.)

Roger Brooke Taney

The octogenarian chief justice from Maryland was the personification of judicial opposition to Lincoln. Andrew Jackson's chief lieutenant in the controversy over the Bank of the United States in the early 1830s, Taney had achieved a respectable record as a jurist before issuing his inflammatory opinion in the *Dred Scott* case in 1857. Arguably the worst decision ever made by the Supreme Court, *Dred Scott* excited antislavery opinion throughout the country and, by inspiring much of the Lincoln-Douglas debates of 1858, helped to elevate Abraham Lincoln to the presidency. *Dred Scott* revealed Taney's pervasive pro-Southern bias, a bias that animated almost every judicial thought he expressed during the war. His sharpest challenge to Lincoln came in *Ex parte Merryman* in early 1861, in which he held that the president's suspension of habeas corpus was unconstitutional. But the range of his disagreements with the president was wide enough to cover the blockade, conscription, legal tender, the federal income tax, and the imposition of martial law. Although Taney agreed that secession was unconstitutional, he also believed that the government had no power to coerce secessionist states back into the Union. Tall, thin, and stooped, with a mane of unruly hair, a pinched face, and tobacco-stained teeth, Taney had a quiet yet authoritative manner that adversaries found difficult to deal with. When he died in October 1864 at the age of eighty-seven, many believed that he had outlived the spirit of his age.

(Photo credit: Collection of the Supreme Court of the United States.)

John Catron

Born of German ancestry about 1781, probably in Pennsylvania, John Catron became a favorite of Andrew Jackson after he moved to Tennessee early in the nineteenth century and embarked on a career in the law. Largely self-taught, he owed his success at the bar to shrewd common sense and a rigorously logical mind. Jackson nominated him to the Supreme Court on his last day as president in 1837, but the Senate did not confirm him until five days later, so his formal appointment came from Jackson's successor, Martin Van Buren. More than six feet tall, with a large frame, black eyes, dark hair, a large nose, and a prominent, almost combative jaw, Catron was, according to one of his biographers, a man whose "manner attracted attention." He supported slavery and joined in the notorious *Dred Scott* decision of 1857 (though for entirely different reasons than Taney) but took a rigorously pro-Union stance after his home state seceded in 1861. He refused to resign from the Supreme Court and tended diligently to his circuit court duties in Kentucky, Tennessee, and Missouri, where his strong decisions against secession earned him the enmity of Confederates and the praise of Unionists. Prevented by illness from attending court during the 1864–65 term, Catron died at his home in Nashville on May 30, 1865.

SAMUEL NELSON

Associate Justice Samuel Nelson was a Democrat of Scotch-Irish heritage who planned to study for the ministry before he switched to the law. Born in New York in 1792 into a family that supported slavery (his studies at Middlebury College were said to have been financed by his father's sale of a Negro girl), Nelson became known as "a Northern man with Southern principles" after President John Tyler appointed him to the Supreme Court in 1845. He was a capable judge, noted for his proficiency in admiralty and common law, but without keen political instincts. In 1861 he joined with Justice John Archibald Campbell of Alabama in an unsuccessful effort to broker a North-South compromise that would avert secession. If his wartime decisions were not supportive of Lincoln, neither were they aggressively antagonistic. In appearance, Nelson was a stern-looking man with a large head made to appear even larger by his luxuriant hair and full side whiskers that drooped low across his collar. George Templeton Strong, who encountered Nelson one day at a Columbia Law School commencement, described him as looking "leonine and learned enough to represent Ellenborough and Kenyon and Mansfield and Marshall all in one." After twenty-seven years of Supreme Court service, Nelson died in Cooperstown, New York, in 1873, at the age of eighty-one.

ROBERT C. GRIER

Associate Justice Robert C. Grier of Pennsylvania was a Democrat known for industrious work habits, a tendency to make quick decisions, and a sharp, often cutting tongue. Born in 1794 in Cumberland County, Pennsylvania, he graduated from Dickinson College in 1812 and was admitted to the bar in 1817. His political instincts were pro-Southern, but during the Civil War he was rigorously loyal to the Union. After visiting his daughter in Kentucky in 1861, he reported to Justice Clifford that his son-in-law was "a secessionist, as insane as the others," and after the rout of the Union Army at the First Battle of Bull Run, he told Clifford that "we must conquer this rebellion or declare our republican government a failure." Grier's majority opinion in the *Prize Cases* (1863) gave Lincoln his most important judicial victory and was fully as important as a battlefield triumph. A bear of a man, standing more than six feet tall and weighing close to three hundred pounds, Grier had blond hair, blue eyes, and a ruddy complexion. His departure from the Court was one of the saddest in the tribunal's history. Beset by illnesses, including a serious stroke, he was physically immobilized and mentally weakened when in 1870, during deliberations for the *Legal Tender Cases,* his colleagues persuaded him that he was unable to fulfill his duties and should resign. His last day on the Court was January 31, 1870. He died in Philadelphia eight months later.

(Photo credit: Handy Studios, Collection of the Supreme Court of the United States.)

John Archibald Campbell

Associate Justice Campbell of Alabama came to the Court in 1852 after the sitting justices unanimously petitioned President Franklin Pierce to appoint him to a seat left vacant by the death of Justice John McKinley. Only forty-one years old at the time of his appointment, Campbell had already earned a national reputation as a brilliant lawyer, learned in the law and other subjects. He supported slavery, though he realized that it hampered the South both economically and socially, and joined in the notorious *Dred Scott* decision of 1857. Though he defended the constitutional right of secession, and regarded Lincoln's election in 1860 as "a calamity to the country," Campbell sought in early 1861 to work out a compromise that would keep the Southern states in the Union. When the attack on Fort Sumter signaled the failure of the compromise, he resigned from the Court and returned to his home state. Disappointed to learn that his fellow Alabamians had no affection for him, he went to New Orleans, where he practiced law until Union forces occupied the city in early 1862. He then went on to Richmond, Virginia, where he became assistant secretary of war in the Confederate cabinet. After the war Campbell continued his law practice, appearing frequently in important Supreme Court cases. A moderately tall man with a bald head, a pale complexion, gray eyes, and bushy eyebrows that he nervously tugged at when lost in thought, Campbell was gentle, even shy in his manner, but when he spoke he commanded attention. His resignation from the Court cut short a career that might have been one of the most brilliant in the nation's history, and also one of the longest, for his death did not occur until 1889, just short of thirty-six years after his appointment and twenty-eight years after his resignation.

(Photo credit: Handy Studios, Collection of the Supreme Court of the United States.)

NATHAN CLIFFORD

Associate Justice Clifford of Maine was a Northern Democrat
with Southern sympathies who kept a low profile during the war,
neither challenging nor lending notable support for the policies
of the Lincoln administration. Born in New Hampshire in 1803,
he had begun his law practice and political career in Maine,
served as attorney general in President Polk's cabinet, and at the
close of the Mexican War went to Mexico to try to resolve differences arising out of the treaty that had ended the war with
that country. When President Buchanan chose him to replace
the resigned Benjamin Curtis on the Supreme Court in 1857,
the *New York Tribune* attacked his qualifications, saying he was
"just about equal to the trial of a case of assumpsit upon a prom-
issory note in the court of a Justice of the Peace." Though not
on the court at the time the *Dred Scott* case was decided, Clifford made it clear that he agreed with that controversial decision. A big man who tipped the scales at more than three hundred pounds, Clifford was a meticulous and thorough worker,
though characteristically phlegmatic in his manner and almost
totally devoid of any sense of humor. He served on the Court
without much distinction until his death in 1881, just short of
his seventy-eighth birthday.

(Photo credit: Handy Studios, Collection of the Supreme Court of the United States.)

Noah H. Swayne

Associate Justice Swayne of Ohio was Lincoln's first appointment to the Supreme Court and, on the whole, his most disappointing. Though noted as one of Ohio's most successful lawyers, he never made much of an impression as a justice, though he persisted for years in the foolish hope that he would one day be named chief justice. Lincoln chose Swayne because he wanted a justice from Ohio to replace the deceased Justice John McLean, because McLean himself had thought highly of Swayne, and because Swayne had a host of influential supporters. He loyally supported Lincoln's policies during the war but beyond that did little to distinguish himself. Born to a Quaker family in Virginia in 1804, he had moved to Ohio because of his strong opposition to slavery. Originally a Jacksonian Democrat, he became a Republican in the 1850s, when the nation was racked by the growing controversy over the extension of slavery into the territories. By that time he had won a reputation as one of the best trial lawyers in the nation and had built up a clientele that included influential banks, railroads, and other corporations. Like so many of his colleagues, Swayne was a large man, both in height and girth, with a massive head, a ruddy complexion, and dark hair that thinned toward baldness in later years. His photographs reveal a handsome face that was deeply lined as he grew older, a high forehead, and a curious habit of tilting his head to the right. When first encountered he could be charming, but on further acquaintance many felt his charm was contrived and insincere. Swayne served on the Court until his resignation in 1881. He died three years later at the age of seventy-nine.

(Photo credit: Matthew Brady, Collection of the Supreme Court of the United States.)

SAMUEL FREEMAN MILLER

Associate Justice Miller of Iowa was arguably Lincoln's best appointment to the Court, though the president was unacquainted with him before his appointment and had little opportunity to get to know him during the war. Originally a medical doctor, the Kentucky-born Miller had switched to the law and moved to Iowa in the 1840s, where his legal reputation became so great that lawyers, judges, legislators, and governors all along the Mississippi joined to urge that he be appointed to the Supreme Court in 1862. Miller had a commanding intellect and a forceful personality, and when Salmon P. Chase became chief justice late in 1864 he found that Miller was, "beyond question, the dominant personality upon the bench." A large man, with a big head, a square jaw, and a muscular body, Miller wrote opinions in some of the most important cases of the Reconstruction era, including the controversial *Slaughterhouse Cases* of 1873, which provided the first important opportunity for the Court to interpret the Fourteenth Amendment. In all, Miller wrote opinions in more than six hundred cases—almost one hundred of them on constitutional issues—becoming, in his own words, the "organ of the Court" in constitutional issues. He continued to serve on the Court until his death in 1890 at the age of seventy-four.

David Davis

David Davis of Illinois was one of Lincoln's oldest political friends, but as an associate justice of the Supreme Court he became best known for his ringing opinion in *Ex parte Milligan* (1866), rebuking Lincoln's administration (though not the president himself) for its policy of subjecting civilians to military justice in states where the courts were open and functioning. Davis had serious doubts about his qualifications to serve on the Court before Lincoln appointed him in late 1862. Although he had been a trial judge for many years, he had never argued a case on appeal, he was not a legal scholar, and he wrote slowly and with difficulty. Aside from his *Milligan* opinion, he had only a mediocre record as a Supreme Court justice. While on the Court, he continued to dabble in politics, even aspiring at one point to be the presidential nominee of the Liberal Republicans, and in 1877 he resigned to become United States senator from Illinois. An imposing man physically, Davis stood just under six feet in height and, from middle age on, weighed upwards of three hundred pounds. In groups of lawyers, he was more of a listener than a speaker. He had a roaring laugh (which was often set off by Lincoln's stories) and a genial face, and despite occasional flashes of anger, he was almost always good-natured. As the wife of one of the lawyers who practiced regularly in his Illinois court commented, he "had a big head and a big body, a big brain and a big heart." Davis was seventy-one years old when he died in Bloomington, Illinois, in 1886.

(Photo credit: Handy Studios, Collection of the Supreme Court of the United States.)

STEPHEN JOHNSON FIELD

Associate Justice Field of California took his seat as the tenth member of the Supreme Court on December 7, 1863, but because of the illnesses of other judges the full complement of ten justices was actually present for only five court days, from Monday, December 7, through Friday, December 11, 1863. Field's appointment is sometimes cited as a Republican effort to "pack" the Supreme Court with friendly judges, but his appointment owed more to circuit court requirements than to political calculations—specifically, the need to bring the rich and increasingly important state of California under the umbrella of the Supreme Court with the creation of a tenth judicial circuit for the Pacific Coast. Born in Connecticut in 1816, Field belonged to one of the nation's most accomplished families (one of his brothers was a leading attorney in New York City and a frequent Supreme Court advocate, and another laid the first telegraph cable across the Atlantic Ocean in 1858). Field himself was a formidable lawyer and an accomplished judge, with a fine mind, a determined (if combative) personality, and a devotion to the law. A Democrat, he supported the administration during the war but broke with the Republicans over the *Test Oath Cases* in 1867. With his dissent in the *Slaughterhouse Cases* in 1873, Field became the Supreme Court's leading exponent of the controversial doctrine of substantive due process. Field continued to serve until old age dimmed his mind and he was persuaded to resign, effective December 1, 1897. By that time, he had established a record of Supreme Court service (thirty-four years, six months, and eleven days) that broke John Marshall's previous record and stood until it was in turn broken by William O. Douglas's record of more than thirty-six years. The last survivor of Lincoln's five Supreme Court appointments, Field was eighty-four years old when he died on April 9, 1899.

(Photo credit: Collection of the Supreme Court of the United States.)

SALMON P. CHASE

Lincoln waited eight weeks after Roger Taney died before naming Salmon Portland Chase of Ohio as the new chief justice in December 1864. For three years Chase had served ably as Lincoln's secretary of the treasury, but he had used much of that time to further his own presidential ambitions and undermine Lincoln's credibility with Congress and the public. Four or five times he responded to differences with the president by submitting his resignation, confident that Lincoln would decline to accept it. Finally, in June 1864, Lincoln decided that he "could not stand it any longer" and accepted his ambitious secretary's latest resignation. Despite their personal differences, Lincoln apparently never seriously considered appointing anyone other than Chase as chief justice. He conceded that the Ohioan was a man of extraordinary ability, and believed that he shared his own views on the key issues of emancipation and legal tender. In fact, Chase believed that the Legal Tender Act (which he supported as secretary of the treasury) was unconstitutional, and in *Hepburn v. Griswold* (1870) he struck it down. He served Lincoln's legacy better in *Texas v. White* (1869), in which he condemned secession and held that the Constitution created "an indestructible Union composed of indestructible states." A tall man with a handsome face, an aversion to alcohol, a hatred of slavery, and an appalling lack of humor, Chase continued to aspire to the presidency until his death in 1873. After his passing, he was remembered as a man of great attainments and even greater (and unfulfilled) ambitions.

(Photo credit: Collection of the Supreme Court of the United States.)

WILLIAM STRONG

Associate Justice Strong of Pennsylvania was nominated to the
Court on February 7, 1870, by President Ulysses S. Grant, and
approved by the Senate on February 18. Although Strong had
no personal contact with Lincoln and was not on the Court during the war, his appointment (and that of Joseph Bradley, made
on the same date) helped to bring closure to an important issue
raised by the conflict, for Strong and Bradley joined three other
justices in *Knox v. Lee* and *Parker v. Davis*, two cases collectively
referred to as the *Legal Tender Cases* (1872), to declare the Legal
Tender Act constitutional, overruling the earlier decision announced by Chief Justice Chase in *Hepburn v. Griswold* (1870)
and providing constitutional sanction to this important war
measure. Formerly a judge of the Pennsylvania Supreme Court,
Strong's opinion on the legal tender issue was well known before
his appointment, for he had made a Pennsylvania decision in favor of the legal tender. On the Supreme Court, Strong was a
forceful and articulate judge who directed most of his energies to
the business issues that were then becoming more and more important to the nation's life. Strong was seventy-two years old
when he retired from the Court on December 14, 1880. He was
still in good health and mentally acute, but he wished to provide
an example to other judges (among them Noah Swayne and Nathan Clifford) then suffering the ravages of old age. As his
daughter explained, he thought it better to leave while people
would still ask, "Why does he?" than to wait until they asked,
"Why doesn't he?" Strong lived fifteen years after his retirement,
dying at the age of eighty-seven in 1895.

(Photo credit: Matthew Brady, Collection of the Supreme Court of the United States.)

JOSEPH P. BRADLEY

Like William Strong, Associate Justice Bradley of New Jersey was nominated by President Grant on February 7, 1870. While Strong's nomination was confirmed on February 18, Bradley's confirmation came a month later. Strong and Bradley were decisive votes in the controversial *Legal Tender Cases* (1872), upholding the constitutionality of the wartime measure that had been so important in financing the war. An outstanding technician of the law, Bradley served on the Court for twenty-two years, until his death on January 22, 1892, at the age of seventy-eight.

(Photo credit: Matthew Brady, Collection of the Supreme Court of the United States.)

6   The Boom of Cannon

On March 10, 1863, THE day the decision in the *Prize Cases* was announced, the Senate confirmed the appointment of a new associate justice to the Supreme Court. Stephen J. Field was forty-six years old and in his sixth year as chief justice of the Supreme Court of California when he received news of his appointment to serve in a newly created tenth seat on the nation's highest tribunal. The fact that he was a Democrat, and a partisan in California politics, would not ordinarily have recommended Field to President Lincoln. But the spring of 1863 was not an ordinary time in the country's history, and events in Washington and far-off San Francisco were conspiring in a special way to make the Californian's appointment all but inevitable.

Field was a man of energy and ability, a member of one of the most accomplished families in the nation, and an experienced jurist. Born in Connecticut in 1816, he was raised in Stockbridge, Massachusetts, the son of David Dudley Field, a prominent Congregationalist minister and author. As testimony to the Reverend Field's faith in the virtues of hard work and piety, four of his nine children went on to national and even international prominence, and a fifth became the mother of one of the country's leading jurists. The eldest of the Field sons, named David Dudley Field for his father, became one of the most prominent lawyers in New York City and the leader of a movement to replace antiquated legal procedures with modern, simplified judicial practices. His proposed legal code (known in later years as the Field Code) replaced the outdated and technical forms of the old English common law with clear and simple legal directives. It was adopted in New York in 1848 and later enacted in nearly two dozen other states. Another of the sons, Cyrus Field, became a successful businessman in New York City. After making an early fortune in the paper business, Cyrus Field invested in a small telegraph company and, in 1858, succeeded in laying the first telegraph cable across the Atlantic Ocean.[1] It was an amazing achievement that revolutionized communications between the Old World and the New. A fourth son, Henry Martyn Field, became an internationally famous minister and a popular travel writer. And one of the Field daughters, Emilia, became the mother of David J. Brewer, a lawyer and judge who was an associate justice of the United States Supreme Court from 1890 to 1910, serving for part of that time with his uncle, Stephen J. Field.

Like his brothers, Stephen Field pursued his higher education at Williams College, then went to New York City to practice law. He left New York in 1848 to travel in Europe, but came back to the United States when he heard reports of gold discoveries in far-off California. Arriving in San Francisco late in 1849, he plunged into the tumultuous legal life of the gold-rush state, establishing a law practice, serving for a short time as an alcalde (a Spanish term for an office that combines the functions of mayor and judge), and winning election to the state legislature, where he was instrumental in securing California's adoption of the Field Code. He ran (unsuccessfully) for the state senate as a Democrat, and in 1857 he won a bitterly contested election (again as a Democrat) for chief justice of the state supreme court. Field's service on the California Supreme Court gave him special familiarity with the land laws that that state had inherited from Mexico and Spain. Those laws, which the United States was obligated to respect under the Treaty of Guadalupe Hidalgo, governed the titles to huge tracts of contested land in the state.[2] Beginning in the late 1850s and continuing into the Civil War years, the Supreme Court in Washington found itself confronted with a flood of California land cases. Stephen Field's familiarity with California's Spanish and Mexican land laws was one of the factors that recommended him for Supreme Court service.[3]

Field's political experience was a less important qualification, though Lincoln did not ignore it. Field had always been a Democrat, although his brother David Dudley Field had left the party, first to support the Free Soil candidacy of Martin Van Buren in 1848, and after 1856, to become a Republican. David Dudley Field opposed the extension of slavery into the western territories and supported the Wilmot Proviso, a congressional proposal (never enacted) that would have excluded slavery from any of the territories acquired from Mexico. He was one of the distinguished New Yorkers who sat on the stage of New York's Cooper Union in February 1860, when Lincoln delivered the speech that first raised expectations that he might become president of the United States.[4] David Dudley Field was close to Salmon P. Chase and supported his presidential candidacy at the Republican convention in Chicago, but when it became clear that Chase was out of the race he threw his support to Lincoln. After Chase became Lincoln's secretary of the treasury, David Dudley Field continued to act as one of Chase's informal advisers.

Stephen Field made it clear in his political campaigns in California that he was not an abolitionist and that he staunchly defended the right of individual states to decide whether they should or should not have slavery (federal officials, he said, had "no more right to meddle with slavery in the different States, than they have with slavery in Turkey").[5] This did not differ much from Lincoln's own position on that issue. Although Field's political views on other issues were not well known in Washington, it was clear that he supported the Union, for in October 1861 he declared his position on that issue in one of the first messages sent by transcontinental telegraph. As chief justice of California, he sent the message to the president in the temporary absence of the state's governor, declaring that the new telegraph system would strengthen "the attachment which binds both the East & West to the Union" and help the people "express their loyalty to that Union & their determination to stand by the Government in this its day of trial."[6]

Field seemed satisfied with his position as chief justice of California when, in January 1863, Matthew Hall McAllister submitted his resignation from the U.S. Circuit Court for California.[7] Congress's reorganization of the circuit system in 1862 had left California untouched, in part because the Pacific Coast was so far from the nation's other population centers, and in part because Judge McAllister's administration of the circuit court there had been problem-free. But Judge McAllister was now sixty-two years old and in declining health. In April 1862, he asked for and received a six-month leave of absence due to illness, and nine months later he resigned.[8]

California was the only independent circuit in the nation and, as such, a judicial anomaly, but California was in many ways an anomalous state. One of the newest members of the Union (admitted in 1850 as part of Henry Clay's last great compromise), it already boasted a large (and rapidly increasing) population and one of its most spectacular cities (San Francisco was the nation's fifteenth largest city in 1860). Richly endowed with mineral wealth, it also included immense tracts of undeveloped land. It stood with the Union in the face of Southern secession but had some prominent elected leaders who were sympathetic to the Confederacy (if not openly, at least secretly).

Asked if he would be willing to replace McAllister on the U.S. circuit court, Field said that he would rather retain his position as the highest state judge in California. But "if a new justice were added to the Supreme Court of the United States," he added, "I would accept the office if tendered to me."[9] Senators continued to press Lincoln to nominate him to the circuit court, and he did so, believing that a new Supreme Court seat would soon be created and Field would then be in line to fill it. Before the circuit court nomination could be confirmed, however, Congress created the tenth seat, along with a new judicial circuit that included Oregon as well as California.[10] The congressional delegations from both states unanimously urged Lincoln to nominate Field to the new position on the Supreme Court, as did California's governor Leland Stanford.[11]

If these recommendations were not enough to convince Lincoln that Field should be nominated, the wishes of David Dudley Field may have been the clincher. According to Henry Martyn Field, a New Yorker named John A. C. Gray, a mutual friend of David Dudley Field and the president, paid a personal call on the president to discuss the nomination. He found that, while Lincoln "agreed entirely in the fitness of Judge Field," he had one question to ask: "Does David want his brother to have it?" When Gray answered yes, the president responded, "Then he shall have it."[12] After the nomination was discussed in a meeting of the president's cabinet, Gideon Welles wrote in his diary: "Appointments considered yesterday and to-day. Generally conceded that Field of California was the man for the Supreme Court."[13] On March 6, Lincoln sent Field's nomination to the Senate, and on March 10 it was unanimously confirmed.[14]

It has been charged that Stephen J. Field's appointment represented an effort by Lincoln and the Republicans to "pack" the Supreme Court; that the closeness of the vote in the *Prize Cases* had convinced the powers that be in

Washington that another pro-administration justice was necessary to ensure that the Court would support the government's war policies.[15] After the war, Kentucky's senator Garrett Davis charged that Field's appointment was ideologically driven; that Congress had been "preeminently radical, and determined, if possible, to make the Supreme Court radical also. A tenth judge was added to the bench," Davis stated, "and it was the purpose of the leaders that the place should be filled with a Radical, and they so hoped even after his appointment."[16]

If the Republicans were concerned about Supreme Court challenges to their war measures, it would hardly have been surprising, for administration policies had been under almost continuous attack, at least since Chief Justice Taney issued his opinion in the *Merryman* case. But the circumstances of Stephen Field's appointment to the Supreme Court do not support the charge that "court packing" was the sole, or even the primary, motivation. There is no evidence that McAllister's resignation was politically motivated (he was born and had spent most of his life in Georgia, and it is unlikely that he would have cooperated in a plan to strengthen Lincoln's hand in the Supreme Court), and Field could not have been appointed if McAllister had not stepped down. Field's expertise in California land law was genuinely needed in Washington— in fact, when Field retired from the Court thirty-four years later, he specifically stated that the tenth seat was created to bring him to Washington so that he could help to bring order out of the "confusion" caused by the conflicting Spanish and Mexican land titles, and the mining laws of the Pacific Coast.[17] Further, plans had already been made to create a tenth seat on the Supreme Court before the *Prize Cases* squeaked through the high tribunal on a vote of five to four. If the Republicans had wanted to fill the Court with "reliable" judges who would affirm all of their measures, they could have tried to do so in 1862, or even in 1861, when the war effort seemed most vulnerable to judicial attack—when Taney's *Merryman* opinion was a topic of conversation all over the country, and there was genuine concern that other influential judges might join the chief justice's crusade against Lincoln's war measures.

Historian Stanley I. Kutler has pointed out that the proposal to create a tenth Supreme Court seat prompted almost no debate in Congress. If Lincoln and the Republicans were trying to "pack" the Court, there would have been a storm of protest from the administration's critics, "but the Democratic party in

Congress remained quiescent," and Democratic newspapers (never reluctant to take issue with the Republicans on other issues) "withheld comment." According to Kutler, this silence suggests that the proposal was not seen as a Republican grab for power but as a prudent initiative designed to improve the judiciary by extending the Supreme Court's representation to a part of the country that had never before been represented.[18]

In fact, several motives prompted the addition of the tenth seat in 1863— the unexpected resignation of the circuit judge in San Francisco, the willingness of an able California jurist to move to Washington, and the hope that an additional judge would strengthen the administration's position in the high court. There was never any guarantee that Field would support all of the president's war policies. That Field was favored by "radicals" in Congress, as Garrett Davis asserted, is not at all clear from the record. Save Field's belief in the need to preserve the Union, his political views were almost totally unknown in Washington in 1863. To say that the circumstances of his appointment amounted to "court packing" is to stretch that phrase well beyond its usual meaning.

Field's joining the Court occasioned little interest in Eastern newspapers, for there were other, more vital interests at stake in the spring of 1863. In California, however, the papers took more notice. One California journal proclaimed that "the appointment of such a man to the highest judicial tribunal of the nation is fortunate for the country, and will be universally regarded on this coast as a wise exercise of the appointing power."[19] A San Francisco paper declared: "As a judicial officer, the appointee has not now, nor ever has had, his superior on the bench, and his selection for this responsible position will give unalloyed satisfaction to citizens generally throughout the state."[20] And another San Francisco journal wrote that Field "has a logical mind, accompanied with motive industry" and that his work "never gets behind." This paper, however, thought his land law expertise was his best qualification: "People are tired of having all the decisions affecting property overturned every time a new man goes on the bench. Nearly every man of substance had been at some time victimized in the course of the legal revolutions which the almost annual crop of judges has given us. These considerations will make many cheerfully acknowledge the new judge, who would have opposed him were his antecedents only those of lawyer Field."[21]

Field received word of his appointment by telegraph; using the same means, he asked for permission to postpone the beginning of his service until May 20, which would be his father's birthday (the patriarch of the Field clan was about to turn eighty-two).[22] In addition to honoring his father, Field wanted to finish some pending state supreme court cases. On the appointed day, he took his oath of office in San Francisco as a justice of the United States Supreme Court.[23] During the summer he heard cases in the federal circuit court, and in the fall he boarded a steamboat for the long journey from California to Washington, via Panama and New York. It was an arduous trip but one that Field would get used to in the years ahead, for however important his vote was on cases that had to be decided in Washington, his circuit duties on the Pacific Coast would occupy most of his time and energy during his many years of service on the Supreme Court. On Monday, December 7, 1863, the judges of the high tribunal gathered in Washington for the opening of their new term. With the addition of Justice Field, ten justices were present.

Many years later, Field reminisced about his early days in Washington and the war atmosphere that pervaded the city when he arrived there in 1863. The mood of war penetrated even into the chambers of the Supreme Court: "When I came here the country was in the midst of war. Washington was one great camp, and now and then the boom of cannon could be heard from the other side of the Potomac. But we could not say *inter arma silent leges* ["in war the laws are silent"]. This court met in regular session, never once failing in time or place, and its work went on as though there were no sound of battle."[24]

FIELD HAD BEEN IN Washington only six weeks when the Supreme Court convened to hear arguments in one of the most important—and potentially explosive—cases of the war. It was Friday, January 22, 1864, and Justice Wayne was presiding in the absence of Chief Justice Taney, who was again too ill to come to the Capitol. The case was *Ex parte Vallandigham,* and it came before the Court on petition for a writ of certiorari to the judge advocate general of the army, Joseph Holt of Kentucky. Holt was a Democrat who had served President Buchanan as postmaster general and secretary of war before Lincoln appointed him to his army post in September 1862. Despite his political differences with the president, Holt was a Union loyalist and an accomplished lawyer—in fact, his legal abilities were so widely admired that he had been mentioned by both Democrats and Republicans as a potential Supreme Court nominee. Holt was on hand on January 22 to argue the government's case in *Ex parte Vallandigham*. The case for the petitioner, Clement Laird Vallandigham of Ohio, was argued by George E. Pugh. Both Pugh and Vallandigham were prominent Democratic politicians in Ohio and vocal critics of Lincoln's war policies. Pugh had been his state's attorney general from 1852 to 1854 and a United States senator from 1855 to 1861 (he lost his bid for reelection to Salmon P. Chase, soon to become Lincoln's treasury secretary). Vallandigham was perhaps the North's loudest and most determined critic of the president's war policies—and it was the very loudness and dogged determination of his criticism that had led to his legal difficulties.

Vallandigham was a conservative Democrat who defended the interests of yeoman farmers and low-wage laborers against the expanding interests of urban merchants, manufacturers, and financiers. He opposed the war because he believed in the "absolute sovereignty of the states," and he resisted emancipation because he believed that blacks were inferior to whites.[25] Like Roger Taney, he argued that the benefits of citizenship could never be extended to the Negro, not just because of his "descent from slaves" but "because he is the descendant of a servile and degraded race."[26] He sensed that a Northern victory in the war would effect a profound transformation in the political, social, and economic life of the nation, changing it from a loosely knit league of rural communities into a commercial and industrial nation committed to expanding concepts of political and social equality. He sought to summarize his position on the war with the slogan: "The Constitution as it is, the Union as it was." But one of his followers added a revealing phrase to the rallying cry: "The Constitution as it is, the Union as it was, *and the Niggers where they are.*"[27]

Vallandigham's views were not shared by most Northerners—not even by most Northern Democrats, who supported the war (with varying degrees of enthusiasm) and identified themselves as War Democrats. But they did accurately reflect the opinions of the antiwar wing of his party, generally called the Peace Democrats, although Republicans called them "Copperheads," in allusion to the poisonous snakes of the same name.

The strength of the Copperhead movement during the Civil War has been the subject of sharp disagreement among historians. For more than a generation, the late Frank L. Klement of Marquette University argued that the Copperhead threat was largely illusory, a kind of "fairy tale" threat that was the subject of wild exaggeration by Unionists, especially Republicans.[28] A more recent study by Jennifer L. Weber of the University of Kansas indicates that Copperheadism was in fact strong throughout the conflict, although the number of its sympathizers varied, rising and falling in inverse relation to the Union's military fortunes. When the North prevailed on the battlefield, Copperhead sympathies waned, but when the war effort stalled, or was in danger of failure, the number and influence of the Copperheads swelled.[29] The movement was a real threat to the war effort, Weber says, and was recognized as such by Lincoln, who told Massachusetts senator Charles Sumner that he feared a "fire in the rear" (meaning the antiwar Democrats) more than he feared the Union's military chances.[30] Throughout the conflict, Clement Vallandigham was the most articulate and vociferous spokesman for the antiwar movement in the North. Weber has called him "the most notorious Copperhead in the nation."[31]

Born in New Lisbon, Ohio, in 1820, to parents with Southern roots, Vallandigham was a talented lawyer and an ambitious politician. Originally a Jacksonian, he had strongly defended President Polk's prosecution of the war with Mexico in the mid-1840s (a fact that caused him some embarrassment after he took his aggressive antiwar stance in the 1860s). After moving to Dayton, he published a newspaper for a couple of years and then resumed his law practice. A handsome man and a spellbinding speaker, he won a tough contest for election to the U.S. House of Representatives in 1858. Originally a supporter of Stephen Douglas's doctrine of "popular sovereignty," he broke with the Little Giant after the Confederate attack on Fort Sumter, opposing Lincoln's war policies (which Douglas supported) and arguing against all military measures designed to resist secession.

Vallandigham opposed Lincoln's call for militiamen in 1861; he opposed the president's proclamation of a blockade; he opposed the issuance of legal-tender notes ("greenbacks") to finance the war; and he opposed the conscription laws passed by Congress in 1862 and 1863, arguing that they proved that the people of the North did not support the war. He condemned the idea of emancipation, labeling calls for an end to slavery as "mingled fanaticism and hypocrisy." "I see more of barbarism and sin," he said, "a thousand times, in the continuance of this war, the dissolution of the Union, the breaking up of this government, and the enslavement of the white race, by debt and taxes and arbitrary power." After the final Emancipation Proclamation was issued on January 1, 1863, he denounced it on the floor of the House of Representatives, arguing that "if this Union cannot endure 'part slave and part free,' then it is already and finally dissolved."[32] He excoriated arbitrary arrests in the North, condemning Lincoln as a despot and suggesting that, if he continued to behave as he had, he should be impeached.[33] Eager to take to the platform wherever he could find a large audience, he traveled to New York to vent his antiwar views, then returned to Ohio where, in the election of 1862, he lost his seat in Congress. Undeterred, he announced his candidacy for governor of Ohio.

Vallandigham's new campaign met a stumbling block in the spring of 1863, when Lincoln ordered Major General Ambrose Burnside to take command of the military's Department of the Ohio, headquartered in Cincinnati. Burnside had been removed from his command of the Army of the Potomac because of the irresolution he had displayed at the Battle of Fredericksburg the previous December. In his new department (which included Illinois, Indiana, Michigan, Wisconsin, and part of Kentucky as well as Ohio) Burnside encountered widespread and often intemperate agitation against the war, and on April 13, 1863, he issued a military order (General Orders, No. 38) designed to suppress the agitation. It declared that "all persons found within our lines who commit acts for the benefit of the enemies of our country will be tried as spies or traitors, and, if convicted will suffer death." It also provided that the "habit of declaring sympathy for the enemy will not be allowed in this department. Persons committing such offenses will be at once arrested, with a view to being tried as above stated, or sent beyond our lines into the lines of their friends. It must be distinctly understood that treason, expressed or implied, will not be tolerated in this department."[34]

When Vallandigham learned about Burnside's order, he openly ridiculed it. It was "a base usurpation of military power," he said; he could "spit upon it and stamp it under foot," as his right to criticize the government was based upon "General Orders, No. 1," the Constitution of the United States. "The sooner the people inform the minions of usurped power that they will not submit to such restrictions upon their liberties," he insisted, "the better." Meanwhile, Burnside learned that Vallandigham was planning to speak at a large outdoor rally in Mount Vernon, Ohio, on May 1. Suspecting that he intended to make more inflammatory statements, Burnside sent two members of his staff and ten citizens of Cincinnati to "observe" the speech and take notes on what was said. According to Frank Klement's biography of Vallandigham, the former congressman learned in advance that Burnside's men would be in Mount Vernon and, "needing martyrdom to gain his goals, intended to make the most of his opportunity."[35] Speaking provocatively and flamboyantly, he delivered a nearly two-hour-long tirade against Lincoln and the Republicans that won him wild applause from the crowd and a secure, if controversial, place in the history of the Civil War.

Back in Cincinnati, Burnside's men reported that Vallandigham had addressed an audience of some 20,000 at Mount Vernon; and that he had expressed virulent antiwar sentiments, declaring the war "a wicked, cruel, and unnecessary war; . . . a war not being waged for the preservation of the Union; . . . a war for the purpose of crushing out liberty and erecting a despotism; . . . a war for the freedom of the blacks and the enslavement of the whites" and charging "that the Government of the United States was about to appoint military marshals in every district, to restrain the people of their liberties, to deprive them of their rights and privileges."[36]

On orders from Burnside, Vallandigham was arrested in his home early on the morning of May 5 and taken before a military commission in Cincinnati. There he was charged with "publicly expressing . . . sympathy for those in arms against the government of the United States, and declaring disloyal sentiments and opinions with the object and purpose of weakening the power of the government in its efforts to suppress an unlawful rebellion."[37]

From the outset, Vallandigham denied the jurisdiction of the military commission to try him. He pointed out that he was not a member of the military and argued that he was not subject to military law. If it was charged that he had committed any crime, he said, he was entitled to be tried in a civil court according to due process of law. In any event, citizens had the right to criticize public policy and public servants. And he avowed that "he had never counseled disobedience to the Constitution, or resistance to laws and lawful authority."[38]

Vallandigham's argument did not persuade the military commissioners who tried him. They found him guilty and sentenced him to imprisonment for the duration of the war. Two days later, ex-Senator Pugh appeared before Judge Humphrey Leavitt of the U.S. circuit court in Cincinnati and petitioned for a writ of habeas corpus on behalf of Vallandigham. Burnside responded by in-forming the judge that he had authority from the president of the United States to arrest and try Vallandigham. Pugh argued that Vallandigham was en-titled to his release on habeas corpus because military commissions have no ju-risdiction over civilians; under the Constitution, he said, civil rights are "not subject to the whim of military men." Leavitt conducted a full hearing and concluded that he had no authority to review a decision of a military commis-sion. Vallandigham's petition was denied.[39]

Vallandigham's arrest and trial were extensively covered in newspapers all over the country. Supporters of the Northern war effort generally applauded Burnside's action, although Vallandigham's supporters, and virtually all of the Copperheads of the North, saw it as a vicious attack on civil liberty. His arrest and conviction were, in their view, "a great blunder" and "the most atrocious outrage ever perpetrated in any civilized land." A headline in Vallandigham's hometown newspaper condemned his arrest as "A Dastardly Outrage!!!" and protested that "The Hour for Action Has Arrived."[40]

Lincoln had no prior knowledge of Vallandigham's arrest and had not au-thorized it.[41] He had, however, created a climate in which arrests such as this could take place, for on September 24, 1862, he had issued a proclamation stat-ing that "all persons discouraging volunteer enlistments, resisting militia drafts, or guilty of any disloyal practice, affording aid and comfort to Rebels . . . shall be subject to martial law and liable to trial and punishment by Courts Martial or Military Commission." In the same proclamation, he had ordered the sus-pension of the writ of habeas corpus "in respect to all persons arrested, or who are now, or hereafter during the rebellion shall be, imprisoned in any fort, camp, arsenal, military prison, or other place of confinement by any military authority or by the sentence of any Court Martial or Military Commission." The proclamation was intended to restrain "disloyal persons" from interfer-ing with the draft and "giving aid and comfort in various ways to the insurrec-tion."[42] Burnside might well have thought that his General Orders, No. 38, fell within its terms. But the general did not report the order to his superiors or seek their permission before ordering Vallandigham's arrest, and the arrest itself was a major embarrassment to the president. Public clamor about Vallandigham's case made it inevitable that Lincoln would be asked to look into the matter.

Knowing only what he had read about the case, the president telegraphed

Burnside to ask if the newspaper stories were correct, while at the same time assuring him that he would support his efforts to maintain law and order. Burnside's reply was vague; he thanked the president for his "kind assurance of support" but gave him no details of Vallandigham's case.[43] On May 18, Major General U.S. Grant began his siege of Vicksburg, Mississippi, defended by a Confederate army under Major General John C. Pemberton. Lincoln was concerned with news of Vicksburg when, the following day, he discussed the Vallandigham case with his cabinet. As Gideon Welles noted in his diary, the cabinet generally agreed that the arrest was "arbitrary and injudicious" and an infringement on "the constitutional rights of the parties." Every member, Welles said, "regrets what has been done." But the cabinet did not want to rebuke Burnside or undermine confidence in his authority, and they sought a way out of the dilemma. Burnside's order had provided that persons could be punished by death, imprisonment, or being "sent beyond our lines into the lines of their friends." Lincoln and his cabinet picked up on the last option. Accordingly, Secretary of War Stanton, acting pursuant to Lincoln's direction, ordered that Vallandigham be sent under secure guard to the headquarters of General W. S. Rosecrans in Tennessee and thence turned over to Confederate authorities. If he should return and be arrested, he was to be "kept in close custody for the term specified in his sentence" (that is, the duration of the war).[44]

Vallandigham was delivered into the custody of Confederate general Braxton Bragg on May 26. He was treated well by his Confederate hosts, but he was not happy in the Land of Dixie. He was a candidate for political office in the North and wanted to resume his campaign there. So he made his way to Wilmington, North Carolina, where he boarded a ship bound for Bermuda. From there he was carried by another ship to Canada, and he eventually came to rest in Windsor, Ontario, just across the river from Detroit and less than fifty miles from the northern border of Ohio. In Canada, Vallandigham resumed his campaign for the Ohio governorship (his running mate as Democratic candidate for lieutenant governor was his attorney George Pugh). He wrote letters, met supporters, and conferred with Democratic strategists—but to no avail. When the votes were counted in October, Vallandigham's Union Party opponent, John Brough, won by an unprecedented majority.

In the meantime, Pugh had taken Vallandigham's case to the United States Supreme Court on a petition for a writ of certiorari. Certiorari is an extraordinary writ issued by an appellate court to a lower court, commanding it to certify its record in a particular case for review. It is issued at the discretion of the appellate court to examine and pass on the validity of the lower court's judgment when appeal is not a matter of right.[45] In the Vallandigham case, Judge Leavitt's decision could not be appealed directly to the Supreme Court because he had issued it alone, without the participation of the circuit judge, and appeal was available only when both the district judge and the circuit judge had heard the case together and issued a certificate of division. (Justice Noah Swayne was the circuit judge for Ohio at the time of Vallandigham's arrest, but he was either unavailable to participate in the hearing or intentionally chose to absent himself.) Even if it were procedurally possible, a direct appeal might not have suited Vallandigham's purpose, for Leavitt had passed only on the legality of the Ohioan's detention. A review on certiorari, in contrast, would permit the Supreme Court to examine the legality of all of the proceedings against Vallandigham—his arrest, trial, sentence, and exile.[46]

Pugh argued that the military commission that tried Vallandigham was a court, at least for purposes of review by the Supreme Court, and that the writ of certiorari was the proper device for bringing it before the Court. For the government, Judge Advocate General Holt argued that the Supreme Court had no jurisdiction to review the proceedings of a military commission, either by certiorari or habeas corpus. Courts-martial and military commissions derived their authority from the president under Article II of the Constitution, Holt pointed out, while the Supreme Court had authority under Article III of the Constitution. These two sources of authority were separate and distinct. Holt quoted from Chief Justice Taney's opinion in *Luther v. Borden,* which had broadly justified the exercise of military power in time of insurrection.[47]

Justice Wayne announced the Court's decision on February 15, 1864. He reviewed the constitutional and statutory provisions delineating the Supreme Court's jurisdiction and concluded that the Supreme Court had no jurisdiction over military tribunals. A military commission was not a "court" for purposes of the Supreme Court's jurisdiction, Wayne said, and thus the legality of Vallandigham's arrest, trial, and conviction were all beyond the purview of the Court. Vallandigham was not entitled to a writ of certiorari, and Pugh's petition was denied.[48] Justices Nelson, Grier, and Field concurred in Wayne's opinion. The official reports noted that Justice Miller was not present at the argument and took no part in the decision. Only five justices were noted in the reports.[49] What of the other five? We know that Taney was ill, and Catron probably was too. But what of Justice Clifford, the doughface Democrat? And what of Lincoln's appointees, Justices Swayne and Davis? Perhaps they agreed with Wayne's decision and simply did not register their votes in the reports. Perhaps they agreed, but tepidly; or perhaps they disagreed, but not so strongly that they wished to file dissents. With only four justices registering their votes in the official reports, it was a somewhat puzzling decision but a decision nonetheless, and one that sustained Lincoln's conduct of the war, albeit in a round-about way.

Thus, with a short jurisdictional discussion ("legal jargon," historian Frank Klement called it), the Supreme Court avoided the necessity of passing on the substantive questions raised by Vallandigham's case.[50] Did Vallandigham have a right under the Constitution to criticize the president during a time of civil insurrection? Did his arrest deny his rights of free speech? Was he, as a civilian, properly subject to military arrest and trial? Was the whole Vallandigham case a denial of basic constitutional rights? An example of the kind of tyranny and despotism that Vallandigham himself had so often condemned? The Supreme Court did not answer these questions, either because it could not do so—or did not choose to do so. If it had provided answers, the answers would almost certainly have been damaging to the president and his conduct of the war. They would have subjected the national government to condemnation, inevitably weakening the president's authority. If the Court had addressed all of these issues, it might have struck a blow for civil liberties but also undermined the government's war efforts. Perhaps, in the end, the Court avoided the issues it could have decided because it wanted to support the government of which it was a part, oppose the secession, and help the president bring the war to an end.

Lincoln was uneasy about the Vallandigham case, despite his Supreme Court "victory." He knew that Burnside had overstepped his bounds—and said as much in his discussion with the cabinet. When Burnside went a step further and used his General Orders, No. 38, to shut down the *Chicago Times,* a newspaper that was aggressively antagonistic to Lincoln and the Northern war effort, the president decided to intervene. He told Secretary of War Stanton to revoke Burnside's order and permit the newspaper to resume publication.[51]

The president was still troubled by the issue of civil liberties when a group of Democrats meeting in Albany, New York, passed a set of resolutions condemning his approval of military arrests and charging him with trampling on the Constitution. He had been thinking for some time about constitutional rights in wartime and decided to take advantage of the opportunity presented by the Albany resolutions to put his thoughts down on paper. He addressed a long letter to Erastus Corning, chairman of the Albany meeting, and released it on June 12 to the *New York Tribune*. In the letter (commonly known as the "Corning letter"), he explicitly rejected the notion that the Constitution did not apply in time of rebellion or insurrection. On the contrary, he argued, it contained provisions specifically designed to meet the present crisis. He wrote:

> Ours is a case of Rebellion—so called by the resolutions before me—in fact a clear, flagrant and gigantic case of Rebellion; and the provision of the Constitution that "The privilege of the writ of Habeas Corpus shall not be suspended, unless when in cases of Rebellion or Invasion, the public safety may require it," is *the* provision which specially applies to our present case. This provision plainly attests the understanding of those who made the Constitution, that ordinary Courts of justice are inadequate to "Cases of Rebellion"—attests their purpose that, in such cases, men may be held in custody whom the Courts, acting on ordinary rules, would discharge. Habeas Corpus does not discharge men who are proved to be guilty of defined crime; and its suspension is allowed by the Constitution on purpose that men may be arrested and held, who can not be proved to be guilty of defined crime, "when in cases of Rebellion or invasion, the public safety may require it." This is precisely our present case, a case of Rebellion, wherein the public safety does require the suspension.[52]

Lincoln specifically denied that Clement Vallandigham had been arrested merely because he criticized the administration: "If this assertion is the truth and the whole truth—if there was no other reason for the arrest, then I concede that the arrest was wrong." But Vallandigham had been laboring, "with some effect," to interfere with the raising of troops, to encourage desertions, and thus to impair the government's ability to suppress the rebellion. "He was not arrested because he was damaging the political prospects of the administration," Lincoln insisted, "or the personal interests of the commanding general; but because he was damaging the army, upon the existence, and vigor of which, the life of the nation depends." Realizing that purely legalistic arguments often fall on deaf ears, Lincoln exercised the "lawyerly" skills that had so often enabled him to persuade juries in Illinois and presented a homely example that would drive home his point:

> Long experience has shown that armies cannot be maintained unless desertion shall be punished by the severe penalty of death. The case requires, and the law and the Constitution, sanction this punishment. Must I shoot a simple-minded soldier boy who deserts, while I must not touch a hair of a wiley [sic] agitator who induces him to desert? This is none the less injurious when effected by getting a father, or brother, or friend, into a public meeting, and there working upon his feelings, till he is persuaded to write the soldier boy that he is fighting in a bad cause, for a wicked administration of a contemptable [sic] government, too weak to arrest and punish him if he shall desert. I think that in such a case, to silence the agitator, and save the boy, is not only constitutional, but, withal, a great mercy.[53]

The Albany Democrats were unpersuaded by Lincoln's argument, although they acknowledged that it was based *on the Constitution* and not *in spite of it*.[54] Elsewhere, however, the letter was received favorably. The *New York Times* said it was "full, candid, clear and conclusive." The Massachusetts educator and statesman Edward Everett (who a few months later would share the rostrum with Lincoln in a commemorative ceremony at Gettysburg, Pennsylvania) said that, although he would not have counseled Vallandigham's arrest, he deemed Lincoln's "defence of the step complete." Lincoln's Corning letter was printed all over the country in newspapers and pamphlets, eventually reaching an estimated ten million readers. If the opinion of Justice Wayne in *Ex parte Vallandigham* did not convincingly settle the legal issues raised by Vallandigham's arrest, the Corning letter did much to assuage popular doubts on the issue. The people found Lincoln's logic persuasive and, as historian Doris Kearns Goodwin has written, "popular sentiment began to shift."[55] The shift was subtle, but undeniable. And it was in favor of the war.

7 The Old Lion

THE SUPREME COURT'S CASELOAD seemed to increase after Stephen Field took his seat on the bench in late 1863.[1] To do his part in handling the load, the new justice plunged into his work, setting an example of industry and energy that served as a model for his colleagues. Observers could not help but notice the sharp contrast between the junior judge and the old justices, and particularly the chief justice. Field was forty years younger than Taney, but that was not their only difference. Both men were tall and, in their way, impressive figures, but Field sat upright in his chair, while Taney seemed to drape over his like a loose piece of clothing. When standing, Taney was habitually stooped while Field was ramrod straight. Field's hair was dark brown and curly, save for on the top of his head, which was growing bald. His eyes were grayish blue, only faintly obscured by a pair of wire-rimmed glasses, and his long face was adorned with a luxuriant beard—the first full beard on the Supreme Court, where facial adornment would in years to come be the rule more than the exception. Taney, with his mop of tousled hair hanging carelessly over his forehead and ears, reminded some of an old lion. To others, however, his pinched mouth and suspicious eyes made him look more like a wizened goat.[2] In personality and demeanor, the judges also contrasted. Taney spoke softly but with a self-assured tone in his voice. Field's speech was crisp and sometimes angry. If Field had any overbearing fault, it was a tendency to lose his temper. Taney was also capable of anger, but his was a slow-burning, enduring kind of anger—the kind that grows over months and years, even decades.

Taney was in his twenty-eighth year as chief justice when Field came to the bench. He had long since become set in his judicial methods and thought processes. His opinions had all been formed, tried, and tested years before. He remembered the Supreme Court when it was dominated by the ideas and attitudes of his old mentor, Andrew Jackson, and though there were still relics of that era on the bench, the winds of change were now blowing through Washington. If nothing else, the war itself had transformed the capital city. John Archibald Campbell, who left Washington for the Confederacy in 1861, reflected a sense of sympathy for the old chief justice when he wrote him on his departure:

> In taking leave of the court I should do injustice to my own feelings, if I were not to express to you the profound impression that your eminent qualities as a magistrate and jurist have made upon me. I shall never forget the uprightness, fidelity, learning[,] thought and labor, that have been brought by you to the consideration of the judgments of the court, or the urbanity, gentleness, kindness and tolerance that have distinguished your intercourse with the members of the court and bar. From your hands I have received all that I could have desired and in leaving the court, I carry with me feelings of mingled reverence, affection and gratitude.[3]

Campbell had been appointed by Franklin Pierce, but he felt a kinship with the Jacksonians on the Court, and Taney reciprocated the sentiment. Not long after Campbell wrote his letter to Taney, the chief justice himself wrote Pierce, then in retirement in New Hampshire, to thank him for a letter approving of his *Merryman* decision. The former president was a Northerner, but also a doughface, and pleased by any decision that showed the errors of the Republican administration. Taney's letter to Pierce is instructive, not only because it shows the close political ties that bound the chief justice and the former Democratic leader but also because of the light it sheds on Taney's views about secession.

Since the constitutionality of secession never came before Taney in an official capacity, he did not have an opportunity to publicly record his opinions on the issue. But opinions he *did have*. In an unpublished, eight-page memorandum, apparently prepared late in January 1861 for use in a court decision, if and when the issue should come before him, he addressed secession head-on.[4] In the memorandum, Taney reiterated his support for slavery and argued that Northern states were obligated to respect the institution, because they "bound themselves by the social compact of the Constitution to uphold it." Then he wrote: "The South contends that a state has a constitutional right to secede from the Union formed with her sister states. In this I submit the South errs. No power or right is constitutional but what can be exercised in a form or mode provided in the constitution for its exercise. Secession is therefore not constitutional, but revolutionary; and is only morally competent, like war, upon failure of justice."[5]

But this did not end the question. Taney went on to express views like those James Buchanan asserted in his last message to Congress, arguing that even though the Constitution did not recognize a right to secession, it did not recognize any power in the federal government to "coerce" a seceding state to remain in the Union or, once having left, to return to it.[6] Taney argued that "federal laws can, by the constitution, be enforced in a state only by its own citizens." He further argued that federal power could enter a state only "at the call of that state" and that there was "no rightful power to bring back by force the states into the Union."[7]

In the letter he wrote to Pierce after the *Merryman* decision, Taney went beyond the question of the *constitutionality* of secession to discuss the wisdom and justice of Lincoln's efforts to resist secession. He wrote:

> The paroxysm of passion into which the country has suddenly been thrown, appears to me to amount almost to delirium. I hope that it is too violent to last long, and that calmer and more sober thoughts will soon take its place: and that the North, as well as the South, will see that a peaceful separation, with free institutions in each section, is far better than the union of all the present states under a military government, and a reign of terror preceded too by a civil war with all its horrors, and which end as it may will prove ruinous to the victors as well as the vanquished. But at present I grieve to say passion and hate sweep everything before them.[8]

By stating his belief that "peaceful separation" was "far better than . . . a civil war with all its horrors," Taney was aligning himself with advocates of secession, if not on strictly constitutional theory, at least on practical grounds. It was a peculiar position for a chief justice of the United States Supreme Court to take, publicly continuing to function as the highest judicial officer in the land while privately condoning the efforts of a huge section of the land to split it in two.[9]

As 1861 gave way to 1862 and then 1863, and as it became apparent that Taney's hope for a short war (which many others had shared) was unrealistic, he began to resign himself to a long ordeal. There had never been any real doubt that his sympathies lay with the South and that, in any struggle between the sections, his heart (if not his brain) would be below the Mason-Dixon Line. It was a feeling that informed his great opinions—his declaration in *Dred Scott* that the Constitution protected slavery and that Congress was powerless to restrict its spread, and his condemnation in *Ex parte Merryman* of Lincoln's decision to suspend habeas corpus in Maryland. If on the one hand he condemned a whole race to permanent subservience, and on the other staunchly defended civil liberties against the assaults of a "despotic" executive, he was in both cases pleading the cause of his region. *Dred Scott* favored the South in 1857 (or so its defenders believed at the time), and *Merryman* favored the South in 1861 by undermining the legitimacy of the Republican president's war measures. As Taney's biographer, Carl Brent Swisher, has written, the chief justice's "limitations derived from a provincialism too rigid to expand to the scope of full national vision." And his opinions were tinged "with an unadmitted sense of some kind of guilt." Swisher suggests that the guilt may have originated within himself or simply have resulted from the realization that, on the great issues facing the country, his own opinions were not those of most Americans; that, in asserting his own deeply held views, he faced "a powerful and determined majority who disagreed with him."[10]

In 1855, Taney had experienced that guilt in a personal way. It was his custom to vacation in the summer at Old Point Comfort in Virginia, a quaintly genteel resort on the northern shore of Hampton Roads, where cool breezes from Chesapeake Bay gave Southerners relief from the heat and humidity of the season. His daughter Anne and her husband, J. Mason Campbell of Baltimore, had begun to travel in the summer to Newport, Rhode Island, a Northern resort that was more fashionable than Old Point Comfort, and the chief justice's youngest daughter, Alice, had begged him for permission to go with them. He wrote angrily to Campbell:

> I have not the slightest confidence in [the] superior health of Newport over Old Point, and look upon it as nothing more than that unfortunate feeling of inferiority in the South, which believes every thing in the North to be superior to what we have. Yet I am willing that Alice shall go with you if she wishes it and her mother wishes it, and it will not cost more than $100. I would take that much from my increased salary but am unable to spare more without injustice to others. And it must be distinctly understood, that nothing additional must come from you. Until I see you have provided for your wife and children, I will accept nothing from you for mine.[11]

Bowing to her father's displeasure, Alice accompanied Taney and his wife to Old Point Comfort for their summer ritual. It was colder there than usual in July, with stiff winds that forced the family to close their doors and windows, but they stayed on. Then news began to drift into the resort that an epidemic of yellow fever had stricken New Orleans and was spreading north. The Taneys were concerned, but still they stayed on at Old Point. Mrs. Taney became unwell toward the end of the summer, and Alice also fell ill. In September Mrs. Taney suffered a stroke. Taney sought in vain to get medical care for his wife, but it was too late, and she died on September 29. At first it was thought that paralysis was the cause of her death, but it was soon discovered that yellow fever had invaded her body. A few hours after Mrs. Taney succumbed, Alice Taney also died, also of yellow fever. Taney, then seventy-eight years old, was crushed, as were the Campbells, safe in their vacation home at Newport. The chief justice sadly went home, never again to return to Old Point Comfort.[12]

BACK ON THE BENCH, Taney divided his time between the Supreme Court's headquarters in Washington and his circuit assignments in Baltimore. Compared with the long distances the other justices had to travel (Field's circuit duties in California compelled him to travel an amazing 12,000 miles each year), Taney's trips between Washington and Baltimore were short and relatively undemanding. In Baltimore in 1862 and 1863, indictments for treason were brought against many who had attempted to aid the Confederate cause by burning bridges or otherwise attempting to thwart Union army operations. There were eventually some sixty cases listed on the docket of the circuit court in Baltimore. Some of the defendants were released on bail, while others languished in jail awaiting trial. Observers were anxious to see how Taney would deal with these defendants in his capacity as circuit judge. He sat with District Judge William F. Giles in many of these cases. If observers hoped for an early resolution of the cases, however, they were disappointed, for both Giles and Taney had apparently decided on a strategy of delay. They postponed the trials that were pending at the end of 1861 until the April term of 1862. When that term began, it was announced that Taney was "indisposed," and the trials were again postponed.

In the fall of 1862, the chief justice was so ill that he was unable to attend the November term of the circuit court, and the trials were again postponed. As Swisher observed: "It is clear that his sympathies were with the persons accused of treason, and that he felt unable to guarantee them a fair trial under the circumstances. He may therefore have welcomed an excuse for absenting himself from court, in so far as his absence provided a reason for further postponing the cases."[13] Taney was apprehensive, however, that Judge Giles would be pressured to hear the cases. He thought that some of the trials might result in death sentences and believed that a district judge, sitting alone, could not hear a case that raised the possibility of capital punishment. He wrote Giles, explaining that if both of them sat on a case that raised a new and doubtful question of criminal law, they could certify it to the Supreme Court. If the case was heard only by the district judge, however, there could be no certification. Giles shared Taney's sympathies and did his best to resist trials. Supreme Court historian Charles Fairman has commented on the "interesting contrast" between Taney's insistence in May 1861 that *Ex parte Merryman* should be decided without a moment's delay, and his later willingness to let serious criminal indictments go unresolved for months, even years.[14]

The U.S. district attorney in Baltimore, William Price, was aware of the dilatory tactics of the two federal judges. In September 1862, Price wrote Attorney General Bates in Washington: "You are aware from the constitution of the court [that] if the Chief Justice should be on the bench, the treason cases will have to be made very plain and conclusive if we expect a conviction."[15]

Price tried to have another judge assigned to the Baltimore court so the cases could be tried, but he was unsuccessful, and the prosecutions continued to stand in abeyance. By the spring of 1864, Taney was still dragging his heels. He wrote Justice Nelson in May of that year, saying that he doubted he would be able to go to Baltimore to hear the treason cases, but insisting that if he did, he would not cooperate in the prosecutions. He thought it would be impossible to give the defendants fair and impartial trials, for witnesses and jurors would be intimidated by the fear of arbitrary arrest if their testimony did not please the military authorities. Defiantly he told Nelson: "I will not place the judicial power in this humiliating position, nor consent thus to degrade and disgrace it, and if the district attorney presses the prosecutions I shall refuse to take them up."[16] It was an irony that may have been lost on the chief justice that in May of 1861 he had considered the civil courts of Maryland fully competent to try John Merryman and others charged with sabotaging the Union military effort, but in September 1862 he decided that it would be impossible to give accused traitors fair trials in Maryland.

Taney's resistance to administration policies did not stop with his opposition to the treason trials in Maryland. He continued to point with pride to his *Merryman* decision, insisting (against some criticism) that it struck a blow for civil liberties. He joined the dissenting judges in the *Prize Cases*, taking the position that Lincoln's declaration of a blockade had been unauthorized because Congress had not first declared war. In his capacity as circuit judge, he decided several cases against the blockade, upholding Judge Giles in one case and reversing him in another, using the latter occasion to denounce spying tactics used by the government.

In the summer of 1863, Taney took issue with a regulation issued by Treasury Secretary Salmon P. Chase. Aimed at Marylanders who were doing business with the Confederacy, the regulation forbade the shipment without a permit of goods from Baltimore to any point in Maryland south of the railroad between Washington and Annapolis. The chief justice condemned the regulation on two grounds: first, because the Treasury Department was usurping the legislative authority of Congress in attempting to prescribe rules for trade; and second, because not even Congress could interfere with trade within the bounds of a state, which was a matter over which the state has exclusive control. Taney wrote:

A civil war or any other war, does not enlarge the powers of the federal government over the states or the people beyond what the compact has given to it in time of war. A state of war does not annul the 10th article of the amendments to the Constitution, which declares that "the powers not delegated to the United States by the Constitution, nor prohibited by it to the states, are reserved to the states respectively or to the people."

Nor does a civil war or any other war absolve the judicial department from the duty of maintaining with an even and firm hand the rights and powers of the federal government, and of the states, and of the citizen, as they are written in the Constitution, which every judge is sworn to support.[17]

Taney's opinion was vigorously disputed by U.S. District Attorney Price, who wrote the assistant attorney general in Washington to express the belief that, if the matter was passed upon by the full Supreme Court, Taney's opinion would be reversed. But, like many other cases decided during the war, it never reached the high court.

Taney continued to protest government war measures. In both 1861 and 1862, Congress passed income tax laws, subjecting incomes to modest taxes for the support of the war effort. The bill signed by Lincoln on July 1, 1862, imposed taxes of 3 percent on incomes between $600 and $10,000, and 5 percent on incomes above $10,000. Secretary Chase interpreted the law as applying to the salaries of federal judges, despite the objection that this violated Article III, Section 1, of the Constitution, which provides (in relevant part): "The judges, both of the supreme and inferior courts, . . . shall, at stated times, receive for their services, a compensation, which shall not be diminished during their continuance in office." Chase did not believe that taxing the judges' salaries "diminished" them within the meaning of the constitutional provision and ordered that the prescribed amounts be deducted from their pay. Taney took the position that the provision was violated. He also believed that the deductions worked a hardship on the judges, since their pay was not high to begin with (associate justices received $6,000 per year and the chief justice $6,500) and the inflation caused by the war was making it more and more difficult for them to make ends meet.[18] But he could not force the issue into the courts, for it was

improper for any judge to preside over a case in which his own economic interest was at stake. Still, he was not inclined to suffer in silence. In February 1863,
he wrote Chase to protest the application of the income tax to judges' salaries:

> The Act in question, as you interpret it, diminishes the compensation
> of every Judge three percent; and if it can be diminished to that ex-
> tent by the name of a tax, it may, in the same way, be reduced from
> time to time at the pleasure of the Legislature.
>
> The Judiciary is one of the three great departments of the govern-
> ment created and established by the Constitution. Its duties and pow-
> ers are specifically set forth, and are of a character that requires it to
> be perfectly independent of the other Departments. And in order to
> place it beyond the reach, and above even the suspicion, of any such
> influence, the power to reduce their compensation is expressly with-
> held from Congress, and excepted from their powers of legislation. . . .
>
> Having been honored with the highest judicial station under the
> Constitution, I feel it to be more especially my duty to uphold and
> maintain the constitutional rights of that Department of the govern-
> ment; and not by any act or word of mine have it to be supposed that I
> acquiesce in a measure that displaces it from the independent position
> assigned to it by the statesmen who framed the Constitution. And in
> order to guard against any such inference, I present to you this re-
> spectful, but firm and decided, remonstrance against the authority you
> have exercised under this Act of Congress.[19]

Chase did not answer this letter, so a few weeks later Taney sent a copy to
Attorney General Bates with the message that a number of the judges of the
Supreme Court and other federal courts shared his view as to the unconstitutionality of Chase's order. Bates, however, followed Chase's lead and refused to
answer the letter. Frustrated, Taney had it entered on the records of the Supreme Court, to serve as notice of his protest.

Though Taney's disagreement with Chase over the income tax law was un-
questionably principled, it also had a personal dimension. Well into the ninth
decade of his life, the chief justice was in precarious financial condition, with
two daughters (one unmarried and the other a widow) who depended on him
for their support and no resources other than his salary to fall back on. In an-

other expression of his pro-Southern partisanship, Taney had some years earlier invested his modest life savings in securities issued by the State of Virginia. After it seceded, Virginia passed a law forbidding any payments to persons in loyal states. Wherever his heart might be, Taney was a legal resident of Maryland, and Maryland was still loyal to the Union. Knowing Taney's sympathies were with them, however, some Virginians suggested that an exception should be made in his case so that payments to him could continue. But he was not naive enough to believe that people would tolerate such an arrangement. In the North he would be condemned as a traitor; in the South he would be excoriated as a man who would not act on his convictions and resign his seat on the Supreme Court, as Justice Campbell had. Assuming the posture (as he often did) of an innocent victim of unfair criticism, he instructed his personal attorney and friend in Baltimore, David M. Perine, to refuse the Richmond offer. He wrote:

> I am sensible that this proposition has arisen from the personal kindness of friends in Richmond who know that public life has not enriched me. And I am very sure that it never entered their minds that any one would suspect them of unworthy motives in offering it or me in receiving it. But yet I think the offer was made inadvertently—and under the impulses of kind feelings which prevented them from looking at the interpretation, which baser minds might put upon the offer. Malignity would not fail to impute unworthy motives to them and to me—and in the present frenzied state of the public mind—men who do not know my Virginia friends or me, would be ready to believe it.[20]

TANEY'S QUARRELS WITH THE Lincoln administration were not limited to Salmon P. Chase's interpretation of the income tax law. Predictably, he found himself in sharp disagreement with a whole host of government measures, and growing ever more frustrated by his inability to express his opposition to them. Cases raising a wide range of issues related to the conduct of the war were bubbling up through the federal courts in various parts of the country, but it took time for district and circuit judges to express themselves on the issues, and with every month that passed it seemed increasingly unlikely that the issues would reach the Supreme Court in time for Taney to rule on them. More and more, the old judge was confined to his Washington home, too feeble to make the short trip to the Capitol to hear arguments in the Court. At home, he spent much of his time in his bed, smoking cigars and brooding about the war. When he was able to take up his pen, he wrote out his thoughts on the great constitutional issues of the war, to be used as judicial opinions if and when the issues should come before him.[21] In his writings he took strong positions, and they were invariably contrary to the actions taken by Lincoln and his administration. He was apparently so sure of his opinions that he did not feel it necessary to confer with the other judges or to hear arguments from attorneys before reaching his conclusions. Litigants whose cases came before the Supreme Court during the Civil War were entitled (as are litigants in any other time) to plead their cases before judges who had not already decided key issues against them. Taney's practice of writing out constitutional opinions in cases that had not yet come before him raises the alarming specter of a judge whose mind had already been made up and who was not even trying to maintain the appearance that it was open.

In 1862, Congress began to experiment with innovative measures for financing the war, including the income tax, large bond issues, and the issuance of "greenbacks" (treasury notes that were not backed by either gold or silver but that were declared to be "legal tender" for the payment of all debts, public and private). The law requiring that greenbacks be accepted in payment of debts was known as the Legal Tender Act, and it raised a storm of controversy throughout the country.[22] Taney, predictably, believed that the measure was unconstitutional. He wrote out an opinion in which he argued that Congress's power to coin money did not include the power to issue paper money, and that the power to borrow did not include the power to force irredeemable currency on private creditors. "I am therefore of the opinion that the law declaring these Notes a legal tender is unconstitutional and void."[23]

In 1862 and again in 1863, Congress passed conscription acts, requiring eligible men to serve in the armed forces of the United States, but granting certain exceptions (notably for men who could pay for substitutes). The *New York Times* called the 1863 act "the grandest pledge yet given that our Government means to prevail and will prevail."[24] Taney did not share the *Times*'s enthusiasm for conscription. At home, he wrote out a document titled "Thoughts on the Conscription Law of the U. States," in which he argued that the law was unconstitutional because it violated the separation of state and federal govern-ments. If the federal government could force members of the state militias to serve in its armies, Taney asserted, it could destroy the militias. The federal power might even extend to the conscription of the elected civil officers of the states, thus bringing the state governments to a practical halt. Since Taney be-lieved that the Constitution gave the federal government no power to do this, he concluded that the conscription law was unconstitutional and that it con-ferred "no power on the persons appointed to execute it."[25]

As with his objections to Secretary Chase's interpretation of the income tax law, Taney's opposition to conscription had a personal dimension. He had sons-in-law and grandsons who were potentially subject to conscription. (One of his sons-in-law, Richard T. Allison, had already been commissioned a major in the Confederate army.)[26] He also had a black "body servant" named Madi-son Franklin, who was subject to the federal law. According to Taney's friend and first biographer, Samuel Tyler, Madison Franklin actually received a con-scription notice. Tyler's brother was the Taney family physician and knew that Franklin had a heart condition that "wholly disqualified him for the duties of a soldier." But when the physician offered to write to the proper officer and have Franklin excused, the chief justice would have none of it. As Tyler remembered (echoing his old friend's chronic sense of being abused): "The Chief Justice said he would rather buy a substitute, and did pay one hundred dollars for a substitute, while the Government of the United States was, in violation of the Constitution, withholding three per cent. of his salary."[27]

If Taney felt it was improper for a man, white or black, to be conscripted to fight for the Union, he apparently had no qualms about young men fighting for the Confederacy. When his wife's grandnephew, McHenry Howard, came to him to say good-bye before starting off to enlist in the Confederate Army, Taney expressed approval for the youth's decision. Howard was the grandson of John Eager Howard, a Maryland patriot who had fought bravely in the Revolution-ary War. Taney told the twenty-two-year-old who was about to become a Con-federate soldier: "The circumstances under which you are going are not unlike those under which your grandfather went into the Revolutionary War."[28]

Lincoln's Emancipation Proclamation was another measure that agitated Taney. The Proclamation was admittedly unprecedented, and it was roundly condemned not only as an unconstitutional usurpation of power by the execu-tive but also as an unconscionable attack on the property rights of slaveholders. No copy of Taney's private opinion condemning the Emancipation Proclamation seems to exist, but Swisher believed that he may have worked out an opinion on this subject, as he did on others.[29]

Taney's disaffection with the Lincoln administration had a personal as well as an official flavor, for he complained even about things that the president clearly had no control over, attributing them to executive overreaching. He complained in a letter to David Perine, who lived outside Baltimore, that Perine probably could not receive the letters Taney sent him because the administration had barricaded the streets in Baltimore.[30] He was an avid reader of reviews, journals, and magazines and complained to his son-in-law J. Mason Campbell when he had trouble receiving publications from outside the United States, accusing the administration of banning newspapers and inspecting the mail:

> My newspaper reading is indeed a good deal curtailed—for although it may be difficult to say what are the boundaries of the President's power at this day, or whether it has any boundaries, I am not willing to admit that he has a *right* to prescribe what news-papers I shall read—although I know from experience that he has the *power* to prescribe what I shall not read.
>
> I fear the detectives will think themselves hardly paid for their trouble by its contents when they have opened and read & resealed this letter.[31]

In another letter to Campbell, he allowed that he might get along without newspapers, but not without cigars. "You know I can smoke none but Schumacher's Principes," he told Campbell in September 1861, "and my stock is getting low—and will hardly last the week."[32] Three years later, he told his grandson that he had tried to give up cigars in favor of a pipe, but abandoned the attempt because "all the pipe tobacco will now be of northern growth—and very unpalatable to one who is accustomed to Spanish cigars."[33]

Taney's personal relations with Lincoln and his cabinet were proper but distant. The chief justice and the president had little occasion to meet face to face, and Taney did not encourage any contact that was not necessary. Edward Bates, whose duties as attorney general required him to maintain good relations with all of the federal judges, visited the Court from time to time, sometimes to inquire into the upcoming docket, sometimes to listen to attorneys argue their cases. Bates was uniformly polite and deferential, not only because he was a thorough gentleman but also because he realized that the judges held great power and, with an adverse decision in an important case, could thwart all of the efforts of the cabinet, the army, and the navy to bring the war to a conclusion. Bates made his first personal call on the justices in November 1861, and he reported in his diary that he had "an agreeable talk" with Justice Wayne and "a conversation much more pleasant than I expected" with the chief justice.[34] Taney was, like Bates, a gentleman—albeit a "Southern" gentleman—and coolly polite no matter what personal resentments were stirring inside him.

It was the custom of the Supreme Court justices to call on the president at the beginning of each year, but when their first opportunity to call on Lincoln arrived on January 1, 1862, Taney declined to accompany his colleagues. He wrote Justice Wayne the day before the visit to explain why he would not go with the other judges. "I expect some friends to-morrow," he said blandly, "and as there is no established Etiquette which requires the court to wait on the President on the 1st of January, as a matter of official courtesy, I am sure my Brethren will excuse me for not joining them tomorrow."[35]

Taney was rigorously correct in his relations with the other justices. He could also be warm when he felt a personal attachment to one of his colleagues, or even when he did not, for he knew from long experience that collegiality was essential to the smooth operation of a multijudge tribunal, and that a jurist who wished his views to prevail had to forge alliances.

Despite all of this, however, he found it increasingly difficult as the war proceeded to carry out his official duties. He had complained for so many years of his chronic illnesses and "weak constitution" that it was difficult to recognize real disabilities when they came on him. But as 1862 melted into 1863, it became evident that the chief justice was approaching the end of his career. He was often unable to come to the Capitol and had to rely on the senior associate justice, James Wayne of Georgia, to preside in his absence. In 1864, Taney was absent more often than he was present.

EDWARD BATES WAS PLEASED to find Taney on the bench on April 12, 1864, and wrote in his diary that the chief justice seemed "more cheerful and active" than he had been recently. All of the judges were present that day except Grier, who was sick at home. But there were dispiriting signs among those who were present. "Taney, Wayne, Catron, and Grier, are evidently failing," Bates noted, "being obviously, less active in mind and body, than at the last term." Old age was implicated in the decline of all four of these judges, for Grier was seventy, Wayne seventy-four, and Catron approaching eighty. Taney, at eighty-seven, exceeded all of the others in age—though not in seniority, for Wayne had begun his service on the Court a year and two months before the chief justice (Wayne was, in fact, the only surviving justice who had served with the venerated Chief Justice John Marshall). Bates thought that all four of the judges would "gladly resign" if the government would only provide them with pensions. There was a bill then pending in Congress to do just that (Bates supported it strongly), but the lawmakers had not yet taken any action on it. "But most of them, if not all," Bates wrote in his diary, "cannot afford to resign, having no support but their salaries." Bates then added this note to his diary entry: "I might perhaps, as well have said 5, as 4; for Mr. Justice Nelson shews [sic] as plainly as the other 4 signs of decay. He walks with a firmer step it is true, but I do not see that his *mind* stands more erect than theirs, or moves onward with a steadier gait."[36] Nelson was then seventy-one years old and beginning his twentieth year on the Court.

While at least half of the Supreme Court was growing feeble, observers naturally focused most of their attention on Taney, for he was Lincoln's chief judicial antagonist, and it was generally supposed that he would be the first to leave the Court. The wife of Union major general (later U.S. senator) John A. Logan was a long-time Washington resident with a keen eye for the comings and goings in the city. Years later, she wrote of Taney's odd appearance during this period:

> There was no sadder figure to be seen in Washington during the years of the Civil War than that of the aged Chief Justice. His form was bent by the weight of years, and his thin, nervous, and deeply-furrowed face was shaded by long, gray locks, and lighted up by large, melancholy eyes that looked wearily out from under shaggy brows, which gave him a weird, wizard-like expression. He had outlived his epoch, and was shunned and hated by the men of the new time of storm and struggle for the principles of freedom and nationality.[37]

Though more and more a shut-in, Taney still liked to have attention focused on him. In 1862 he had asked each of his fellow judges to call on him before they left Washington at the end of the Court's term. At his home on Indiana Avenue, he told them that he had a presentiment that he would die soon and would not see them again. He managed to come back in 1863 but continued to have forebodings of imminent death. He wrote David Perine in that year that he hoped to linger until the next term of the Court, when Lincoln's newest appointee, Stephen J. Field, would join as the tenth justice. But he could not help complaining: "Very different however that Court will now be from the Court as I have heretofore known it. Nor do I see any ground for hope that it will ever again be restored to the authority and rank which the Constitution intended to confer upon it. The supremacy of the military power over the civil, seems to be established—and the public mind has acquiesced in it & sanctioned it. We can pray for better times—and submit with resignation to the chastisements which it may please God to inflict upon us."[38]

For years there had been rumors that Taney was about to leave the Court. Even the deferential Edward Bates had speculated as early as 1859 about who would become the chief justice "if Taney would only die out of the way."[39] So long as James Buchanan was president and could name Taney's successor, the chief justice's detractors had hoped that he would stay on, for a younger successor who shared Taney's views on the great constitutional issues of the day would, in their estimation, be disastrous. And Taney stayed on to administer Lincoln's oath of office, to sternly rebuke him in *Merryman*, and to dissent from the majority opinion in the *Prize Cases*. Now Taney's detractors were wondering how much longer he would continue to linger. In a frank (and uncharitable) comment, Ohio's abolitionist senator Benjamin Wade said: "I prayed with earnestness for the life of Taney to be prolonged through Buchanan's Administration, and by God I[']m a little afraid I have overdone the matter."[40]

Taney grew weaker in the summer of 1864. He had been suffering for a long time from an intestinal disease, and it was now causing him severe pain. The two daughters who lived with him called in the doctors, who agreed that the end was near. While the chief justice was lying on his bed, one of the doctors read to him from the newspapers. The people of Maryland were about to vote on a new constitution, the papers said. The new constitution, which had been adopted on September 6 by a convention meeting in Annapolis, proposed that slavery be abolished in Maryland. The chief justice must have been dazed.

Hearing the same news, Lincoln was deeply satisfied. The presidential election was fast approaching. The president was cautiously optimistic about his chances for reelection, and Maryland's move to abolish slavery cheered him. "I had rather have Maryland upon that issue," he told newspaper reporter Noah Brooks, "than have a State twice its size upon the Presidential issue; it cleans up a piece of ground."[41] The new Maryland constitution also proposed an oath of allegiance to the United States, much like one Lincoln had proposed for secessionist states. Taney's doctor asked the old judge if a man might properly take the oath if it violated his conscience. Taney deplored the suggestion, insisting that there must be no compromise of "principles."[42]

Taney received the last rites of the Catholic Church, to which he had been faithful all his life, and spoke quietly with his daughters and a few intimate friends. Then, about ten o'clock in the evening on October 12, 1864, he died.[43] At 7:13 the following morning, Secretary of War Stanton telegraphed Salmon P. Chase (no longer a member of the president's cabinet): "Chief Justice Taney died last night."[44]

Attorney General Bates noted Taney's passing in his diary, commenting that the chief justice "was a man of great and varied talents; a model of a presiding officer; and the last specimen within my knowledge, of a graceful and polished old fashioned gentleman." Bates was in a generous mood when he recalled the many high offices—attorney general of Maryland, secretary of the treasury, and attorney general and chief justice of the United States—that Taney had filled, "generally, with applause." But he admitted that the "lustre of his fame, as a lawyer and judge, is for the present, dimmed by the bitterness of party feeling arising out of his unfortunate judgment in the Dred Scott case." Bates thought that decision "was a great error; but it ought not and will not, for long, tarnish his otherwise well earned fame."[45]

The day after Taney's death, the voters of Maryland gave final approval to the new state constitution abolishing slavery. Virtually overnight, an institution integrally tied up with the history and traditions of Maryland, and one that Taney had defended throughout his judicial career, vanished from his native state. In New York, the diarist George Templeton Strong noted the irony of the almost simultaneous passing of the old chief justice and the end of slavery in Maryland, writing that "two ancient abuses and evils were perishing together."[46]

On Friday, October 14, Taney's death was discussed in the president's cabinet. Secretary of State Seward felt it was his duty to attend the funeral services scheduled for Saturday in Taney's Washington home, but he did not feel he should go on to the church services planned for Frederick, Maryland, where Taney lived early in his legal career. Seward thought that Lincoln should also go to the Taney house. Bates thought it was his duty, and a proper courtesy, to go with the remains to Frederick. Lincoln asked Welles for his opinion. The secretary of the navy agreed that Seward and Lincoln should go to the house. He thought it best, however, that the president let every cabinet member decide for himself what he wished to do. Welles himself "felt little inclined to participate" in the obsequies, later writing in his diary: "I have never called upon him living, and while his position and office were to be respected, I had no honors for the deceased beyond those that were public. That he had many good qualities and possessed ability, I do not doubt; that he rendered service in Jackson's administration is true, and during most of his judicial life he was upright and just. But the course pursued in the Dred Scott case and all the attending circumstances forfeited respect for him as a man or a judge."[47]

Lincoln had made some changes in the cabinet since his first appointments. Edwin Stanton had replaced Simon Cameron as secretary of war, William P. Fessenden of Maine had taken over the Treasury Department from Salmon P. Chase, former governor William Dennison of Ohio had succeeded Montgomery Blair as postmaster general, and John P. Usher of Indiana had replaced Caleb B. Smith as secretary of the interior. Usher and Fessenden told the president they did not intend to go to Taney's funeral. Dennison said he would go to the funeral in Washington, at the Taney house, but not to the service in Frederick. On the morning of Saturday, October 15, Seward, Bates, and Dennison went to the Taney home by carriage. Lincoln arrived at the same destination in a separate carriage. Arrangements for the funeral had been made by Lincoln's friend from Illinois Ward Hill Lamon, who was the United States marshal in Washington and charged with the duty of arranging judicial ceremonies. After a short service, the coffin was carried out of the house by six pallbearers assisted by black servants. The pallbearers included Taney's close friends Samuel Tyler and James M. Carlisle (the latter one of the losing attorneys in the historic *Prize Cases*). A modest procession made its way to the Washington depot of the Baltimore and Ohio Railroad, which had provided two cars to take the body and the mourners from the capital city to Frederick. The procession was led by a Catholic priest, followed by one of Taney's physicians, his daughters, and his son-in-law J. Mason Campbell. Lincoln took a modest position well back in the procession, followed by Seward, Bates, and Dennison.[48]

From the train station, the president returned to the White House and Seward and Dennison to their offices. Bates, as he had intended, went all the way to Frederick, where he joined other mourners in the Catholic church and stood by while the chief justice's body was buried in the churchyard. In the evening, he returned on the train to Washington.[49]

8   A New Chief

SALMON P. CHASE WAS IN Covington, Kentucky, on the day that Taney died, speaking in support of Lincoln's bid for reelection.[1] Chase had no real affection for the president, despite the nearly three and a half years the two men had spent working together. Lincoln had depended heavily on Chase's efforts to bridge the frightening gap between military expenditures and revenues, but the men had never developed a warm relationship, or anything that approached mutual trust.

Chase's decision to take to the campaign trail in the fall of 1864 was, like so many of his actions, a political calculation. If he had never been very impressed by Lincoln's performance as president, he was even less enthusiastic about George B. McClellan, who was hoping to replace him. He had no strong antipathy to the Democratic Party, which had nominated McClellan as its presidential candidate at their convention in Chicago, for he had once been a Democrat himself, and he would become one again in a few years. For now, however, he was a Republican, and he realized that his political fortunes were tied to the Republican candidate. What's more, he disagreed on some fundamental points with the Democratic platform, which condemned government efforts to put down the Southern insurrection as "four years of failure" and demanded an immediate cessation of hostilities, with "the rights of the States unimpaired" (that is, the preservation of slavery). Chase was willing to compromise on some issues, but not on slavery, for which he had an unwavering hatred.

Chase had left Lincoln's cabinet the previous July in a dispute over the control of Treasury Department appointments in New York, but Lincoln was now running for reelection, and Chase rightly calculated that he would probably be reelected. So he decided to take to the hustings, in the words of his biographer, John Niven, "to place the President under obligation."[2] He toured his home state of Ohio, then traveled through Michigan, Missouri, Kentucky, and Pennsylvania, speaking before crowds large and small. Hearing that Roger Taney had at long last died, he finished up his speaking tour and returned to Washington, where Lincoln would soon be naming a new chief justice.

Everybody in official Washington knew that Chase coveted Taney's position, for he had not been shy about dropping hints. He would much rather have been president, as he was convinced that he was better qualified to occupy the chief executive's chair than any man in the nation in 1864—certainly better qualified than the man who now occupied it. But recent military victories led by Major General Philip Sheridan in the Shenandoah Valley, and Major General William T. Sherman's sensational capture of Atlanta on September 2, had strengthened the voters' confidence that the president deserved a second term. Chase had been one of the last to give up hope that the Republicans would turn their backs on Lincoln, for if they did, he believed that they might ask him to lead their ticket. Even after Lincoln's renomination at the Republican convention (renamed the National Union Convention) in June, he thought that a third party might be formed to nominate him. Chase was a man of exceptional intelligence and even more exceptional ambition; if there were limits to his intelligence, there were none to his ambition (or so his detractors claimed).

The death of Taney had been expected for so long that Lincoln had naturally assumed he would be called on to pick his successor. He had talked about the possibility with some of his close associates, discussed the names of likely nominees, and given some thought to their qualifications. Attorney General Bates had broached the subject with him, telling him of his own interest in the chief justiceship, and Chase had done the same. Both were highly qualified lawyers with distinguished careers in public service. Bates, in particular, was noted for his even, sober disposition—what some people might call a "judicial temperament"—and as a member of the cabinet he had always given the president his best. But Bates was not young (he had just turned seventy-one), and he would soon be ready for retirement. Chase was younger (he would turn fifty-seven the following January) and more vigorous, but he had never demonstrated any loyalty to the president. Chase had a host of friends in and out of the government, but he also had many enemies.

In the first days following Taney's death, Lincoln was barraged with recommendations. Bates even sent him a letter reaffirming his own interest in the appointment. "I will only add that I could not desire to close my public life more honorably," Bates wrote, "than by a brief term of service in that eminent position. I would not if I could desire to occupy that place more than two or three years, and so that it would still be within your disposal during your second term. In fact, I desire it chiefly—almost wholly—as the crowning, retiring honor of my life."[3]

Chase did not write the president to solicit the appointment, but he did not have to, for his political associates and admirers were already doing that for him. The day after Taney's death, Lincoln's personal secretary John Hay recorded in his diary that the old chief justice was gone, and then he wrote: "Already (before his poor old clay is cold) they are beginning to canvass vigorously for his successor. Chase men say the place is promised to their *magnifico*. . . . I talked with the President one moment. He says he does not think he will make the appointment immediately. He will be, he says, rather 'shut pan' in the matter at present."[4]

Lincoln had good reason to keep his counsel. The fall elections were approaching, and his reelection was by no means a sure thing. The nomination of a new chief justice would have political ramifications, and whatever name he advanced might roil the political waters unnecessarily. Although Chase had a host of supporters, it was not certain that Lincoln would choose him, for even if the president had previously assured Chase that he would be chosen, much had happened since then. Chase had left the cabinet under unpleasant circumstances, and in the interim he had done all he could to wrest the Republican nomination away from Lincoln.

SALMON PORTLAND CHASE WAS an interesting man with enough interesting characteristics to keep the gossipy tongues of Washington wagging throughout the war years. Born in New Hampshire in 1808, he was the eighth child in a large family from old New England stock, better educated than most of their neighbors but without any substantial wealth. He owed his distinctive first name to the family's tradition of giving its sons memorable (some might say peculiar) first names: one of his uncles was also named Salmon Chase, another uncle was Philander Chase, and his own father was Ithamar Chase. Salmon Portland Chase himself detested his name and as a young man toyed with the idea of changing it to Spencer de Cheyce or Spencer Payne Cheyce.[5] But he stuck with the "awkward, *fishy*" designation and eventually made it famous.

When Salmon was nine years old, his father died and his widowed mother sent him to live and study with his uncle Philander, who had recently become the Episcopal bishop of Ohio. With the bishop acting as his surrogate father, Chase studied at an Ohio boys' school and then at the College of Cincinnati, of which his uncle was president. When Bishop Chase left for England to secure funding for a new college in Ohio (to be called Kenyon College), Salmon returned to New Hampshire and enrolled at Dartmouth. After graduating with a Phi Beta Kappa key, he moved to Washington, D.C., where he taught school and studied law with William Wirt, one of the capital's most distinguished attorneys.

Born in Maryland, Wirt had practiced law in Virginia and the District of Columbia and represented the prosecution in the famous conspiracy trial of Aaron Burr before serving as attorney general of the United States under Presidents James Monroe and John Quincy Adams. Over the course of his long career, Wirt argued more than 170 cases in the Supreme Court. Though advanced in years, he was still attorney general and still an important personage in Washington when Chase read law in his office between 1827 and 1829.

Chase passed the bar in 1829 in Washington and then moved to Cincinnati, where he began his life as a practicing lawyer. Ambitious to build a successful practice, he studied industriously, wrote articles for literary journals, and worked hard to hone his speaking style (he had a lisp that he was eventually able to mask but not entirely eliminate). He represented local businessmen and avoided involvement in politics until 1836, when a dramatic event thrust him into the controversies of the times. A political activist named James G. Birney had recently come to Cincinnati and begun to publish the *Philanthropist*, a weekly newspaper dedicated to the peaceful abolition of slavery. Located across the Ohio River from Covington, Kentucky, Cincinnati depended for much of its thriving trade on commodities produced by slave labor, and local attitudes toward the peculiar institution were volatile. Birney himself had been a slave owner in Alabama and Kentucky before he converted to the abolitionist cause, and his Cincinnati newspaper aroused strong emotions.

Outraged by the abolitionist journal in their midst, a group of Cincinnatians broke into Birney's printing shop, ransacked the building, and tossed his printing press into the river. Hearing that the mob intended to tar and feather Birney and run him out of town, Chase went to the hotel where he lived and planted himself firmly in the front door, defying the mob to pass. He was a fine figure of a man, six feet, two inches tall, with broad shoulders, a massive head, and a handsome face. Impressed by Chase's calm courage, the mob backed away. Reports of the confrontation quickly spread through Cincinnati, earning Chase a justified reputation for bravery and effecting a revolution in his own thinking. He was already disposed by his religious convictions to regard slavery with disgust. Now he became convinced that somebody should oppose the slaveholders, and that he was the best man to do so.

In the years to come, Chase took the cases of free blacks and fugitive slaves who were pursued into Ohio from Kentucky plantations. Convinced that slavery offended God's law, he began to develop innovative legal theories under which Ohio courts could resist the "slave catchers" who came over the river from Covington in search of "runaways." He researched English and American legal precedents, studied the history of the Northwest Ordinance of 1787 (which formed the basis for the law of Ohio and other northwestern states), and became convinced that slavery was not supported by natural law. According to Chase's theory, unless slavery was upheld by the positive provisions of "municipal law" (that is, the statutes or ordinances of a state), it could not be sustained. Thus when a person held in slavery in one of the Southern states was brought into a free state, he or she became free, because there was no municipal law to hold him or her in bondage. It was an important legal theory, and one that would gain some acceptance in the years ahead. Chase took several high-profile cases into the federal courts in Cincinnati, where he established important legal precedents. His reputation began to spread to neighboring states, and even to the nation's capital, where he was referred to as the "Attorney General for Runaway Slaves."

In 1842 Chase became the attorney for a farmer named John Van Zandt, who was charged in the United States Circuit Court in Cincinnati with harboring escaped slaves in violation of the Fugitive Slave Law passed by Congress in 1793.[6] Van Zandt, a former Kentuckian who had moved to Ohio because of his opposition to slavery, had been driving his wagon at night along a road north of Cincinnati when he encountered a party of nine blacks. He stopped his wagon and allowed them to get in, then proceeded on his way, but two white men soon began to pursue the wagon. The blacks were slaves who had recently escaped from their master, a Kentuckian named Wharton Jones, and Jones had hired the two men to catch them and bring them back. Van Zandt tried to elude the pursuers, but they soon caught up with his wagon, seized eight of the black passengers (one was able to escape), and carried them back to slavery in Kentucky. A complicated series of legal procedures then ensued in Ohio, some prosecuted in state court and others in the U.S. Circuit Court, where Supreme Court Justice John McLean presided as circuit judge and Humphrey H. Leavitt as district judge.

With the cooperation of an attorney named Thomas Morris, Chase represented Van Zandt in a jury trial presided over by McLean and Leavitt. After the verdict went against his client, Chase persuaded McLean and Leavitt to certify important questions of law to the Supreme Court in Washington. By that time the case had attracted so much notice that former governor William H. Seward of New York (like Chase, a bitter opponent of slavery) had offered to help. Chase and Seward worked together in preparing Van Zandt's appeal, but the crowded condition of the high court's calendar and the apparent reluctance of some of the justices to take up the case resulted in several postponements. Finally, Seward informed Chase that if the case was to be considered at all it would have to be submitted on written arguments, without any oral presentation. So the Ohioan set about the laborious task of crafting a 108-page brief in which he advanced a series of groundbreaking arguments against slavery and the Fugitive Slave Law.

Chase argued that slavery was inconsistent with the Declaration of Independence's promise that "all men are created equal"; that the Fugitive Slave Act violated provisions of the Bill of Rights, including the Fifth Amendment's guarantee that "No person shall . . . be deprived of life, liberty, or property, without due process of law"; and that Congress had no power under the Constitution to pass the Fugitive Slave Act. Article IV, Section 2, provides (in relevant part): "No person held to service or labor in one state, under the laws thereof, escaping into another, shall, in consequence of any law or regulation therein, be discharged from such service or labor, but shall be delivered up on claim of the party to whom such service or labor may be due." Chase argued that this provision (the Fugitive Slave Clause) was a statement of policy, requiring states to surrender fugitive slaves as a matter of comity but not as a judicially enforceable obligation. It was not one of Congress's "enumerated powers," and it did not give the national legislature any authority to set up a statutory procedure for the return of fugitive slaves.

The case of *Jones v. Van Zandt* was submitted to the Supreme Court in February 1847 and decided the following month. In an opinion by Associate Justice Levi Woodbury of New Hampshire, the Court denied all of Chase's arguments. Woodbury said that the Fugitive Slave Clause was "one of [the] sacred compromises" upon which the Constitution rested, and that, whatever judges might think about the morality of slavery, they were bound to uphold the constitutional provisions that sustained it.[7] The unanimous decision was supported by all of the justices then serving, including Justice McLean and Chief Justice Taney.

Chase lost this high-profile case in the Supreme Court, but he won it in the court of public opinion, for his argument caught the attention of lawyers and judges all over the country, and began to raise hopes in opponents of slavery that effective legal arguments against the hated institution would one day succeed. His legal brief also helped inspire the most powerful literary argument ever advanced against slavery, the best-selling novel *Uncle Tom's Cabin*. The novel's author, Harriet Beecher Stowe, was living in Cincinnati while the Van Zandt case was wending its way through the courts, and she used Van Zandt himself as the inspiration for her fictional John Van Trompe, a courageous conductor on the Underground Railroad who helped the runaway slave Eliza Harris escape through Ohio into Canada. After its publication in the early 1850s, *Uncle Tom's Cabin* raised the level of antislavery fervor throughout the United States.

The Van Zandt case also raised Chase's political profile and encouraged him to make a new effort to win elective office. He had begun his political life as a Whig, winning election to the Cincinnati city council in 1840. But he lost his office the following year because of his strong temperance views and decided to cast his lot with the Liberty Party, an association of antislavery activists that swirled around the abolitionist publisher James G. Birney. In 1848 Chase became one of the organizers of the new Free Soil Party, which persuaded former president Martin Van Buren to carry its banner into the presidential campaign that year. The Free Soil Party had no intention of interfering with slavery in any of the states, for its leaders recognized that the regulation of slavery within states was a matter that the Constitution reserved to the states. But they opposed slavery in any place where Congress had the power to legislate on the question, such as the District of Columbia (where slavery was still open and notorious) and the western territories.

In late 1848, flush with the fame he had won in the case of *Jones v. Van Zandt,* Chase made a successful run for one of Ohio's seats in the United States Senate. In Washington, Chase aligned himself with the Democrats, but he bitterly opposed the efforts of Democratic senator Stephen A. Douglas of Illinois to finesse the controversy over the expansion of slavery by advancing the doctrine of popular sovereignty. Chase believed that Douglas's Kansas-Nebraska Act broke the "sacred pledge" made to the nation when the Missouri Compromise was adopted in 1820. Then, Congress had banned all slavery north of latitude 36° 30′. Now Douglas argued that slavery should be allowed wherever a majority of voters (all of whom, of course, were white and male) could be persuaded to allow it, even in territory north of 36° 30′. When Douglas and his supporters succeeded in passing the Kansas-Nebraska Act in 1854, Chase told his Massachusetts Senate colleague Charles Sumner: "They celebrate a present victory, but the echoes they awake will never rest until slavery itself will die."[8]

Chase was a candidate for governor of Ohio in 1855, this time running as a Republican (though he preferred to call himself a Democratic-Republican) and basing his campaign in large part on opposition to the Kansas-Nebraska Act. His inauguration in 1856 was a milestone, for it was the first time a major state had elected a Republican governor. He used his new platform to launch his first serious bid for a presidential nomination. He was one of the leading contenders for the nomination at the Republican national convention, held that year in Philadelphia; but Ohio's delegation was deeply divided, with some supporting Chase, others the charismatic "Pathfinder" John C. Frémont, and yet others Ohio's perennial presidential aspirant, Justice John McLean of the Supreme Court. Chase's inability to rally his own state's delegates to his candidacy revealed a weakness that would plague him for the rest of his political life: while he always had enthusiastic supporters, he also had equally passionate enemies. Chase was deeply disappointed when Frémont received the Republican nomination and grumbled that the delegates had ignored better men (like him) who "personified the great real issue before the country." McLean was also bitter, but he blamed his defeat on Chase. "Chase is the most unprincipled man politically that I have ever known," the Supreme Court justice declared. "He is selfish beyond any other man."[9]

Chase was reelected to a second term as governor of Ohio in 1857. In 1858, he went to Illinois to campaign for the little-known Springfield lawyer who was seeking to unseat Senator Douglas. Chase shared Lincoln's belief that slavery was a moral issue, and not merely a political one (as Douglas conceived it), and he shared Lincoln's opposition to the Kansas-Nebraska Act. Like Lincoln, he was profoundly disturbed by the Supreme Court's decision in the *Dred Scott* case. He agreed with Lincoln that the issue of slavery in the states was to be decided within those states. Unlike Lincoln, however, he was not willing to concede that the Fugitive Slave Law was constitutional, and he still held out hope that it could be repealed. Chase took to the campaign trail for Lincoln in Illinois, speaking to thousands in Chicago, Galena, Warren, Rockford, and Mendota. In the end, Lincoln lost the senate race to Douglas, but he did not forget the help that Chase had given him.

The Ohio legislature elected the out-going governor Chase to a second U.S. Senate term early in 1860. But that election did not calm his presidential aspirations. Carl Schurz was a prominent Wisconsin Republican who was supporting William H. Seward's bid for the Republican nomination for president that year. Schurz visited Chase at his home in Columbus, Ohio, and found that he had a serious case of "presidential fever." He seemed genuinely hurt by the notion that anyone would prefer Seward (or any other candidate) to himself. Schurz breakfasted with the governor and his beautiful teenage daughter, Kate, who had become a political adviser and hostess for her thrice-widowed father. Kate "had something imperial in the pose of the head," Schurz later wrote, "and all her movements possessed an exquisite natural charm." The conversation inevitably turned to politics. Chase honestly believed, as Schurz put it, "that he owed it to the country and that the country owed it to him that he should be President." Schurz admired Chase but thought his consuming presidential ambitions were "a pathetic spectacle."[10]

Seward and Chase were the two leading candidates for the Republican presidential nomination in 1860, but there were some others as well, "favorite son" candidates like Pennsylvania's Senator Simon Cameron; Missouri's old-line Whig, former congressman Edward Bates; and Illinois's unsuccessful Senate candidate from 1858, Abraham Lincoln. All of these men were opponents of slavery, though they differed on some other issues. Lincoln's convention manager was the affable circuit judge (later Supreme Court justice) David Davis of Bloomington. For his part, Chase did next to nothing to prepare for the balloting, for he was convinced that the fact that he was "the best man" for the presidency would be apparent to all and would automatically put him over the top. But his enemies again surfaced in the Ohio delegation, and his support steadily eroded. It took three ballots to give the nomination to Lincoln. Chase "felt betrayal, indignation, and hurt."[11] But he did not yet feel defeated. He wrote Lincoln to congratulate him on his victory, and then methodically made plans for his own political future.

Chase had not yet begun his new term as senator from Ohio when Lincoln invited him to Springfield, Illinois, in late December 1860. When Chase arrived in Springfield, the president-elect walked to the hotel where Chase was staying and quickly got down to business. "I have done with you," he said, "what I would not perhaps have ventured to do with any other man in the country—sent for you to ask you whether you will accept the appointment of Secretary of the Treasury, without, however, being exactly prepared to offer it to you." The problem, Lincoln explained, was getting support for the nomination in Pennsylvania, where Simon Cameron also expected a high appointment, possibly the Treasury post. Many Republicans thought Cameron unworthy of a cabinet post, but he was an important politician and had done much to help Lincoln win the election. Chase was disappointed, for he thought he was entitled to the highest post in the cabinet, which was secretary of state, but that had already been offered to Seward. Chase and Lincoln continued their discussions in Lincoln's law office, and on Sunday they attended church together. Chase left Springfield on Monday, promising to consider the post of secretary of the treasury "under the advice of friends." After Chase had left, Lincoln wrote Illinois senator Lyman Trumbull that he had decided that Chase's appointment was "not only highly proper, but a *necessity*."[12] On his way back to Ohio, Chase came to the same conclusion.

As finally constituted, Lincoln's cabinet was made up of Seward as secretary of state, Chase as secretary of the treasury, Cameron as secretary of war, Bates as attorney general, Gideon Welles as secretary of the navy, Montgomery Blair as postmaster general, and Caleb Smith as secretary of the interior. Each of these men brought special talents to the cabinet, and Lincoln came to rely on all of them, not only for the management of their own departments but also for advice about diplomatic affairs, military strategies, and financial policies.

Although Chase brought no special experience in financial affairs to the Treasury Department, he had counted some small banks among his clients when he was practicing law in Cincinnati in the 1830s and 1840s. His Democratic Party background was revealed in his deep-seated antipathy to large banks, for a fierce opposition to the Bank of the United States was one of the tenets of Andrew Jackson's political creed—and this antipathy went hand in glove with a hard-money philosophy. Chase believed that bank notes were instruments with which the financial elites oppressed the poor. The only "real money" was specie (gold or silver, or gold or silver certificates backed up by reserves of those metals). The paper money in general circulation before 1860 consisted of notes issued by state banks, generally smaller financial institutions chartered and regulated by the states and not subject to federal control. Chase's hard-money convictions made it difficult for him to deal with the enormous fiscal requirements of the war, but it was a difficulty that many other politicians of the time shared.

When Chase began his work in the Treasury Department, the government had only $3 million on hand and debts that totaled almost $65 million.[13] Military expenditures were growing rapidly, and import duties were no longer being collected in Southern ports, so the Treasury had to borrow large sums of money, issuing interest-bearing bonds and notes for the purpose. Chase shared the general belief in the first weeks after Fort Sumter that the war would be short, but as the fighting dragged on it became obvious that stopgap financing would be inadequate. He proposed a broad array of new taxes, which Congress passed. In 1861, an income tax law was enacted (payable June 30, 1862), imposing a tax of 3 percent per year on all incomes over $800.[14] This was the first federal income tax in the nation's history. Before any revenue was actually collected under the law, however, the rates were increased to 3 percent on all incomes between $600 and $10,000 and 5 percent on all incomes above $10,000.[15] Even these rates eventually had to be increased in 1864, when they rose to 5 percent on incomes between $600 and $5,000, 7.5 percent on incomes from $5,000 to $10,000, and 10 percent on higher incomes.[16]

Until revenues equaled expenditures, however, it was still necessary to borrow huge sums of money. To do this, Chase had to go to the financial centers of Philadelphia, New York, and Boston, where there were adequate stores of specie to meet the government's expenses. In Philadelphia, he made arrangements with the private bank of Jay Cooke & Company to sell government securities on commission. Chase worked closely with banker Jay Cooke, who knew when and where money was available, what interest rates lenders would demand, and what maturities would be most readily marketable. Cooke and his brother Henry also knew how to advertise government securities so they would reach the widest possible number of potential lenders. The Cookes were enthusiastic supporters of the Union cause and devised the idea of asking lenders to lend money on "patriotic principles," knowing that this would help them obtain lower interest rates while also helping to save the Union from the threat of dissolution.[17] Chase made frequent trips to visit Jay Cooke in Philadelphia and other money managers in New York, and when his busy work schedule permitted him to take time away from his Washington office, he frequently spent it at Cooke's palatial mansion outside Philadelphia.

As the government debt increased, the Treasury's notes and bonds encountered market resistance. There was not enough specie in the Treasury's vaults to redeem all of the government's securities—not enough specie in all the vaults of all of the banks and counting houses in Philadelphia, New York, and Boston—so it became necessary to consider the issuance of notes that were not redeemable in gold or silver. Congressman Elbridge G. Spaulding of New York, chairman of the House Ways and Means Committee, recognized the need for issuing "irredeemable" securities and sought to convince Chase that they were appropriate. Irredeemable, non-interest-bearing securities were also called legal tender notes, because the law required that they be accepted in payment of all debts, public and private (except import duties paid to the government and interest on government bonds payable by the government, which would still be paid in specie). Redeemable notes were accepted as money because they could be converted into gold or silver; irredeemable securities, or legal tender notes, were accepted because the law required that they be accepted. Chase at first resisted the concept of legal tender, for it offended his hard-money philosophy. But as expenses soared and tax revenues lagged, it became obvious that some action had to be taken. By February 1862, he had surrendered on the point, writing: "It is true that I came with reluctance to the conclusion that legal tender . . . is a necessity, but I came to it decidedly, and I support it earnestly."[18] On February 25, 1862, Congress authorized the issuance of $150,000,000 worth of legal tender notes; on July 11, 1862, it authorized an additional $150,000,000; and on March 3, 1863, yet another $150,000,000.[19] Popularly called greenbacks, the notes were issued in small denominations and quickly went into wide circulation.

It was one of Chase's responsibilities as secretary of the treasury to employ engravers to design the legal tender notes. Those who knew the secretary to be a vain man were not surprised when he had his own portrait placed in the upper left corner of the one-dollar notes because he knew that those notes would have the widest circulation. He later explained: "I had some handsome pictures put on them; and as I like to be among the people . . . and as the engravers thought me rather good looking, I told them they might put me on the end of the one-dollar bills."[20] Although the greenbacks tended to cause inflation, the inflation rate was tolerable (much less than that suffered by the Confederate currency), and the notes did much to maintain financial liquidity during the darkest days of the war. They also made the handsome face of Salmon P. Chase familiar to millions of Americans who would otherwise have known him only as a name. As Lincoln's personal secretaries John Hay and John Nicolay later noted, his features became "more familiar in the eyes of the people than those of any other man in America."[21]

Chase put his stamp on the nation's finances in another important way, by persuading Congress in 1863 to adopt a law that established a system of national banks, chartered by the federal government and required by law to purchase federal securities.[22] A national bank could be established by any group of five or more individuals who could put up at least $30,000 in federal securities. These banks were empowered to issue national bank notes backed by their federal securities. The new system established a uniform national currency and also helped to underwrite the war debt. Lincoln deferred to Chase on most of his major measures but paid particular attention to the national banking system. The president told John Hay in December of 1863 that the national banking system was "the principal financial measure of Mr. Chase in which he [Lincoln] had taken an especial interest."[23]

In addition to Treasury policies, Chase took an interest in military affairs. It was Chase who first recommended Ambrose Burnside to the president for an important command in the Union army. Burnside had come to Washington in 1861 as a colonel of the Rhode Island militia, traveling with William Sprague, a young millionaire who had recently been elected to the Senate from that state. After Senator Sprague met and fell in love with Chase's daughter Kate, Chase championed Burnside's cause with Lincoln. Senator Sprague eventually married Kate Chase in a lavish Washington wedding, and Burnside went on to command the Army of the Potomac—briefly. Neither the command nor the wedding was particularly successful, for Kate Chase and William Sprague quickly fell to quarreling and their marriage eventually ended in divorce, while General Burnside vacillated and hesitated so much at the disastrous Battle of Fredericksburg that Lincoln had to relieve him of his command and send him into semi-exile in Ohio. For a while Chase ostentatiously took credit for having recommended Burnside to the president, and George B. McClellan as well. McClellan had become acquainted with Chase while he was in Ohio before the war, and his quick advance to the command of the Army of the Potomac was attributable in part to Chase's warm endorsements. It took longer for McClellan to prove himself to be an ineffective field commander than it took Burnside, but thereafter Chase stopped reminding people that he had originally championed the careers of both men.

SALMON CHASE WAS ENERGETIC, diligent, and honest. But his honesty consisted more in personal than in political probity. All through the war, he continued to harbor presidential ambitions, and he was not above using the patronage that he controlled to advance his cause. The Treasury Department employed hundreds of clerks, collectors, accountants, bookkeepers, and assessors in Washington and elsewhere, and Chase zealously defended his right to choose the men who would occupy these positions. Lincoln was generally tolerant of Chase's patronage prerogatives, though on occasion he had to accommodate other cabinet officers. In New York, particularly, Seward wanted to put some of his political friends in influential Treasury posts. When Chase and Seward clashed over appointments, Lincoln tried to mediate.

As the war proceeded, it became evident that Chase and Seward were enemies. They had cooperated years earlier in the Supreme Court case of *Jones v. Van Zandt* because they both hated slavery, but since that time their political ambitions had driven them apart. Seward now regarded himself as too old to be elected president (he was eight years older than Chase and seven years older than Lincoln), and he believed that his service as secretary of state was the final honor of his political career. Seward grew ever closer to Lincoln during the war, while Chase erected a wall of formality between himself and the president. He was courteous, proper, and stiff. Not surprisingly, Lincoln came to feel real affection for Seward but none for Chase.

While Chase was the kind of man that Lincoln could admire, he was never the kind that Lincoln could love. The president was a humorous man, always ready with an anecdote designed to ease tensions and, in the process, draw a lesson from an incident or problem. Seward loved to listen to the president's stories, and at the end of them, his laughter—low and hearty and rumbling—was the sincerest of all. Chase was unable to tell a funny story, and when someone else told one, he could not see the humor in it. While Seward (and, to a lesser extent, Welles and Bates and Blair) welcomed the president's never-ending store of good humor, Chase regarded it as indecorous. As he snidely commented to a friend about Lincoln's sense of humor, "The root of the matter was a difficulty of temperament. The truth is that I have never been able to make a joke out of this war."[24] Lincoln was a modest man, aware of his own abilities and also willing to recognize the qualities of those around him. Chase, in contrast, was a man who could see the faults in others but none in himself. He was rigid, vain, and piously religious (Lincoln's religion was deeply felt but never worn on his sleeve). Chase's archrival in Ohio, Senator Benjamin Wade, commented that "Chase is a good man, but his theology is unsound. He thinks there is a fourth Person in the Trinity, S. P. C. [Salmon P. Chase]."[25]

When it was to Chase's political advantage to commend the president or to express agreement with one of his controversial policies, he did so, and when it was to his advantage to take issue with a measure or initiative, he did that. He and his political friends spread word in 1862 that Lincoln was an ineffectual administrator and that his cabinet had become dysfunctional. He let it be known that Seward was the strongman of the administration and was responsible for the failure of the cabinet officers to get along. Several senators became so agitated about the charges that they asked for an audience with the president and demanded that Seward be dismissed. But Lincoln knew that Chase was behind the story, and he arranged to have the senators and the cabinet all present at the same time and then asked each secretary in turn to tell the senators if the cabinet was functioning well. Chase was stunned and had no choice but to tell the truth—it was. Both Chase and Seward submitted their resignations at this time, but Lincoln refused to accept either one.[26]

As time went on, Lincoln got reports that Chase was letting it be known that he would like to run for the Republican nomination in 1864 and succeed Lincoln as president. Lincoln noticed that, whenever a personnel problem arose, Chase would support him if it was to his advantage to do so and oppose him if it was not. When, in October 1863, Lincoln decided to remove Major General William S. Rosecrans from his command of the Army of the Cumberland after the disastrous battle of Chickamauga, Hay told Lincoln that Chase "would try to make capital" out of the decision. The president laughed and said: "I suppose he will, like the bluebottle fly, lay his eggs in every rotten spot he can find."[27]

Chase's political intrigues increased as the months passed by. He informed his supporters that he was ready to accept the Republican presidential nomination, should it be offered to him, and he enlisted the aid of influential friends (among them Jay and Henry Cooke) in getting flattering articles about himself published in journals and magazines. Edward Bates wrote in his diary that "Chase's head is turned by his eagerness in pursuit of the presidency."[28] John Hay noted in December 1863 that Chase was "at work night and day, laying pipe" (politicking). Lincoln was amused by what he called "Chase's mad hunt after the presidency."[29] Others were not so indulgent. David Davis, now an associate justice of the Supreme Court, thought that Chase was "more ambitious than Douglas ever was" and that he "would join any party for success."[30] In a letter to a friend, Davis wrote: "Eating a man's bread and stabbing him at the same time, may be questioned. Chase is doomed to disappointment. I could tell you some things about him that would astonish you."[31]

Lincoln did not interfere with Chase's politicking, for he still believed that he was an effective secretary of the treasury. He compared Chase's presidential aspiration to "a horsefly on the neck of a ploughhorse," telling Hay "it kept him lively about his work."[32] Twice more Chase submitted his resignations in fits of pique, and twice more Lincoln urged him to stay on the job. Then, in June of 1864, the two came to loggerheads over the appointment of a new assistant United States treasurer in New York. Chase submitted another letter of resignation, expecting the president would again urge him to stay on. Lincoln did not do so.

The president explained the situation to John Hay. "Mr. Chase has resigned & I have accepted his resignation. I thought I could not stand it any longer." Chase's latest letter of resignation was, like all of his others, a kind of ultimatum. As Lincoln put it, "It meant 'You have been acting very badly. Unless you say you are sorry, & ask me to stay & agree that I shall be absolute and that you shall have nothing, no matter how you beg for it, I will go.'"[33] But Lincoln could not surrender to Chase on such terms, so Chase had to go.

The president accepted Chase's resignation on June 30. "Of all I have said in commendation of your ability and fidelity," he wrote, "I have nothing to unsay; and yet you and I have reached a point of mutual embarrassment in our official relation which it seems can not be overcome, or longer sustained, consistently with the public service."[34] Chase was stunned. He wrote in his diary that he "had found a good deal of embarrassment" from Lincoln, "but what he had found from me I could not imagine, unless it has been created by my unwillingness to have offices distributed as spoils or benefits."[35] Others who knew both men were not so much surprised by Chase's departure as relieved. Gideon Welles looked upon it "as a blessing."[36] Bates greeted it with "a vague feeling of relief."[37] And Francis P. Blair, Sr., Montgomery Blair's father, exulted that Chase had "dropped off at last like a rotten pear unexpected to himself & every body else."[38]

After Lincoln was renominated by the Republicans and McClellan chosen by the Democrats, Chase realized that he was out of the presidential picture, at least for 1864. When some of his Ohio supporters put his name before a local convention as a candidate for the House of Representatives, Chase protested that he would accept a nomination only if it was unanimous. It was not—in fact he did not even receive a majority of the votes cast. In a meeting with William P. Fessenden of Maine, his successor as secretary of the treasury, Chase received an indirect offer from Lincoln for a major diplomatic appointment.[39] He would have relished the honor but he realized that such a move would take him out of politics, and he declined.

At Lincoln's invitation, Chase visited the president at the White House and at his summer retreat at the Washington Soldiers' Home. Chase found Lincoln cordial but reserved, "not at all demonstrative either in speech or manner."[40] He had previously dropped hints that he would like to have a judicial nomination. Both men knew that Chief Justice Taney was old and sick, and that it was only a matter of time before the choicest judicial plum in the nation would be available for the plucking, but neither knew exactly when.

LINCOLN RETURNED FROM THE memorial service for Roger Taney to find a pile of letters and telegrams awaiting him. Important officials inside and outside Washington were anxious to give him advice about picking a new chief justice. Not surprisingly, there were many aspirants for the position, some of whom he knew personally and others, only by reputation. Attorney General Bates was one of the first to ask directly for the appointment.[41] Senator Charles Sumner was one of the first to recommend that it go to Chase. Sumner was known for his sharp tongue (in 1857, he had been savagely beaten on the Senate floor in retaliation for a caustic speech he made there). Sumner was in a typically vituperative (but also exultant) mood when he wrote Lincoln from Boston:

> Providence has given us a victory, in the death of Chief Justice Taney. It is a victory for Liberty & for the Constitution.
>
> Thus far the Constitution has been interpreted for Slavery. Thank God! It may now be interpreted surely for Liberty. The importance of this change cannot be exaggerated.

Sumner thought that the new chief justice had to have "an acknowledged mastery of his profession" and also be "an able, courageous, & determined friend of Freedom, who will never let Freedom suffer by concern or hesitation." He also had to have "an aptitude for public law." Sumner thought that Chase fulfilled "more of these requirements than any other person" and strongly urged his nomination. "Let it go forth," Sumner wrote Lincoln "that he is Chief Justice & our cause will gain every where."[42]

Lincoln was nearly deluged with letters and telegrams recommending Chase's appointment. David Dudley Field wrote him from New York, while Field's brother Associate Justice Stephen J. Field sent a telegram from California (together with that state's governor Frederick F. Low). William Cullen Bryant, influential editor of the *New York Evening Post*, wrote a letter, as did Ohio's senator John Sherman (then traveling in Iowa); Speaker of the House

Schuyler Colfax of Indiana; and Joseph Medill, editor of the *Chicago Tribune*.[43] Sherman's letter contained the news that Associate Justice Samuel Miller preferred Chase's appointment to that of any other man, and that Justice Field concurred. (Miller had earlier favored the nomination of Associate Justice Noah Swayne, "but subsequent reflection satisfied him that the public service would be best promoted by the selection of Gov Chase.")[44] Medill's letter crudely suggested that Republican victories in the just-completed gubernatorial and congressional elections in Pennsylvania, Ohio, and Indiana were "too much for old Dred Scott Taney. He saw that it was useless to stay any longer, so he made his exit."[45]

Chase was not the only person thought to be qualified for the appointment. Postmaster General Blair was recommended by William E. Chandler of New Hampshire, Treasury Secretary Fessenden by Vice President Hannibal Hamlin of Maine, John Jay of New York by New Hampshire's radical senator John P. Hale, and Secretary of State Seward by Benjamin H. Brewster of Pennsylvania.[46] Congressman Rufus P. Spalding of Ohio, Governor David Tod of Ohio, and Congressman James K. Moorhead of Pennsylvania wrote in behalf of Secretary of War Edwin Stanton, while George B. Butler and Hiram Davis wrote in behalf of their fellow New Yorker, the brilliant lawyer William Evarts.[47] Sumner himself received at least one recommendation, although there is no indication that he had any interest in the position, while Justice Swayne was favored by Justice David Davis and by a well-respected Ohio attorney named Morrison R. Waite, who would in a few years occupy the chief justice's chair himself.[48]

Secretary of War Stanton's wife was anxious for her husband to be appointed. In a personal conversation with Orville Browning, she implored him to speak to Lincoln in support of her husband. Browning acknowledged that Stanton was "an able lawyer, learned in his profession, and fond of it," but he suspected that Lincoln favored Chase. "I fear Mr. Chase's appointment," Browning wrote in his diary, "and am anxious to prevent it."[49] When Browning called on Lincoln to plead Stanton's cause, the president listened quietly, acknowledged Stanton's abilities, and refused to make any commitment.[50]

Justice Davis was one of Chase's bitterest opponents. He wrote Lincoln from his home in Illinois, where he was suffering from a painful carbuncle on his neck, to tell him that he felt "deeply and earnestly on the subject." He and the president had discussed the matter the previous winter, when it appeared that Taney was near death. Davis had called on Lincoln then and told him that a majority of the current Supreme Court justices favored Justice Swayne as Taney's successor. Davis agreed with the others and begged Lincoln "not to appoint Chase."[51] Now writing from Illinois, Davis reminded Lincoln that Swayne was not an active political partisan. "No regular partisan ought to be elevated to such a place," Davis wrote. "Judicial life should be kept as free as possible from party politics. To place a mere partisan in such a position weakens an administration and lessens the respect that should attach to the decisions of the Court.[52]

Edward Bates shared Davis's distaste for Chase. In late November, Isaac Newton, Lincoln's commissioner of agriculture, told Bates that he had discussed the Supreme Court appointment with the president, who had expressed a willingness to give it to Bates. But he was "overborne" by others, Newton said, and "Chase was turning every stone to get it." Bates realized that he had little prospect of being appointed, and wrote in his diary that failure to get it "will be no painful disappointment for my mind is made up to private life and a bare competency."[53] By November 24, Bates had given up all hope of receiving the appointment and informed Lincoln that he would resign as attorney general, effective November 30. He had served three years and nine months in the office and, some months earlier, had informed the president that he intended to leave after the elections. Bates and Lincoln parted on good terms and with each feeling genuine respect for the other. James Speed, a Kentucky attorney and the brother of one of Lincoln's oldest friends, Joshua Speed, was named to replace Bates.

Sumner realized that Chase had determined opponents and sought to answer their arguments. On October 24, he wrote Lincoln from Boston that "anti-Slavery men are all trembling, lest the opportunity should be lost of appointing a Chief Justice, who, in his interpretation of the Constitution & of the War Powers, would deal a death-blow to Slavery." Sumner insisted that the new chief justice "must believe in Liberty & be inspired by it," and he assured Lincoln that the nomination of Chase "would cause a glow of delight throughout the Country among all the best supporters of the Administration . . . [T]he sooner it is made the better![54]

LINCOLN WAITED EIGHT WEEKS before announcing his choice to succeed Taney. The delay is not hard to explain. The presidential voting was not completed until November 8, and Lincoln was much occupied with the campaign in the weeks leading up to the election. If he was leaning toward the appointment of Chase, he may have realized that an early announcement of his intention to name Chase would antagonize conservative voters, for Chase was widely regarded as a radical on issues of slavery and reconstruction. In any event, the Supreme Court was not in session during this time, and Congress was not due to reconvene until December 5, so the Senate could not have taken up the nomination before that date. On December 6, the day after the opening of the Thirty-eighth Congress, Lincoln submitted a formal nomination of Salmon P. Chase to the Senate. The nomination was considered the same day and unanimously confirmed.[55]

Lincoln's nomination of Chase was hardly unexpected. He had dropped hints here and there that he was favorably disposed to Chase, and the recommendations he had received were persuasive. Moreover, there did not seem to be any other logical candidate. Stanton was a brilliant lawyer, but Lincoln felt he could not find anyone to take Stanton's place in the War Department, and the secretary himself wanted to finish his work there.[56] Montgomery Blair was an able lawyer, but his views about reconstruction (which was becoming an increasingly divisive issue in the government) were more conservative than Lincoln's, and he was given to outbursts of temper. The president had confided one evening in Ward Hill Lamon, telling his old friend that he had "looked over the ground" and was "satisfied that the appointment of Governor Chase would satisfy the country." What's more, he told Lamon that the unhappy incident between Chase and himself "was not to be taken into account."[57] When Chase's enemies reminded the president of Chase's constant efforts to undermine him politically, Lincoln answered directly: "Now, I know meaner things about Governor Chase than any of those men can tell me; but I am going to nominate him."[58]

Lincoln later gave a longer explanation of the appointment to New York congressman Augustus Frank. There was no question of Chase's ability or of his "soundness on the general issues of the war," Lincoln said. Then he added: "I should despise myself if I allowed personal differences to affect my judgment of his fitness for the office of Chief Justice." But Lincoln did have some doubts about Chase's continuing political ambitions. As he told Connecticut's senator Lafayette Foster: "Mr. Chase will make an excellent judge if he devotes himself exclusively to the duties of his office and don't meddle with politics. But if he keeps on with the notion that he is destined to be President of the United States, and which in my judgment he never will be, he will never acquire that fame and usefulness as Chief Justice which he would otherwise certainly attain."[59]

Noah Brooks, who came to know the president very well in the last years of the war, believed that Lincoln had intended to appoint Chase all along. "I will venture to say that the President never desired to appoint any other man than Chase to the Chief Justiceship," Brooks wrote; "he never, I believe, had any other intention."[60] Brooks reported that Lincoln was visited by members of the Electoral College from Maryland not long after he sent Chase's nomination to the Senate, and they informed him that they were pleased with the appointment. Lincoln replied that "he trusted the appointment would be for the best." There were "two points of national importance," Lincoln said, on which the country needed assurances. Brooks summarized Lincoln's remarks:

> By the appointment of Mr. Chase all holders of United States securities in America and Europe felt assured that the financial policy of the Government would be upheld by its highest judicial tribunal. In sustaining that policy, Judge Chase would be only sustaining himself, for he was the author of it. The other point to which Lincoln referred was that relating to the constitutionality of the emancipation policy of the Government. He said that other distinguished gentlemen had been named as competent to undertake the great trust now borne by Judge Chase; but these did not bear the same relations to those important issues that Chase did, although they were doubtless equally sound.[61]

After Chase was nominated, Congressman George S. Boutwell of Massachusetts told Lincoln that he was "very glad that he had decided to appoint Mr. Chase." Boutwell later recalled Lincoln's reply:

> There are three reasons in favor of his appointment, and one very strong reason against it. First, he occupies the largest place in the public mind in connection with the office, then we wish for a Chief Justice who will sustain what has been done in regard to emancipation and the legal tenders. We cannot ask a man what he will do, and if we

should, and he should answer us, we should despise him for it. Therefore we must take a man whose opinions are known. But there is one very strong reason against his appointment. He is a candidate for the Presidency, and if he does not give up that idea it will be very bad for him and very bad for me.[62]

Chase's views on emancipation might certainly have recommended him to Lincoln, for Lincoln was never confident that the Supreme Court would sustain his Emancipation Proclamation.[63] He firmly believed in the Proclamation's constitutionality, but he was well aware that his emancipation policy had a host of enemies, in the North as well as in the South, and it was reasonable to assume that Chase would vote to uphold it. Chase's intimate connection with the Legal Tender Act and the issuance of greenbacks was also a positive recommendation. He had been the principal architect of the administration's financial measures during the war and understood them as well as any other man. Why would he vote to strike down his own measures?[64]

Less than a week after Chase was appointed, Gideon Welles recorded in his diary that Lincoln had told Senator Zachariah Chandler of Michigan "that he would rather have swallowed his buckhorn chair than to have nominated Chase."[65] But nominate him he did. The conclusion is obvious that he did so not because of personal preferences but in spite of them, because he believed that Chase was well qualified to be chief justice, and because he believed that Chase shared his views on key war issues that were likely to come before the Supreme Court for review. And he made the nomination in spite of substantial personal doubts about the man.

Chase wrote Lincoln as soon as he learned of his nomination. He thanked him for "this mark of your confidence, & especially for the manner in which the nomination was made. . . . Be assured that I prize your confidence & good will more than nomination or office."[66]

John Nicolay, one of Lincoln's private secretaries, was not sure if Chase's appointment was in all respects wise and appropriate. But he was sure that it reflected well on the president, showing him to be a man who would not hold a grudge against a political adversary. Chase had treated Lincoln poorly, and Lincoln had reciprocated by appointing him to one of the highest offices in the land. "Probably no other man than Lincoln," Nicolay said, "would have had, in this age of the world, the degree of magnanimity to thus forgive and exalt a rival who had so deeply and so unjustifiably intrigued against him."[67]

But it was characteristic of Lincoln to disregard personal animosities when making important appointments. In the first year of the war he had appointed James Shields as a brigadier general, despite the fact that Shields was one of his oldest and bitterest political rivals from Illinois (Shields had even challenged him to a duel in 1842).[68] And he had appointed Edwin Stanton as secretary of war early in 1862, despite the fact that Stanton had insulted him when the two men were working on an important trial together in 1855 (Stanton had then called him a "d——d long armed Ape" who "does not know anything"),[69] and he kept Stanton in his post after he was told that the secretary had called him a "d——d fool." ("If Stanton said I was a d——d fool," Lincoln replied, "then I must be one, for he is nearly always right, and generally says what he means.")[70] Shields and Stanton and Chase all went on to serve their country honorably— and in Stanton's case, brilliantly.

THE SUPREME COURT OPENED its term on December 7. Thomas Ewing of Ohio, a former senator and member of the cabinets of Presidents William Henry Harrison and Zachary Taylor, presented a memorial from the Supreme Court bar expressing sorrow for Taney's death and offering sympathy to his family, after which Justice Wayne of Georgia read a long tribute to the departed chief justice.[71]

On December 15, Chase appeared in the Supreme Court's Capitol chamber to take his oath as the nation's sixth chief justice. The room was filled with dignitaries, among them Thomas Ewing, Secretary of State Seward, Senator Benjamin Wade, Chase's daughters, Kate and Nettie, and his son-in-law, Senator William Sprague of Rhode Island. Noah Brooks saw Senator Sumner leaning against one of the marble columns "in a fine and studied pose; his handsome features plainly showed his inward glow of gratification." After Chase took his oath, Brooks met Senator Wade outside the courtroom. Wade was one of Chase's bitterest political enemies, and one of the capital's wickedest wits. Wade's eyes "actually suffused with tears," Brooks wrote, as he said: "Lord, now lettest thou thy servant depart in peace, for mine eyes have seen thy salvation."[72]

One of the new chief justice's first duties was to administer the oath of office to Lincoln on the occasion of his second inauguration, March 5, 1865. The oath was administered before a large audience gathered on the east front of the Capitol to hear the president deliver his inaugural address, one of the shortest but most memorable in the nation's history (it would later be acclaimed by many historians as his "greatest speech"). Chase, as always, stood tall and dignified. The clerk of the Supreme Court handed the chief justice a Bible, and Lincoln placed his right hand on the page open to Isaiah 5. Chase led the president in the words of the prescribed oath, which Lincoln ended with the emphatic words: "So help me God."[73]

Chase maintained polite relations with Lincoln after he began his duties as chief justice. Official letters were exchanged, and Chase made some personal visits to the White House. On Friday, April 14, 1865, the chief justice planned to call on the president to explain his views on extending suffrage to the former slaves. It was an issue that was much discussed in Washington in the early months of 1865, and one upon which Chase had some definite opinions. Five days earlier, General Robert E. Lee had surrendered the Army of Northern Virginia to Lieutenant General U. S. Grant at Appomattox Court House in Virginia; three days before, Union troops under Major General E. R. S. Canby had entered Mobile, Alabama, following the Confederate evacuation of the city; and just the day before, Union troops under Major General William T. Sherman had occupied Raleigh, North Carolina. Lincoln was cheered by the good news from his generals but still burdened by the difficult issues that loomed on the horizon. Realizing how busy the president was, Chase decided that he would forgo his personal visit to the White House. He was asleep in his Washington home some time after 10:15 that evening when a servant woke him and called him downstairs. A Treasury agent had come to tell him that Lincoln had been shot at Ford's Theater, just a few blocks away, and was hovering near death. Three other government employees appeared soon afterward to tell Chase that Seward had also been attacked and that guards were being posted at the homes of all high government officials. Chase thought immediately of dressing and going to the theater. But on second thought he concluded that he would not be of any help, so he stayed home.

Still alive but unconscious, Lincoln was taken out of the theater and moved into a small room in the Peterson boarding house across the street. There Secretary Stanton took charge of the growing crowd. All of the members of the cabinet (except the badly wounded Seward) filed into the little room where Lincoln lay dying, paying their respects, shedding tears, offering prayers. Chase walked to Peterson's the next morning and was told that the president was dead. He continued on to the Kirkwood House, the hotel where Vice President Andrew Johnson lived. There he met the new attorney general, James Speed, and the new secretary of the treasury, Hugh McCulloch. Speed and McCulloch left for the attorney general's office to examine provisions of the Constitution and federal statutes relating to the succession to the presidency in the event of the president's death. They also looked for precedents relating to the two previous presidents who had died in office, William Henry Harrison, who was succeeded by John Tyler in 1841, and Zachary Taylor, who was succeeded by Millard Fillmore in 1850.

They were back at the Kirkwood House at ten o'clock, where Johnson, Chase, Montgomery Blair, Francis Blair, Sr., Edwin Stanton, and a half dozen other people were waiting in the parlor. After Chase administered the presidential oath to Johnson, the new president repeated the words Lincoln had repeated outside the capital six weeks earlier: "So help me God." Chase answered: "May God guide, support and bless you in your arduous duties."

9 A Law for Rulers and People

CHASE DID NOT TAKE easily to his new role as chief justice. For most of the previous decade he had administered large bureaucracies, with secretaries, clerks, and assistants to accept his orders and carry out his decisions. It had been years since he had appeared in a court to try a case or argue an appeal, and though there was never any doubt that he had a keen legal mind, he had rarely used it in recent years for anything other than staking out political positions on controversial issues. As presiding judge of the Supreme Court, Chase was obliged to work alone, without even a secretary or clerk to help him with his legal research and opinion writing, and with a paltry salary to recompense him for his efforts.

As governor of Ohio, as a United States senator, and as a member of Lincoln's cabinet, Chase had been admired as a statesman, not a mere lawyer, and he shared the beliefs of his most ardent admirers that he would elevate the Court. He was confident, moreover, that his service there would help him achieve his ultimate goal, which was the presidency. But how could he demonstrate his powers of statesmanship when he had to spend long hours alone in his library, reviewing the records of cases, looking up statutes and precedents, and writing out opinions? Chase found his new work "unfamiliar and tedious," and in a letter to a friend he complained about "the painful monotony of hearing, reading, thinking and writing on the same class of subjects and in the same way, all the time—morning, noon, evening and night."[1]

Three hundred sixty cases were on the Court's docket when Chase became chief justice, and litigants typically had to wait two years for their hearings. Most cases did not present difficult issues, and the most daunting task for the judges was reading the records and reviewing the evidence collected in the lower courts. Reverdy Johnson who, in addition to his duties as senator from Maryland, was one of the busiest attorneys in the Supreme Court, stated on the floor of the Senate that "at least one half the cases in the Supreme Court are more or less troublesome because of their obligation to examine into the facts." Johnson said that the records were "generally very large, the testimony being generally very voluminous, and as the court is obliged, as the law now stands, to examine into the whole record in order to pass judgment upon the facts as well as the law, it takes a great deal of their time."[2]

To relieve the tedium of his work, Chase continued to cultivate his political contacts. While Lincoln was still president, he offered him advice on important issues, particularly the question of black suffrage. Chase insisted that the right to vote should be extended to all adult males, regardless of race or previous condition of servitude. Lincoln was sympathetic to this claim but unwilling to embrace it as his own. Throughout his political career, he had been cautious about espousing unprecedented causes, particularly if they did not have enough support to prevail. During the war, he had advanced cautiously on the issue of emancipation, resisting it when Frémont issued his first proclamation in Missouri in 1861, but concluding a year later that a general emancipation of slaves in rebellious states was demanded not only by justice but also by military necessity. Once Lincoln had adopted a position he did not retreat from it, and emancipation was a point on which he was now unyielding. He enthusiastically supported the effort that began in Congress in 1864 to amend the Constitution to end slavery throughout the nation, reminding wavering congressmen that the amendment would settle the fate, "for all coming time, not only of the millions now in bondage, but of unborn millions to come."[3] The amendment (which would become the Thirteenth) read:

Section 1. Neither slavery nor involuntary servitude, except as a punishment for crime whereof the party shall have been duly convicted, shall exist within the United States, or any place subject to their jurisdiction.

Section 2. Congress shall have power to enforce this article by appropriate legislation.

Lincoln rejoiced when the amendment reached final passage on January 31,
1865, calling it an occasion of "congratulation to the country and to the whole
world." The amendment was "a King's cure for all the evils" of slavery, he said.
"It winds the whole thing up." But he reminded supporters that it still had to
be ratified and urged them "to go forward and consummate by the votes of the
States that which Congress so nobly began."[4]

The issue of suffrage was neither as clear nor as commanding as emancipation. While blacks could not vote in the slave slates, they were denied the
same right in many Northern states, including Lincoln's own Illinois, and Lincoln knew that any effort to require universal suffrage would meet strong opposition all over the country. In his last public address, delivered on April 11,
1865, Lincoln commented on the new constitution of Louisiana, noting that it
contained an emancipation provision but that "the elective franchise is not
given to the colored man." He said that he would personally prefer to see the
vote given to "very intelligent" blacks and to "those who serve our cause as soldiers." But he was willing to accept Louisiana's new constitution as a good start
toward bringing the state back into its "proper practical relation with the
Union." He had not settled on any "exclusive, and inflexible plan" for the reconstruction of the rebellious states, favoring instead a cautious approach.[5] As
Supreme Court historian Charles Fairman has written: "Lincoln always distinguished between the distant goal and the immediately practicable advance,
and kept both in view."[6]

After Andrew Johnson became president, Chase drafted proclamations
for his signature, tried to persuade Johnson to adopt his views on suffrage, and
gave him advice on some important legal questions. For example, he counseled
the president against any attempt to put the captured Confederate president
Jefferson Davis on trial for treason. If Davis was in fact guilty of treason (a fact
that was subject to vigorous debate), his treason had occurred in the South
and he would have had to be tried before a Southern jury, for Article III,
Section 2, of the Constitution provides (in relevant part): "The trial of all
crimes, except in cases of impeachment, shall be by jury; and such trial shall

be held in the state where the said crimes shall have been committed." Chase reasoned that a Southern jury would effectively insulate Davis from any conviction. Further, thousands of captured Confederate soldiers and officers had already been treated as prisoners of war rather than traitors, and Chase believed that it would be unfair not to accord the same treatment to Davis. Beyond this, he believed that trying Davis would be a needless act of vengeance that would have negative political consequences.[7]

At first it seemed that the chief justice and the new president might find some common ground. As the months passed, however, it appeared that they had very different ideas about how the South was to be governed after the war, and about whether blacks were to be given voting rights.

Chase's strong personality made him a commanding figure on the Court, but it also put him in conflict with the other strong-minded judges there. When he first came on the Court he found that Justice Miller was "beyond question, the dominant personality upon the bench, whose mental force and individuality [were] felt by the court more than any other."[8] Miller was energetic and purposeful, sometimes blunt, but always deserving of respect. Chase got along well with Justice Field, who liked to regale his colleagues with tales of his adventurous life in gold-rush California. Like Miller, Field had a first-class intelligence, but he could also be argumentative and sanctimonious. Chase's and Field's views seemed at first to be close, but differences soon appeared. Chase was never comfortable with his fellow Ohioan, Justice Swayne.[9] Although the two men shared some political views, Swayne resented the fact that he had been passed over for chief justice. Justice Davis was absent from Washington during the whole of the 1864–65 term, still in Illinois suffering neck pain. When he returned, he established polite relations with Chase, though the two men found little on which they agreed.[10] Chase found Justice Clifford dull and plodding, but hoped that he could influence his views on constitutional questions.

The other justices—Catron, Wayne, Nelson, and Grier—tottering relics of the *Dred Scott* era, were growing weaker with each passing year. Catron was approaching eighty years of age and, due to illness, was absent from the Court during all of the 1864–65 term. Wayne was seventy-five and the senior justice in point of service, but he still managed to contribute to the Court's work.

Nelson was seventy-two and in relatively good health but neither as energetic nor as assertive as he had been in earlier years. Grier was seventy and in failing health.

THOUGH MUCH OF THE COURT'S work in early 1865 was pedestrian, the judges were aware that potentially explosive issues could arise at any time. Many men had been arrested during the war, held without benefit of habeas corpus, and denied trials and bail.[11] Some were civilians who had been tried by military commissions and sentenced to imprisonment or, in some cases, death. The legal community was sharply divided as to the constitutionality of these trials, and petitions seeking to set them aside had been filed in federal courts. Lincoln had been aware of the challenges and was almost resigned to the fact that the Supreme Court would eventually rule on them. He had chosen Chase as chief justice in large part because Chase shared his war aims and could be depended on to sustain his most important war measures. But he knew that a Supreme Court judge could never commit himself in advance to a particular ruling, and that it was always possible one of his appointees (there were five in all) would disappoint him.

Cases challenging military commissions had reached the court before Chase became chief justice, but, like the potentially explosive Ex parte Vallandigham, they had been dismissed on jurisdictional grounds.[12] In March 1863 Congress had passed a comprehensive statute on the subject of habeas corpus, intending not only to defuse the hotly contested issue of whether the power to suspend rested with the president or with Congress (the question that Taney had decided against Lincoln in Merryman), but also to establish a regularized procedure under which persons arrested by military authorities in the loyal states would have access to the courts.[13] The new statute provided, first, that the president "is authorized" to suspend the writ anywhere in the United States, "whenever, in his judgment the public safety may require it." (It did not say that the president "is hereby authorized" to suspend the writ.)[14] Second, it required the secretary of state and the secretary of war to prepare lists of all citizens of loyal states who were held as prisoners (other than as prisoners of war) by order of the president or either of the secretaries, and to furnish the lists to the judges of the federal district and circuit courts. Third, it provided that, if a grand jury adjourned without indicting a person named on a list, the person was entitled to release upon taking an oath of allegiance to the federal government.[15]

In February 1865, a petition for habeas corpus and for certiorari was filed in the Supreme Court on behalf of a man named John Dugan, who had been arrested on charges of robbing an army paymaster in the District of Columbia. In January, the Supreme Court of the District of Columbia had issued a writ of habeas corpus on behalf of Dugan, directed to the superintendent of the Old Capitol Prison. The superintendent declined to comply because Lincoln had personally ordered that the writ of habeas corpus be suspended in Dugan's case.[16]

When the court declined to proceed further, Dugan's attorneys filed their petition in the U.S. Supreme Court, asking that a writ of certiorari be issued to the lower court and a writ of habeas corpus to the prison superintendent. Lincoln was concerned. Gideon Welles was also concerned, for he believed that Chase might use this opportunity to strike a blow for judicial independence by invalidating Lincoln's suspension. The secretary of the navy suspected that Chase intended "to make himself felt by the Administration when he can reach them."[17] Welles wrote in his diary: "There is no man with more fierce aspirations than Chase, and the bench will be used to promote his personal ends."[18]

On February 27, the Supreme Court granted certiorari "returnable forthwith" in Dugan's case. Since the Court was nearing its adjournment, it could have put the hearing over until the following term, which would begin in December. But habeas corpus was one of the cornerstones of liberty, and it took precedence over other matters. Dugan's attorney asked the Court to proceed to a hearing without delay. But Attorney General Speed urged the justices to wait until the official record was brought up from the lower court. The Court agreed with Speed and, on March 3, ordered that the case of *In Re John Dugan* be continued to the next term. But by then the fighting was over, Dugan had regained his freedom, and his attorney asked that his petition be dismissed.[19] Thus did Lincoln and his administration narrowly miss an arrow aimed at the heart of their war program in February 1865.

ON WEDNESDAY MORNING, February 1, 1865, Senator Charles Sumner entered the chamber of the Supreme Court in the company of an attorney from his state who was seeking admission to the bar. At eleven o'clock, the judges filed into the room and took their seats. Chief Justice Chase stood for a moment, bowed to the assembled attorneys, and took his seat with what a newspaper reporter described as "a great presence." Sumner then rose to address the judges: "May it please the Court, I move that John S. Rock, a member of the Supreme Court of the State of Massachusetts, be admitted to practice as a member of this Court."[20] The chief justice nodded his head as he granted the motion, confident that on that day he had struck a blow for freedom and equality, for Rock was not simply a Massachusetts attorney but the first African American attorney ever admitted to the bar of the Supreme Court.

Sumner, who shared Chase's passion for racial equality, was thrilled. The new attorney was a man of impressive attainments, a native of New Jersey whose free-black parents had sacrificed mightily so he could stay in school until he was eighteen years old. After graduation, Rock taught school and studied dentistry, medicine, and finally law. He was active with abolitionist societies in Philadelphia and Boston, where he settled in the mid-1850s, and he became an effective speaker and writer on abolitionist issues. Ill health forced him in 1859 to travel to Paris for special medical treatment. His trip there was made difficult by the *Dred Scott*–like ruling of James Buchanan's secretary of state, Lewis Cass, that blacks were not eligible to carry U.S. passports because they were not citizens. Back in Boston, Rock practiced law, continued his work with abolitionist societies, and, in 1863, helped recruit African American soldiers for the Fifty-fourth Massachusetts Regiment. In 1864 he wrote Senator Sumner to ask for his help in gaining admission to practice before the Supreme Court, but he was told that nothing could be done so long as Roger Taney was the chief justice. "I suppose," Rock wrote to a friend, "the old man lives on out of spite."[21] After Taney died, Rock renewed his request, and Sumner told him to come to Washington. His admission to the Supreme Court on February 1 was also accompanied by a friendly welcome in the hall of the U.S. House of Representatives.

Sumner believed that Rock's admission would settle a host of difficult issues for African Americans, for if they were good enough to practice law in the highest court in the land, it would be "difficult for any restriction on account of color to be maintained any where." "Street cars," Sumner said, "would be open afterwards."[22] But Sumner was too optimistic. Even in the Supreme Court there was a backlash against the black man's admission. Justice Davis was not in Washington when Rock made his appearance there, but he learned of it in Illinois and thoroughly disapproved. He complained that Sumner's "radicalism" was running athwart "every body's prejudices" and asked: "What object of swearing in the negro man, as an attorney of [the] U.S. Supreme Court[?] He had no business there & never would. . . . The negro can never be elevated to social & political rights in this country & all wise statesmen know it. But republics make politicians & not statesmen."[23]

Although Davis's views were clearly racist by the standards of later generations, they were not unusual for a man of his time and region, born in Maryland, educated in Ohio, and grown to maturity in central Illinois, where he was surrounded by men and women from slaveholding states. Davis was a firm defender of the Union and an opponent of slavery, but he never indulged in "radical" notions of racial equality. Justice Wayne's biographer, Alexander A. Lawrence, suggests that Wayne was also offended by Rock's admission. He points out that the Georgian was absent from court on February 1 and suggests that Rock's admission was "more than a Judge who had concurred in the still unreversed Dred Scott decision could stomach."[24] But Charles Fairman has noted that Wayne was absent for several days before and after the black attorney's appearance and that he "was not a Judge who made resentful demonstrations."[25]

If Lincoln was aware of Rock's admission to the Supreme Court, there appears to be no record that he made any comment on it. It was not customary for the president to follow the day-to-day operations of the Supreme Court, and if he did hear of it, it is difficult to imagine that he would have objected to the admission of an African American attorney. Although his own views on racial equality had evolved over the years, he had never denigrated blacks. The day of Rock's admission to the Supreme Court was also the day on which Lincoln celebrated the passage of the Thirteenth Amendment, a day of triumph for the president and for African Americans.

On several occasions during the war, Lincoln had invited the African American abolitionist and editor Frederick Douglass (whom he called "one of the most meritorious men in America") to visit him, both at the White House and at his summer retreat at the Soldiers' Home in Washington. Douglass later wrote that, in Lincoln's company, he was "never in any way reminded of my humble origin, or of my unpopular color." And on the day of his second inauguration, when Lincoln caught sight of Douglass across the crowded East Room in the White House, he called out, "Here comes my friend Douglass." Douglass later said that he was sure that Lincoln called out to him in such a voice so "that all around could hear him."[26] "I saw you in the crowd today, listening to my inaugural address," the president said. "How did you like it?"

Douglass replied: "Mr. Lincoln, I must not detain you with my poor opinion, when there are thousands waiting to shake hands with you." "No, no," Lincoln said. "You must stop a little[,] Douglass; there is no man in the country whose opinion I value more than yours."[27] It is hard to imagine that such a president would have taken umbrage at the honor accorded John Rock in the Supreme Court.

But honors do not always translate into real accomplishments. Despite his distinction as the first member of his race to be admitted to practice in the Supreme Court of the United States, John Rock would never live to see the day when he or his fellow African Americans could freely "ride on streetcars," much less vote, or hold office, or live where they pleased. "Black codes" were already being enacted in both Northern and Southern states that would deny equal rights on the basis of race, and Rock was destined to die an unexpected death on December 3, 1866, at the age of forty-one—less than two years after Lincoln's own death—knowing that slavery had been outlawed in his native land but that other basic rights had yet to be extended to members of his race.

THE SUPREME COURT adjourned on March 10, 1865, fourteen weeks after it began its December term. The justices whose health permitted them to travel then set out for their homes and circuit duties. Chase headed first to Baltimore, for he had fallen heir to Taney's old Fourth Circuit, which included Delaware, Maryland, Virginia, and North Carolina. After sitting for a short time in Baltimore, the chief justice was back in Washington on April 14, when Lincoln was assassinated. After administering the presidential oath to Andrew Johnson, he had to decide whether to go into Virginia on circuit duty. He conferred with Justice Wayne, who had a similar decision to make; Wayne's Fifth Circuit included South Carolina, Georgia, Alabama, Mississippi, and Florida. Wayne had not gone on circuit duty since the war began, and he did not feel the time was yet ripe to do so. Military commissions were still operating in the South, and habeas corpus was still suspended. Chase and Wayne agreed that it was "unbecoming" for them to travel to the South under these circumstances.[28] As soon as the new president thought it "wise and safe" to revoke the suspension of habeas corpus, Chase said, he would be willing to hold court anywhere in the circuit assigned to him.[29]

David Davis, who had been in Illinois during all of the Court's 1864–65 term, was attending to his circuit court duties in Chicago when he received news of Lincoln's death. Though his neck was still painful, he sent a messenger to all of the local judges, asking them to adjourn their courts and bring the lawyers before him. On Saturday, April 15, speaking from his circuit court bench, he told the assembled lawyers that the nation had been "stricken by a great calamity and a great sorrow. My sorrow is a double one. I sorrow not only as a citizen of the United States but as a personal and devoted friend of the President."[30]

From Washington, Robert Todd Lincoln, the deceased president's eldest son, telegraphed Davis, asking him to "come at once to Washington and take charge of my father's affairs."[31] Although exhausted and still in pain, Davis dropped all of his Illinois business to head East, where he met with the Lincoln family and made arrangements to administer the president's estate in Sangamon County, Illinois. For the next several months, Davis took great care to provide for Mrs. Lincoln and her two children, even accepting an appointment to act as guardian of the fourteen-year-old Tad Lincoln. He was able to invest Lincoln's assets wisely, so that by the time they were ready to be distributed two years later, they had doubled in value. Against the insistence of the grateful Robert Todd Lincoln, Davis refused to accept any fee for his work for the Lincoln family. Mrs. Lincoln wrote him: "Permit me to say, that in no hands save your own could our interest have been so advantageously placed. Please accept my grateful thanks for all your kindness to myself & family."[32]

While Chase was administering the oath to Andrew Johnson and David Davis was taking charge of Abraham Lincoln's estate, John Catron remained gravely ill at his home in Nashville. The Tennessean's advanced age and long illness had prepared his colleagues for his imminent death, which came on May 30, 1865. President Johnson made no immediate effort to nominate a successor. Catron had been absent from the Court for so long that his death did not make a practical difference in the Court's operations, and there was a general feeling that ten judges was not a practical number. With an even number of judges, it was always possible that a vote would be equally divided, in which case the judgment appealed from would be affirmed without a ruling on the merits. If the Court were expanded to eleven, it would be unwieldy. For the time being at least, the Court would continue its work with just the remaining nine judges.

DAVID DAVIS WAS WELL enough to resume his circuit-court work in Indiana in the spring. He went to Indianapolis, where David McDonald had recently been appointed as the federal district judge. Working together, Davis and McDonald took up some serious cases in the circuit court. One was a petition for habeas corpus filed on behalf of a man named Lambdin P. Milligan, who was held prisoner near Indianapolis under authority of a military commission. Milligan was a lawyer and a minor politician (he had made an unsuccessful bid for the Democratic nomination for governor of Indiana in 1864) with well-known Southern sympathies. Arrested on October 5, 1864, by order of Brevet Major General Alvin P. Hovey, commander of the military district of Indiana, Milligan was charged with "conspiracy against the government of the United States," "affording aid and comfort to rebels against the authority of the United States," "inciting insurrection," "disloyal practices," and "violation of the laws of war."[33] Between October 21 and December 6, Milligan and four other men, Horace Heffren, William A. Bowles, Stephen Horsey, and Andrew Humphrey, were tried before a military commission organized by order of General Hovey. All of the men were members of the Sons of Liberty, a secret "army" dedicated to ending the war on terms favorable to the South. (Ohio's Clement L. Vallandigham was the "Supreme Commander" and Milligan a "major general" of the Sons of Liberty.) They objected vigorously to the commission's jurisdiction, arguing that they were entitled to be indicted and tried in a civil court under the Habeas Corpus Act of 1863. But their arguments were overruled, largely on the basis of the Supreme Court's ruling in Ex parte Vallandigham that it had no jurisdiction to review the proceedings of military commissions.[34] In the second week of the trial, charges against Heffren were dropped when he agreed to testify against the other defendants. The evidence of guilt was strong (although not without some conflict) and, after due deliberations, the commission convicted Milligan, Bowles, Horsey and Humphrey. Humphrey was sentenced to hard labor for the duration of the war, while the others were ordered to be hanged.[35]

Faced with a death sentence, Milligan arranged for Joseph E. McDonald, a prominent Indianapolis lawyer and Democratic politician, to become his attorney. (McDonald was a former congressman and state attorney general and had beaten Milligan for the gubernatorial nomination in 1864.) McDonald went to Washington to plead Milligan's case with President Lincoln. In spite of the president's busy schedule, Lincoln and the attorney sat up until almost eleven o'clock at night reviewing the papers in the case. Lincoln told McDonald he found "certain errors and imperfections in the record" and would send it back to Indiana for correction. "You may go home, Mr. McDonald," he said, with a pleased expression, "and I'll send for you when the papers get back; but I apprehend and hope there will be such a jubilee over yonder" (pointing to the hills of Virginia just across the river) "we shall none of us want any more killing done."[36] Until that time, however, Lincoln would keep Milligan and his fellow defendants "in prison awhile to keep them from killing the Government."[37]

But Lincoln was assassinated and Andrew Johnson became president before Milligan's record could be corrected and sent back to Washington. When the papers finally got back to the White House, Andrew Johnson was in a mood to "make treason odious." The trial of those implicated in Lincoln's assassination had begun on May 13 in Washington before a military commission, pursuant to Johnson's own order. Johnson approved all three of the Indiana sentences and directed that Milligan and his fellow defendants be executed on May 19, 1865.

On May 10, a petition for writ of habeas corpus was filed on behalf of Milligan and the others in the circuit court in Indianapolis. Now frantic efforts began to save the men's lives. Indiana's Republican governor Oliver P. Morton (who had earlier urged that Milligan be tried) sent Schuyler P. Colfax, the Republican speaker of the House of Representatives, to Washington with a letter protesting the scheduled executions. And Justice Davis and Judge McDonald wrote President Johnson, urging him to issue a stay so the case could be reviewed in the federal courts, and ultimately in the Supreme Court. In their letter, the judges said they did not "call in question the guilt of these men. We are satisfied that their trial had a most salutary effect on the public mind by developing and defeating a most dangerous and wicked conspiracy against our government." But, they pointed out, the military commission under which Milligan and the others were tried was "a new tribunal unknown to the Common Law," and there were "serious doubts" about its jurisdiction over civilians. "Would it not be wiser," Davis and McDonald asked, "to defer the execution of these men until the Supreme Court of the United States have passed on the question of the jurisdiction of the court that tried them?" Johnson responded by commuting all of the sentences to life imprisonment.

Back in Indianapolis, Davis and McDonald proceeded to hear Milligan's petition. It was apparent that the judges were strongly inclined in Milligan's favor on the issue of jurisdiction, but they wanted to submit the matter to the Supreme Court for a final and authoritative pronouncement. So they issued a certificate of division and framed three questions for answer by the high tribunal:

1. Should a writ of habeas corpus be issued?
2. Should Milligan be discharged from custody?
3. Did the military commission have jurisdiction to try and sentence Milligan?[38]

The record in *Ex parte Milligan* was filed in the Supreme Court on December 27, 1865. On February 5, 1866, the Court ordered that arguments begin on Monday, March 5. On March 2, Attorney General Speed filed a motion to dismiss the case for lack of jurisdiction, and the Court directed that arguments on this motion be heard at the same time as the argument on the merits.[39]

While the justices were waiting for arguments to begin in *Ex parte Milligan*, another important issue was working its way toward them. The Supreme Court had convened for its December term on Monday, December 6, 1865. Two days later, Reverdy Johnson had appeared to ask for early hearing of a petition filed on behalf of Augustus H. Garland, an attorney from Arkansas who had formerly been a member of the Supreme Court bar but whose membership had lapsed during the war. Garland's petition to reinstate his membership was complicated by an enormous issue then shaking the legal and political communities in both the North and the South: the requirement that ex-Confederates demonstrate their loyalty to the United States by taking so-called test oaths. The issue of the oaths, while important, was only part of the even larger issue of how the states formerly in rebellion should be "reconstructed," and whether men who had taken up arms against the United States during the war were now to be included in the political life of the nation, or wholly excluded from it.

As early as July 1862, Congress had enacted what was known as the Iron-Clad Oath, which required all civil and military officers of the United States (except the president himself) to swear (or affirm) that they had never voluntarily borne arms against the United States (after becoming citizens); that they had never voluntarily given "aid, countenance, counsel, or encouragement" to persons engaged in armed hostility against the government; that they had never sought or accepted any office under any authority hostile to the United States, or voluntarily supported such an authority; and that they would in the future support and defend the Constitution of the United States against all enemies, foreign and domestic.[40] In January 1865 the law was amended to require all persons seeking admission to the bar of any federal court (or appearing in such a court by reason of a previous admission) to take the same oath.[41] In accordance with the federal statute, the Supreme Court on March 10, 1865, adopted the requirement as one of its rules.[42]

Oath requirements were also being enacted in many states. Missouri signified its intention of requiring an oath in a new state constitution that was narrowly adopted by the state's voters in June 1865. The new constitution stated that designated persons must swear they had never been in "armed hostility to the United States"; never given "aid, comfort, countenance, or support to persons engaged in any such hostility"; never "in any manner, adhered to the enemies, foreign or domestic, of the United States"; never "advised or aided any person to enter the service of such enemies"; and never expressed "sympathy with those engaged in exciting or carrying on rebellion against the United States."[43] Missouri's oath applied broadly to public officers, officers of public and private corporations, professors and teachers, trustees, attorneys, bishops, priests, deacons, ministers and other clergymen, and even ordinary voters. Any person who held an office, practiced a profession, or exercised a function specified in the state constitution, after having failed to take the oath, was subject to a fine in the amount of $500 and imprisonment in the county jail for up to six months. Falsely taking the oath would subject a guilty person to prosecution for perjury and imprisonment for not less than two years.[44] It was a draconian measure, and one that was almost sure to arouse fierce opposition in a state whose wartime population was bitterly divided on the great questions of secession and slavery.

Augustus H. Garland was unable to take the new oath required by the Supreme Court's rules because he had a record of high-profile participation in the

Confederate government. Born in Tennessee in 1832, he had moved to Arkansas in the 1850s to practice law, and there became involved in politics. He was a delegate to the Arkansas secession convention in 1861, a delegate to the Confederate Provisional Congress from 1861 to 1862, a representative from Arkansas to the Confederate Congress from 1862 to 1864, and a member of the Confederate Senate from 1864 to 1865. His previous practice in the Supreme Court in Washington did not excuse him from having to take the oath now required by the rules. Garland and vocal oath opponents like Reverdy Johnson were anxious to argue the constitutionality of the oath requirement and obtain an early order of the Supreme Court striking it down. Garland's case, together with that of a Louisiana attorney named Robert Marr, who had also participated in the Confederate government, was set down for early argument.

The Missouri test oath was contested when a young Catholic priest named John Cummings was arrested and charged with performing his priestly duties without first having taken the oath. After offering Mass and preaching to his congregation, Father Cummings was arrested, indicted, and convicted in the Pike County Circuit Court. When he refused to pay his $500 fine, he was clapped into jail. Local attorneys quickly noticed his plight and made arrangements to challenge the required oath in court. The first case was heard in the Missouri Supreme Court, which sustained the oath. Then a writ of error was obtained from the United States Supreme Court, alleging the violation of a right under the United States Constitution.[45] The issues raised by Father Cummings's arrest were similar to those raised by Garland's bid to resume his practice in the Supreme Court, so the two cases were set down for argument together. Referred to as the *Test Oath Cases,* they were scheduled to be heard immediately after the arguments in *Ex parte Milligan.*

A formidable array of legal talent was on hand when arguments began in *Ex parte Milligan* on March 5, 1866. Appearing for Milligan were his Indianapolis attorney Joseph E. McDonald, former U.S. attorney general Jeremiah Sullivan Black, Justice Field's brother David Dudley Field, and a thirty-three-year-old congressman from Ohio named James A. Garfield. Field may have been the most eminent of Milligan's attorneys, though he was rivaled by Black, who had not only served three years as Buchanan's attorney general but had also spent four years as chief justice of the Supreme Court of Pennsylvania and two years as reporter of decisions for the United States Supreme Court. Black had served briefly as Buchanan's secretary of state and then, on February 5, 1861, been nominated to sit on the Supreme Court. He missed confirmation because Lincoln had already been elected president and the Senate was in no mood to confirm any nominee of the lame-duck Buchanan. Garfield was a learned lawyer and a college president as well as a successful major general in Union army operations in Kentucky and Tennessee. Almost everybody in the courtroom in March 1866 knew that Chief Justice Chase aspired to be president; nobody could have guessed that Garfield was the only man in the room that day who would actually attain that office, winning election in 1880 and serving briefly as president before he, like Lincoln, was felled by an assassin's bullet in 1881.

The government was represented by the new attorney general, James Speed, former Ohio attorney general Henry Stanbery, and Benjamin F. Butler, the blustery Massachusetts lawyer and Union major general who had earned the sobriquet "Beast Butler" during the six months he served as military governor of Louisiana in 1862. Butler was appearing in the capacity of special counsel for the United States.

McDonald opened the argument for Milligan, reviewing the facts of the case and arguing that his client should never have been tried before a military commission, because the Constitution and the laws of Congress both guaranteed him a trial in civilian courts, with all of the procedural guarantees of fairness provided in such courts. Garfield examined precedents in English and American law relating to the jurisdiction of military tribunals, arguing that the acts with which Milligan and his codefendants had been charged were clearly criminal in nature, and that they should have been charged under criminal statutes, not military orders. Black's argument was long and forceful. He characterized the military commission that tried Milligan as a "strange tribunal" and charged that it had jurisdiction over neither the parties nor the subject matter of the case. He invoked the provisions of the Habeas Corpus Act of 1863 and stated that Milligan and his codefendants fell squarely within its terms. They were being held pursuant to orders of the president and had not been indicted by a grand jury. They were thus entitled to their liberty under the terms of the act. More important, they were entitled to their liberty under terms of the Constitution. There was no fighting in Indiana when Milligan was arrested—he was a civilian, and the courts in his state were open and functioning. Under those circumstances, Black argued, the Constitution clearly required that Milligan be tried in a civilian court.

For the government, Stanbery argued that the case was not properly before the Court because a certificate of division was issuable only in a contest between adverse parties, and this was an ex parte matter, with only one party before the Court. Attorney General Speed and Benjamin Butler argued the merits of the action. They emphasized the president's "sovereignty in carrying on war" and argued that he was "the sole judge of the exigencies, necessities, and duties of the occasion." Speed argued that the constitutional requirements for trial in civil cases were "all peace provisions of the Constitution" and fell "silent amidst arms." It was a foolish argument and provoked Justice Miller to comment (in a private letter) that Speed was "certainly one of the feeblest men who has addressed the Court this term."[46]

The *Milligan* arguments continued for six and a half days, from March 5 through March 13, at which time the Court took up the *Test Oath Cases*. David Dudley Field was once again before the bar, now representing Cummings and Garland. (Apparently neither of the Field brothers felt any embarrassment on account of their close relationship, or ever suggested that it would be improper for one brother to sit in judgment in a case in which the other was an advocate.) Reverdy Johnson also appeared for Cummings and Garland, and Montgomery Blair, Lincoln's former postmaster general and one of the attorneys of record in *Dred Scott v. Sandford*, filed a brief on their behalf. The state of Missouri was represented by George P. Strong, a St. Louis attorney, and Missouri's U.S. senator John B. Henderson.

Field, Johnson, and Blair argued that the challenged oaths were invalid under the United States Constitution because they amounted to ex post facto laws and bills of attainder. The Constitution contains two provisions dealing with laws of this kind. Article I, Section 9, clause 3 (which applies to Congress) provides: "No bill of attainder or ex post facto law shall be passed." And Article I, Section 10, clause 1 provides (in relevant part): "No state shall . . . pass any bill of attainder [or] ex post facto law."

An ex post facto law is a law that imposes a punishment for an act that was not punishable when it was committed; or imposes additional punishment for the act; or changes the rules of evidence so that less or different testimony is required to convict a person for commission of the act. A bill of attainder is a legislative act that imposes a punishment without a judicial trial. Field, Johnson, and Blair argued that depriving a person of the right to practice a profession or business, to hold public or private office, or to vote, was a punishment that offended both of these provisions of the Constitution, for it was not illegal during the war merely to "encourage" the Southern insurrectionists, to express "sympathy" for their cause, or a "desire for their triumph." The new oath requirements made all of those things illegal, they argued, and did so retroactively, imposing punishments on all those who could not take the prescribed oaths.

It was also argued on behalf of Father Cummings that imposing the oath requirement on a clergyman was a violation of freedom of religion, for it purported to prevent a duly ordained priest from ministering to his flock in accordance with the mandates of his church. And it was argued on behalf of Augustus Garland that the oath requirement unconstitutionally deprived him of the benefits of the pardon that President Andrew Johnson had given him in July 1865. In that action, the president had pardoned Garland for "all offences" committed by him in connection with the Southern rebellion, and the pardon was conditioned only upon his taking an oath to faithfully support and defend the Constitution, the Union, and all laws and proclamations relating to emancipation. Garland had taken that oath. Article II, Section 2 of the Constitution states: "The President . . . shall have power to grant reprieves and pardons for offenses against the United States, except in cases of impeachment." Subjecting Garland to the new Supreme Court oath deprived him, his attorneys argued, of the benefits of the presidential pardon.

THE ARGUMENTS IN *Ex parte Garland* continued from March 13 to March 15, while those in *Cummings v. Missouri* extended from March 15 through March 20. In all, the Court devoted six days to the arguments in the *Test Oath Cases*. But even this was not enough to reach a decision. On April 2, President Johnson issued a proclamation declaring that the insurrection in the Southern states was at an end.[47] The following day, Chief Justice Chase announced from the bench that, on the facts stated in the petition and exhibits, the Court had reached a decision in Ex parte Milligan, answering the three questions that had been certified from Indiana:

1. A writ of habeas corpus ought to be issued.
2. Milligan ought to be discharged from custody according to the Habeas Corpus Act of 1863.
3. The military commission had no jurisdiction to legally try and sentence Milligan.[48]

There was no statement of reasons for the decision, and Chase announced that the Court's opinion would be read at the next term, set to begin in December, "when such of the dissenting judges as see fit to do so will state their grounds of dissent." On the same date, Chase announced that Cummings v. Missouri would be continued to the next term, "curia advisari vult" (the court will be advised). This Latin phrase signaled that the Court had not yet reached a decision on the test oaths and had ordered a delay for further consideration. With this somewhat puzzling order, the Supreme Court adjourned on April 3, and the justices left Washington for their circuits.

The Court's vote in Ex parte Milligan had been divided five to four, with Nelson, Grier, Clifford, Davis, and Field in the majority and Chase, Wayne, Miller, and Swayne in the minority. Under the long-established rules of the Court, if the chief justice was in the majority, he would designate one of the judges to write the opinion, but if he was in the minority, the designation would be made by the senior associate justice in the majority—in this instance, Samuel Nelson. Nelson assigned the Milligan opinion to David Davis. (Neither Nelson nor Davis apparently thought there was anything wrong with the same judge deciding the case in both the circuit court and the Supreme Court. In later years, a judge who had decided a case in the circuit court would routinely decline to participate in the decision of the same case in the Supreme Court.)[49] Davis had no doubt that the military commission that had tried Milligan was unconstitutional, but he was not sure of all the legal reasons for reaching that conclusion. He had never regarded himself as a legal scholar, and opinion writing did not come easily to him.[50] He was determined, however, to research the law and, when doubts occurred to him, to write his fellow justices for help. Davis left Washington, attended to his circuit court work, and then headed home to Bloomington, Illinois, to spend the rest of the summer composing his opinion.[51]

While Davis was laboring over his *Milligan* opinion, reports were circulating in the newspapers that the *Test Oath Cases* had also been decided. The newspapers reprinted a letter written by Reverdy Johnson, to the effect that the judges had decided that the oaths were unconstitutional but had deferred the announcement of a decision to give one of the judges more time to write an opinion. The reports created a lot of controversy in Missouri, where elections were coming up in the fall and the validity or invalidity of the Missouri oath could well have a decisive effect on the outcome. (If the oaths were struck down, many Democrats who would otherwise be ineligible to vote would be able to cast ballots.) Justice Miller heard the reports and wrote to Chase: "Whatever may be our guesses at the individual conclusions of the members of the Court, it is certainly false that the Court ever decided the case, or even took a vote upon it. Not only so but there are several members of the Court, who have never as far as I know *expressed* any opinion on the subject."[52] Chase agreed, though he had to admit that he had "no memoranda of what took place" when the case was discussed. Later statements made by Grier and Nelson indicated that Field had been wavering on the question of the Missouri oath and that Grier had suggested that decisions in both cases be postponed to allow Field time for more reflection. Whatever the cause, there was a serious misunderstanding among the judges. Chase had kept no records on their discussion of the case, and it was his responsibility as chief justice to do so. This lapse, coupled with the suggestion that Chase was personally interested in the case and wanted to affect its outcome, led historian Charles Fairman to condemn his "loose" administration and to write that: "Danger attended this way of doing business, especially in any situation where Chase had a strong personal concern for the outcome."[53]

THE JUSTICES WERE BACK in Washington on December 3 for the opening of the Court's new term. Two weeks later, on December 17, Justice Davis read his opinion in *Ex parte Milligan*.

He began by stating that the controlling question in the case was whether the military commission convened by General Hovey in Indianapolis had jurisdiction to try and sentence Milligan, who was a civilian. "No graver question was ever considered by this court," Davis wrote, "nor one which more nearly concerns the rights of the whole people; for it is the birthright of every American citizen when charged with crime to be tried and punished according to law. . . . If there was law to justify this military trial, it is not our province to interfere; if there was not, it is our duty to declare the nullity of the whole proceedings."[54] Davis referred to key provisions of the Constitution protecting the rights of those accused of crime: the freedom from unreasonable search and seizure guaranteed by the Fourth Amendment; the right to a grand jury indictment guaranteed by the Fifth Amendment; the right to due process of law, as guaranteed by that same Fifth Amendment; the right to a speedy and public trial by an impartial jury, as guaranteed by the Sixth Amendment; and the right to be tried by a jury, as guaranteed by Article III, Section 2.[55]

Davis noted the difference between a suspension of the privilege of the writ of habeas corpus (as had occurred in Ex parte Merryman) and a trial and conviction by a military commission. If the privilege of the writ has been validly suspended, the government is not required to produce an arrested person in answer to a writ of habeas corpus. But the "Constitution goes no further," Davis said. "It does not say, after a writ of habeas corpus is denied a citizen, that he shall be tried otherwise than by the course of the common law." Even if the writ is suspended, an accused person cannot be tried, convicted, and punished unless he is first accorded his constitutional rights of trial by jury and due process of law.

The law permits an exception when "martial law" has been validly declared. Martial law can be declared in cases of foreign invasion or civil war, Davis said, if "the courts are actually closed, and it is impossible to administer criminal justice according to law." But martial law is proper only "where war really prevails," where "there is a necessity to furnish a substitute for the civil authority . . . to preserve the safety of the army and society." In such a case, as "no power is left but the military, it is allowed to govern by martial rule until the laws can have their free course."[56] There was no war in Indiana when Milligan was arrested, and the courts were open and functioning. Under those circumstances, trial by a military commission was neither necessary nor constitutionally permissible. Davis continued with a memorable statement, one of the "thunderously quotable" phrases that, when uttered, take on an importance beyond their literal meaning.[57] He wrote:

The Constitution of the United States is a law for rulers and people, equally in war and in peace, and covers with the shield of its protection all classes of men, at all times and under all circumstances.

Pursuant to this "law for rulers and people," Milligan and his fellow defendants were entitled to their freedom.

Contrary to the announcement he made when the court adjourned in April, Chief Justice Chase did not dissent from Davis's decision. Instead, he filed a concurring opinion in which he agreed that Milligan was entitled to be released under a writ of habeas corpus, but for different reasons than those asserted by Davis. He referred to the Habeas Corpus Act of 1863, which provided that persons held under military authority were entitled to release if they were not indicted by the grand jury convened in their district. Milligan and his codefendants had been named on a list provided to the district judge in Indianapolis as required by the act. However, they had not been indicted by the grand jury. For this reason, they were entitled to be released under the terms of the act itself.

Chase noted that the crimes with which Milligan was charged "were of the gravest character" and that the record in his case amply demonstrated his guilt. But he agreed with Davis that it was "more important to the country and to every citizen that he should not be punished under an illegal sentence . . . than that he should be punished at all." Since the Habeas Corpus Act was ample justification for Milligan's release, he objected to the implication in Davis's opinion that Congress had no power under the Constitution to enact such a statute. "Congress has the power not only to raise and support and govern armies," Chase wrote, "but to declare war. It has therefore the power to provide by law for carrying on war." Indiana was a military district at the time Milligan was arrested; it "had actually been invaded in the past"; and it "was constantly threatened with invasion." Chase had no doubt that, "in such a time of public danger," Congress was empowered under the Constitution to organize military commissions, and when it enacted the Habeas Corpus Act it had done just that. The fact that the federal courts were open was not sufficient grounds for denying Congress the power to authorize military commissions, for the courts "might be open and undisturbed in the execution of their functions, and yet wholly incompetent to avert threatened danger or to punish, with adequate promptitude and certainty, the guilty conspirators."[58] Justices Wayne, Swayne, and Miller joined in Chase's concurring opinion.

THE COURT'S DECISIONS in the *Test Oath Cases* were announced on January 14, 1867. *Cummings v. Missouri* and *Ex parte Garland* were, like *Milligan*, five-to-four decisions. Justice Field, joined by Wayne, Nelson, Grier, and Clifford, delivered the majority opinions in both cases. Miller, joined by Chase, Swayne, and Davis, issued a powerfully argued dissent that was applicable to both cases.

Field acknowledged that in Missouri during the war there had been a "struggle for ascendancy . . . between the friends and the enemies of the Union" and that the struggle had aroused "fierce passions." It would have been "strange," Field said, if the Missouri constitution had not exhibited "some traces of the excitement" amidst which it was adopted. But the framers of the United States Constitution had intended to guard against this kind of excitement and passion. Field found the severity of the Missouri oath "without any precedent that we can discover." It embraced "more than thirty distinct affirmations or tests." It was retrospective rather than prospective. It embraced "all the past from this day; and, if taken years hence, it will also cover all the intervening period." Further, the Missouri oath referred not only to overt acts of hostility against the government but also to "words, desires, and sympathies." "If one has ever expressed sympathy with any who were drawn into the Rebellion," Field noted, "even if the recipients of that sympathy were connected by the closest ties of blood, he is as unable to subscribe to the oath as the most active and the most cruel of the rebels."

Field carefully examined the constitutional rules relating to bills of attainder and ex post facto laws and found both provisions offended by the Missouri oath. The Missouri oath purported, in some cases, to punish conduct that was not illegal when it was committed, and in others, to increase the penalties for conduct previously declared to be illegal. It reversed the constitutional rule of the presumption of innocence by requiring oath takers to deny their guilt to escape the punishment. And depriving a person of a vocation, a position, an honor, or a privilege open to others was "punishment, and can be in no otherwise defined."

Field found the oath in *Ex parte Garland* subject to objections much like those in *Cummings v. Missouri*. Requiring attorneys who wished to practice (or continue to practice) in the federal courts to take the oath punished them for past conduct. The law imposing the oath was thus objectionable as an ex post facto law and a bill of attainder. Beyond that, the oath deprived Augustus Garland of the benefits of his presidential pardon. The power of the president to grant pardons and reprieves, Field said, is "unlimited," except for the stated case of impeachment. The power was not subject to legislative control and could not be diminished by an act of Congress requiring a pardoned person to swear that he had not committed the offense for which he was pardoned. If Congress could thus exact further punishment from the oath taker, "the pardon may be avoided, and that accomplished indirectly which cannot be reached by direct legislation." Field thus concluded that Garland was entitled to practice in the Supreme Court, as was Robert Marr, whose legal situation was identical.[59]

Miller's dissent was filed in *Ex parte Garland*, but it applied to *Cummings v. Missouri* as well. He carefully analyzed the legal history of bills of attainder and ex post facto laws and determined that both terms contemplated criminal proceedings that inflicted punishment. He denied that the oaths before the Court imposed any punishments at all. They merely required that the affected persons declare their loyalty to the United States. Oaths were required all the time of officeholders, attorneys, and other persons, he said. Their purpose was to establish qualifications for an office, a profession, or a calling. It was well within the power of Congress "to require loyalty as a qualification of all who practice in the national courts." Miller noted that the Constitution required that the president and vice president be natural-born citizens.[60] "Is this a punishment to all those naturalized citizens who can never attain that qualification?" he asked. In some states, the law prescribed that judges could not be more than sixty years of age. "To a very large number of the ablest lawyers in any State," Miller said, "this is a qualification to which they can never attain, for every year removes them further away from the designated age. Is it a punishment?" Since establishing a qualification for an office did not "punish" those who could not meet the qualification, Miller said, Garland's presidential pardon was irrelevant. The pardon relieved Garland of any punishment for his association with the Confederate government. It did not, and could not, relieve him of the qualifications imposed on all persons who sought to practice law in the Supreme Court of the United States.[61]

After the opinions of Field and Miller had been read, the Supreme Court rescinded its rule requiring the test oath.[62] Garland, Marr, and all other affected attorneys were now eligible to practice in the Supreme Court.

For Garland, at least, the rescission was a triumph. He continued, almost uninterrupted, the high-profile career he had begun before the war. A former Confederate senator, he was elected to the United States Senate from Arkansas in 1867. Although the radical Republicans refused to seat him in the Senate, he later served as governor of Arkansas from 1874 to 1876 and was elected a second time to the Senate in 1876. This time his qualifications were not challenged, and he served in that body until 1885, when he resigned to become United States attorney general under Democratic president Grover Cleveland. He left the attorney general's office in 1889 to resume his private law practice and was arguing a case in the Supreme Court in Washington in January 1899 when he suffered a stroke and died.[63]

THE COURT CONTINUED to hear arguments and deliver opinions through the spring of 1867. None of its decisions, however, aroused as much raw emotion as *Milligan, Cummings,* and *Garland.* Press comments on the three cases ranged from praise to condemnation, and even to warnings that the decisions endangered the victory just won on the battlefield.

Democratic newspapers generally hailed the *Milligan* decision as a great blow for freedom. The *New York World* (which had opposed Lincoln throughout the war) praised Davis's opinion as "a triumphant vindication of the Democratic party and a happy augury of the future."[64] And the *Louisville Democrat* expressed satisfaction "that in the worst days of party insanity and misrule, there is one conservative department of the Government unawed and uninfluenced by the arbitrary power of Jacobinism. . . . *God save the Union and the Supreme Court.*"[65]

Republican newspapers were less enthusiastic. The *New York Herald* ridiculed Davis's opinion as "constitutional twaddle" and said it would "no more stand the fire of public opinion than the Dred Scott decision."[66] The *New York Times* lamented that the majority had not expressed "the common sense doctrine that the Constitution provides for the permanence of the Union, and for such exercise of authority by Congress as may be necessary to preserve the National existence." The *Philadelphia North American* compared Davis to Confederate president Jefferson Davis and charged that Lincoln had "made a mistake in appointing a Judge of the fatal name of Davis."[67] The *Independent* noted the peculiar effect the *Milligan* decision might have on other military trials. The men (and one woman) implicated in Lincoln's assassination had been tried by a military commission in Washington, sentenced, and then hanged. Was their trial subject to the same constitutional infirmities as Milligan's? If so, the *Milligan* decision "virtually declares" that these assassins "suffered a juridico-military murder."[68]

Other newspapers struck a more balanced tone. In Illinois, the *Springfield Republican* said that *Milligan* was "simply a reaffirmation of the sacred right of trial by jury."[69] The *Chicago Tribune* noted that the majority and concurring opinions both agreed that Milligan was entitled to his liberty, disagreeing only on the issue of whether Congress had power to provide for commissions, and it criticized Davis for leaving the impression that Congress had no power to do so.[70]

It has occasionally been argued that the *Milligan* decision was guided by the earlier opinion of Roger Taney in *Ex parte Merryman*. Warren wrote that *Milligan* "strongly upheld" the principles laid down in *Merryman,* and David Silver stated that *Milligan* was a "vindication for Chief Justice Taney."[71] Except that both dealt with arrests in wartime, however, *Merryman* and *Milligan* were different cases. The issue before Taney in 1861 was whether the president or Congress had the power to suspend the writ of habeas corpus. He decided that only Congress could do that. It is true that his opinion (delivered without listening to any arguments from Lincoln or his administration) expounded at length on the proper role of courts and executives in time of war, but the facts of *Merryman* contrasted sharply with those of *Milligan*. Maryland was in a turmoil caused by street riots and sabotage when John Merryman was arrested. Notwithstanding this, Merryman was never tried by a military commission—or tried at all. Indiana was (if we may accept Justice Davis's description) in a state of peace when Lambdin Milligan was taken before a military commission, tried, and sentenced to be hanged. There was no question in *Milligan* whether Congress or the president could suspend the writ of habeas corpus, for Congress had spoken in the Habeas Corpus Act of 1863, authorizing the president to suspend the writ.[72]

Justice Davis was a sensitive man who, as Charles Fairman has observed, "set great store upon the good opinion of others."[73] He was chagrined by criticism of his *Milligan* decision, particularly when it came from men in whom he reposed special confidence. One such person was his brother-in-law, Julius Rockwell, a prominent Republican politician in Massachusetts. Rockwell had long been speaker of the Massachusetts House of Representatives, had served in the national House of Representatives, and had served a brief term in the U.S. Senate from 1854 to 1855. Since 1859 he had been a highly respected judge of the Massachusetts Superior Court. When Rockwell did not immediately write him about *Milligan,* Davis concluded that "he does not like my opinion." When Rockwell finally wrote, it was to express agreement with Chief Justice Chase's concurring opinion, which reasoned that Milligan was entitled to release under the act of Congress and that it was unnecessary to decide the case upon constitutional grounds. But he complimented Davis on the "great felicity of language and the true spirit of Judicial dignity and candor" shown in his opinion.[74] Davis's reply to Rockwell mixed resignation with resolution. "It w[oul]d be folly to say that I am indifferent to criticism," he admitted, "but I can conscientiously say, that I do not *wilt* under it." He told his brother-in-law that "this Court w[oul]d be a hell on earth to me, unless I can decide questions according to the light which God has given me. I hope that God will give me strength to utter my convictions & never to quail before any political tempest."[75]

Davis knew that *Ex parte Milligan* was the most important case he had ever decided—probably the most important he would ever decide. And to the end of his days he remained convinced that he had decided it "according to the light which God has given me." Thousands of Americans—perhaps millions— were also satisfied that he had done just that and, in the process, earned a firm place in the history of the Court and his country.

10   The Union Is Unbroken

CHASE PRESIDED OVER THE Court during one of the most turbulent eras
of its history, for the war had settled the great questions of secession, union,
and slavery on the battlefield but not in the law books. The radical Republicans in Congress were determined to remake the states of the old South in a
new mold, using military power and political compulsion to "reconstruct" their
constitutions, their elections, and their governments, while Democrats generally (and former Confederates particularly) were determined to resist the radicals and to enlist the support of any legislators, executives, or judges who might
help them to do so. Chase was a forceful personality but never a good administrator. He tried to have his own way on questions not only of judicial administration but also of constitutional jurisprudence, and his efforts to coerce his fellow judges aroused resentment and resistance.[1]

The death of John Catron in May 1865 marked the beginning of five years
during which the size of the Court fluctuated, sometimes in response to exter-
nal demands, sometimes in response to its own needs. When Field joined the
Court in 1863, its membership was set by law at ten justices, but Catron's long
illness had for practical purposes reduced that number to nine. Andrew Johnson waited nearly a year before he nominated a replacement. His eventual
choice was Henry Stanbery of Cincinnati, the well-known former Ohio attorney general who had participated in the arguments of Ex parte Milligan and Ex
parte Garland on the government's side.[2] Stanbery's professional qualifications
were high, but in March 1866 he had been the principal draftsman of Johnson's

message vetoing the Civil Rights Act that Congress had just passed, and this aroused senatorial hackles. The precedent-breaking act declared "all persons born in the United States and not subject to any foreign power" to be citizens of the United States, and it guaranteed all citizens a broad range of equal rights, regardless of race, color, or previous condition of servitude. Congress overrode Johnson's veto and the act became law on April 9, 1866.[3] One week later, Johnson sent Stanbery's nomination to the Senate. Senators who resented his role in the civil rights veto quickly moved to sideline the nomination.[4]

Movement had already begun in Congress to reorganize the Supreme Court to improve its efficiency and reduce its caseload. With the approval of all of the justices except Clifford, Senator Ira Harris of New York proposed to create an intermediate appellate court within each circuit. The court would be administered by a new circuit justice working with the Supreme Court justice assigned to the circuit, and it would have broad jurisdiction. Appeals to the Supreme Court would be limited to more important cases.[5] Another proposal, made by Congressman James F. Wilson of Iowa, would reduce the authorized size of the Supreme Court from ten to nine justices. Wilson defended his proposal on the ground that the existing court was too large for efficient administration and that an even number of justices risked a tie vote. He also thought that further reductions in the size of the Court might be justified as vacancies occurred.[6] Justice Miller hoped that the Senate bill would pass, for intermediate appellate courts would do much to reduce the court's substantial backlog.

While the Supreme Court was out of session, Chase took it upon himself to intervene with the House judiciary committee. Without consulting the other justices, he asked that the legislation before Congress be amended to increase the salaries of Supreme Court judges (associate justices would receive $10,000 per year and the chief justice $12,000) and to change his title from "Chief Justice of the Supreme Court" to "Chief Justice of the United States." And he agreed that no new judges should be appointed until the Court's membership was reduced to seven.[7] (Reducing the number of justices would, he thought, make the higher salaries more acceptable to Congress.) As finally passed, the bill reduced the number of judges to seven and changed Chase's title, but it did not increase the judges' salaries or create intermediate appellate courts. As thanks for his meddling, Chase got part of what he wanted (a grander title, though it was so effectively buried in the legislation that the public took no notice of it), and Miller and the other judges got nothing. The final act was submitted to President Johnson and signed by him on July 23, 1866.[8] By signing the bill, the president acknowledged that Stanbery's nomination would die. Three days earlier, Johnson had nominated Stanbery to be attorney general, as successor to James Speed, who had resigned.[9] The nomination was promptly confirmed by the Senate.[10]

It has often been asserted that the bill reducing the Court from ten to seven justices was designed to deprive Andrew Johnson of the power to make any Supreme Court appointments.[11] Johnson was, by this time, in a bitter struggle with the radical Republicans in Congress over reconstruction and a host of other issues. Justice Davis, who was not in Washington when Congress reduced the size of the Court, was "puzzled by the bill," primarily because it left the justices' circuit court assignments in doubt. But he "supposed" the bill was passed "simply to prevent the Presdt fr[om] appointing Supreme Judges & that it might be changed hereafter."[12] A careful analysis of the chronology of the legislation indicates that Davis's supposition was mistaken. In fact, the idea of reducing the Court to seven justices predated the radicals' difficulty with Johnson, and it found its way into the 1866 legislation when Chase suggested it as an offset for higher salaries. It was only in the last days of the legislative process that the final bill emerged with a reduced court and no intermediate appellate courts to help the justices with their work. Johnson (who was never reluctant to veto acts of Congress that he disagreed with) had readily signed the reduction bill and acquiesced in its results.[13] Further, Congress did not have to reduce the size of the Court to make sure that Johnson would not make unacceptable appointments, for the radicals had enough votes in the Senate to reject any nominees they disapproved. As Fairman has observed: "It is no wonder that the President made no contest over the bill."[14]

JANUARY 14, 1867, MARKED the thirty-second anniversary of Justice James M. Wayne's accession to the Supreme Court. Entering his seventy-seventh year, the justice from Savannah was the longest-serving judge remaining on the Court. He had begun his service when Chief Justice John Marshall presided and had served during the administrations of eleven presidents. Though frail, he was not in bad health and still contributed to the Court's work, even giving occasional lectures at universities in Washington.[15] But the summer of 1867 was hot and humid, and typhoid was in the capital. Sometime early in the summer, Wayne fell victim to the disease, and on July 5, he died.[16] He had completed thirty-two years, five months, and twenty-one days of service on the high court, a record exceeded up to that time only by Marshall himself, who served thirty-four years, five months, and two days before his death in 1835.

Wayne's contribution to the Supreme Court was measured not only by time served but also by his important decisions. While he had been a member of the majority that handed down the notorious *Dred Scott* decision in 1857, during the war he had provided indispensable support for some of Lincoln's key measures. He sided with the majority to sustain the blockade in the *Prize Cases* in 1863 (his vote in those cases made the difference between victory and a crushing defeat for the administration), and in 1864 he wrote the opinion in *Ex parte Vallandigham* that denied the Supreme Court's jurisdiction to hear an appeal from a military commission and enabled the president to avoid a potentially disastrous decision.[17] In *Ex parte Milligan,* he declined to join Justice Davis's opinion striking down the military commissions as unconstitutional, agreeing with Chase's concurring opinion that Milligan was entitled to his release but that the military commission that tried him did not violate the Constitution.[18] And he had, by orders made in circuit court cases in Washington, sustained the administration's position in key habeas corpus cases.[19] In late December 1866, Wayne had considered a petition for habeas corpus filed on behalf of Dr. Samuel A. Mudd, one of the eight persons convicted for complicity in Lincoln's assassination. The Supreme Court's recent decision in *Ex parte Milligan* had persuaded Mudd's lawyers that he was entitled to release from his imprisonment on the Dry Tortugas in Florida because his conviction, like Milligan's, had been by a military commission. Wayne, however, refused to order Mudd's release; as did Chief Justice Chase, to whom Mudd's lawyers appealed after Wayne turned them down.[20] Only in the *Test Oath Cases* did Wayne oppose the government's position, joining with Field, Nelson, Grier, and Clifford to strike down the oaths.[21]

In all, Wayne's record was one of dependable support for the government in its efforts to deal with secession. He had paid dearly for his Union loyalty, losing his property in Savannah early in the war and forfeiting the opportunity to go home. He had, however, earned a reputation as a judge of principle and character. Wayne's death reduced the Supreme Court to eight judges. By terms of the act of July 23, 1866, no successor was appointed.

A POTENTIALLY EXPLOSIVE case raising some of the same issues that the Court faced in *Milligan* arrived in Washington a few months after Wayne's death. A fiercely racist newspaper editor named William McCardle had published articles in a Vicksburg, Mississippi, newspaper attacking the government's reconstruction policies. Military authorities found the articles "incendiary and libelous" and had McCardle arrested and held for trial by a military commission. The commission had been established pursuant to the Reconstruction Act of 1867, in which Congress authorized military commanders in the former insurrectionary states to organize military commissions when they deemed them necessary "for the trial of offenders."[22] McCardle filed a petition for a writ of habeas corpus in the federal circuit court, but it was denied. He then appealed to the Supreme Court in Washington, which made a preliminary finding that it had jurisdiction to hear the case.[23]

The merits of McCardle's petition were extensively argued between March 2 and 9, 1868, by a panel of distinguished lawyers that included, among others, Jeremiah Sullivan Black, David Dudley Field, and Senator Lyman Trumbull of Illinois. Justice Field later said that he had rarely heard arguments of such "learning, ability and eloquence." Reports soon began to circulate that the arguments against the validity of military commissions had been so persuasive that the majority of the justices were almost certain to strike down the reconstruction laws. Congress heard the reports and decided to take action.

It had been generally agreed, at least since 1789, that Congress had extensive power to define and limit the jurisdiction of the Supreme Court, for Article III, Section 2, of the Constitution provides that "the Supreme Court shall have appellate jurisdiction, both as to law and fact, with such exceptions, and under such regulations as the Congress shall make."[24]

By giving Congress the power to make "exceptions" and "regulations," the Constitution gave the legislature a large degree of control over the Court's appellate jurisdiction. McCardle's petition was brought under an 1867 act of Congress giving the Supreme Court jurisdiction to hear appeals in habeas corpus cases when any person was deprived of liberty "in contravention of the constitution or laws of the United States."[25] Before the Court could announce its decision in McCardle's case, however, Congress began to consider a bill repealing the part of the 1867 law that gave the Supreme Court jurisdiction of the case. When the justices assembled for their conference, the bill had passed in both houses of Congress but had not yet been signed by President Johnson. Conceding that Congress had the power to repeal the 1867 law, and believing, as Justice Davis later explained, that it was "unjudicial to run a race with Congress," the justices withheld their decision.[26] When the bill got to Johnson, he vetoed it, but Congress promptly passed it over his veto. After the bill finally became law, the Court postponed McCardle's case to the next term, to give the judges and attorneys the opportunity to fully consider the effect of Congress's action.[27]

In April 1869, after hearing extensive arguments, Chase announced that the case was to be dismissed. The chief justice conceded Congress's power to make "exceptions" to the Court's appellate jurisdiction and stated that it was "hardly possible to imagine a plainer instance of positive exception. . . . Without jurisdiction the court cannot proceed at all in any cause. Jurisdiction is power to declare the law, and when it ceases to exist, the only function remaining to the court is that of announcing the fact and dismissing the cause."[28]

But there were protests. Orville Browning (now Andrew Johnson's secretary of the interior) condemned the Court's failure to decide McCardle before Congress repealed its jurisdiction as an "exhibition of cowardice."[29] Gideon Welles complained that the justices had "caved in, fallen through, failed, in the McCardle case."[30] And on the Court itself, Justice Grier (joined by Justice Field) prepared a written statement in which he condemned the initial postponement. Grier argued that the case involved the liberty not only of McCardle but also of "millions of our fellow-citizens," and that it deserved a prompt decision. He charged that his fellow justices had "evaded the performance of a duty imposed on us by the Constitution" and added: "I am not willing to be a partaker either of the eulogy or opprobrium that may follow."[31]

The views expressed by Browning, Welles, and Grier had an effect on later appraisals of Ex parte McCardle, prompting some historians to call the case an abdication of judicial responsibility. If the Court had stood up to Congress in the battle over jurisdiction, these historians argued, it could have restrained some of the excesses of Reconstruction, striking a blow for civil liberty at the same time that it upheld its independence. By failing to do so, it badly impaired its prestige and dignity.[32] These criticisms, however, do not take account of a decision the Court rendered just a year later.

At the end of his *McCardle* opinion, Chase dropped a hint. It was a mistake, he said, to conclude that Congress had repealed all of the Court's appellate jurisdiction in habeas corpus cases. It had repealed only the 1867 provision authorizing appeals from the federal circuit courts.[33] Left untouched was a general provision in the Judiciary Act of 1789 granting the Supreme Court jurisdiction to issue writs of habeas corpus.[34] Taking the hint, attorneys for a Mississippian named Edward Yerger petitioned for Yerger's freedom from a military prison in Mississippi, where he was held on charges of having murdered an army officer. Yerger first petitioned the federal circuit court for habeas corpus under the Judiciary Act of 1789 and, when it denied relief, he applied to the Supreme Court for a writ of certiorari reviewing the circuit court's denial, and a writ of habeas corpus ordering his release. In *Ex parte Yerger*, decided on October 25, 1869, Chase upheld the Court's habeas corpus jurisdiction. He said that "the general spirit and genius of our institutions has tended to the widening and enlarging of the habeas corpus jurisdiction of the courts; . . . and this tendency, except in one recent instance [*McCardle*], has been constant and uniform." The Court could not exclude from its habeas jurisdiction "any cases not plainly excepted by law." Since *Yerger* was "a case of imprisonment alleged to be unlawful," it was the Court's responsibility to exercise its jurisdiction and hear the case.[35]

Viewed in the light of *Yerger*, *McCardle* does not seem so much a judicial abdication as a recognition of realities. Congress had power under the Constitution to create an "exception" to the Court's appellate jurisdiction, and in *McCardle* it did so. In *Yerger*, the Court forcefully asserted its general habeas jurisdiction, proving that it need not (and perhaps would not) acquiesce in all cases to congressional "exceptions." As Supreme Court historian Stanley Kutler has written: "The Court's full position in *McCardle*, and its later behavior in the *Yerger* case, are clearly inconsistent with the usual charges of judicial impotence and cowardice. . . . [I]n the light of prevailing political passions, the Court's counter-response in the two cases indicates the quintessence of judicial independence and courage, besides being a clever bit of judicial strategy."[36]

RELATIONS BETWEEN ANDREW JOHNSON and the radical Republicans in Congress deteriorated badly after 1865. Siding with Southern whites who opposed the extension of suffrage and other civil rights to former slaves, Johnson stubbornly resisted Republican efforts to "reconstruct" the former insurrectionary states. He pardoned ex-Confederates and publicly expressed his defiance of the radical leadership in Congress. And he dismissed federal officeholders who opposed his policies. To prevent the president from filling offices with his own supporters, Congress passed the Tenure of Office Act, providing that federal officials whose appointments required Senate confirmation could be removed only with the advice and consent of the Senate. The president could suspend an official for cause when the Senate was not in session, but if the Senate did not concur in the suspension when it reconvened, the official had to be reinstated. Johnson believed that the Tenure of Office Act was unconstitutional and vetoed it, but his veto was overridden, and it became law on March 2, 1867.[37]

Congress was in recess in the summer of 1867 when Johnson decided to remove Edwin Stanton from his post as secretary of war. Stanton had allied himself with the radicals and become increasingly hostile to the president. When Johnson demanded his resignation, Stanton refused to resign, forcing the president to suspend him from office. In January 1868, the new Senate met and refused to concur in Stanton's removal. Johnson responded by formally dismissing Stanton. But Congress was determined to assert its authority.

Article II, Section 4, of the Constitution provides: "The President, Vice President and all civil officers of the United States, shall be removed from office on impeachment for, and conviction of, treason, bribery, or other high crimes and misdemeanors." And Article I, Section 2, clause 5, provides (in relevant part): "The House of Representatives shall . . . have the sole power of impeachment." By a formal vote on February 24, 1868, the House of Representatives adopted eleven articles of impeachment, charging Andrew Johnson with violation of the Tenure of Office Act and attempting "to bring into disgrace, ridicule, hatred, contempt and reproach the Congress of the United States."[38] Chase watched the growing storm with special interest, knowing that he would be called on to preside over the impeachment trial, for according to Article I, Section 3, clause 7 of the Constitution: "The Senate shall have the sole power to try all impeachments. . . . When the President of the United States is tried, the Chief Justice shall preside: And no person shall be convicted without the concurrence of two thirds of the members present."

No president had ever before been impeached, so Chase had to make unprecedented decisions about his role in the trial. He insisted that it should be conducted with judicial formality. He demanded the right to rule on the competency of witnesses and the admissibility of evidence, subject to appeal to a vote of the senators. He also demanded that he have a vote in case of a tie. Chase decided privately that if the senators did not agree with his stipulations, he would refuse to preside, leaving the Senate in the embarrassing position of having to proceed in a manner unauthorized by the Constitution. Recognizing the strength of his position, the senators agreed to his stipulations.[39]

The impeachment trial began on March 4 and continued for eleven weeks. Chase conducted himself with dignity, making rulings that were generally admired for their fairness and judiciousness. But some of his rulings seemed to favor Johnson and angered the radicals. They had once considered Chase as one of their number—now they began to suspect that he had "gone over to the enemy." In late May, the Senate voted. With thirty-five senators voting to convict and nineteen to acquit, Johnson escaped removal from office by only one vote. On May 26, Stanton advised Johnson that he was relinquishing his office.[40]

The end of Johnson's impeachment trial coincided with the beginning of the presidential election season. On May 20 and 21, the Republican convention in Chicago nominated Ulysses S. Grant for president and Schuyler Colfax for vice president. With the Democratic convention scheduled to open in New York City on July 4, Chase began a letter-writing campaign in which he let it be known that, while he had no presidential "ambitions," under appropriate conditions, "I would not be at liberty to refuse the use of my name."[41] His strong record of support for universal male suffrage would ordinarily have made him unacceptable to the Democrats, for they were opposed to admitting former slaves to the polls; but he dropped hints that he would be willing to compromise on the issue. Reversing his earlier stand that equal voting rights should be guaranteed by the federal government, he announced that he now believed that suffrage was a question "for the people of the States themselves, not for outsiders."[42] (He knew full well that if the decision was left to white voters in the former Confederate states, African Americans would never be permitted to vote.)

He disingenuously repeated his denials of presidential ambitions while continuing to make concessions to the Democratic leaders. He even went so far as to say that Clement Vallandigham, now returned from his Canadian ex- ile and participating vigorously in the Democratic convention, was a man "of whose friendship one may well be proud."[43] In a letter to August Belmont, the New York financier who was chairman of the Democratic National Commit- tee, he bragged of his Democratic credentials. "For more than a quarter of a century," Chase told Belmont, "I have been, in my political views and senti- ments, a Democrat."[44] As John Niven has written: "The bright side of his char- acter, the oft-spoken belief in common humanity, was swinging slowly to the dark side of political expediency and even cynicism."[45]

Chase's daughter, Kate Sprague, moved to the Fifth Avenue Hotel in New York to take personal charge of her father's campaign. But things went badly for Chase at the convention. With 263 votes required for the nomination, Chase received only 4. Chagrined, he toyed with the possibility of mounting an inde- pendent candidacy, but quickly found there was no support for the idea.

When the votes were counted in the general election on November 3, the Republicans Grant and Colfax won, with 214 electoral votes to only 80 for the Democratic candidates Horatio P. Seymour of New York and Francis P. Blair, Jr., of Missouri. Noting how desperately Chase had made concessions in his ef- forts to win political support, editors of the Nation derisively commented that "no weight whatever will hereafter attach to any judgment of his on any one of the great constitutional questions arising out of the rebellion and reconstruc- tion which will doubtless come before his Court."[46]

Chase, of course, did not agree. He went back to his work on the Supreme Court, still dreaming of another presidential bid in 1874.

ONE OF THE "great constitutional questions" referred to by The Nation found its way to the Supreme Court in 1869. It was the constitutionality of the legal tender notes that Chase himself had issued in great quantities during the war— the so-called greenbacks that bore his portrait and his imprimatur as chief steward of the nation's finances.[47] Chase's roots in the Democratic Party had inclined him strongly in favor of "hard money" before the war broke out, and he stated that his approval of the legal tender notes in 1862 was a strategic de- cision, designed to meet the exigencies of the war and not a general endorse- ment of paper money. But the greenbacks had served their purpose well, raising hundreds of millions of dollars for the U.S. Treasury that would have been unobtainable through conventional borrowing or taxation. With vast numbers of greenbacks in circulation all over the country, the war had been won and the economy had survived.

But the power of the federal government (or, more particularly, of Congress as the legislative branch of the government) to issue the greenbacks had never been clear. It was universally agreed that the United States was a government of limited powers, and that a power could not be exercised unless it was granted (or "enumerated") in the Constitution itself. Article I, Section 8, contains a list (or enumeration) of eighteen powers that the Constitution has granted to Congress. The list includes (among other things) the powers:

> To borrow money on the credit of the United States . . . ;
> To regulate commerce with foreign nations, and among the several states
> . . . ;
> To coin money, regulate the value thereof . . . ;
> To raise and support armies . . . ;
> To provide and maintain a navy . . . ;
> To provide for calling forth the militia to execute the laws of the union, suppress insurrections and repel invasions;
> To provide for organizing, arming, and disciplining the militia, and for governing such part of them as may be employed in the service of the United States . . . ; and
> To make all laws which shall be necessary and proper for carrying into execution the foregoing powers, and all other powers vested by this Constitution in the government of the United States, or in any department or officer thereof.

None of these enumerations expressly authorizes the issuance of paper money, much less laws making paper money legal tender, though they might be extended to cover the situation under the "necessary and proper" clause as expounded by John Marshall in *McCulloch v. Maryland* (1819). In his decision in that case, one of the great landmarks of constitutional interpretation, Marshall upheld Congress's charter of the Second Bank of the United States over the claims of Jeffersonians that the Constitution gives Congress no power to charter corporations or banks. Speaking for a unanimous Court, Marshall ruled that the bank was justified under the "necessary and proper" clause because it furthered the exercise of Congress's enumerated powers to lay and collect taxes, borrow money, regulate commerce, declare and conduct war, and raise and support armies and navies. A constitution that contained a detailed statement of all of the government's powers would, in Marshall's words, "partake of the prolixity of a legal code, and could scarcely be embraced by the human mind. . . . Its nature, therefore, requires, that only its great outlines should be marked, its important objects designated, and the minor ingredients which compose those objects, be deduced from the nature of the objects themselves," for as Marshall proclaimed in one of his immortal phrases, "we must never forget that it is a constitution we are expounding." Whether the exercise of a particular power was "necessary and proper" was to be determined in the first instance by Congress, and the Court was to reject Congress's judgment only in the case of a clear abuse. Marshall wrote: "Let the end be legitimate, let it be within the scope of the constitution, and all means which are appropriate, which are plainly adapted to that end, which are not prohibited, but consist with the letter and spirit of the constitution, are constitutional."[48]

Support for greenbacks had generally been high during the war, though there were dissenting voices, and those voices were often heard in the courts. One of the first serious challenges to the Legal Tender Act was raised in New York by James Roosevelt (father of future president Franklin D. Roosevelt) in 1863. A man named Meyer was indebted to Roosevelt on a mortgage that had been executed before February 25, 1862, the effective date of the Legal Tender Act. Meyer tendered $8,171 in greenbacks in payment of the mortgage, but Roosevelt insisted that he had a right to be paid in gold and that, by requiring him to accept greenbacks, the Legal Tender Act deprived him of valuable constitutional rights. His attorney pointed out that the market value of the greenbacks at the time they were tendered was only $7,844.22, or $326.78 less than the amount of the debt. After Roosevelt's claim was denied in the New York Court of Appeals, his attorney brought a writ of error to the U.S. Supreme Court. Under the Judiciary Act of 1789, the Supreme Court could hear an appeal from a state supreme court when the state court denied the validity of a federal statute.[49] Here, however, the state court had upheld the federal statute. On December 21, 1863, the Supreme Court dismissed the appeal in *Roosevelt v. Meyer* for lack of jurisdiction. Justice Wayne announced the decision for the Court, and Justice Nelson dissented without opinion.[50]

Another important legal tender case that came before the Supreme Court under Chief Justice Chase was *Bronson v. Rodes,* which reached the Court in 1865. This case involved the enforceability of a contract made in 1851 to pay $1,400 "in gold or silver coin, lawful money of the United States." The payment was to be made in 1857. Writing for the majority, Chase declined to decide whether the Legal Tender Act was or was not constitutional, ruling instead that payment in this case had to be "in coined lawful money" because that was "the lawful intent and understanding of the parties." Chase said that the contract was "in legal import, nothing else than an agreement to deliver a certain weight of standard gold, to be ascertained by a count of coins."[51] Justice Miller dissented, pointing out that, in 1851, gold and silver was the only legal tender in the United States and that everybody who accepted a note payable in dollars contemplated that it would be paid in coin. He had no doubt, he said, that the Legal Tender Act was intended to make notes "a legal tender for all private debts then due, or which might become due on contracts then in existence, without regard to the intent of the parties on that point."[52]

Veazie Bank v. Fenno was another legal tender dispute that reached the Court in 1869. This case turned not on the validity of the legal tender notes themselves but on Congress's decision to impose a 10 percent tax on state bank notes.[53] The tax was clearly designed to drive the state notes out of circulation and leave the field clear for greenbacks. Again without expressing an opinion on the constitutionality of the legal tender notes, Chase upheld the 10 percent tax against the charge that Congress had no power to impose it. He admitted that the Constitution contained no "enumerated power" to impose such a tax, but pointed out that Congress was empowered to provide for the circulation of coin and to emit bills of credit. Thus it was empowered to make its bills "a currency, uniform in value and description, and convenient and useful for circulation." If Congress could do all of these things, it followed under the "necessary and proper" clause that Congress could also "restrain, by suitable enactments, the circulation as money of any notes not issued under its authority. Without this power, indeed, its attempts to secure a sound and uniform currency for the country must be futile."[54] Justices Nelson and Davis dissented.

The Court had, up to this point, avoided the central issue of the constitutionality of the Legal Tender Act, presuming it to be constitutional (every act of Congress is presumed to be constitutional until the contrary is shown) but finding it to be inapplicable to a whole host of cases by carefully construing contractual language. The case of *Hepburn v. Griswold,* which had been on the Court's docket for several years, finally forced the judges to address the constitutionality issue head on.

On June 20, 1860, Susan Hepburn signed a note promising to pay Henry Griswold $11,250 on February 20, 1862. The note did not specify the form of the payment, stating merely that it was to be in "dollars." In 1860, however, the only lawful money of the United States in which the debt could be paid was gold and silver coin. Five days after the note came due, Congress passed the Legal Tender Act, providing that legal tender notes would be "lawful money and a legal tender in payment of all debts, public and private, within the United States, except duties on imports and interest." Hepburn did not pay her note until 1864, after Griswold had brought suit in the Chancery Court in Louisville, Kentucky, to enforce it. The amount due was paid, in legal tender, into the court, which upheld the constitutionality of the Legal Tender Act. But on appeal to the Court of Errors of Kentucky, the judgment was reversed. Hepburn then appealed to the U.S. Supreme Court, where the case was argued two times and, in November 1869, considered at length in the judges' regular conference.

There were eight justices on the Court when it took up the *Hepburn* case, but one was substantially disabled. Pennsylvania's seventy-five-year-old Justice Robert Grier had suffered a stroke in the summer of 1867, and it had left him partially paralyzed. Grier could walk only with extreme difficulty and even had trouble wielding a pen or a pencil. Taking heavy law books down from high shelves was a near impossibility.[55] He had hung on to his Court seat, hoping that living space could be found for him in the Capitol. This proved impossible, so the judge struggled on, painfully climbing stairs, laboring to write simple letters, and trying to keep his mind focused on lawyers' arguments.

Andrew Johnson had left the White House in March 1869, surrendering his office to Ulysses S. Grant, who enjoyed good relations with the Republican Congress. Mindful of Justice Grier's disability and Justice Samuel Nelson's advanced years (the New Yorker would turn seventy-seven on November 11, 1869), Congress had in April provided for the first retirement pensions in the Court's history. The new law allowed Supreme Court judges who had served at least ten years and were at least seventy years of age to retire at full salary. And in the same act that provided for the pensions, Congress had once again reorganized the judicial system, increasing the size of the Supreme Court from eight to nine justices and providing for the appointment of a new class of circuit judges, who were required to reside in each of the nine circuits and who had the same powers within the circuits as the Supreme Court justices. The law was designed to encourage Grier and Nelson to retire, but even if they did not, Grant would be entitled to appoint one Supreme Court justice, to bring the Court up to its full complement of nine. By its terms, however, the law was not to become effective until December 6, 1869, the date set for the opening of the Court's next term.[56]

Hepburn was discussed for three or four hours in the Court's conference room on November 27. It was a vigorous discussion, for Chase had finally made it clear that he considered the Legal Tender Act unconstitutional, at least insofar as it applied to debts incurred before its effective date, and Miller was equally convinced that the act was constitutional. All of the justices had the opportunity to express their opinions. When the vote was taken, the count was four to four, with Justice Grier voting to reverse the judgment of the Kentucky Court of Errors and sustain the constitutionality of the act. One of the judges (unnamed) who voted to sustain the Kentucky court suggested that Grier had not understood the question on which he had just voted. But Grier said that he understood that the Kentucky court had declared the Legal Tender Act unconstitutional and that he voted to reverse that judgment. So the vote still stood at four to four. In the discussion of the next case on the conference list, however, Grier made a statement that seemed to be inconsistent with his vote in *Hepburn,* and one of the justices (again unnamed) called the inconsistency to his attention. At this, Grier changed his vote on *Hepburn,* so that there were now five votes to sustain the Kentucky court and three to overrule it. Grier was obviously confused.[57]

Justice Miller later prepared a confidential "Statement of Facts" in which he recorded his recollections of what happened during the *Hepburn* deliberations. The statement was signed by Miller, Swayne, and Davis to affirm its accuracy.[58] These three justices felt unable to do anything about Grier's vote (he was, after all, one of their brethren, and they respected his long record of Court service), but they were aware of the great consequences that attended the outcome of the case and concerned about Grier's muddled mind. Hundreds of millions of dollars in legal tender notes were still circulating all over the United

States. Americans had expressed their confidence in the currency, using the greenbacks to finance businesses, purchase property, meet payrolls, and fund investments. If the notes were suddenly declared unconstitutional, the reaction of the markets could only be guessed at. And all of this was because Justice Grier was allowed to change his vote in conference. "We do not say he did not agree to the opinion," Miller, Swayne, and Davis said. "We only ask, of what value was his concurrence, and of what value is the judgment under such circumstances?"[59] All of the justices agreed, however, that Grier was no longer able to perform the duties of his office. A week after their *Hepburn* conference, they chose three of their number to call on him and persuade him to submit his resignation.[60] The new retirement pension provided by Congress was an additional inducement. Bowing to the inevitable, Grier submitted his resignation to President Grant, effective February 1, 1870.[61]

The president had already taken steps to bring the Court up to its full membership. On December 15, he nominated his attorney general, Ebenezer R. Hoar of Massachusetts, to the new ninth seat. Hoar was eminently qualified for the position, but he had antagonized many senators by opposing their efforts to win judicial nominations for various political favorites, and they dragged their heels on his nomination. After Grier announced his retirement, Grant moved on December 20 to nominate Edwin Stanton to succeed the retiring justice.[62] The former secretary of war was an accomplished lawyer (Lincoln had had great confidence in his legal abilities) and popular with the radicals in Congress. Grant hoped that Stanton's popularity might persuade some senators also to support Hoar. Stanton was immediately confirmed by a Senate vote of forty-six to eleven, but Hoar's nomination was not considered until February 3, when it was rejected by a vote of twenty-four to thirty-three.[63] Tragically, Stanton suffered a coronary thrombosis and died on December 24, only four days after his confirmation. He was only fifty-four years old and had not yet taken up his duties on the Court.

Chase's majority opinion in *Hepburn v. Griswold* was read in the Court's conference on January 29. The chief justice was anxious to announce it, but the dissenters asked for time to prepare their opinion. Accordingly, the announcement was postponed until February 7. By that time, Justice Grier was no longer a member of the Court. Of the seven justices still serving on that date, only four supported the decision and three opposed it. Everybody knew that

Grant would soon appoint two new judges, one to succeed Grier and the other to fill the new ninth seat, and that the Court would then be up to its full strength. "Under these circumstances," Miller later wrote in his "Statement of Facts, "the minority begged hard for delay until the bench was full. But it was denied."[64]

Chase's opinion concluded that the Legal Tender Act was unconstitutional as applied to preexisting debts. He admitted that John Marshall's opinion in *McCulloch v. Maryland* provided guidance on the key question of whether legal tender was "necessary and proper" for the execution of any of Congress's enumerated powers. Was the "end . . . legitimate" and "within the scope of the constitution"? Were the means adopted by Congress "appropriate" and "plainly adapted" to the end? Were the means "not prohibited, but consistent with the letter and spirit of the constitution"?[65] Examining Marshall's words, Chase bore down heavily on the great chief justice's reference to the "spirit of the constitution." He referred to the so-called contracts clause in Article I, Section 10, which provides (in relevant part): "No state shall . . . pass any . . . law impairing the obligation of contracts." This clause applies to the states and not to Congress (there is no comparable limitation on the power of Congress), but Chase reasoned that "the spirit of the Constitution" made it applicable to Congress as well. To apply the Legal Tender Act to preexisting debts would, he said, impair the "obligation of contracts" and thus violate the Constitution.

He also referred to the "due process" and "takings" clauses of the Fifth Amendment, which state: "No person shall be . . . deprived of life, liberty, or property, without due process of law; nor shall private property be taken for public use, without just compensation." He found the Legal Tender Act similarly inconsistent with these provisions for, in his judgment, they deprived certain persons (creditors) of property without "due process of law," and took their property for public use without "just compensation." In Chase's view, an act that made irredeemable paper money legal tender for the payment of previously contracted debts was not "a means appropriate, plainly adapted, really calculated to carry into effect any express power vested in Congress." It was "inconsistent with the spirit of the Constitution" and thus prohibited by it.[66]

Chase was conscious (as was everybody who heard him deliver his opinion) that the conclusion he had now reached was diametrically opposed to the conclusion he had reached while he was secretary of the treasury. Then he had declared legal tender a "necessity" and said that he supported it "earnestly."[67] Now he said that it was inconsistent with the "spirit of the Constitution." How could he explain this apparent contradiction? Decisions were made during the war, he said, "under the influence of apprehensions for the safety of the Republic." Then, the time "was not favorable to considerate reflection upon the constitutional limits of legislative or executive authority." Power was assumed "from patriotic motives." Now, "under the influence of the calmer time," supporters of legal tender had reconsidered their opinions and changed their conclusions. The new conclusions, Chase wrote, "seem to us to be fully sanctioned by the letter and spirit of the Constitution."[68]

Miller's dissent (which was joined by Swayne and Davis) pointed out that the power to control money was specifically forbidden by the Constitution to the states, for Article I, Section 10, provides: "No state shall . . . coin money; emit bills of credit; make anything but gold and silver coin a tender in payment of debts." No such prohibition is placed on the power of Congress. Miller acknowledged that some matters are expressly forbidden to Congress, "but neither this of legal tender, nor of the power to emit bills of credit, or to impair the obligation of contracts, is among them."[69] Miller referred to Marshall's statement in McCulloch that the Constitution's "necessary and proper" clause was inserted to give Congress some flexibility in choosing the means to exercise its enumerated powers. Marshall had said that the Constitution was "intended to endure for ages to come" and "to be adapted to various crises of human affairs." If Congress's enumerated powers were rigidly circumscribed, it would be without power to meet "exigencies which, if foreseen at all, must have been but dimly, and which can best be provided for as they occur."[70] Miller thought that Marshall's words were "almost prophetic," for without the flexibility they allowed, Congress could not have carried on the great war to save the Union; it could not have raised the money necessary to fund the war; and the whole effort would have been rendered "nugatory." Congress would have been stripped of the power, in Miller's words, "to avail itself of experience, to exercise its reason, and to accommodate its legislation to circumstances, by the use of the most appropriate means of supporting the government in the crisis of its fate."[71]

Miller disagreed with Chase's argument that the Legal Tender Act, by impairing the obligation of a contract made before its effective date, was inconsistent with the "spirit of the Constitution." He pointed out that the Constitution clearly authorized Congress to pass bankruptcy laws. Article I, Section 8, gives Congress the power "to establish . . . uniform laws on the subject of bankruptcies throughout the United States." Congress had up until that time passed three bankruptcy laws, and they all applied to debts contracted before their effective dates. Miller asked how it could be in accordance with the "spirit of the Constitution" to directly destroy a creditor's rights to benefit an individual debtor and in violation of the same "spirit" to remotely impair the value of money "for the safety of the nation."[72] The "spirit of the Constitution" seemed altogether too abstract and intangible a concept for Miller. "It would authorize this court to enforce theoretical views of the genius of the government, or vague notions of the spirit of the Constitution and of abstract justice, by declaring void laws which did not square with those views." It would, Miller said, substitute the justices' own "ideas of policy for judicial construction, an undefined code of ethics for the Constitution, and a court of justice for the National legislature."[73]

On the same day that the decision in *Hepburn* was announced, President Grant nominated two new justices to the Supreme Court. William Strong was a sixty-one-year-old lawyer and former United States congressman from Philadelphia who had served eleven years on the Pennsylvania Supreme Court. In that capacity, he had made important decisions that favored the government's war efforts, including one that sustained the conscription law and another that upheld the Legal Tender Act.[74] Strong was a highly respected lawyer who had frequently been mentioned as a candidate for the Supreme Court. The other nominee, Joseph P. Bradley, was a lawyer from Newark, New Jersey, who specialized in patent, corporate, and commercial law and had achieved a reputation for his representation of the powerful Camden and Amboy Railroad. Bradley was a week shy of his fifty-seventh birthday when Grant sent his nomination to the Senate. Strong's nomination was confirmed on February 18 and Bradley's a month later.

Soon after the new justices took their seats, the Court was confronted with several cases that mixed legal tender issues with other questions. These were cases in which creditors complained that they were entitled to additional payments because the market value of legal tender notes was less than that of gold coin. Miller, Swayne, Davis, and the new justices felt it proper to reargue the central question of the constitutionality of legal tender. Chase believed that the question was settled. But *Hepburn* had decided only that legal tender was unconstitutional as applied to preexisting debts, leaving open the question as to debts incurred after the effective date of the act. Miller and his supporters believed that the entire issue should be reargued, not only because *Hepburn* had only partially settled it, but also because *Hepburn* had been decided by an incomplete court and, even more important, because the whole question was of "immense importance to the government, to individuals and to the public." The justices noted that the legal profession still had doubts on the question. "If it is ever to be reconsidered," Miller wrote at the end of April, "a thing which we deem inevitable, the true interests of all demands that it be done at the earliest practicable moment."[75] Attorneys whose clients had benefited from the *Hepburn* ruling naturally argued that the whole matter was settled, while their opponents disagreed. Chase tried at every turn to side with the former, but Miller and his supporters were finally able to force the issue. Miller later wrote that there had been "a desperate struggle in the secret conference of the court for three weeks" and that Chief Justice Chase had "resorted to all the stratagems of the lowest political trickery" to prevent the legal tender issue from being reargued.[76]

ON MAY 1, 1871, THE Supreme Court announced its decisions in *Knox v. Lee* and *Parker v. Davis*, two cases that had been combined for argument and were collectively referred to as the *Legal Tender Cases*. Opinions in the cases were delivered on January 15, 1872.[77]

In *Knox v. Lee*, Mrs. Lee (a loyal citizen of Pennsylvania) owned a flock of sheep in Texas. Confederate authorities confiscated the sheep in March 1863 and sold them to a man named Knox. After the war, Mrs. Lee brought suit against Knox for the value of the sheep, claiming that she was entitled to the value in gold coin and not in legal tender notes. Knox argued that, since U.S. Treasury notes were legal tender in 1863, Mrs. Lee was not entitled to anything else.

In *Parker v. Davis*, a man named Parker had agreed some time before the effective date of the Legal Tender Act to sell a parcel of land in Massachusetts to another man named Davis. When Parker failed to convey the land, Davis sued him for specific performance of the contract. In 1867, the Massachusetts court ordered Davis to pay the agreed price into court and Parker to execute a deed conveying title to Davis. Davis paid the money in legal tender notes and Parker objected, arguing that he was entitled to payment in gold coin.

These *Legal Tender Cases* raised issues as to the constitutionality of the Legal Tender Act as it applied to debts incurred both before and after its effective date. It was clear that Mrs. Lee's sheep were taken from her in 1863, after the act became effective, and although Davis's promise to pay Parker for his land was made before the effective date, the court order requiring him to pay the specified sum into court was made thereafter.

Justice Strong delivered the majority opinion, which was joined in by Swayne, Miller, and Davis. Justice Bradley delivered his own opinion, agreeing with and supplementing Strong's. Strong repeated many of the same arguments made in Justice Miller's dissent in *Hepburn*. He opened by describing the consequences that were likely to flow from the Court's decisions in these cases, saying:

> They will affect the entire business of the country, and take hold of the possible continued existence of the government. If it be held by this court that Congress has no constitutional power, under any circumstances, or in any emergency, to make treasury notes a legal tender for the payment of all debts (a power confessedly possessed by every independent sovereignty other than the United States), the government is without those means of self-preservation which, all must admit, may, in certain contingencies, become indispensable. . . . It is also clear that if we hold the acts invalid as applicable to debts incurred, or transactions which have taken place since their enactment, our decision must cause, throughout the country, great business derangement, widespread distress, and the rankest injustice.

Strong continued:

> It is not indispensable to the existence of any power claimed for the Federal government that it can be found specified in the words of the Constitution, or clearly and directly traceable to some one of the specified powers. Its existence may be deduced fairly from more than one of the substantive powers expressly defined, or from them all com-

bined. It is allowable to group together any number of them and infer from them all that the power claimed has been conferred.[78]

Strong carefully analyzed Chase's argument that legal tender impaired "the obligation of contracts" and denied "due process" and thus was inconsistent with "the spirit of the Constitution," and he rejected it. His opinion was carefully reasoned and powerfully stated. And it concluded with a specific statement overruling *Hepburn v. Griswold* and questioning the circumstances under which that case was decided:

> That case was decided by a divided court, and by a court having a less number of judges than the law then in existence provided this court shall have. These cases have been heard before a full court, and they have received our most careful consideration. . . . We have been in the habit of treating cases involving a consideration of constitutional power differently from those which concern merely private right. We are not accustomed to hear them in the absence of a full court, if it can be avoided. Even in cases involving only private rights, if convinced we had made a mistake, we would hear another argument and correct our error. And it is no unprecedented thing in courts of last resort, both in this country and in England, to overrule decisions previously made. We agree this should not be done inconsiderately, but in a case of such far-reaching consequences as the present, thoroughly convinced as we are that Congress has not transgressed its powers, we regard it as our duty so to decide and to affirm both these judgments.

Chase's dissent was joined in by Justices Nelson, Clifford, and Field. Thus, by a vote of five to four, legal tender was sustained.

Not surprisingly, the Court's handling of the legal tender issue provoked heated comment. Chase's conclusion that the Legal Tender Act was unconstitutional was the most controversial aspect of the whole episode, for it repudiated his most important wartime policy. Lincoln had appointed him chief justice at least in part because he believed that Chase would sustain the government's position on legal tender, and in the end he did not. While the armies were in the field, he had endorsed the issue of greenbacks, but as chief justice he concluded that they were illegal. The *Washington Chronicle* noted that in 1862 Chase had endorsed the legal tender law as "appropriate" and "adapted" to giving effect to the government's war power. "To say now that the same clause was unconstitutional," the *Chronicle* continued, "is to say that, in the opinion of the Chief Justice, the Constitution was so ingeniously framed as to tie the hands of the people whose liberties it was intended to secure and prohibit the Government from doing the thing most obviously essential to its own preservation."[79] *Harper's Weekly* said that the Court had "overstepped the just line of its authority and attempted to restrict Congress in this matter, when the framers of the Constitution decided to leave them free of such restrictions."[80] And the *Nation* argued that the complicated questions of how to raise armies in a modern industrial community and "how to get money to support them without plunging business into confusion and disheartening the people" were best left to Congress and not the Supreme Court. "There is no way to submit them to a court," the *Nation* added; "a court which was competent to pass on them would no longer be a court."[81]

Chase, of course, had his defenders. One of the strongest was Justice Field, who saw the chief justice's inconsistency on the legal tender issue as a strength rather than a weakness. His shifts on the great constitutional question, in Field's judgment, represented "intellectual integrity." Chase "preferred to be the honest judge rather than the consistent statesman," Field said.[82] (Chase's judgment on legal tender was, of course, identical to Field's.)

In years to come, Chase's and Field's decision on the legal tender issue did not prevail. It was the judgment of Miller and Strong and Bradley that came to be the settled law of the United States. The Court's decision in the *Legal Tender Cases* upholding the constitutionality of legal tender was reaffirmed in 1884 in *Julliard v. Greenman*, this time by a vote of eight to one (only Justice Field remained to dissent).[83]

Whether or not legal tender was consistent with "the spirit of the Constitution," later generations of Americans could not seriously doubt that their government had the same power to issue paper money and compel its acceptance in financial markets that the governments of sovereign nations around the world exercised on a routine basis. In *Hepburn*, Chase took a stand against legal tender. But he was overruled by the tide of history.

IF CHASE'S DECISION in *Hepburn v. Griswold* was widely criticized, the same could not be said of his decision in another case that excited passions all over the country and posed an even more critical question. Lincoln had consistently maintained, both before and during the war, that the Union had to be defended against its enemies; that it could not be rent asunder by the unilateral action of any state or group of states, or by any ordinance or ordinances of secession. In his First Inaugural Address, the president stated his position as clearly and forcefully as a lawyer might have stated it in a Supreme Court argument:

> I hold, that in contemplation of universal law, and of the Constitution, the Union of these States is perpetual. Perpetuity is implied, if not expressed, in the fundamental law of all national governments. It is safe to assert that no government proper, ever had a provision in its organic law for its own termination. Continue to execute all the express provisions of our national Constitution, and the Union will endure forever—it being impossible to destroy it, except by some action not provided for in the instrument itself.

Lincoln was addressing his remarks to a great crowd assembled to hear him take his oath of office as president—a political audience gathered before the national Capitol on the eve of a war that would test the survival of the nation he had been elected to lead. Yet he spoke like a lawyer addressing a jury, or seeking to persuade a panel of judges:

> The Union is much older than the Constitution. It was formed in fact, by the Articles of Association in 1774. It was matured and continued by the Declaration of Independence in 1776. It was further matured and the faith of all the then thirteen States expressly plighted and engaged that it should be perpetual, by the Articles of Confederation in 1778. And finally, in 1787, one of the declared objects for ordaining and establishing the Constitution, was "*to form a more perfect Union.*"
>
> But if destruction of the Union, by one, or by a part only, of the States, be lawfully possible, the Union is less perfect than before the Constitution, having lost the vital element of perpetuity.
>
> It follows from these views that no State, upon its own mere motion, can lawfully get out of the Union,—that *resolves* and *ordinances* to that effect are legally void; and that acts of violence, within any

State or States, against the authority of the United States, are insur-rectionary or revolutionary, according to circumstances.

I therefore consider that, in view of the Constitution and the laws, the Union is unbroken; and to the extent of my ability, I shall take care, as the Constitution itself expressly enjoins upon me, that the laws of the Union be faithfully executed in all the States. Doing this I deem to be only a simple duty on my part; and I shall perform it, so far as practicable, unless my rightful masters, the American people, shall withhold the requisite means, or in some authoritative manner, direct the contrary.[84]

In 1867, the State of Texas filed an original suit in the United States Su-preme Court against George W. White and John Chiles to recover 135 bonds that Texas owned at the beginning of the war but that the secessionist govern-ment of the state transferred to White and Chiles in January of 1865. The bonds, each with a face value of $1,000 and by their terms payable to the bearer, were originally issued to Texas by the United States in settlement of a disputed boundary claim. Most had been paid before 1860, but some remained in the state treasury after Texas joined the Confederacy in 1861. After the re-bel forces in Texas were disbanded in May 1865, Texas adopted a new constitu-tion and elected a new governor, who now sought to recover the bonds (or their value) from White and Chiles. The theory of the suit was that the rebel government of the state had wrongfully appropriated the bonds during the war, transferring them without any authority to do so. The state asked for an in-junction restraining White and Chiles from collecting any payments on the bonds from the federal government, and compelling them to surrender the bonds to the state.

In their defense, White and Chiles argued that the State of Texas had no right to maintain a suit in the Supreme Court because it had seceded in 1861 and, by that action, surrendered its rights as one of the states of the Union. It was conceded that, if Texas had retained its status as a state at the time it filed its suit, the Court had jurisdiction to hear it, for Article III, Section 2 provides that "in all cases . . . in which a state shall be party, the Supreme Court shall have original jurisdiction." If Texas was no longer a state, however, the Court had no jurisdiction.

Chase began his opinion in *Texas v. White* by acknowledging the importance of the issue the Court was asked to decide. "We are very sensible of the magnitude and importance of this question," he wrote, "of the interest it excites, and of the difficulty, not to say impossibility, of so disposing of it as to satisfy the conflicting judgments of men equally enlightened, equally upright, and equally patriotic." He began by discussing the nature of a "state." As the word was used in the Constitution, he deemed it to be "a people or political community, as distinguished from a government." It was in this sense, he said, that the word was used in Article IV, Section 4, of the Constitution: "The United States shall guarantee to every state in this union a republican form of government, and shall protect each of them against invasion."

Chase traced the history of Texas from the time of its admission to the Union in December 1845, and reviewed its experience with secession and the Confederate government. He then asked: "Did Texas, in consequence of these acts, cease to be a State? Or, if not, did the State cease to be a member of the Union?" Under the Articles of Confederation, he said, "the Union was solemnly declared to 'be perpetual.'" And when the Articles were found to be inadequate to the country's needs, "the Constitution was ordained 'to form a more perfect union.'" Echoing Lincoln, Chase said: "It is difficult to convey the idea of indissoluble unity more clearly than by these words. What can be indissoluble, if a perpetual Union, made more perfect, is not?"[85]

But the states did not lose their individual existence after they became part of the "more perfect Union." They retained their own powers, their own jurisdiction. He referred to the words of the Tenth Amendment: "The powers not delegated to the United States by the Constitution, nor prohibited by it to the states, are reserved to the states respectively, or to the people."

He quoted from *Lane County v. State of Oregon*, decided during the same term of the Court, in which he wrote that "the people of each State compose a State, having its own government, and endowed with all the functions essential to separate and independent existence," and that "without the States in union, there could be no such political body as the United States."[86] He continued: "Not only, therefore, can there be no loss of separate and independent autonomy to the States, through their union under the Constitution, but it may be not unreasonably said that the preservation of the States, and the maintenance of their governments, are as much within the design and care of the Constitution as the preservation of the Union and the maintenance of the National government." Chase then enunciated the most memorable phrase in all of his constitutional jurisprudence: "The Constitution, in all its provisions, looks to an indestructible Union, composed of indestructible States."[87]

It was an eminently quotable phrase, as clear as it was strong. Fairman has called it "the most enduring thing Chase ever said."[88] Simple yet forceful, it was justification enough for Chase's decision in favor of the State of Texas, holding that, despite all of the sorrows and tragedies of the war, the lost lives, the maimed bodies, the shattered illusions and unfulfilled hopes, Texas was still a sovereign state, a member of the "more perfect Union" formed in 1789, and entitled to maintain its suit in the Supreme Court.

With Chase in the chief justice's chair, the Supreme Court had affirmed in *Texas v. White* that the United States was an "indestructible Union." With Lincoln in the White House, the nation had proved by its valor and tenacity that the Union was "unbroken." Despite their political rivalry, their conflicting ambitions, and the rupture in their working relationship, Lincoln and Chase came in the end to the same conclusion. The nation was indestructible. The Union was unbroken.

11   History in Marble

ON FEBRUARY 23, 1865, LYMAN Trumbull of Illinois rose in the United States Senate to call for the consideration of a bill just reported out of the Judiciary Committee, of which he was chairman. The bill, which called for an appropriation of $1,000, had previously passed the House of Representatives without opposition. In the Senate, however, it encountered immediate resistance.

"What is that?" Senator Charles Sumner of Massachusetts snapped, after Trumbull read the bill's number.

"A bill reporting for a bust of the late Chief Justice Taney," Senator Trumbull answered, "to be placed in the Supreme Court Room of the United States."

The proposal was not unexpected. Marble busts had been placed along the walls of the Supreme Court's chamber commemorating all four of Taney's predecessors as chief justice, John Jay (1789–1795), John Rutledge (1795), Oliver Ellsworth (1796–1800), and John Marshall (1801–1835). It was a high honor but also a customary one, sanctioned by tradition and, in years past, never the subject of legislative disagreement. It was not to be so in the case of Roger Taney, just four months dead that February.

"I object to that," Sumner stated; "that now an emancipated country should make a bust to the author of the *Dred Scott* decision."

It was clear to everyone in the Senate that day that Sumner's opposition focused on the Supreme Court's now-famous (or infamous) 1857 decision regarding slavery in the United States, and particularly in the federal territories. *Dred Scott* was the most controversial decision in the Court's history, and though eight years had passed since it was handed down, it still grated on many Americans. In those eight years, the legal effect of the decision had been largely, if not entirely, mooted by the Civil War and events surrounding it, notably the Emancipation Proclamation of 1863 and the passage in January 1865 of the Thirteenth Amendment (which, upon ratification by three-fourths of the states, would end slavery for once and for all throughout the country). But the raw nerves *Dred Scott* had exposed, and the hatreds it stirred, were still throbbing.

Both Trumbull and Sumner were Republicans and political associates of Lincoln. But the senator from Illinois was identified with the conservative Republicans, while Sumner was at the forefront of the radicals, the congressional leaders who sought in the expected aftermath of the war (Appomattox was still two months in the future) to elevate the condition of former slaves, erase traces of the old racist regime in the South, and "punish" Confederates who had led the secessionist states into "treason" against the United States. Sumner, more than most others, was uncompromising in his anti-Southern views. He was moralistic, self-righteous—and adept at the forensic arts of rebuke and scorn.

Trumbull responded to Sumner's challenge by pointing out that Taney had presided over the Supreme Court for more than a quarter of a century and that, in that time, he had "added reputation to the character of the judiciary of the United States throughout the world." Such a judge, Trumbull argued, was not to be "hooted down by an exclamation that the country is to be emancipated." Trumbull added: "Suppose he did make a wrong decision. No man is infallible. He was a great and learned and an able man. I trust the Senate will take up the bill, and not only take it up, but pass it."[1] Unpersuaded, Sumner responded: "The Senator from Illinois says that this idea of a bust is not to be hooted down. Let me tell the Senator that the name of Taney is to be hooted down the page of history. Judgment is beginning now; and an emancipated country will fasten upon him the stigma which he deserves. The Senator says that he for twenty-five years administered justice. He administered justice at last wickedly, and degraded the judiciary of the country, and degraded the age."[2]

Maryland's Senator Reverdy Johnson took immediate exception to Sumner's charge. Johnson was one of Taney's old friends, a veteran of Supreme Court litigation and one of the lead attorneys in the *Dred Scott* case itself. He expressed "astonishment" at Sumner's tirade, saying that Sumner would be "very happy" if, when the judgment of history was finally passed, he stood "as pure and as high upon the historic page as the learned judge who is now no more." Johnson continued:

> The honorable member seems to suppose that the decision in the Dred Scott case was a decision of the Chief Justice alone. It was not so. In that decision a majority of the court concurred. Whether that decision is right or not, permit me to say to the honorable member there are men belonging to the profession at least his equals, who think it to have been right; but whether right or wrong, those who know the moral character of the Chief Justice as well as I did would blush to say that his name is to be execrated among men.[3]

Johnson affirmed that Taney was a "learned jurist" and that "a brighter intellect never adorned the judicial station," asking: "Does the honorable member wish to have it unknown in future times that there was such a Chief Justice? I suppose he does; I presume he does; and why? Because he differed with him." If Sumner considered it his duty "to assail the memory of a departed, and a great, and a virtuous man," then Johnson considered it his duty "to rise up and say a word in his vindication."

California's James McDougall deplored "the rude, the very rude, remarks" of Sumner and charged that the Massachusetts senator was not worthy "to stand at the door" of Taney's chamber. Sumner scoffed, rejecting the "familiar saying" that "nothing but good" should be said of the dead and arguing: "If a man has done evil during his life he must not be complimented in marble." Sumner read from portions of Taney's *Dred Scott* decision, including the now-famous assertion that, when the Declaration of Independence and the Constitution were adopted, Negroes were regarded as "so far inferior that they had no rights which the white man was bound to respect."[4] Sumner denied that this was a fact (many others, including Lincoln, had argued against the historical truth of the assertion) and continued: "Sir, it is not fit, it is not decent, that such a person should be commemorated by a vote of Congress; especially at this time when liberty is at last recognized."[5]

Trumbull disagreed with the *Dred Scott* decision—he had always disagreed with it—but he thought it wrong to denounce a "great jurist" merely because he "made an erroneous decision." If Sumner himself were chief justice for nearly thirty years, Trumbull argued, he would "be more than man if he did not make any erroneous decision."

New Hampshire's John P. Hale also opposed Trumbull's bill, though he was less anxious than Sumner to denounce Taney. Perhaps, Hale speculated, Taney was "as good a judge as the Senator from Maryland thinks him to have been, or as my friend from Illinois thinks." But his name would always be associated with the *Dred Scott* decision, which was "a reproach to the civilization and humanity of the age." The decision was "discreditable," Hale thought, though not "disgraceful." When Congress and the people erect a bust of a man in a public place, it indicates that they "cherish his fame and take this mode of perpetuating his name and memory in enduring marble." If it does not mean that, it means nothing at all. Better to "let Judge Taney alone," Hale argued, "let his memory alone, let his fame go for what it is worth," and let his record be judged by "impartial posterity."[6]

Sumner's Massachusetts colleague Henry Wilson was next to speak, disclaiming the wish "to follow any man to the grave with reproaches," but determined not "to perpetuate in marble the features of the judge who pronounced the Dred Scott decision." Wilson thought the "loyal millions" who deplored the decision in 1857 would find it strange to see the Senate in 1865 "voting honors" to its author, "the man who did more than all other men that ever breathed the air or trod the soil of the North American continent to plunge the nation into this bloody revolution."[7]

Reverdy Johnson asserted that, when *Dred Scott* was decided, Taney was "but one of eight or nine judges who concurred with him." (In fact, only six others voted as he did, and their reasons for doing so were bewilderingly various.) But he correctly recalled that three justices who steadfastly served the cause of Union loyalty during the war—Georgia's James Wayne, Tennessee's John Catron, and Pennsylvania's Robert Grier—had all voted with Taney in *Dred Scott*. And he argued that it was "wrong in point of fact" as well as "illogical and unjust" to attribute the views of these judges to Taney's influence.

Ohio's Senator Benjamin Wade now joined the fray. Wade's tongue was as sharp as Sumner's, and his opposition to the proposed bust of Taney every bit as firm, but his wit was more agile. Wade thought it was a mistake for Trumbull and Johnson to refer to Taney's learning and wisdom. "The greater you make Judge Taney's legal acumen," the Ohioan argued, "the more you dishonor his memory by showing that he sinned against light and knowledge. It would be more for his fame if you could prove him a fool." In an obvious reference to Reverdy Johnson, Wade proclaimed his opinion of the *Dred Scott* decision (and those of Sumner, Wilson, and Hale) to be "as reliable as that of the feed attorney in the case." Johnson, of course, took offense, asking Wade what authority he had to call him a "feed attorney" in *Dred Scott*. Wade pointed out that he was an attorney in the case, and argued that, if he had volunteered, "so much the worse."

"I did volunteer," Johnson answered.

"I am sorry for it," Wade retorted. "I was in hope you were only induced to embark on so bad a cause by an enormous fee."

Wade would not relent. Taney's opinion in *Dred Scott* had "gone down to posterity with utter contempt and disgrace," he said, "and the people of Ohio, whose representative I am, and whose opinions I profess to represent on this floor, would pay $2,000 to hang this man in effigy rather than $1,000 for a bust to commemorate his merits."[8]

John S. Carlile, one of the loyalist senators from Virginia (elected after secession, by the pro-Union government in Virginia) was the last senator to enter the debate. Considering his consistently proslavery (though pro-Union) stance throughout the war, it was not surprising that Carlile supported Trumbull's bill. "I do not believe we can honor Chief Justice Taney by perpetuating his features in marble," Carlile said, "but I do believe the Senate by voting to embody the features of Taney in marble will do honor to itself." Carlile predicted that Taney's memory would be "cherished by the wise and the good long after the names of those who now strut their little hour upon the political stage will have been forgotten." It was a simple "mark of respect," Carlile argued, to give Taney the same honor previously given to John Jay and John Marshall, and failure to do so would place a "stigma" on the record of the Senate.[9]

But Sumner was determined. "I am sorry to be drawn into this debate," he said disingenuously. "But they who seek to canonize one of the tools of slavery are responsible. Taney shall not be recognized as a saint by any vote of Congress if I can help it."[10]

Trumbull and Johnson and Carlile knew, of course, that the senator from Massachusetts *could* help it—and would; so, after an evening recess, they permitted the bill to die by an indefinite postponement, without any vote.[11] No bust would be erected by the Senate to honor Roger Taney.

SALMON P. CHASE, TANEY'S successor as chief justice, died on May 7, 1873. Seven months later, in December 1873, the United States Senate took up consideration of a bill providing for marble busts of both Chase and Taney to be placed in the Supreme Court's Capitol chamber.[12] The custom that had been followed after the deaths of Jay, Rutledge, Ellsworth, and Marshall, but rejected after Taney's passing, was to be revived, this time to honor the author of the anti-secessionist pronouncement, *Texas v. White,* along with the author of the proslavery *Dred Scott* decision. The two busts would be produced and delivered to the Supreme Court at a total cost of $2,500. This time there was no debate. The measure passed in the Senate without opposition on January 16, and in the House on January 26, 1874. President Ulysses S. Grant signed it into law on January 29.[13]

In 1874 Charles Sumner was the last survivor of the quartet of senators who in 1865 argued against a bust for Taney. Hale, Wade, and Wilson had all left the Senate—as had Taney's 1865 supporters, Reverdy Johnson, James McDougall, and John S. Carlile. Lincoln himself had been dead for eight years, but it is not difficult to imagine that something of his spirit hovered over the Senate chamber in 1873, as it did over much of the nation. He had been, in Edwin Stanton's immortal words, consigned "to the ages" by an assassin's bullet, only six months after Roger Taney succumbed to the ravages of old age.[14] Reverdy Johnson, who had supported Lincoln on the preservation of the Union and Taney on slavery (but ultimately joined Lincoln in supporting the Thirteenth Amendment), had enjoyed one of his last bursts of fame as one of the attorneys for Mary Surratt, one of eight persons (and the only woman) tried before a military commission for conspiring to murder Lincoln.[15] His defense was unsuccessful—Mrs. Surratt was hanged—but Johnson, a good lawyer to the end, earned respect for offering his services in an unpopular cause. Sumner had worked with Lincoln during the war (not always smoothly, for his politics were always harder and more severe than the president's), and he had become a friend of Mrs. Lincoln, who enjoyed his good looks and Northeastern erudition.[16]

If there was still a spirit of animosity against Roger Taney in 1873, it did not find expression in the Senate chamber. Lincoln himself, after all, had been known for his magnanimity. He had not blamed the South for the terrible ordeal the nation had gone through, much less those, like Taney, whose hearts had been with the South during the struggle. In his Second Inaugural Address, he had called on Americans to "judge not that we be not judged." And he had spoken (as he so often did) words that would live far into the future: "With malice toward none; with charity for all; with firmness in the right, as God gives us to see the right, let us strive on to finish the work we are in; to bind up the nation's wounds; to care for him who shall have borne the battle, and for his widow, and his orphan—to do all which may achieve and cherish a just, and a lasting peace, among ourselves, and with all nations."[17]

Charles Sumner did not speak a word in opposition to the bill honoring Taney and Chase in 1873, despite his earlier boast that Taney "would not be recognized as a saint" if he could help it. Sumner had vigorously championed Chase's appointment as chief justice in 1864 and would not have objected to a bust honoring him. But why did he not speak out again against Taney? Though only sixty-two years old in 1873, Sumner was a sick man, suffering from heart disease that caused him repeated bouts of chest pain. His biographer, David Herbert Donald, has written that he was too ill during this period to make regular appearances in the Senate, and he died on March 11, 1874.[18] But the Congressional Record shows that Sumner did attend some Senate sessions in December 1873 and in January and February 1874, when the bill for the two busts was taken up and passed, and he did express his views on some issues that seemed to him important. The bust of Roger Taney was not one of them.

Perhaps Sumner was too weak to restate his deeply felt grievances against the departed chief justice. Perhaps he realized that the argument about Dred Scott was over, that his side (and Lincoln's) had won the debate—not Taney's. By 1873 the Thirteenth Amendment had been finally ratified, as had the Fourteenth, which wrote national citizenship into the Constitution and guaranteed equal protection and due process of law to all Americans, and the Fifteenth, which declared that the right to vote could not be denied on account of race, color, or previous condition of servitude.[19] Dred Scott was now a relic of America's past, a painful chapter in a painful history that had led up to the terrible struggle between North and South. But there were other, more positive chapters in the Supreme Court's history, some of which did honor to the chief justice from Maryland. Perhaps Sumner had absorbed some of the spirit of Lincoln's magnanimity. Perhaps he had come to realize, as had most members of Congress by 1873 and 1874, that Roger Taney would not be judged more favorably by history because his marble likeness adorned a wall in the Supreme Court. John Hale had said in 1865 that it was better to let "impartial posterity" judge Taney and his record. And Hale had argued that that could best be done by refusing to place Taney's bust in the Supreme Court. By 1874, however, Congress had decided otherwise, concluding that posterity would not be swayed by marble. Perhaps, in the end, even Charles Sumner agreed.

The Legacy

A HISTORY OF LINCOLN and the Supreme Court would be incomplete without some reflection on the broader meaning of the history and the lessons that can usefully be drawn from it. What cases decided by the high court during the Civil War and in its aftermath (when justices appointed by Lincoln continued to dominate the Court) still rank as controlling precedents in modern Supreme Court jurisprudence? If Lincoln was, as surveys of scholarly and public opinion assure us, one of the two greatest presidents in the history of the United States (only George Washington rivals him for the top position), what qualities did he display that can serve as guides for modern presidents? How did his experiences with Supreme Court justices affect the discharge of his official duties (for good or for ill), and can modern presidents derive any insights from them?

Opinions of Lincoln's performance as president are inevitably tied to the outcome of the war. That the side he led ultimately prevailed colors our judgment about the decisions he made and the policies he adopted. At the outset of the war, he insisted that the Union was indissoluble, and at the end of the war the Union remained "unbroken." During the war, he embraced the emancipation of slaves as a necessary (and morally worthy) goal, and shortly after the war ended slavery was, through the Thirteenth Amendment (which he worked assiduously to pass), abolished throughout the United States. He took sometimes drastic measures to further his war aims, some that were firmly within his constitutional powers, some that were arguably beyond those powers, and many that lay in the vast gray area between. Lincoln shared the doubts of his severest critics about the constitutionality of some of his actions, but he never took any action that he believed was clearly beyond the legitimate powers conferred on him by the Constitution. He never, for example, gave any thought to cancelling the congressional elections of 1862, which posed the very real threat of ousting Republicans from control of the national legislature and ushering in an antiwar Democratic majority. Nor did he consider the possibility of cancelling (or postponing) the presidential election of 1864 that at one time seemed likely to turn him out of the White House. The elections were mandated by the Constitution, and they went forward, unmolested by any action of the president.

Because Lincoln ultimately prevailed, we may be more willing to concede the doubtful issues to him than if he had failed. After all, he won the war, he saved the Union, he freed the slaves. But if he had not been successful in accomplishing those goals—if the South had succeeded in breaking its constitutional ties to the North, if African Americans had emerged from the war as firmly saddled with the burden of slavery as when they entered it—history would have judged Lincoln more harshly. Bitter critics of Lincoln often ask if the terrible costs of the war—more than 600,000 deaths, nearly 500,000 wounded, tens of thousands arrested, and property losses in the billions of dollars—were "worth it." Disregarding the obvious objection that it was never within the power of Lincoln (or any other person) to neatly balance the costs and the benefits of the conflict (both of which were unknowable until the last shot had been fired), it is reasonable to assume that such a "cost-benefit analysis" would have been less favorable to Lincoln if he had lost the war. A chief executive who leads a nation into a great war is ultimately responsible for its outcome. If it ends in victory, he is acclaimed as a hero; if in defeat, he is condemned as a villain or a fool (or pitied as a tragic victim of a fate beyond his control). Great presidents who have led the United States in successful wars—Lincoln, Wilson, and Franklin D. Roosevelt—are assigned high positions in history. But Lyndon B. Johnson, a president who presided over the unsuccessful war in Vietnam, is saddled with the stigma of the loss, despite his very substantial domestic accomplishments.

Granting that Lincoln prevailed in the Civil War, however, does not answer the questions of how he did it, how the Constitution fared while he did it, and what lessons can be drawn from his experience as chief executive and his interactions with the Supreme Court.

THE MEASURES FOR WHICH Lincoln is most often criticized fall generally into three groups. First are the actions that he took without congressional authorization, relying merely on his authority as commander in chief. Second are the actions that infringed on the civil liberties of Americans in the loyal states, subjecting them to arbitrary arrest and denying them access to the courts to enforce their constitutional rights. And third are the war measures that he adopted against the South, some of which were unprecedented in the history of war.

Lincoln responded to the Confederate assault on Fort Sumter by summoning 75,000 state militiamen to suppress the Southern rebellion. His proclamation calling forth the troops recited that he was acting "in virtue of the power in me vested by the Constitution and laws." In the same proclamation, he summoned both houses of Congress to assemble in Washington on July 4, 1861, "then and there to consider and determine, such measures, as, in their wisdom, the public safety, and interest may seem to demand."[1] Article II, Section 2, of the Constitution states (in relevant part): "The President shall be commander in chief of the Army and Navy of the United States, and of the militia of the several states, when called into the actual service of the United States." And Article II, Section 3, provides that the president "may, on extraordinary occasions, convene both Houses, or either of them."

But Article I, Section 8, clause 15, clearly gives Congress the power "to provide for calling forth the militia to execute the laws of the union, suppress insurrections and repel invasions." And Article I, Section 9, clause 7, provides that "no money shall be drawn from the treasury, but in consequence of appropriations made by law." Further, Article I, Section 8, clause 12, gives Congress (not the president) power "to raise and support armies."

Lincoln clearly had the power to summon Congress to a special session. The bombardment and capture of a federal fort by an army acting in the name of a confederation of secessionist states was certainly an "extraordinary occasion" justifying the exercise of the president's convening powers. But what constitutional power did Lincoln have to call forth the militia? And what power did he have to call for volunteers to augment the regular army? A president who presumes to decide on the size of the army, or to increase its size, treads dangerously on the powers of Congress. What power did he have to pay the troops that came to Washington without congressional appropriations? Congress had not appropriated any money to pay the militia summoned to Washington, and nothing in the Constitution gives the president any powers of appropriation. But reality dictated that the army could not survive on proclamations alone. Money was needed to pay the soldiers, feed them, clothe them, arm them, house them, and transport them while Congress was not in session. There was money in the federal treasury, and Lincoln used it to make the army functional.

And what of Lincoln's decision to impose a blockade of Southern ports? Article I, Section 8, clause 11, of the Constitution gives Congress the power "to declare war, grant letters of marque and reprisal, and make rules concerning captures on land and water." Congress never declared war against the Southern states. Indeed, in Lincoln's estimation, it would have been wrong to do so, for those states were still part of the Union, and a declaration of war is appropriate only for a war against a foreign power. A vigorous argument was made in the Supreme Court that, because war had never been declared, the blockade was illegal. The implication was clear from this argument that other measures the president had taken without congressional authorization were also illegal. But the Supreme Court answered these arguments in the *Prize Cases,* in which Justice Grier stated that "a civil war is never solemnly declared" and that the president was bound to meet the war "in the shape it presented itself, without waiting for Congress to baptize it with a name."[2] It was the most significant vindication that Lincoln ever received from the Court.

Lincoln acted quickly and decisively to counter the Southern insurrection. His critics argued that he stretched his constitutional powers to do so. Surely he exposed himself to enormous risk if it should later be determined that he had acted illegally. But in the message he sent to the special session of Congress he convened on July 4, 1861, he explained that the dire necessity raised by the insurrection forced him to call out the "war power" of the government, and "so to resist force, employed for its destruction, by force, for its preservation." He believed that the measures he took were "strictly legal," but "whether strictly legal or not" they were taken "under what appeared to be a popular demand, and a public necessity; trusting then as now, that Congress would readily ratify them."[3] After Congress came into its special session, it declared that all of the acts taken by the president after March 4, 1861, respecting the army and navy and calling out the militia, were "approved and in all respects legalized and made valid . . . as if they had been issued and done under the previous express authority and direction of the Congress of the United States."[4] As Justice Grier stated in the *Prize Cases*, if there was any defect in the president's original actions, Congress's ratification "operated to perfectly cure the defect."[5] For purposes at least of Lincoln's initial response to the Southern insurrection, the president and Congress had thus joined forces, linking the constitutional powers of the executive branch of the government with those of the legislative branch, winning the approbation of the judicial branch, and effectively removing any constitutional objection to the president's actions.

Lincoln's suspension of the privilege of the writ of habeas corpus was initially a unilateral action, taken without congressional authorization. Chief Justice Taney's opinion in *Ex parte Merryman* condemning the suspension was based primarily on the argument that the Constitution gave the power of suspension exclusively to Congress.[6] But in the same act in which Congress ratified Lincoln's call-up of the militia, his unauthorized payment of the troops, and his blockade of Southern ports, Congress also approved his suspension of habeas corpus. By August 6, 1861, when the ratification became effective, Taney's condemnation of the suspension had effectively been nullified. Lincoln had claimed the power to suspend habeas corpus without congressional approval for a little more than three months, and in two of those months Congress was not in session and could not have acted. Because the Constitution itself does not state whether habeas corpus is to be suspended by Congress or the president; because Lincoln suspended it at a time when Congress was not in session and thus was powerless to act; and, further, because the government was then facing a clear danger, Lincoln's argument that the framers could hardly have intended that "the danger should run its course" before Congress could be called together has some resonance.

In fact, the precise question of whether the president may suspend habeas corpus when Congress cannot do so has never been decided by the high court, although some justices have expressed the opinion that he may not do so.[7] The question was briefly touched on in 2004 in *Hamdi v. Rumsfeld*, a case arising during the War on Terror and involving an American citizen who was captured in Afghanistan, declared an "enemy combatant," and confined by U.S. military authorities, first in Guantanamo Bay, Cuba, and thereafter in South Carolina. Speaking for a plurality of the Court, Justice Sandra Day O'Connor stated that, "*unless Congress acts to suspend it*, the Great Writ of habeas corpus allows the Judicial Branch to play a necessary role in maintaining this delicate balance of governance, serving as an important judicial check on the Executive's discretion in the realm of detentions."[8]

In a dissenting opinion in the same case, Justice Antonin Scalia wrote: "Our Federal Constitution contains a provision explicitly permitting suspension. . . . Although this provision does not state that suspension must be effected by, or authorized by, a legislative act, it has been so understood, consistent with English practice and the Clause's placement in Article I." Justice Scalia cited *Ex parte Merryman* as authority for this proposition and referred to Lincoln's suspension as "unauthorized."[9] But Justice O'Connor explicitly noted in *Hamdi*: "All agree suspension of the writ has not happened here."[10] Thus both her statement and that of Scalia relating to the power of suspension were dicta and not binding as precedent in future cases.

Further, the facts of *Hamdi* contrasted sharply with those under which Lincoln suspended habeas corpus in *Merryman*. By the time Hamdi's case arrived at the Supreme Court, he had been held prisoner for more than two years, while Merryman had been held for only three days when Taney ordered his release. If exigent circumstances justify suspension by the president rather than by Congress, it is hardly reasonable to suppose that the exigency will continue for years. During that time, there would be ample opportunity for Congress to weigh in, either ratifying the president's action or disapproving it.

The peculiar circumstances of Lincoln's first suspension of habeas corpus did not continue for the duration of the Civil War. After March 3, 1863, the president was authorized by act of Congress to suspend the writ anywhere in the United States, "whenever, in his judgment the public safety may require it."[11] However, the act authorizing suspension required that lists of all persons detained under the president's order (other than as prisoners of war) be furnished to federal courts in the appropriate districts and that listed persons be released if they were not indicted by grand juries in those districts. This put the government to the choice of trying arrested persons in the civil courts or giving them their freedom.

Later Supreme Court decisions help us understand the importance of Congress's decision to ratify Lincoln's initial response to Southern secession (including his initial suspension of habeas corpus) and later to give him broad discretion to suspend habeas. One of the most notable explanations of the intersection of executive and congressional power came in the 1952 Supreme Court decision in *Youngstown Sheet & Tube Co. v. Sawyer*. During the Korean War, President Harry S. Truman ordered his secretary of commerce to seize and operate the nation's steel mills. Apprehensive that a threatened strike by steelworkers would harm the country's war production, Truman believed that government seizure and operation of the mills would avert the strike. He cited as authority for his action "the Constitution and laws of the United States" and his office as "President of the United States and Commander in Chief of the Armed Forces."

Very quickly, the controversy was brought before the Supreme Court, which decided that Truman's power as commander in chief could not be stretched so far as to seize a private industry by executive order. Six justices, led by Justice Hugo L. Black, wrote separate opinions condemning the seizure. The opinion of Justice Robert Jackson became the most influential because of the cogency of its analysis. Jackson divided the powers of the president into three broad categories. In the first, the president acts "pursuant to an express or implied authorization of Congress." In such a case, Jackson said, "his authority is at its maximum, for it includes all that he possesses in his own right plus all that Congress can delegate." In the second category, the president acts "in absence of either a congressional grant or denial of authority." When he does this, "he can only rely upon his own independent powers." But there is in this area "a zone of twilight in which he and Congress may have concurrent authority, or in which its distribution is uncertain," so that an actual test of power "is likely to depend on the imperatives of events and contemporary imponderables rather than on abstract theories of law." In the third category, Jackson continued, the president "takes measures incompatible with the expressed or implied will of Congress." In such a case, his power is at its "lowest ebb, for then he can rely only upon his own constitutional powers minus any constitutional powers of Congress over the matter."[12] Truman's seizure of the steel mills fell into the third category, for Congress had previously passed a comprehensive statute regulating labor strikes (the Taft-Hartley Act), and the statute did not permit the president to seize an industry. In Lincoln's case, the actions he took to respond to the threat of Southern secession may have initially fallen in the second category described by Jackson. After Congress ratified and approved them, however, they moved to the first category, where his authority was at its maximum.[13]

EVEN IF IT IS ASSUMED that Lincoln's initial suspension of habeas corpus was constitutional (either because he acted pursuant to his own constitutional power or because Congress came to his aid by ratifying the suspension), the issue of how the suspension might affect other constitutional rights must be addressed. In *Ex parte Merryman,* Chief Justice Taney ruled that the constitutional rights of John Merryman to a jury trial and due process of law had been abridged by Lincoln's suspension, and in *Ex parte Milligan* Justice David Davis ruled that Lambdin P. Milligan's rights to a grand jury indictment, to a speedy and public trial by an impartial jury, and to freedom from unreasonable search and seizure were all violated when he was tried and sentenced by a military commission in Indiana. Because the *Merryman* decision was not made by the full Supreme Court, *Milligan* has drawn the most attention from constitutional scholars and has most often been cited in later Supreme Court opinions.

Historians have been generous in their praise of Davis's decision in *Milligan*. Writing in the 1920s, Supreme Court historian Charles Warren called *Milligan* "one of the bulwarks of American liberty" and celebrated Davis's opinion as "immortal."[14] In the 1960s, historian Allan Nevins described *Milligan* as "a great triumph for the civil liberties of Americans in time of war."[15] And in a book published in 1971, Charles Fairman called it "a landmark of constitutional liberty."[16]

In the 1980s, historian Mark Neely acknowledged that *Milligan* was "the most famous Supreme Court decision" of the Civil War era. But he argued that the decision had had "little practical effect" and failed to clear up "all the complex civil liberties issues caused by the Civil War."[17] Despite the Supreme Court's decision, trials of civilians by military commissions continued for at least five years after Lincoln was assassinated. Most took place in the South as part of the reconstruction program authorized by Congress. Justice Davis's decision did little or nothing to stop these trials. Nor did Davis himself expect that it would, for in 1867 he admitted that in his opinion "not a word" was said "about reconstruction," adding that "the power is conceded in insurrectionary States."[18]

In his book about the president's wartime powers, Chief Justice William Rehnquist wrote that *Milligan* "is justly celebrated for its rejection of the government's position that the Bill of Rights has no application in wartime."[19] But he questioned the decision's general applicability to circumstances that arise during war. He recalled the Latin maxim *Inter arma silent leges* ("In war the laws are silent") and said that, though it could not be used to justify the denial of law in times of military crisis, it had "validity in at least a descriptive way." "There is no reason to think that future wartime presidents will act differently from Lincoln, Wilson, or Roosevelt," he wrote, "or that future Justices of the Supreme Court will decide questions differently from their predecessors." Rehnquist believed that the historic trend against the curtailment of civil liberty in wartime would continue, but that civil liberties would never occupy as favored a position in times of military conflict as they do in peace. "The laws will thus not be silent in time of war," Rehnquist wrote, "but they will speak with a somewhat different voice."[20]

In support of Neely's and Rehnquist's observations, it is interesting to note how little practical effect the *Milligan* decision has had in modern wars. Neely has pointed out that it was totally irrelevant during World War I, when President Woodrow Wilson sent American troops to fight on foreign soil, and it was all but ignored during World War II, when the United States was engaged in one of the bloodiest military struggles in the history of the world.[21]

Two notable Supreme Court decisions addressed the issue of military trials of civilians during World War II. The first was *Ex parte Quirin,* in which eight German spies (including one who was an American citizen) were tried by a military commission created by President Franklin D. Roosevelt. The spies had crossed the Atlantic on German submarines with the intent of landing, assuming the identities of civilians, and carrying out sabotage. Four came ashore on Long Island, where they buried their German uniforms, put on civilian clothes, and headed for New York City. The other four came ashore on the coast of Florida and headed for Jacksonville. All were armed with explosives, fuses, and incendiary devices. The spies were eventually captured, tried by the military commission, and sentenced to death. Denying their petitions for habeas corpus, the Supreme Court in 1942 held that the spies (including the American citizen) were properly subject to military justice and that President Roosevelt, as commander in chief, had constitutional authority to create the military commission that tried them. Writing for the Court, Chief Justice Harlan Fiske Stone held that *Milligan* was not applicable. The German spies were plainly within the "boundaries of the jurisdiction of military tribunals," Stone said, and their acts were "an offense against the law of war which the Constitution authorizes to be tried by military commission."[22]

Four years later, in *Duncan v. Kahanamoku*, the Supreme Court reviewed the convictions of two civilians in Hawaii who had been tried by military tribunals in 1942. One was a stockbroker who was charged with embezzling stock belonging to another civilian, and the other was a shipfitter at a local navy yard who was charged with engaging in a brawl at the yard. The tribunals had been established after the territorial governor transferred total control of the Hawaiian government to U.S. military authorities. All of the civilian courts in Hawaii were closed, and the military presumed to exercise all of the judicial functions in the islands, including authority over ordinary crimes. The Supreme Court struck down the convictions of both civilians. In his opinion for the majority, Justice Hugo L. Black cited *Milligan* for the proposition that "civil liberty and this kind of martial law cannot endure together." However, he decided the case on statutory grounds, ruling that the Hawaii Organic Act of 1900, which was the asserted basis for the governor's orders, did not authorize the transfer of ordinary judicial power to military authorities.[23]

The authority of military tribunals established by President George W. Bush after the terrorist attacks of September 11, 2001, has been challenged many times. In 2004, the Supreme Court handed down three important decisions relating to these tribunals. The first was *Rumsfeld v. Padilla*, which arose out of the detention of José Padilla, an American who had flown from Pakistan to Chicago, where he was detained as a material witness in a grand jury investigation into the 9/11 attacks. Thereafter, President Bush issued an order designating Padilla as an enemy combatant and authorizing military authorities to confine him, first in New York and thereafter in South Carolina. In New York, his attorney petitioned the U.S. district court for a writ of habeas corpus. On appeal, the Supreme Court declined to rule on the thorny issue of whether Padilla's initial arrest and subsequent detention were legal, concluding merely that his petition for habeas corpus should have been filed in South Carolina rather than New York, because the district court in New York lacked jurisdiction to proceed.[24] *Milligan* played no part in the Court's decision.

Rasul v. Bush arose out of the imprisonment at Guantanamo Bay, Cuba, of two Australians and twelve Kuwaitis who were captured in Afghanistan during the U.S. military campaign against al-Qaeda. Denying that they had ever been combatants against the United States, the prisoners sought writs of habeas corpus. The government argued that federal courts had no jurisdiction over Guantanamo, since the United States occupied it only under a lease and ultimate sovereignty remained with Cuba. The Supreme Court rejected this argument. In an opinion by Justice John Paul Stevens, the Court ruled that the applicable statute gave federal courts habeas corpus jurisdiction over Guantanamo. Stevens cited *Milligan* for the limited purpose of showing that persons held by military authorities may petition for habeas corpus when the court has proper jurisdiction, but *Milligan* alone did not establish that jurisdiction. The federal habeas corpus statute did so.[25]

In *Hamdi v. Rumsfeld* (previously mentioned in connection with the suspension of habeas corpus), a petition was filed challenging President Bush's authority to hold Yaser Esam Hamdi without any charges or trial. The Supreme Court granted relief, stating that Hamdi's detention as an enemy combatant was legal but that he had the right under congressional enactments to challenge his detention before a neutral decision maker. Although no single opinion was supported by a majority of the justices, Justice O'Connor delivered an important opinion that was concurred in by Chief Justice Rehnquist and Justices Anthony Kennedy and Stephen Breyer. O'Connor said that the president could not hold a U.S. citizen indefinitely without according him the basic protections of due process of law. But she did not base her ruling on *Milligan*. She stated explicitly that the famous Civil War case had been "updated" and "clarified" by the World War II decision in *Ex parte Quirin*, which provided the Court "with the most apposite precedent that we have on the question of whether citizens may be detained in such circumstances." She continued:

> *Ex parte Milligan*, 4 Wall. 2, 125 (1866), does not undermine our holding about the Government's authority to seize enemy combatants, as we define that term today. In that case, the Court made repeated reference to the fact that its inquiry into whether the military tribunal

had jurisdiction to try and punish Milligan turned in large part on the fact that Milligan was not a prisoner of war, but a resident of Indiana arrested while at home there. . . . That fact was central to its conclusion. Had Milligan been captured while he was assisting Confederate soldiers by carrying a rifle against Union troops on a Confederate battlefield, the holding of the Court might well have been different. The Court's repeated explanations that Milligan was not a prisoner of war suggest that had these different circumstances been present he could have been detained under military authority for the duration of the conflict, whether or not he was a citizen.[26]

Hamdan v. Rumsfeld, decided in 2006, arose out of the detention of Salim Ahmed Hamdan, a citizen of Yemen who was captured in Afghanistan and thereafter detained by U.S. military authorities in Guantanamo Bay. After Hamdan was designated as an enemy combatant, military authorities prepared to try him before a military commission for conspiracy to commit terrorism. Hamdan admitted that he had once been a driver for al-Qaeda leader Osama bin Laden, but he denied that he had ever engaged in terrorism and petitioned the U.S. district court for habeas corpus. Issuing six separate opinions, a highly fractured Supreme Court held that President Bush had authority to detain Hamdan but not to try him or punish him, because the military commission established for that purpose did not satisfy the requirements of the Uniform Code of Military Justice and the Geneva Conventions. This result was reached by reference to statute and treaties, however, and not by invoking the constitutional principles laid down in *Milligan*.[27]

If the Supreme Court's decisions during the War on Terror have not been compelled by *Milligan*, they have not been inconsistent with it. Even as Justice O'Connor refused to apply *Milligan* to the facts of *Hamdi*, she made it clear that the overarching principle of *Milligan* still has broad application. "We have long since made clear," O'Connor declared in *Hamdi*, "that a state of war is not a blank check for the President when it comes to the rights of the Nation's citizens."[28] If *Milligan* arose during a domestic insurrection and *Hamdi* during a foreign war; if Lambdin Milligan was arrested, tried, and sentenced to death in Indiana during a time when the courts were open and functioning, and Yaser Hamdi was captured on a battlefield in a foreign country contested by opposing armies, there was good reason for distinguishing the two cases. There was no reason, however, for turning back from the broad principle that, in the American system of justice, the power of military courts is limited by the Constitution; that the president, whether he be Abraham Lincoln, Franklin D. Roosevelt, or George W. Bush, is constrained by basic principles of constitutional law; that the courts, headed by the Supreme Court of the United States, will always exercise their independent power to review the actions of military courts, compare them to the Constitution, and strike them down when violations are found.

THERE IS NO REASON TO suspect that Lincoln himself did not accept this principle. While Justice David Davis was writing his *Milligan* opinion, he was asked by William H. Herndon, Lincoln's former law partner in Springfield, for a statement about the deceased president. Herndon was gathering material for a projected Lincoln biography and sought information from men who had known the president well. In answering Herndon, Davis naturally thought about Lincoln's own views on the military trials. He told him:

> Mr. Lincoln was advised, and I also so advised him, that the various military trials in the Northern and Border States, where the courts were free and untrammelled, were unconstitutional and wrong; that they would not and ought not to be sustained by the Supreme Court; that such proceedings were dangerous to liberty. He said he was opposed to hanging; that he did not like to kill his fellow-man; that if the world had no butchers but himself it would go bloodless. . . . I am fully satisfied therefore that Lincoln was opposed to these military commissions especially in the Northern States, where everything was open and free.[29]

Whether Justice Davis's recollection was entirely accurate, it is clear that Lincoln took no pleasure from the military commissions, or from any of the other measures whereby the legal rights of ordinary citizens were denied during the war. He made it clear that military arrests and trials rested on grounds of military necessity and would continue only so long as the necessity continued. After the necessity was over, the arrests would cease. In his "Corning letter" of June 1863, in which he defended his suspension of the writ of habeas corpus,

Lincoln said that he was unable to "appreciate the danger . . . that the American people will, by means of military arrests during the rebellion, lose the right of public discussion, the liberty of speech and the press, the law of evidence, trial by jury, and Habeas Corpus, throughout the indefinite peaceful future, which I trust lies before them, any more than I am able to believe that a man could contract so strong an appetite for emetics during temporary illness, as to persist in feeding upon them through the remainder of his healthful life."[30] The president was saying that, just as "emetics" are necessary when a man is sick but not when he regains his health, so military arrests and trials are necessary when a nation's security is threatened by forces that the civil courts are incompetent to deal with, but not when the normal function of the courts is restored. He saw no danger that his temporary measures would lead to a permanent loss of liberty. In his annual message to Congress in December 1864, with victory on the horizon but not yet attained, Lincoln admitted that the "executive power itself would be greatly diminished by the cessation of actual war."[31] That is, in time of peace, the power of the commander in chief to suspend habeas corpus and to order military arrests and trials would not be what it was while the war raged on.

Milligan is less important as a rule of law than as a reaffirmation of judicial independence. It is hard to imagine that a case will ever again arise in which an American citizen, not engaged in combat and not acting as an enemy agent, is arrested, tried, and convicted by a military commission in a state in which there is no fighting and in which the courts are open and functioning—and in which the Supreme Court is called to pass upon the constitutionality of the proceedings only after the conflict is over. The fact that the fighting was already over when *Milligan* was decided may help to explain why it was not decided in the same manner as *Ex parte Vallandigham* or *Ex parte Quirin*. When Justice Wayne denied jurisdiction in *Vallandigham*, and when a unanimous Supreme Court upheld the military commission in *Quirin*, war was still being waged. When Justice Davis decided *Milligan*, the war was won, the fighting had stopped, and the national security was no longer in peril.

Despite all of this, *Milligan* still stands tall among decisions of the Civil War Court, for it affirms the proposition, indispensable in a society that values the rule of law, that the Supreme Court will not turn its back on the Constitution. The federal judiciary will not mindlessly accede to the wishes of the executive or legislative branches of the government when vital constitutional principles are at stake. The case also stands for the proposition that partisan loyalties will not trump important constitutional principles, for the opinion in *Milligan* was written by a Republican judge appointed by a Republican president and announced at a time when Republicans controlled Congress. Yet the judge rendered a decision that defied his own party, honored the Constitution, and did honor to the Court.

ONE OF LINCOLN'S MOST notable actions was taken without any authorization or ratification by Congress. He issued the Emancipation Proclamation on his own authority as commander in chief and spurned suggestions that Congress should join him as its author. Twice during the war Congress passed "confiscation acts," providing in various terms that slaves owned by Southern rebels would be forfeited to the use of the Union army.[32] Lincoln had little enthusiasm for these acts, which he believed had serious constitutional objections, and he was hesitant about enforcing them. He always recognized that Congress had no constitutional power to decree an emancipation of slaves within any states. When some of his generals took steps to free slaves in their military districts, he countermanded their orders, reserving to himself "as Commander-in-Chief of the Army and Navy" the power to "declare the Slaves of any state or states, free."[33] And when, on January 1, 1863, he issued his final proclamation of emancipation, it was drafted in sternly legalistic language, carefully chosen for its constitutional import. The proclamation recited that it was issued "by virtue of the power in me vested as Commander-in-Chief of the Army and Navy of the United States in time of actual armed rebellion against [the] authority and government of the United States, and as a fit and necessary war measure for suppressing said rebellion." It was directed only against states, or parts of states, "wherein the people thereof respectively, are this day in rebellion against the United States." And it concluded with a statement that the proclamation was "sincerely believed to be an act of justice, warranted by the Constitution, upon military necessity."[34]

The Emancipation Proclamation has been criticized because it did not apply generally to all of the slaves in all of the country. It had no application to Missouri, Kentucky, Maryland, or Delaware, slave states that never seceded from the Union, nor to Tennessee or the counties in Louisiana and Virginia that were occupied by Union troops when the proclamation was issued. When asked why the proclamation did not apply nationally, Lincoln explained that it had "no constitutional or legal justification, except as a military measure" and that certain areas were exempted "because the military necessity did not apply to the exempted localities." If he extended it into those localities, he said, he would do so "without the argument of military necessity, and so, without any argument, except the one that I think the measure politically expedient, and morally right." "Would I not thus give up all footing upon constitution or law?" he asked. "Would I not thus be in the boundless field of absolutism?"[35] As constitutional scholar Akhil Reed Amar has stated, the very fact that the proclamation did not apply throughout the country "reinforced Lincoln's legal authority to make it. The holes and exceptions were themselves proof that Lincoln's was indeed a *military* (and thus executive) decision as distinct from a *moral* one (which would have required express legislative backing)."[36]

The proclamation has also been criticized on the ground that it lacks the eloquence and passion of Lincoln's other great utterances, the Gettysburg Address and the Second Inaugural. In 1948, historian Richard Hofstadter grumbled that the proclamation "had all the moral grandeur of a bill of lading."[37] More recently, however, historian Allen C. Guelzo has explained what Hofstadter apparently did not understand, that the Proclamation was "a legal document" and that "legal documents cannot afford very much in the way of flourishes."[38] Lincoln knew that his Emancipation Proclamation would be subjected to the most rigorous analysis in the courts, possibly by Chief Justice Taney himself. And so he took pains to articulate his constitutional authority for issuing it—his own powers as commander in chief, and the military necessity posed by the Southern rebellion. Lincoln was not so naive, however, as to believe that all of his critics would accept his constitutional justification for the proclamation. He knew that it might fall before judicial attack, and so he joined other opponents of slavery who sought to amend the Constitution to prohibit slavery throughout the country. Their efforts were crowned with success in 1865 when the Thirteenth Amendment passed Congress and was ratified by the requisite number of states. The constitutional amendment removed the possibility that the Supreme Court might one day issue its own "proclamation" against the Emancipation Proclamation.

If Lincoln is most often criticized today for his suspension of habeas cor-

pus, and for abridging the constitutional rights of civilians, he was most enthusiastically praised in the years immediately following the war for his Emancipation Proclamation, and for his preservation of the Union. Whether the
criticism or the praise comes closer to the mark is perhaps a matter of opinion.
For those who benefited from emancipation and the preservation of the Union,
however, for those who shared the president's own exultation in the "new birth
of freedom" he described at Gettysburg, the answer will always be clear.

Notes

AJP-LC	Andrew Johnson Papers, Library of Congress
AL	Abraham Lincoln
ALP-LC	Abraham Lincoln Papers, Library of Congress
CG	*Congressional Globe*
CW	*Collected Works of Abraham Lincoln*, ed. Roy P. Basler
DDP-LC	David Davis Papers, Library of Congress
DMPP-MHS	David M. Perine Papers, Maryland Historical Society
EBWP-LC	Elihu B. Washburne Papers, Library of Congress
EMSP-LC	Edwin McMasters Stanton Papers, Library of Congress
FED. CASES	*Federal Cases*
JEHP-MHS	John Eager Howard Papers, Maryland Historical Society
JSBP-LC	Jeremiah Sullivan Black Papers, Library of Congress
LC	Library of Congress
LTP-LC	Lyman Trumbull Papers, Library of Congress
MHS	Maryland Historical Society
NYEP	*New York Evening Post*
NYH	*New York Herald*
NYT	*New York Times*
NYTRIB	*New York Tribune*
OR	*The War of the Rebellion: A Compilation of the Official Records of the Union and Confederate Armies*
RBT	Roger B. Taney

RBTP-LC	Roger B. Taney Papers, Library of Congress
RBTP-MHS	Roger B. Taney Papers, Maryland Historical Society
S. CT.	*Supreme Court Reporter*
SPC	Salmon P. Chase
SPCP-LC	Salmon P. Chase Papers, Library of Congress
STATS.	United States Statutes at Large
U.S.	*United States Supreme Court Reports*
USC	United States Constitution
WHSP-LC	William H. Seward Papers, Library of Congress

Introduction

1. Simon, *Lincoln and Chief Justice Taney*.
2. See Farber, *Lincoln's Constitution*, 30–31, 44, 49, 51–52, 58, 68, 77, 79–85, 87–91.
3. CW, 1:112.
4. Steiner, *An Honest Calling*, 56.
5. CW, 1:112.
6. Bruce, *Lincoln and the Riddle of Death*, 14.
7. *The Law Practice of Abraham Lincoln: Complete Documentary Edition* (Champaign: University of Illinois Press, 2000), a DVD publication, lists twenty of Lincoln's cases that were appealed to the U.S. Supreme Court. In some, he represented a party only at the trial level, in others at an intermediate appellate level. In *Moore v. Brown*, 11 How. (52 U.S.) 413 (1850), he filed the record in the U.S. Supreme Court but did not argue the case. In *Forsyth v. Reynolds*, 15 How. (56 U.S.) 358 (1853), he filed a brief but did not participate in the oral argument. In *Lewis v. Lewis*, 7 How. (48 U.S.) 776 (1849), he presented an oral argument. See discussion in Chapter 1.
8. CW, 2:82.
9. Ibid.
10. *Dred Scott v. Sandford*, 19 How. (60 U.S.) 393 (1857). See Chapter 2 for discussion.
11. Holzer, *Lincoln at Cooper Union*, 28, 51–54.
12. Ibid., 144, 233.
13. AL to Albert G. Hodges, April 4, 1864, ALP-LC.
14. USC, Art. I, Sec. 8, clause 17 (District of Columbia); Art. IV, Sec. 3, clause 2 (territories). See discussion in Chapter 2.
15. USC, Art. IV, Sec. 2, clause 3.
16. AL, Notes for Speech in Kansas and Ohio, September 16–17, 1859, ALP-LC.
17. See Davis's Farewell Speech to the U.S. Senate, January 21, 1861, CG, 36th Congress, 2nd Session, 1861, 487; also Inaugural Address as Provisional Presi-

dent of the Confederacy, February 18, 1861, Crist and Dix, *Papers of Jefferson Davis*, 46–50.

18. Richardson, *Compilation*, 7:3161–3162, 3166–3167; for further discussion, see Chapter 1.

19. Taney's views as to the constitutionality of secession were expressed in an untitled, eight-page memorandum in his own handwriting that was donated to the Library of Congress in 1929. This memorandum has been labeled (apparently by a library archivist) "Fragment of a Manuscript Relating to Slavery in the United States," RBTP-LC. Although the memorandum is undated, internal evidence indicates that it was written between January 26 and February 1, 1861. It was Taney's practice during the war to set forth his views on controversial constitutional issues for possible use in Supreme Court opinions, if and when those issues should come before the Court. For description and discussion of this memorandum, see Fehrenbacher, *Dred Scott Case*, 554–555, 711n.5; for further discussion of Taney's views on secession, see Chapter 7.

20. Lincoln expressed these views in his First Inaugural Address. CW 4:252; see discussion in Chapter 1. See also Farber, *Lincoln's Constitution*, 78–79, 86, 102, 108–109, 111.

21. USC, Art. II, Sec. 2.

22. USC, Art. II, Sec 1; for discussion of Lincoln's First Inaugural Address, see Chapter 1.

23. CW, 2:401.

24. Ibid.

25. Donald, *Lincoln Reconsidered*, 148–149.

26. Borrett, *Letters from Canada and the United States*, 252–253.

27. Steiner, *An Honest Calling*, 40–41.

28. The jurisdiction of the federal courts extends only to "cases" or "controversies" arising under the Constitution or laws of the United States. USC, Art. III, Sec. 2.

29. USC, Art. III, Sec. 1.

30. Kohn, "Failing Justice," 91.

31. Swisher, "Mr. Chief Justice Taney," 212, 226–227.

32. Rehnquist, *All the Laws but One*, 222.

1. A Solemn Oath

1. NYT, March 5, 1861, p. 1.

2. Ibid.

3. NYTrib, March 17, 1857, p. 5.

4. Swisher, *Roger B. Taney*, 322.

5. See Chapter 2.

6. Fehrenbacher, *Dred Scott Case*, 560.

7. Swisher, *Roger B. Taney*, 154.

8. For Taney's views on slavery and race, see Finkelman, "'Hooted Down the Page of History': Reconsidering the Greatness of Chief Justice Taney," 89–93.

9. Richardson, *Compilation*, 7:3161–3162, 3166–3167.

10. See "Fragment of a Manuscript Relating to Slavery in the United States," RBTP-LC. Fehrenbacher, *Dred Scott Case*, 553–554, describes this memorandum in detail. For further discussion, see Chapter 7.

11. RBT to James Mason Campbell, October 19, 1860, JEHP-MHS.

12. *Dred Scott v. Sandford*, 19 How. (60 U.S.) 393, 405, 412, 416 (1857).

13. *Ross v. Duval*, 13 Pet. (38 U.S.) 45 (1839).

14. *Lewis v. Lewis*, 7 How. (48 U.S.) 776, 779–780 (1849).

15. Frank, *Lincoln as a Lawyer*, 80–81.

16. *The Law Practice of Abraham Lincoln: Complete Documentary Edition* (Champaign: University of Illinois Press, 2000), a DVD publication, lists twenty of Lincoln's cases that were ultimately appealed to the U.S. Supreme Court. In some, he represented a party only at the trial level, in others at an intermediate appellate level. In *Moore v. Brown*, 11 How. (52 U.S.) 413 (1850), he filed the record in the U.S. Supreme Court but did not argue the case. In *Forsyth v. Reynolds*, 15 How. (56 U.S.) 358 (1853), he filed a brief but did not participate in the oral argument.

17. Swisher, *Taney Period*, 717.

18. CG, 35th Congress, 1st Session, 941.

19. Tyler, *Memoir of Roger Brooke Taney*, 391.

20. Nicolay and Hay, "Lincoln's Inauguration" 273.

21. Fehrenbacher, *Dred Scott Case*, 227.

22. RBT to David M. Perine, May 9, 1860, DMPP-MHS.

23. Swisher, *Taney Period*, 726.

24. Warren, *Supreme Court in United States History*, 2:10.

25. Black to Charles R. Buckalew, January 28, 1861, JSBP-LC.

26. Weisenburger, *John McLean*, 226–227.

27. Swisher, *Taney Period*, 48.

28. Ibid., 47.

29. See Donald, *Lincoln*, 243.

30. NYTrib, April 14, 1860, p. 5.

31. Lawrence, *James Moore Wayne*, 128–129.

32. "Memoranda," 3. Wall. (70 U.S.) ix.

33. Chandler, "The Centenary of Associate Justice John Catron," 34.

34. Lawrence, *James Moore Wayne*, 134.

35. Strong, *Diary of George Templeton Strong*, 370.

36. Swisher, *Taney Period*, 220.

37. Fehrenbacher, *Dred Scott Case*, 234.

38. Gatell, "Robert C. Grier," 883.

39. NYTrib, March 17, 1857, p. 5.
40. Lawrence, *James Moore Wayne*, 134.
41. Saunders, *John Archibald Campbell*, 11.
42. Ibid., chap. 4.
43. Ibid., 62.
44. Ibid., 21.
45. NYTrib, March 17, 1857, p. 5.
46. For more on Benjamin Curtis, see Chapter 2.
47. Gillette, "Nathan Clifford," 967.
48. See Philip Greely Clifford, *Nathan Clifford, Democrat*, vii.
49. Fairman, *Reconstruction and Reunion*, 77.
50. Angle, *Lincoln Reader*, 336 (quoting Henry Watterson).
51. Fugitive Slave Law: Act of February 12, 1793, chap. 7, 1 Stat. 302; Act of September 18, 1850, chap. 60, 9 Stat. 462.
52. AL, First Inaugural Address—Final Text, March 4, 1861, CW, 4:262–271.
53. NYT, March 5, 1861, p. 1.
54. Nicolay and Hay, "Lincoln's Inauguration," 284.
55. NYT, March 5, 1861, p. 1.
56. "Proceedings in Relation to the Death of the Late Judge Daniel," 24 How. (65 U.S.) iii.
57. *Prigg v. Pennsylvania*, 16 Pet. (41 U.S.) 539 (1842).
58. Act of February 12, 1793, chap. 7, 1 Stat. 302, Sec. 1.
59. *Kentucky v. Dennison*, 24 How. (65 U.S.) 66, 109–110 (1861).
60. *Gaines v. Hennen*, 24 How. (65 U.S.) 553 (1861).
61. USC, Art. VI, provides that "all executive and judicial officers, both of the United States and of the several states, shall be bound by oath or affirmation, to support this Constitution." However, the Constitution does not prescribe the words of the oath. The Judiciary Act of 1789 prescribed the form of the oath (or affirmation) as follows: "I, A. B., do solemnly swear or affirm, that I will administer justice without respect to persons, and do equal right to the poor and to the rich, and that I will faithfully and impartially discharge and perform all the duties incumbent on me as _____, according to the best of my abilities and understanding, agreeably to the Constitution, and laws of the United States. So help me God." Act of September 24, 1789, chap. 20, Sec. 8, 1 Stat. 73, 76.

2. Dred Scott

1. *Federalist* No. 78.
2. Oliver Wendell Holmes, Jr., *The Common Law*, ed. Mark De Wolfe Howe (Cambridge, MA: Harvard University Press, 1963), 1.
3. Finkelman, *Dred Scott v. Sandford*, 2.

4. Fehrenbacher, *Dred Scott Case*, 239–240.

5. Finkelman, *Dred Scott v. Sandford*, 16.

6. *Winny v. Whitesides*, 1 Mo. 472 (1824).

7. Finkelman, *Dred Scott v. Sandford*, 20.

8. *Somerset v. Stewart*, 1 Lofft (G. B.) 1 (1772).

9. *Scott v. Emerson*, 15 Mo. 576, 582–587 (1852).

10. Act of September 24, 1789, chap. 20, Sec. 25, 1 Stat. 73.

11. *Strader v. Graham*, 10 How. (51 U.S.) 82, 92–97 (1850).

12. Kaufman, *Dred Scott's Advocate*, 4, 14, 70, 94, 182.

13. Act of September 24, 1789, chap. 20, Sec. 11, 1 Stat. 73.

14. Kaufman, *Dred Scott's Advocate*, 189.

15. Fehrenbacher, *Dred Scott Case*, 280.

16. Swisher, *Taney Period*, 613.

17. Richardson, *Compilation*, 7:2962.

18. *Dred Scott v. Sandford*, 19 How. (60 U.S.) 393, 407 (1857).

19. Ibid., 452.

20. Ibid., 463–465.

21. Ibid., 524–529.

22. Swisher, *Taney Period*, 239.

23. *Dred Scott v. Sandford*, 19 How. (60 U.S.) 393, 576 (1857).

24. Ibid., 619.

25. Fehrenbacher, *Dred Scott Case*, 316.

26. NYTrib, March 7, 1857, p. 4.

27. *Independent*, March 19, 1857, p. 1.

28. *Chicago Daily Tribune*, March 19, 1857, p. 2.

29. *Richmond Enquirer*, March 10, 1857, p. 2.

30. *Daily Picayune*, March 21, 1857, p. 1.

31. *Charleston Mercury*, April 2, 1857, p. 2.

32. NYT, March 9, 1857, p. 4.

33. *Charleston Mercury*, April 2, 1857, p. 2.

34. CW, 2:404.

35. Holzer, *Lincoln-Douglas Debates*, 224.

36. See Swisher, *Taney Period*, 646n53.

37. For discussion, see Chapter 1.

38. CW, 2:400–401.

39. Ibid., 2:495.

40. Holzer, *Lincoln-Douglas Debates*, 304.

41. Ibid., 77.

42. CW, 3:339.

43. *Ableman v. Booth*, 21 How. (61 U.S.) 506, 521 (1859).

44. Holzer, *Lincoln at Cooper Union*, 185, 252–267.
45. Ibid., 265.
46. Swisher, *Taney Period*, 664.
47. Fehrenbacher, *Dred Scott Case*, 457.
48. Ibid., 510.
49. Warren, *Supreme Court in United States History*, 2:357.
50. Fehrenbacher, *Dred Scott Case*, 421, 568.
51. "Visit to Dred Scott—His Family—Incidents of His Life—Decision of the Supreme Court," *Frank Leslie's Illustrated Newspaper*, June 27, 1857, pp. 49–50.

3. *First Blood*

1. *Habeas Corpus. The Proceedings in the Case of John Merryman*, 3–4.
2. NYT, May 29, 1861, pp. 4–5.
3. Swisher, *Taney Period*, 845.
4. Brown, *Baltimore and the Nineteenth of April, 1861*, 49–53.
5. Ibid., 58–59.
6. Trumbull to AL, April 21, 1861, ALP-LC.
7. Browning to AL, April 22, 1861, ALP-LC.
8. AL to Scott, April 25, 1861, ALP-LC (emphasis added).
9. Carter, *Blaze of Glory*, 304–308. See *Johnson v. Duncan*, 6 Am. Dec. 675 (1815).
10. *Luther v. Borden*, 7 How. (48 U.S.) 1, 45 (1849).
11. Act of September 24, 1789, chap. 20, Sec. 14, 1 Stat. 73.
12. AL, Message to Congress, July 4, 1861 (handwritten draft), ALP-LC.
13. See Duker, *Constitutional History*, 167n110.
14. Randall, *Constitutional Problems*, 121.
15. Francis B. Carpenter, "A Day with Governor Seward at Auburn July 1870," in WHSP-LC (Folder 6634).
16. CW, 4:347. See Neely, *Fate of Liberty*, 8.
17. Randall, *Constitutional Problems*, 163n45; Swisher, *Taney Period*, 843–844.
18. Brown, *Baltimore and the Nineteenth of April, 1861*, 84.
19. Statement Cadwalader to RBT, May 26, 1861, in OR, Series II, 1:576.
20. NYT, May 30, 1861, p. 4.
21. *Ex parte Merryman*, 17 Fed. Cases 144, 145 (C.C.D. Md. 1861).
22. Ibid., 146, 147.
23. NYT, May 31, 1861, p. 2.
24. *Ex parte Merryman*, 17 Fed. Cases 144, 146 (C.C.D.Md. 1861); also OR, Series II, 1:576.
25. Hyman, *A More Perfect Union*, 84.
26. Tyler, *Memoir of Roger Brooke Taney*, 427.

27. Brown, *Baltimore and the Nineteenth of April, 1861*, 89.
28. *Ex parte Merryman*, 17 Fed. Cases 144, 147 (C.C.D.Md. 1861).
29. Swisher, *Taney Period*, 847–848.
30. *Baltimore Daily Republican*, May 28, 1861.
31. Brown, *Baltimore and the Nineteenth of April, 1861*, 90.
32. NYT, May 30, 1861, p. 4.
33. Brown, *Baltimore and the Nineteenth of April, 1861*, 90.
34. Ward Hill Lamon, "Habeas Corpus," in Ward Hill Lamon Papers, Huntington Library.
35. See Fehrenbacher, *Dred Scott Case*, 716n20.
36. The full opinion is in *Ex parte Merryman*, 17 Fed. Cas. 144 (C.C.D.Md. 1861), and in *War of the Rebellion: A Compilation of the Official Records of the Union and Confederate Armies*, Series II, 1:577–85.
37. "The suspension of the privilege of the writ of habeas corpus does not suspend the writ itself. The writ issues as a matter of course, and, on the return made to it, the court decides whether the party applying is denied the right of proceeding any further with it." See *Ex parte Milligan*, 4 Wall. (71 U.S.) 2, 130–131 (1866). Although it is technically correct to speak of "suspension of the privilege of the writ," constitutional historians customarily refer to "suspension of the writ" or "suspension of habeas corpus." That custom is followed in this book.
38. Duker, *Constitutional History*, 135–137.
39. *Ex parte Bollman*, 4 Cranch (8 U.S.) 75, 101 (1807).
40. *Ex parte Merryman*, 17 Fed. Cas. 144, 152 (C.C.D.Md. 1861). USC, Amend. V, provides (in relevant part): "No person shall be . . . deprived of life, liberty, or property, without due process of law." Amend. VI, provides (in relevant part): "In all criminal prosecutions, the accused shall enjoy the right to a speedy and public trial, by an impartial jury of the state and district wherein the crime shall have been committed, which district shall have been previously ascertained by law, and to be informed of the nature and cause of the accusation."
41. *Ex parte Merryman*, 17 Fed. Cas. 144, 153 (C.C.D.Md. 1861).
42. Tyler, *Memoir of Roger Brooke Taney*, 423, 659.
43. Binney, *The Privilege of the Writ of Habeas Corpus under the Constitution*.
44. Swisher, *Taney Period*, 917–918.
45. Curtis, *Executive Power*. Also in Curtis, *A Memoir of Benjamin Robbins Curtis*, 2:309–335.
46. *Baltimore Sun*, June 4, 1861, p. 2.
47. See, e.g., Smith, *Roger B. Taney*, 197; "*Ex parte* Merryman: Proceedings of Court Day, May 26, 1861," 392; Sheads and Toomey, *Baltimore during the Civil War*, 35; Steiner, *Life of Roger Brooke Taney*, 500; Simon, *Lincoln and Chief Justice Taney*, 197; Downey, "The Conflict between the Chief Justice and the Chief Executive," 275.

48. NYH, June 2, 1861, p. 5.

49. CW, 4:390.

50. Message to Congress, July 4, 1861 (handwritten daft), ALP-LC; Wilson, *Lincoln's Sword*, 83–85.

51. CW, 4:430.

52. NYT, May 29, 1861, p. 4.

53. Hyman, *A More Perfect Union*, 127.

54. Donald, *Lincoln Reconsidered*, 163.

55. Steiner, *An Honest Calling*, 40.

56. CW, 4:431.

57. OR, Series II, 2:20–30.

58. See USC, Art. II, Sec. 1 (president's oath); Art. VI (oath of executive and judicial officers).

59. *Marbury v. Madison*, 1 Cranch (5 U.S.)137 (1803).

60. Act of August 6, 1861, chap. 63, Sec. 3, 12 Stat. 326.

61. Madison, *Debates in the Federal Convention of 1787*, 427, 477; Farber, *Lincoln's Constitution*, 160–161; Randall, *Constitutional Problems*, 126.

62. *Ex parte Bollman*, 4 Cranch (8 U.S.) 75 (1807); see discussion in Randall, *Constitutional Problems*, 133–134; Jackson, "The Power to Suspend Habeas Corpus," 29–31.

63. Hyman, *A More Perfect Union*, 94.

64. Act of April 30, 1790, chap. 9, Sec. 1, 1 Stat. 112.

65. Act of February 28, 1795, chap. 36, Sec. 1, 1 Stat. 424.

66. *Luther v. Borden*, 7 How. (48 U.S.) 1, 43 (1849).

67. Hyman, *A More Perfect Union*, 90.

68. Farber, *Lincoln's Constitution*, 199.

69. In 1807, President Jefferson asked Congress to authorize him to suspend the writ of habeas corpus. The Senate passed a bill suspending the writ for three months, but the House rejected it decisively. See Warren, *Supreme Court in United States History*, 1:302–303; Duker, *Constitutional History*, 135–137.

70. Bernard C. Steiner, *Life of Roger Brooke Taney*, 500.

71. Randall, *Lincoln the President: Midstream*, 164–165.

72. Lewis, *Without Fear or Favor*, 533.

73. Rehnquist, *All the Laws but One*, 44.

74. But the decision was not published in *Federal Cases* until 1895, more than thirty years after Taney's death.

75. Act of April 29, 1802, chap. 31, 2 Stat. 156, Sec. 6: "Whenever any question shall occur before a Circuit Court upon which the opinions of the judges shall be opposed, the point upon which the disagreement shall happen, shall, during the same term, upon the request of either party or their counsel, be stated under the direction of the judges and certified under the seal of the court to the Supreme Court at

their next session to be held thereafter; and shall by the said court be finally decided: And the decision of the Supreme Court and their order in the premises shall
be remitted to the Circuit Court and be there entered of record, and shall have effect according to the nature of the said judgment and order: Provided, That nothing herein contained shall prevent the cause from proceeding, if, in the opinion of
the court, further proceedings can be had without prejudice to the merits." Justice
David Davis and District Judge David McDonald issued a certificate of division in
1865 while sitting in the circuit court in Indianapolis in the case of *Ex parte
Milligan*, 4 Wall. (71 U.S.) 2 (1966). According to Charles Fairman, the certificate
was probably issued not "because of any disagreement on the law, but because of
Justice Davis' sense of the importance of getting the case into the Supreme Court."
Fairman, *Reconstruction and Reunion*, 135. According to Allen, *Origins of the Dred
Scott Case*, 28, Supreme Court justices sitting on circuit "considered the division of
opinion a good mechanism for shepherding potentially important cases before the
full court."

76. For debate on the interesting point of whether Taney's opinion is properly regarded as a decision of a circuit judge or a Supreme Court justice, see Vladeck,
"The Field Theory: Martial Law, the Suspension Power, and the Insurrection Act,"
n. 2; Rehnquist, *All the Laws but One*, 44; and Simon, *Lincoln and Chief Justice Taney*, 190, who characterize it as a circuit court decision. Fehrenbacher, *Dred
Scott Case*, 574, says it was "a proceedings [sic] at chambers with which the rest
of the Court had nothing to do." Rossiter, *The Supreme Court and the Commander
in Chief*, 20, says that Taney made the decision "not, as is commonly asserted,
in the capacity of circuit judge, but as Chief Justice of the United States pure
and simple." Swisher, *Taney Period*, 845, 849n26, states that Taney always treated
it as a decision of the chief justice "at chambers." Hartnett, "The Constitutional
Puzzle of Habeas Corpus," 279–280, states that the writ "was issued by Chief Justice Roger Taney in his capacity as an individual justice [of the Supreme Court]."

77. Judiciary Act of 1789, chap. 20, 1 Stat. 73, Sec. 14. The modern statute provides
that "writs of habeas corpus may be granted by the Supreme Court, any justice
thereof, the district courts and any circuit judge within their respective jurisdic-
tions." 28 United States Code Sec. 2241(a).

78. USC, Art. III, Sec. 2. In *Marbury v. Madison*, 1 Cranch (5 U.S.) 137 (1803), the
Supreme Court held that Congress cannot constitutionally add to the original jurisdiction of the Supreme Court. In *Ex parte Bollman*, 4 Cranch (8 U.S.) 75, 100–
101 (1807), it held that the full court can grant writs of habeas corpus, but only to
revise the decisions of inferior courts (i.e., only in the exercise of their appellate jurisdiction).

79. "The Constitution specifically limits the original jurisdiction of the Court, though
the individual justice in chambers or on circuit is subject to no such limit." Duker,

Constitutional History, 165n89. "Although the power of the Court itself to issue habeas . . . depends on whether the particular case involves original or appellate jurisdiction, an individual Justice has the power to grant habeas whether the particular
case involves original or appellate jurisdiction. Put slightly differently, the power of
an individual Justice to issue a writ of habeas corpus is *both* original and appellate:
appellate if the particular case involves the revision of another court's judgment,
and original if the particular case does not." Hartnett, "The Constitutional Puzzle
of Habeas Corpus," 26.
80. *In re Kemp*, 16 Wis. 359 (1863).
81. Bates to Stanton, January 31, 1863, EMSP-LC.
82. See Rehnquist, *All the Laws but One*, 41.
83. Paludan, *The Presidency of Abraham Lincoln*, 76.
84. Hyman, *A More Perfect Union*, 81.
85. See Jackson, "The Power to Suspend Habeas Corpus," for a thoughtful discussion
of the weaknesses of Taney's reasoning but a final conclusion that the framers intended to give Congress the power to suspend habeas corpus.
86. In *Ex parte Milligan*, 4 Wall. (71 U.S.) 2 (1866), a bare majority of the Supreme
Court endorsed the substance of Taney's view (though without citing his *Merryman*
opinion) that civilians cannot constitutionally be subjected to military arrest and
trial where the courts are open and functioning. The president's power to suspend
the writ of habeas corpus was not addressed, because the suspension was under authority of Congress's habeas corpus act passed March 3, 1863. See Act of March 3,
1863, chap. 81, 12 Stat. 755. See also discussion in Chapter 9.
87. Jackson, "The Power to Suspend Habeas Corpus," 12, states: "The question of
which branch of government has the power under the Constitution to suspend the
privilege of the writ of habeas corpus remains unanswered."
88. Swisher, *Taney Period*, 850.

4. Judges and Circuits

1. Swisher, *Taney Period*, 724.
2. Ibid., 726.
3. Saunders, *John Archibald Campbell*, 103–104, 110–112.
4. *Dred Scott v. Sandford*, 19 How. (60 U.S.) 393 (1857); Saunders, *John Archibald Campbell*, 67.
5. Saunders, *John Archibald Campbell*, 139.
6. Ibid., 143.
7. Ibid., 145.
8. Connor, *John Archibald Campbell*, 155.
9. Saunders, *John Archibald Campbell*, 152.

10. Woodward, *Mary Chesnut's Civil War*, 92.
11. Weisenburger, *Life of John McLean*, 216.
12. "Death of Judge McLean," 1 Black (66 U.S.) 8, 12.
13. AL to Crittenden, November 4, 1858, in CW, 3:335–336.
14. NYT, March 7, 1861, p. 1.
15. Hicks to AL, March 11, 1861, ALP-LC.
16. Stanton to AL, March 6, 1861, ALP-LC.
17. Silver, *Lincoln's Supreme Court*, 25.
18. Swisher, *Taney Period*, 813.
19. D. Rees to SPC, April 5, 1861, SPCP-LC.
20. Henry Winter Davis to AL, March 6, 1861, ALP-LC.
21. Act of September 24, 1789, chap. 20, Sec. 4, 1 Stat. 73 (Judiciary Act of 1789).
22. Swisher, *Taney Period*, 248–49; Fairman, *Reconstruction and Reunion*, 85.
23. See USC, Art. III, Sec. 2; Warren, *Supreme Court in United States History*, 1:19n2 (until 1866, suits in federal circuit courts "were practically confined to cases based on diverse citizenship"). For further discussion of diversity jurisdiction, see Chapter 2.
24. See Rehnquist, *Supreme Court*, 58.
25. Silver, *Lincoln's Supreme Court*, 59.
26. Swisher, *Taney Period*, 815.
27. Browning to AL, April 9, 1861, ALP-LC.
28. Ibid.
29. William A. Bradley to Elihu B. Washburne, July 10, 1861, EBWP-LC.
30. Swisher, *Taney Period*, 889.
31. Ibid., 865.
32. CG, 37th Cong., 3rd sess., 1139.
33. Swisher, *Taney Period*, 858.
34. Ibid., 861.
35. Ibid., 857.
36. Ibid., 858.
37. NYTrib, July 14, 1861, p. 7.
38. Swisher, *Taney Period*, 859.
39. Catron to William T. Carroll, October 9, 1861, ALP-LC.
40. See Lawrence, *James Moore Wayne*, 174.
41. Ibid., 71–74, 98–99, 144–145.
42. Ibid., 55, 63–65, 66, 71–73, 94–97, 110, 111, 115, 160; *Smith v. Turner*, 7 How. (48 U.S.) 283, 411 (1849).
43. Lawrence, *James Moore Wayne*, 178 ("That Campbell was forty-nine and Wayne seventy perhaps explains much concerning their respective courses").
44. Ibid., 170.

45. Ibid., 168, 170, 189–190.

46. NYTrib, August 5, 1861, quoted in the *Southern Confederacy*, August 13, 1861, p. 2.

47. NYH, August 4, 1861, quoted in the *Southern Confederacy*, August 13, 1861, p. 2.

48. *Southern Confederacy*, August 13, 1861, p. 2.

49. See CW, 5:41.

50. Act of March 2, 1855, chap. 142, 10 Stat. 631.

51. Kens, *Justice Stephen Field*, 95; Swisher, *Taney Period*, 776–777.

52. CW, 5:41–42.

53. Ibid., 5:42.

54. *Chicago Tribune*, March 4, 1861, p. 2.

55. NYTrib, June 10, 1861, p. 4, quoted in Silver, *Lincoln's Supreme Court*, 42–43.

56. CG, 37th Cong., 2nd sess., 1861, 8.

57. USC, Art. III, Sec. 1.

58. CG, 37th Cong., 2nd sess., 1861, 26.

59. Swisher, *Taney Period*, 824; see *Ex parte Merryman*, 17 Fed. Case. 144, 145 (C.C.D. Md. 1861), and the discussion in Chapter 3.

60. CG, 37th Cong., 2nd sess., 1861, 27.

61. Ibid., 27, 28.

62. Ibid., 28.

63. See Donald, *"We Are Lincoln Men,"* 122–127.

64. Act of August 6, 1861, chap. 60, 12 Stat. 319.

65. CW, 4:506.

66. Browning to AL, September 11, 1861, ALP-LC.

67. CW, 4:531–532.

68. Warren, *Supreme Court in United States History*, 2:378.

69. Silver, *Lincoln's Supreme Court*, 60.

70. NYEP, January 27, 1861, p. 2.

71. Silver, *Lincoln's Supreme Court*, 61.

72. Act of July 15, 1862, chap. 178, 12 Stat. 576.

73. Ross, *Justice of Shattered Dreams*, 1–74.

74. Samuel F. Miller to Mrs. James Grimes, August 28, 1888, in *Iowa Historical Record* (1891), 7:88–89.

75. Silver, *Lincoln's Supreme Court*, 66–67.

76. Ibid., 67; Ross, *Justice of Shattered Dreams*, 79.

77. CW, 5:336–337.

78. Ibid., 5:350.

79. Guelzo, *Lincoln's Emancipation Proclamation*, 123.

80. NYT, September 18, 1862, p. 4.

81. Donald, *"We Are Lincoln Men,"* 120–121.

82. Beale, *Diary of Edward Bates,* 244; RBT to Clifford, August 2, 1862, Nathan Clifford Collection, Maine Historical Society.
83. Donald, *"We Are Lincoln Men,"* 124.
84. Medill to Trumbull, July 4, 1862, LTP-LC.
85. King, *Lincoln's Manager,* 20–35.
86. Davis to William Orme, January 27, 1862, DDP-LC.
87. Davis to Usher, May 15, 1862, DDP-LC.
88. King, *Lincoln's Manager,* 195–196.
89. Donald, *"We Are Lincoln Men,"* 125.
90. Swett to Mrs. Swett, August 10, 1862, DDP-LC.
91. AL to Davis, August 27, 1862, DDP-LC.
92. Davis to AL, September 1, 1862, DDP-LC.
93. King, *Lincoln's Manager,* 199.
94. Washington appointed Thomas Johnson in 1791 and John Rutledge in 1795. Adams appointed Bushrod Washington in 1798; Jefferson appointed Brockholst Livingston in 1806; Monroe appointed Smith Thompson in 1823; Van Buren appointed John McKinley in 1837; Polk appointed Levi Woodbury in 1845; and Fillmore appointed Benjamin R. Curtis in 1851.
95. Bates to AL, October 15, 1862, ALP-LC.
96. King, *Lincoln's Manager,* 199–200.

5. *The Prizes*

1. CW, 4:338–339.
2. USC, Art. I, Sec. 8, provides (in relevant part): "The Congress shall have power to lay and collect taxes, duties, imposts and excises, to pay the debts and provide for the common defense and general welfare of the United States; but all duties, imposts and excises shall be uniform throughout the United States."
3. CW, 4:338.
4. Ibid., 4:346–347.
5. USC, Art. I, Sec. 8, cl. 11, gives Congress power to "declare war, grant letters of marque and reprisal, and make rules concerning captures on land and water." Letters of "marque and reprisal" (more often called "letters of marque") are government licenses authorizing private citizens to engage in reprisals against enemy vessels. When properly issued by competent government authorities, they have the effect of legalizing conduct that would otherwise constitute piracy. Piracy is generally any robbery, kidnaping, or other criminal violence committed at sea. In his proclamation of April 19, Lincoln gave notice that any person who, "under the pretended authority" of the seceding states, molested a United States ship or the persons or cargo on board would "be held amenable to the laws of the United States for the prevention and punishment of privacy." CW, 4:339.

6. See Scott to Seward, March 3, 1861, ALP-LC ("you as chief of his Cabinet"); Elliott, *Winfield Scott*, 724 ("Scott's Anaconda").

7. McPherson, *Battle Cry of Freedom*, 91–92.

8. William C. Davis, *Jefferson Davis*, 304–305.

9. Welles, *Lincoln and Seward*, 122–123.

10. CW, 4:265.

11. Ibid., 4:338.

12. Wheaton, *Elements of International Law*, 8th ed., 564–565.

13. Adams, *Great Britain and the American Civil War*, 1:263.

14. Newton, *Lord Lyons*, 1:36.

15. Act of August 6, 1861, chap. 63, Sec. 3, 12 Stat. 326.

16. Act of July 13, 1861, chap. 3, Sec. 4, 12 Stat. 255, 256.

17. Welles to AL, August 5, 1861, ALP-LC.

18. Segal, *Conversations with Lincoln*, 114.

19. Pease and Randall, *Diary of Orville Hickman Browning*, 1:488–489.

20. Welles, *Lincoln and Seward*, 124.

21. Adams, *Great Britain and the American Civil War*, 1:88, 94–95.

22. United States Naval War Records Office, *Official Records of the Union and Confederate Navies in the War of the Rebellion.*, Series I, 5:784.

23. See USC, Art. III, Sec. 2 (judicial power of United States extends to "all cases of admiralty and maritime jurisdiction"); Act of September 24, 1789, chap. 20, Sec. 9, 1 Stat. 73 (district courts to have "exclusive original cognizance of all civil causes of admiralty and maritime jurisdiction, including all seizures under laws of impost, navigation, or trade of the United States"); Act of June 26, 1812, chap. 107, Sec. 6, 2 Stat. 759 (district courts to have original cognizance "in the case of all captured vessels, goods, and effects which shall be brought within the jurisdiction of the United States").

24. Bernath, *Squall Across the Atlantic*, 8.

25. Adams, *Richard Henry Dana*, 2:415; Shapiro, *Richard Henry Dana, Jr.*, 117–118.

26. *Decisions of Hon. Peleg Sprague*, 2:131.

27. See USC, Art. II, Sec. 2.

28. *Decisions of Hon. Peleg Sprague*, 2:134.

29. Ibid., 2:160.

30. See Browning, *From Cape Charles to Cape Fear*, 263

31. Bates to AL, February 9, 1863, ALP-LC.

32. Dana to Welles (endorsed by Sprague), May 18, 1863, ALP-LC; Shapiro, *Richard Henry Dana, Jr.*, 118.

33. Blatchford, *Reports of Cases in Prize*, 4.

34. Ibid., 16–22.

35. Ibid., 22–23.

36. Marvin, *A Treatise on the Law of Wreck and Salvage*.

37. Silver, *Lincoln's Supreme Court*, 107.
38. *Philadelphia Public Ledger*, July 1, 1862, p. 1.
39. Swisher, *Taney Period*, 883–884.
40. *Washington Republican*, February 12, 1863, as quoted in NYT, February 15, 1863, p. 2.
41. Adams, *Richard Henry Dana*, 2:268.
42. Swisher, *Taney Period*, 887.
43. *Preciat v. United States*, 17 Law. Ed. 459, 462 (1862).
44. Swisher, *Taney Period*, 886.
45. Beale, *Diary of Edward Bates*, 281.
46. *Preciat v. United States*, 17 Law. Ed. 459, 465–468 (1862).
47. Adams, *Richard Henry Dana*, 2:269.
48. Ibid.
49. Ibid., 2:270–271.
50. Ibid., 2:266–267.
51. Ibid., 2:267.
52. See *United States v. Castillero*, 2 Black (67 U.S.) 17, 166–169 (1863).
53. *Prize Cases*, 2 Black (67 U.S.) 635, 666–667 (1863).
54. Ibid., 635, 670.
55. Ibid., 635, 671.
56. NYT, March 13, 1863, p. 4.
57. "Downward Steps to Despotism," *New York World*, May 15, 1863, p. 4.
58. Adams, *Richard Henry Dana*, 2:415.
59. Ibid., 2:269.
60. Warren, *Supreme Court in United States History*, 2:381.
61. Adams, *Richard Henry Dana*, 2:264–265.
62. Ibid., 2:274.
63. Ibid., 2:273–274.
64. Henry Wheaton, *Elements of International Law*, 8th ed., edited, with notes, by Richard Henry Dana, Jr. (Boston: Little, Brown, 1866).

6. *The Boom of Cannon*

1. Although the 1858 cable broke after a brief period of service, Cyrus Field was successful in laying a permanent cable in 1866.
2. The Treaty of Guadalupe Hidalgo, Arts. VIII and IX, provided that absentee Mexican landholders would have their property "inviolably respected" and others would "be maintained and protected in the free enjoyment of their liberty and property." See Richard Griswold del Castillo, *The Treaty of Guadalupe Hidalgo: A Legacy of Conflict* (Norman: University of Oklahoma Press, 1990), 62–63.
3. "Correspondence between Mr. Justice Field and the Other Members of the Court

with Regard to His Retiring from the Bench," Appendix, 168 U.S. 713, 715 (1897).

4. Holzer, *Lincoln at Cooper Union*, 106, 147, 243.

5. Kens, *Justice Stephen Field*, 35.

6. Field to AL, October 25, 1861, ALP-LC.

7. Swisher, *Taney Period*, 829.

8. Silver, *Lincoln's Supreme Court*, 91.

9. Field, *Personal Reminiscences*, 115.

10. Act of March 3, 1863, chap. 100, 12 Stat. 794.

11. Field, *Personal Reminiscences*, 116; Kens, *Justice Stephen Field*, 97; see Milton S. Latham, James A. McDougall, Frederick F. Low, A. A. Sargent, and Timothy G. Phelps to AL, February 27, 1863, ALP-LC.

12. Field, *Life of David Dudley Field*, 196.

13. Beale and Brownsword, *Diary of Gideon Welles*, 1:245.

14. Field, *Personal Reminiscences*, 116.

15. See Swisher, *Stephen J. Field*, 115–116 (closeness of vote in *Prize Cases* and apprehension that future cases might be "sabotaged" by judges not committed to successful prosecution of war led to demand that Court personnel be changed so "the country would be in no further danger from that quarter"); Silver, *Lincoln's Supreme Court*, 84 (prudence "dictated a packed Court"); Rehnquist, *Supreme Court*, 209–213 (Lincoln's appointments amounted to "packing the Court"); Kens, *Justice Stephen Field*, 95 (Republicans "wanted to pack the Court with judges who would 'help keep the power of the Court right'").

16. CG, 40th Cong., 2nd sess., 1868, 498.

17. "Correspondence between Mr. Justice Field and the Other Members of the Court with Regard to His Retiring from the Bench," Appendix, 168 U.S. 713, 715 (1897).

18. Kutler, *Judicial Power and Reconstruction Politics*, 19. Kutler argues that the timing of the decision in the *Prize Cases* and the creation of the tenth Supreme Court seat was coincidental. Kutler points out that Franklin D. Roosevelt's proposal to add up to six new members to the Supreme Court in 1937 was opposed by Republicans and "disenchanted" Democrats, who "united and fought tenaciously against the bill." Roosevelt's proposal, unlike Lincoln's, was recognized as a genuine court-packing plan.

19. Swisher, *Stephen J. Field*, 117.

20. Ibid., 118.

21. Ibid.

22. "Correspondence between Mr. Justice Field and the Other Members of the Court with Regard to His Retiring from the Bench," Appendix, 168 U.S. 713, 715 (1897).

23. Swisher, *Stephen J. Field*, 118.

24. "Correspondence between Mr. Justice Field and the Other Members of the Court with Regard to His Retiring from the Bench," Appendix, 168 U.S. 713, 715 (1897). *Inter arma silent leges* is a quotation attributed to Cicero.
25. Klement, *Limits of Dissent*, 21, 39, 41, 42.
26. Curtis, "Lincoln, Vallandigham, and Anti-War Speech in the Civil War," 113.
27. Klement, *Limits of Dissent*, 90, 106.
28. Klement, *Copperheads in the Middle West*.
29. Weber, *Copperheads*, 2, 9, 48.
30. Ibid., 81–82.
31. Ibid., 27.
32. Ibid., 76.
33. Klement, *Limits of Dissent*, 66.
34. OR, Series I, 23 (Pt. 2): 237.
35. Klement, *Limits of Dissent*, 152.
36. *Ex parte Vallandigham*, 28 Fed. Cases 874, 875 (1863).
37. Ibid.
38. Ibid., 874, 875–876.
39. Ibid., 874, 924 (1863).
40. Klement, *Limits of Dissent*, 160.
41. Ibid., 175.
42. CW, 5:436–437.
43. Klement, *Limits of Dissent*, 175–176.
44. OR, II, V, 657; CW, 6:215–216.
45. The writ of certiorari is usually used to examine questions of law.
46. Swisher, *Taney Period*, 928–929.
47. *Luther v. Borden*, 7 How. (48 U.S.) 1 (1849); for discussion, see Chapter 3.
48. *Ex parte Vallandigham*, 1 Wall. (68 U.S.) 243, 254 (1864).
49. Ibid., 243, 254.
50. Klement, *Limits of Dissent*, 259; see also Klement, "The Indianapolis Treason Trials and *Ex parte Milligan*," 111.
51. OR, Series I, 23 (pt. 2): 386; Series II, 5:723–724.
52. AL to Erastus Corning and others, June 1863 (Copy No. 1), ALP-LC.
53. Ibid.
54. Erastus Corning and others to AL, June 30, 1863, ALP-LC.
55. Goodwin, *Team of Rivals*, 525.

7. The Old Lion

1. "Correspondence between Mr. Justice Field and the Other Members of the Court with Regard to His Retiring from the Bench," Appendix, 168 U.S. 713, 715 (1897).

2. Swisher, "Mr. Chief Justice Taney," 228.
3. Campbell to RBT, April 29, 1861, *Maryland Historical Magazine*, 5 (1910): 35.
4. In the Taney Papers in the Library of Congress, this memorandum has been labeled (apparently by an archivist) "Fragment of a Manuscript Relating to Slavery in the United States." The memorandum recites that six states had left the Union. Louisiana was the sixth state to secede, on January 26, 1861. Texas became the seventh state when it seceded on February 1. Thus it is possible to date the memorandum between those two dates. See Fehrenbacher, *Dred Scott Case*, 711n5.
5. "Fragment of a Manuscript Relating to Slavery in the United States," RBTP-LC.
6. Richardson, *Compilation*, 7:3161–3162, 3166–3167; for discussion, see Chapter 1.
7. "Fragment of a Manuscript Relating to Slavery in the United States," RBTP-LC. Fehrenbacher, *Dred Scott Case*, 553–554, describes this memorandum and states that it was acquired by the Library of Congress in 1929. See also discussion in Chapter 1.
8. RBT to Pierce, June 12, 1861, in *American Historical Review*, 10 (1905): 368.
9. Taney's opinion that secession was unconstitutional is discussed in Fehrenbacher, *Dred Scott Case*, 553–555; Tyler, *Memoir of Roger Brooke Taney*, 418; Lewis, *Without Fear or Favor*, 465; Allen, *Origins of the Dred Scott Case*, 220. Fehrenbacher analyzes the question in persuasive detail. Simon, *Lincoln and Chief Justice Taney*, 3, 112, 194, confuses Taney's opinion as to the constitutionality of secession with his view that "a peaceful separation" was "far better than . . . a civil war with all its horrors." Simon supports his conclusion that Taney believed secession was constitutional with authorities that do not support his conclusion, and he overlooks the eight-page memorandum in the Library of Congress that states the contrary.
10. Swisher, "Mr. Chief Justice Taney," 212, 226–227, 228.
11. Swisher, *Roger B. Taney*, 466.
12. Ibid., 466–469.
13. Ibid., 557–558.
14. *Ex parte Merryman*, 17 Fed. Cases 144, 145 (C.C.D. Md. 1861); see Chapter 3. Fairman, *Mr. Justice Miller and the Supreme Court*, 90.
15. Swisher, *Roger B. Taney*, 558.
16. Ibid., 559.
17. *Baltimore Sun*, June 20, 1863, p. 1.
18. The salaries were fixed by statute in 1855. See Act of March 3, 1855, chap. 175, 10 Stat. 643, 655.
19. RBT to SPC, January 1863, handwritten copy in DMPP-MHS.
20. RBT to Perine, July 18, 1861, DMPP-MHS.
21. Swisher, *Roger B. Taney*, 570–572, refers to these writings as "opinions."
22. Act of February 25, 1862, chap. 33, 12 Stat. 345; for discussion, see Chapters 8 and 10.
23. RBT, "Paper Money Made a Legal Tender in the Payment of Debts by Acts of Con-

gress:—Is the Law Constitutional?—Thoughts upon That Subject," eight-page handwritten document, in bound volume "Opinions of Chief Justice Taney," DMPP-MHS.

24. NYT, February 20, 1863, p. 4.
25. RBT, "Thoughts on the Conscription Law of the U. States,—Rough Draught Requiring Revision," twenty-two-page handwritten manuscript, in bound volume "Opinions of Chief Justice Taney," DMPP-MHS.
26. Swisher, *Taney Period*, 962.
27. Tyler, *Memoir of Roger Brooke Taney*, 482.
28. Howard, *Recollections*, 327.
29. Swisher, *Roger B. Taney*, 571–572.
30. Swisher, *Taney Period*, 963.
31. RBT to James Mason Campbell, September 13, 1861, JEHP-MHS.
32. RBT to James Mason Campbell, September 18, 1861, JEHP-MHS.
33. RBT to Roger Brooke Taney Campbell, September 13, 1864, JEHP-MHS.
34. Beale, *Diary of Edward Bates*, 204–205.
35. RBT to Wayne ("copy made from recollection Jan. 2, 1862"), RBTP-MHS.
36. Beale, *Diary of Edward Bates*, 358.
37. Logan, *Thirty Years in Washington*, 413.
38. RBT to Perine, August 6, 1863, DMPP-MHS.
39. Beale, *Diary of Edward Bates*, 79.
40. Burlingame and Ettlinger, *Inside Lincoln's White House*, 76–77.
41. Brooks, *Lincoln Observed*, 138.
42. Swisher, *Roger B. Taney*, 576–577.
43. Ibid., 577.
44. Delaplaine, "Lincoln after Taney's Death," 151.
45. Beale, *Diary of Edward Bates*, 418.
46. Strong, *Diary of George Templeton Strong*, 251.
47. Beale and Brownsword, *Diary of Gideon Welles*, 2:177.
48. Delaplaine, "Lincoln after Taney's Death," 154–155.
49. Beale, *Diary of Edward Bates*, 419.

8. A New Chief

1. Niven, *Salmon P. Chase*, 373.
2. Ibid.
3. Bates to AL, October 13, 1864, ALP-LC.
4. Burlingame and Ettlinger, *Inside Lincoln's White House*, 241.
5. SPC to Charles D. Cleveland, February 8, 1830, in Niven, *Salmon P. Chase Papers*, 2:48.

6. Act of February 12, 1793, chap. 7, 1 Stat. 302. Under Section 4, any person who harbored or concealed another person, after notice that he or she was a fugitive from labor, was subject to a penalty of $500, recoverable by the person claiming the fugitive in an action of debt.

7. *Jones v. Van Zandt*, 5 How. (46 U.S.) 215, 231 (1847).

8. Niven, *Salmon P. Chase*, 152.

9. Ibid., 187.

10. Schurz, *Reminiscences*, 2:169–172.

11. Niven, *Salmon P. Chase*, 221.

12. CW, 4:171.

13. Niven, *Salmon P. Chase*, 250.

14. Act of August 5, 1861, chap. 45, 12 Stat. 292, Sec. 49.

15. Act of July 1, 1862, chap. 119, 12 Stat. 432, Sec. 90.

16. Act of June 30, 1864, chap. 173, 13 Stat. 223, Sec. 116.

17. Larson, *Jay Cooke*, 106, 107.

18. Niven, *Salmon P. Chase*, 297.

19. Act of Feb. 25, 1862, chap. 33, 12 Stat. 345; Act of July 11, 1862, chap. 142, 12 Stat. 532; Act of March 3, 1863, chap. 73, 12 Stat. 709.

20. Niven, *Salmon P. Chase*, 338.

21. Nicolay and Hay, *Abraham Lincoln: A History*, 9:395.

22. Act of February 25, 1863, chap. 58, 12 Stat. 665.

23. Burlingame and Ettlinger, *Inside Lincoln's White House*, 133.

24. Hart, *Salmon Portland Chase*, 318.

25. Burlingame and Ettlinger, *Inside Lincoln's White House*, 77.

26. CW, 6:12.

27. Burlingame and Ettlinger, *Inside Lincoln's White House*, 103.

28. Beale, *Diary of Edward Bates*, 310.

29. Burlingame and Ettlinger, *Inside Lincoln's White House*, 103.

30. King, *Lincoln's Manager*, 201.

31. Ibid., 213.

32. Burlingame and Ettlinger, *Inside Lincoln's White House*, 78.

33. Ibid., 212, 213.

34. CW, 7:419.

35. Niven, *Salmon P. Chase*, 366.

36. Beale and Brownsword, *Diary of Gideon Welles*, 2:63.

37. Beale, *Diary of Edward Bates*, 381.

38. Smith, *Francis Preston Blair Family in Politics*, 2:271.

39. Niven, *Salmon P. Chase*, 371.

40. Ibid., 373.

41. Bates to AL, October 13, 1864, ALP-LC.

42. Sumner to AL, October 12 [*sic*], 1864, ALP-LC. Since Taney died late in the evening of October 12, Sumner's letter was either misdated or written in anticipation of the chief justice's imminent death.

43. David Dudley Field to AL, October 14, 1864; Bryant to AL, October 14, 1864; Medill to AL, October 15, 1864; Low and Stephen J. Field to AL, October 15, 1864; Sherman to AL, October 22, 1864; Colfax to AL, October 23, 1864, ALP-LC.

44. Sherman to AL, October 22, 1864, ALP-LC.

45. Medill to AL, October 15, 1864, ALP-LC.

46. Chandler to AL, October 15, 1864; Hamlin to AL, October 15, 1864; Hale to AL, October 16, 1864; Brewster to AL, October 14, 1864, ALP-LC.

47. Spalding to AL, October 13, 1864; Tod to AL, October 17, 1864; Moorhead to AL, October 19, 1864; Butler to AL, October 18, 1864; Davis to AL, October 18, 1864, ALP-LC.

48. C. Tower to AL, October 14, 1864 (recommending Sumner); Davis to AL, October 22, 1864; Waite to AL, October 22, 1864, ALP-LC. Morrison R. Waite (1816–1888) was appointed chief justice by President U. S. Grant in 1874. He served for fourteen years, until his death in 1888.

49. Pease and Randall, *Diary of Orville Hickman Browning,* 1:686–687.

50. Ibid., 688.

51. Fairman, *Reconstruction and Reunion,* 12.

52. David Davis to AL, October 22, 1864, ALP-LC.

53. Beale, *Diary of Edward Bates,* 428.

54. Sumner to AL, October 24, 1864, ALP-LC.

55. Niven, *Salmon P. Chase,* 374.

56. Goodwin, *Team of Rivals,* 677.

57. Niven, *Salmon P. Chase,* 374.

58. Brooks, "Personal Reminiscences of Lincoln," 677.

59. Niven, *Salmon P. Chase,* 374.

60. Brooks, *Lincoln Observed,* 153.

61. Brooks, *Washington in Lincoln's Time,* 177.

62. Boutwell, *Reminiscences of Sixty Years in Public Affairs,* 2:29. The authenticity of this quotation has been challenged, mainly by participants in later contests over Supreme Court appointments. Boutwell is apparently the only witness who reported that Lincoln said that "we cannot ask a man what he will do." To the extent that Lincoln seems to be saying that Supreme Court nominees should not be questioned about their views on controversial issues, those who favor intense questioning have called the statement foolish, or "un-Lincolnian." To the extent that the statement merely means that a nominee should not be asked to prejudge an issue likely to come before the Court, it seems to be reasonable and in character. Lin-

coln did know (or at least thought he knew) Chase's opinions on emancipation and legal tender and thus did not have to question him about those issues. In the end, he proved to be wrong on legal tender, but Chase himself may not have known his constitutional view on that issue at the time he was appointed. Understood in context, this quotation does not seem to be less credible than many other Lincoln statements remembered by only one person. The extent to which a judicial nominee may legitimately be questioned during the confirmation process was not widely discussed in the nineteenth century, and there is no reason to suspect that Boutwell manufactured this comment out of thin air. Don E. Fehrenbacher and Virginia Fehrenbacher, *Recollected Words of Abraham Lincoln,* 38, have assigned the statement a grade of C on a scale of A to E, suggesting that although it was not recorded contemporaneously it may nevertheless be authentic.

63. See AL, "Response to a Serenade," CW, 8:254; see also Guelzo, *Lincoln's Emancipation Proclamation,* 198, 211, 229.

64. It is worth noting that Lincoln never considered the possibility that Chase might recuse himself from cases in which he had personally been involved. In later years, a Supreme Court justice would decline to participate in such a case. In Lincoln's and Chase's time, however, there was no ethical bar to full participation.

65. Beale and Brownsword, *Diary of Gideon Welles,* 2:196.

66. SPC to AL, December 6, 1864, ALP-LC.

67. Niven, *Salmon P. Chase,* 375.

68. AL to Simon Cameron, August 19, 1961, CW, 4:491–492.

69. Donald, *Lincoln,* 186–187.

70. Julian, *Political Recollections,* 211–212.

71. "Memoranda," 2 Wall. (69 U.S.) ix–xii (1869).

72. Brooks, *Washington in Lincoln's Time,* 175, 176.

73. White, *Lincoln's Greatest Speech,* 180–181.

9. *A Law for Rulers and People*

1. Niven, *Salmon P. Chase,* 376.

2. CG, 39th Cong., 1st sess., 1866, 1718.

3. John B. Alley, in Rice, *Reminiscences of Abraham Lincoln,* 586. Vorenberg, *Final Freedom,* 180, says: "No piece of legislation during Lincoln's presidency received more of his attention than the Thirteenth Amendment."

4. CW, 8:254.

5. Ibid., 8:399–405.

6. Fairman, *Reconstruction and Reunion,* 96.

7. Niven, *Salmon P. Chase,* 395, 408–410.

8. Ibid., 378.

9. Ibid.

10. Ibid.

11. According to Neely, "thousands and thousands" of civilians were arrested by military authorities during the war. However, most were citizens of the Confederate states, and most arrests had nothing to do with dissent or political opposition to the Lincoln administration. "There were more arrests, but they had less significance for traditional civil liberty than anyone has realized." Neely, *Fate of Liberty*, xii, 137, 138.

12. *Ex parte Vallandigham*, 1 Wall. (68 U.S.) 243 (1864); see discussion in Chapter 6.

13. *Ex parte Merryman*, 17 Fed. Case. 144 (C.C.D. Md. 1861); see discussion in Chapter 3.

14. Farber, *Lincoln's Constitution*, 159, argues that this language was "carefully ambiguous" about whether Congress was enforcing its own power to suspend the writ or merely recognizing a power to suspend in the hands of the president.

15. Act of March 3, 1863, chap. 81, 12 Stat. 755.

16. CW, 8:233–234.

17. Beale and Brownsword, *Diary of Gideon Welles*, 2:242–243.

18. Ibid., 2:245–246.

19. Fairman, *Reconstruction and Reunion*, 58.

20. *Independent*, February 9, 1865, p. 1.

21. Nygaard, "Cracking the High Court," 37.

22. Palmer, *Selected Letters of Charles Sumner*, 2:260.

23. Fairman, *Reconstruction and Reunion*, 60.

24. Lawrence, *James Moore Wayne*, 194.

25. Fairman, *Reconstruction and Reunion*, 60n111.

26. White, *Lincoln's Greatest Speech*, 199.

27. Oakes, *The Radical and the Republican*, 242.

28. Fairman, *Reconstruction and Reunion*, 146.

29. SPC to G. W. Brooks, March 20, 1866, AJP-LC.

30. King, *Lincoln's Manager*, 226.

31. Ibid.

32. Ibid., 243.

33. Klement, "The Indianapolis Treason Trials and *Ex parte Milligan*," 110.

34. *Ex parte Vallandigham*, 1 Wall. (68 U.S.) 243 (1864).

35. Klement, "The Indianapolis Treason Trials and *Ex parte Milligan*," 114.

36. Statement of Joseph E. McDonald to Jesse W. Weik, August 28, 1888, in Herndon and Weik, *Herndon's Life of Lincoln*, 449.

37. Statement of David Davis to William H. Herndon, September 10, 1866, in Herndon and Weik, *Herndon's Life of Lincoln*, 449.

38. *Ex parte Milligan*, 4 Wall. (71 U.S.) 2, 8 (1866).

39. Fairman, *Reconstruction and Reunion*, 200.

40. Act of July 2, 1862, chap. 128, 12 Stat. 502.

41. Act of January 24, 1865, chap. 20, 13 Stat. 424.

42. "General Rules," 69 U.S. [2 Wall.] vii.

43. *Cummings v. Missouri*, 4 Wall. (71 U.S.) 277, 280–281 (1867).

44. Ibid., 277, 281.

45. See Act of September 24, 1789, chap. 20, Sec. 25, 1 Stat. 73 (Judiciary Act of 1789).

46. Fairman, *Mr. Justice Miller and the Supreme Court*, 118.

47. Proclamation No. 1, April 2, 1866, 14 Stat. 811.

48. *Ex parte Milligan*, 4 Wall. (71 U.S.) 2, 107 (1866).

49. In 2006, Chief Justice John Roberts took no part in the consideration or decision of *Hamdan v. Rumsfeld*, 126 S.Ct. 2749 (2006) because he had participated in the decision of the same case in the Court of Appeals for the District of Columbia Circuit.

50. King, *Lincoln's Manager*, 201.

51. Ibid., 254.

52. Fairman, *Reconstruction and Reunion*, 153.

53. Ibid., 157–158.

54. *Ex parte Milligan*, 4 Wall. (71 U.S.) 2, 118–119 (1866).

55. Ibid., 119–120.

56. Ibid., 127.

57. Neely, *Fate of Liberty*, 176.

58. *Ex parte Milligan*, 4 Wall. (71 U.S.) 2, 132, 140–141 (1866).

59. *Ex parte Garland*, 4 Wall. (71 U.S.), 333, 374–381.

60. USC, Art. II, Sec. 1, provides: "No person except a natural born citizen, or a citizen of the United States, at the time of the adoption of this Constitution, shall be eligible to the office of President." USC, Amend. XII, provides: "No person constitutionally ineligible to the office of President shall be eligible to that of Vice-President of the United States."

61. *Ex parte Garland*, 4 Wall. (71 U.S.) 333, 382–399 (1866).

62. "General Rules," 4 Wall. (71 U.S.) vii.

63. NYT, January 27, 1899, p. 7; Newberry, *Life of Mr. Garland*, 93–95.

64. Warren, *Supreme Court in United States History*, 2:437.

65. *Louisville Daily Democrat*, January 5, 1867, p. 2.

66. Warren, *Supreme Court in United States History*, 2:432.

67. Ibid., 2:433n1.

68. *Independent*, January 10, 1867, p. 4.

69. Fairman, *Reconstruction and Reunion*, 219.

70. *Chicago Tribune*, January 5, 1867, p. 2.

71. Warren, *Supreme Court in United States History*, 2:374. Silver, *Lincoln's Supreme Court*, 233.

72. Woldman, *Lawyer Lincoln*, 318, 319, admits that *Milligan* did not deal with the president's power to suspend habeas corpus but inconsistently claims that *Milligan* "completely vindicated" Taney's *Merryman* decision.

73. Fairman, *Reconstruction and Reunion*, 229.

74. Ibid., 231.

75. Ibid., 234.

10. *The Union Is Unbroken*

1. Fairman, *Reconstruction and Reunion*, 26.

2. *Ex parte Milligan*, 4 Wall. (71 U.S.) 2 (1866); *Ex parte Garland*, 4 Wall. (71 U.S.) 333 (1866); for discussion, see Chapter 9.

3. Act of April 9, 1866, chap. 31, 14 Stat. 27, Sec. 1.

4. Fairman, *Reconstruction and Reunion*, 162.

5. Ibid., 160–161.

6. CG, 39th Cong., 1st sess., 1866, 1259.

7. Fairman, *Reconstruction and Reunion*, 163–167.

8. Act of July 23, 1866, chap. 210, 14 Stat. 209.

9. U.S. Congress, Senate Exec. Journal, 39th Cong., 1st sess., July 20, 1866, 994.

10. Ibid., July 23, 1866, 1043.

11. See, e.g., Warren, *Supreme Court in United States History*, 2:422–423; Schwartz, *History of the Supreme Court*, 157; Kutler, *Judicial Power and Reconstruction Politics*, 4, 63; Abraham, *Justices, Presidents, and Senators*, 93; Lurie, *Chase Court*, 73; King, *Lincoln's Manager*, 260.

12. Fairman, *Reconstruction and Reunion*, 172.

13. The bill reducing the number of judges was presented to President Johnson on July 20, 1866, and signed by him on July 23, 1866. See Act of July 23, 1866, chap. 210, 14 Stat. 209.

14. Fairman, *Reconstruction and Reunion*, 170.

15. Lawrence, *James Moore Wayne*, 213.

16. Ibid., 214.

17. *Ex parte Vallandigham*, 1 Wall. (68 U.S.) 243 (1864); for discussion, see Chapter 6.

18. *Ex parte Milligan*, 4 Wall. (71 U.S.) 2 (1866).

19. Fairman, *Reconstruction and Reunion*, 569–570.

20. Ibid., 237–239.

21. *Cummings v. Missouri*, 4 Wall. (71 U.S.) 277 (1867); *Ex parte Garland*, 4 Wall. (71 U.S.) 333 (1866); for discussion, see Chapter 9.

22. Act of March 2, 1867, chap. 153, Sec. 3, 14 Stat. 428.

23. *Ex parte McCardle*, 6 Wall. (73 U.S.) 318 (1868).

24. This provision is commonly called the "exceptions clause." A court's "original jurisdiction" is its power to hear a case as an initial matter, while "appellate jurisdiction" is its power to hear an appeal from another court.

25. Act of February 5, 1867, chap. 28, Sec. 2, 14 Stat. 385.

26. King, *Lincoln's Manager*, 264.

27. Act of March 27, 1868, chap. 34, Sec. 2, 15 Stat. 44.

28. *Ex parte McCardle*, 7 Wall. (74 U.S.) 506, 514 (1869).

29. Pease and Randall, *Diary of Orville Hickman Browning*, 2:191.

30. Beale and Brownsword, *Diary of Gideon Welles*, 3:320.

31. This statement was printed, with minor variations, in newspapers around the country. The slightly shortened version here appears in Field, *Personal Reminiscences*, 173.

32. See Kutler, *Judicial Power and Reconstruction Politics*, 5.

33. *Ex parte McCardle*, 7 Wall. (74 U.S.) 506, 515 (1869).

34. Act of September 24, 1789, chap. 20, Sec. 14, 1 Stat. 73, 81–82.

35. *Ex parte Yerger*, 8 Wall. (75 U.S.) 85, 102 (1869).

36. Kutler, *Judicial Power and Reconstruction Politics*, 108.

37. Act of March 2, 1867, chap. 154, 14 Stat. 430. In *Myers v. United States*, 272 U.S. 52 (1926), the Supreme Court held a law requiring the consent of the Senate for removal of certain postmasters unconstitutional as a denial of the president's executive powers under the Constitution.

38. *Supplement to the Congressional Globe Considering the Proceedings of the Senate Sitting for the Trial of Andrew Johnson*, 3–5.

39. Niven, *Salmon P. Chase*, 420.

40. Fairman, *Reconstruction and Reunion*, 527.

41. Ibid., 529.

42. Ibid., 540.

43. Ibid., 544.

44. Ibid., 534.

45. Niven, *Salmon P. Chase*, 429.

46. "The Week," *Nation* 7 (July 16, 1868): 41.

47. For discussion, see Chapter 8.

48. *McCulloch v. Maryland*, 4 Wheat. (17 U.S.) 316, 421 (1819).

49. Act of September 24, 1789, chap. 20, Sec. 25, 1 Stat. 73.

50. *Roosevelt v. Meyer*, 1 Wall. (68 U.S.) 512, 517 (1863). In *Trebilock v. Wilson*, 12 Wall. (79 U.S.) 687 (1872), the Supreme Court conceded that *Roosevelt v. Meyer* was incorrectly decided, for the Judiciary Act of 1789 also permitted appeal to the Supreme Court when a right claimed under the Constitution or a federal statute had been denied in the state court. Since Roosevelt's claim was based on the Con-

stitution, and since it was denied in the New York court, the Supreme Court did have jurisdiction to hear the case. It has sometimes been argued that the Supreme Court chose to deny jurisdiction in *Roosevelt v. Meyer* to avoid deciding the legal tender issue, thus saving the administration from an embarrassing defeat. But Fairman, *Reconstruction and Reunion*, 697–698, argues persuasively that the incorrect decision in *Roosevelt v. Meyer* was inadvertent.

51. *Bronson v. Rodes*, 7 Wall. (74 U.S.) 229, 250 (1868).
52. Ibid., 258.
53. Act of July 13, 1866, chap. 184, Sec. 9, 14 Stat. 98, 146.
54. *Veazie Bank v. Fenno*, 8 Wall. (75 U.S.) 533, 549 (1869).
55. "Resignation of Mr. Justice Grier," 8 Wall. (75 U.S.) vii; Fairman, *Mr. Justice Miller*, 164.
56. Act of April 10, 1869, chap. 22, 16 Stat. 44.
57. "A Statement of Facts Relating to the Order of the Supreme Court of the United States for a Re-argument of the Legal-Tender Question, in April, 1870," in Bradley, *Miscellaneous Writings of the Late Hon. Joseph P. Bradley*, 61–74.
58. William Strong and Joseph P. Bradley, who were shortly to join the Court, also signed the April 1870 statement, although their knowledge of the facts related only to the period after they became justices. Miller prepared the extraordinary document because of concerns about Chase's handling of the legal tender issue. He retained the statement until his death in 1890, when Justice Bradley obtained it and kept it until his death in 1892. Bradley turned it over to his son Charles Bradley with instructions that it should not be made public "as long as any Justice who was on the bench at that time was still living." Justice Field's death in 1899 marked the end of this episode, and Charles Bradley published the statement in 1901.
59. "A Statement of Facts."
60. Ibid., 73–74.
61. "Resignation of Mr. Justice Grier," 8 Wall. (75 U.S.) vii.
62. "Death of the Hon. E. M. Stanton," 8 Wall. (75 U.S.) xxi.
63. Fairman, *Reconstruction and Reunion*, 717.
64. "A Statement of Facts," 71.
65. *McCulloch v. Maryland*, 4 Wheat. (17 U.S.) 316, 421 (1819).
66. *Hepburn v. Griswold*, 8 Wall. (75 U.S.) 603, 623 (1869).
67. Niven, *Salmon P. Chase*, 297.
68. *Hepburn v. Griswold*, 8 Wall. (75 U.S.) 603, 625–626 (1869).
69. Ibid., 627.
70. *McCulloch v. Maryland*, 4 Wheat. (17 U.S.) 316, 415 (1819).
71. *Hepburn v. Griswold*, 8 Wall. (75 U.S.) 603, 631 (1869).

72. Ibid., 637.

73. Ibid., 638.

74. Fairman, *Reconstruction and Reunion,* 720.

75. "A Statement of Facts," 71–72.

76. Fairman, *Mr. Justice Miller,* 170.

77. *Legal Tender Cases,* 12 Wall. (79 U.S.) 457, 528–529 (1870).

78. Ibid., 534.

79. *Washington Daily Morning Chronicle,* February 12, 1870, p. 2.

80. "Legal Tender," *Harper's Weekly,* March 19, 1870, p. 179.

81. "The Legal Tender Decision," *Nation* 10 (February 17, 1870): 100.

82. Hyman, *Reconstruction Justice of Salmon P. Chase,* 169.

83. *Julliard v. Greenman,* 110 U.S. 421 (1884).

84. CW, 4:264–265.

85. *Texas v. White,* 7 Wall. (74 U.S.) 700, 725 (1868).

86. *Lane County v. Oregon,* 7 Wall. (74 U.S.) 71, 76 (1868).

87. *Texas v. White,* 7 Wall. (74 U.S.) 700, 725 (1868).

88. Fairman, *Reconstruction and Reunion,* 628.

11. *History in Marble*

1. CG, 38th Cong., 2nd sess., 1865, 1012.

2. Ibid.

3. Ibid.

4. *Dred Scott v. Sandford,* 19 How. (60 U.S.) 393, 407 (1857); for discussion, see Chapter 2.

5. CG, 38th Cong., 2nd sess., 1865, 1013.

6. Ibid., 1013–1014.

7. Ibid. 1014

8. Ibid., 1016.

9. Ibid.

10. Ibid., 1017.

11. Ibid.

12. *Congressional Record,* 43rd Cong., 1st sess., 1873, 77.

13. Ibid., 1874, 694–695, 929, 1036.

14. See Donald, *Lincoln,* 599, for Stanton's comments: "Now he belongs to the ages."

15. Vorenberg, *Final Freedom,* 96–98, 110–111, 113, 137.

16. Donald, *Lincoln,* 476.

17. CW, 8:333.

18. Donald, *Charles Sumner,* 583.

19. The Thirteenth Amendment was ratified December 6, 1865; the Fourteenth July 9, 1868; and the Fifteenth February 3, 1870.

Afterword: The Legacy

1. CW, 4:331–332.
2. *Prize Cases*, 2 Black (67 U.S.) 635, 669 (1863); for further discussion, see Chapter 5.
3. CW, 4:429.
4. Act of August 6, 1861, chap. 63, Sec. 3, 12 Stat. 326.
5. *Prize Cases*, 2 Black (67 U.S.) 635, 671 (1863).
6. *Ex parte Merryman*, 17 Fed. Case. 144, 148–153 (C.C.D. Md. 1861); for discussion, see Chapter 3.
7. Jackson, "The Power to Suspend Habeas Corpus," 12; see discussion in Chapter 3.
8. *Hamdi v. Rumsfeld*, 542 U.S. 507, 536 (2004), emphasis added.
9. Ibid., 562.
10. Ibid., 525.
11. Act of March 3, 1863, chap. 81, 12 Stat. 755; see Chapter 9.
12. *Youngstown Sheet and Tube Co. v. Sawyer*, 343 U.S. 579, 635–638 (1952).
13. In a footnote to his concurring opinion in the steel seizure case, Justice William O. Douglas noted laconically: "What a President may do as a matter of expediency or extremity may never reach a definitive constitutional decision. For example, President Lincoln suspended the writ of habeas corpus, claiming the constitutional right to do so. See *Ex parte Merryman*, 17 Fed. Cas. No. 9,487. Congress ratified his action by the Act of March 3, 1863. 12 Stat. 755." *Youngstown Sheet and Tube Co. v. Sawyer*, 343 U.S. 579, 634n. 1 (1952).
14. Warren, *Supreme Court in United States History*, 2:427, 439.
15. Nevins, "The Case of the Copperhead Conspirator," 107.
16. Fairman, *Reconstruction and Reunion*, 212.
17. Neely, *Fate of Liberty*, 175–176.
18. Fairman, *Reconstruction and Reunion*, 232.
19. Rehnquist, *All the Laws but One*, 137.
20. Ibid., 224–225.
21. Neely, *The Fate of Liberty*, 181–184.
22. *Ex parte Quirin*, 317 U.S. 1, 46 (1942).
23. *Duncan v. Kahanamoku*, 327 U.S. 304, 324 (1946).
24. *Rumsfeld v. Padilla*, 542 U.S. 426 (2004).
25. *Rasul v. Bush*, 542 U.S. 466 (2004); see 28 United States Code Sec. 2241 (federal habeas corpus statute).
26. *Hamdi v. Rumsfeld*, 542 U.S. 507, 521–522 (2004).

27. *Hamdan v. Rumsfeld*, 126 S. Ct. 2749 (2006).

28. *Hamdi v. Rumsfeld*, 542 U.S. 507, 536 (2004).

29. Herndon and Weik, *Herndon's Life of Lincoln*, 449n.

30. AL to Erastus Corning and others, June 1863 (Copy No. 1), ALP-LC.

31. CW, 8:152.

32. See Act of August 6, 1861, chap. 60, 12 Stat. 319; Act of July 17, 1862, chap. 195, 12 Stat. 589.

33. Guelzo, *Lincoln's Emancipation Proclamation*, 75.

34. CW, 6:28–30.

35. Ibid., 6:428–429.

36. Amar, *America's Constitution*, 357.

37. Hofstadter, *The American Political Tradition and the Men Who Made It*, 131.

38. Guelzo, *Lincoln's Emancipation Proclamation*, 8.

Bibliography

Official Publications

Official Records of the Union and Confederate Navies in the War of the Rebellion. 30 vols. Washington, DC: Government Printing Office, 1894–1922.

The War of the Rebellion: A Compilation of the Official Records of the Union and Confederate Armies. 128 vols. Washington, DC: Government Printing Office, 1880–1901.

Judicial Reports

Blatchford, Samuel. *Reports of Cases in Prize Argued and Determined in the Circuit and District Courts of the United States, for the Southern District of New York, 1861–'65.* New York: Baker, Voorhis, 1866.

Habeas Corpus. The Proceedings in the Case of John Merryman, of Baltimore County, Maryland, before the Hon. Roger Brooke Taney, Chief Justice of the Supreme Court of the United States. Baltimore: Lucas Brothers, 1861.

Decisions of Hon. Peleg Sprague in Maritime, Admiralty, and Prize Causes in the District Court of the United States for the District of Massachusetts, 1854–1864. Boston: Little, Brown, 1868.

Newspapers

Baltimore Daily Republican
Baltimore Sun
Charleston Mercury
Chicago Daily Tribune

Louisville Democrat
New Orleans Daily Picayune
New York Evening Post
New York Herald
New York Independent
New York Times
New York Tribune
New York World
Philadelphia Public Ledger
Richmond Enquirer
Southern Confederacy (Atlanta)
Washington Chronicle (Washington, DC)

Manuscript Collections

Jeremiah Sullivan Black Papers, Library of Congress
Francis Preston Blair Papers, Library of Congress
Salmon P. Chase Papers, Library of Congress
Nathan Clifford Collection, Maine Historical Society, Augusta
David Davis Papers, Library of Congress
John Eager Howard Papers, Maryland Historical Society, Baltimore
Andrew Johnson Papers, Library of Congress
Ward Hill Lamon Papers, Huntington Library, San Marino, CA
Abraham Lincoln Papers, Library of Congress
John Merryman Papers, Maryland Historical Society, Baltimore
David M. Perine Papers, Maryland Historical Society, Baltimore
William H. Seward Papers, Library of Congress
Edwin McMasters Stanton Papers, Library of Congress
Carl Brent Swisher Collection, Library of Congress
Roger B. Taney Papers, Library of Congress
Roger B. Taney Papers, Maryland Historical Society, Baltimore
Lyman Trumbull Papers, Library of Congress
Elihu B. Washburne Papers, Library of Congress
James Moore Wayne Papers, Georgia Historical Society, Savannah

Books and Articles

Abraham, Henry J. *Justices, Presidents, and Senators: A History of the U.S. Supreme
    Court Appointments from Washington to Clinton.* Rev. ed. Lanham, MD: Rowman
    and Littlefield, 1999.

Adams, Charles Francis. *Richard Henry Dana: A Biography*. 2 vols. Boston: Houghton Mifflin, 1890.

Adams, Ephraim Douglass. *Great Britain and the American Civil War*. 2 vols. New York: Russell and Russell, 1925.

Allen, Austin. *Origins of the Dred Scott Case: Jacksonian Jurisprudence and the Supreme Court 1837–1857*. Athens: University of Georgia Press, 2006.

Amar, Akhil Reed. *America's Constitution: A Biography*. New York: Random House, 2005.

Anderson, Burnett. "James M. Wayne." In *The Supreme Court Justices: Illustrated Biographies, 1789–1995*. Edited by Clare Cushman, 2nd ed., 111–115. Washington, DC: Congressional Quarterly, 1995.

———. "John A. Campbell." In *The Supreme Court Justices: Illustrated Biographies, 1789–1995*. Edited by Clare Cushman, 2nd ed., 161–165. Washington, DC: Congressional Quarterly, 1995.

———. "John Catron." In *The Supreme Court Justices: Illustrated Biographies, 1789–1995*. Edited by Clare Cushman, 2nd ed., 126–130. Washington, DC: Congressional Quarterly, 1995.

———. "John McLean." In *The Supreme Court Justices: Illustrated Biographies, 1789–1995*. Edited by Clare Cushman, 2nd ed., 101–105. Washington, DC: Congressional Quarterly, 1995.

———. "Noah H. Swayne." In *The Supreme Court Justices: Illustrated Biographies, 1789–1995*. Edited by Clare Cushman, 2nd ed., 171–175. Washington, DC: Congressional Quarterly, 1995.

———. "Robert C. Grier." In *The Supreme Court Justices: Illustrated Biographies, 1789–1995*. Edited by Clare Cushman, 2nd ed., 151–155. Washington, DC: Congressional Quarterly, 1995.

———. "Samuel F. Miller." In *The Supreme Court Justices: Illustrated Biographies, 1789–1995*. Edited by Clare Cushman, 2nd ed., 176–180. Washington, DC: Congressional Quarterly, 1995.

Anderson, Stuart. "1861: Blockade vs. Closing the Confederate Ports." *Military Affairs* 41, no. 4 (1977): 190–194.

Angle, Paul, ed. *The Lincoln Reader*. New Brunswick, NJ: Rutgers University Press, 1947.

Atkinson, David N. *Leaving the Bench: Supreme Court Justices at the End*. Lawrence: University Press of Kansas, 1999.

Bancroft, Frederic. *The Life of William H. Seward*, 2 vols. New York: Harper, 1900.

Basler, Roy P., ed. *The Collected Works of Abraham Lincoln*. 9 vols. New Brunswick, NJ: Rutgers University Press, 1953–1955.

Beale, Howard K., ed. *The Diary of Edward Bates, 1859–1866*. Washington, DC: Government Printing Office, 1933.

Beale, Howard K., and Alan W. Brownsword, eds. *Diary of Gideon Welles, Secretary of the Navy under Lincoln and Johnson.* 3 vols. New York: W. W. Norton, 1960.

Belz, Herman. *Abraham Lincoln, Constitutionalism, and Equal Rights in the Civil War Era.* New York: Fordham University Press, 1998.

———. "The Supreme Court and Constitutional Responsibility in the Civil War Era." In *The Supreme Court and the Civil War: A Special Edition of the Journal of Supreme Court History.* Edited by Jennifer M. Lowe, 5–8. Washington, DC: Supreme Court Historical Society, 1996.

Bernath, Stuart L. *Squall across the Atlantic: American Civil War Prize Cases and Diplomacy.* Berkeley and Los Angeles: University of California Press, 1970.

Binney, Horace. *The Privilege of the Writ of Habeas Corpus under the Constitution.* Philadelphia: T. B. Pugh, 1862.

Borrett, George Tuthill. *Letters from Canada and the United States.* London: J. D. Adlard, Bartholomew Close, 1865.

Boutwell, George S. *Reminiscences of Sixty Years in Public Affairs.* 2 vols. New York: McClure, Phillips, 1902.

Bradley, Charles, ed. *Miscellaneous Writings of the Late Hon. Joseph P. Bradley.* Newark, NJ: L. J. Hardham, 1901. Reprint, Littleton, CO: Fred B. Rothman, 1986.

Brooks, Noah. *Lincoln Observed: Civil War Dispatches of Noah Brooks.* Edited by Michael Burlingame. Baltimore: Johns Hopkins University Press, 1998.

———. "Personal Reminiscences of Lincoln." *Scribner's Monthly* 15 (1878): 561–569, 673–678.

———. *Washington in Lincoln's Time.* Edited by Herbert Mitgang. New York: Rinehart, 1958.

Brown, George William. *Baltimore and the Nineteenth of April, 1861: A Study of the War.* Baltimore: N. Murray, 1887. Reprint, Baltimore: Johns Hopkins University Press, 2001.

Browning, Robert M., Jr. *From Cape Charles to Cape Fear: The North Atlantic Blockading Squadron during the Civil War.* Tuscaloosa: University of Alabama Press, 1993.

Bruce, Robert V. *Lincoln and the Riddle of Death.* Fort Wayne, IN: Louis A. Warren Lincoln Library and Museum, 1981.

Burlingame, Michael, and John R. Turner Ettlinger, eds. *Inside Lincoln's White House: The Complete Civil War Diary of John Hay.* Carbondale: Southern Illinois University Press, 1997.

Cain, Marvin R. *Lincoln's Attorney General: Edward Bates of Missouri.* Columbia: University of Missouri Press, 1965.

Calhoun, Frederick S. *The Lawmen: United States Marshals and Their Deputies, 1789–1989.* Washington, DC: Smithsonian Institution Press, 1989.

Carter, Samuel, III. *Blaze of Glory: The Fight for New Orleans, 1814–1815.* New York: St. Martin's Press, 1971.

Chandler, Walter. "The Centenary of Associate Justice John Catron of the United States Supreme Court." *Tennessee Law Review* 15 (1937–1939): 32–51.

Clifford, Philip Greely. *Nathan Clifford, Democrat (1803–1881)*. New York: G. P. Putnam's Sons, 1922.

Connor, Henry G. *John Archibald Campbell, Associate Justice of the United States Supreme Court, 1853–1861*. Boston: Houghton Mifflin, 1920. Reprint, Clark, NJ: Lawbook Exchange, 2004.

Cottom, Robert I., Jr., and Mary Ellen Hayward. *Maryland in the Civil War: A House Divided*. Baltimore: Maryland Historical Society, 1994.

Crist, Lynda Lasswell, and Mary Seaton Dix, eds. *The Papers of Jefferson Davis*. Vol. 7. Baton Rouge: Louisiana State University Press, 1992.

Curtis, Benjamin R. *Executive Power*. Boston: Little, Brown, 1862.

———. *A Memoir of Benjamin Robbins Curtis, LL.D.* 2 vols. Boston: Little, Brown, 1879.

Curtis, Michael Kent. "Lincoln, Vallandigham, and Anti-War Speech in the Civil War." *William & Mary Bill of Rights Journal* 7 (1998): 105–191.

Cushman, Clare. "Roger B. Taney." In *The Supreme Court Justices: Illustrated Biographies, 1789–1995*. Edited by Clare Cushman, 2nd ed., 116–120. Washington, DC: Congressional Quarterly, 1995.

———. "Salmon P. Chase." In *The Supreme Court Justices: Illustrated Biographies, 1789–1995*. Edited by Clare Cushman, 2nd ed., 191–195. Washington, DC: Congressional Quarterly, 1995.

———. "Samuel Nelson." In *The Supreme Court Justices: Illustrated Biographies, 1789–1995*. Edited by Clare Cushman, 2nd ed., 141–145. Washington, DC: Congressional Quarterly, 1995.

Davis, William C. *Jefferson Davis: The Man and His Hour*. New York: HarperCollins, 1991.

Delaplaine, Edward S. "Lincoln after Taney's Death." *Lincoln Herald* 79 (1977): 151–157.

Dirck, Brian. *Lincoln the Lawyer*. Urbana: University of Illinois Press, 2007.

Donald, David Herbert. *Charles Sumner*. New York: Da Capo Press, 1996.

———, ed. *Inside Lincoln's Cabinet: The Civil War Diaries of Salmon P. Chase*. New York: Longmans, Green, 1954.

———. *Lincoln*. New York: Simon & Schuster, 1995.

———. *Lincoln Reconsidered: Essays on the Civil War Era*. New York: Vintage Books, 2001.

———. *"We Are Lincoln Men": Abraham Lincoln and His Friends*. New York: Simon & Schuster, 2003.

Downey, Arthur T. "The Conflict between the Chief Justice and the Chief Executive: *Ex Parte Merryman*." *Journal of Supreme Court History* 31 (2006): 262–278.

Duker, William F. *A Constitutional History of Habeas Corpus*. Westport, CT: Greenwood Press, 1980.

Elliott, Charles Winslow. *Winfield Scott: The Soldier and the Man*. New York: Macmillan Company, 1937.

"*Ex Parte* Merryman: Proceedings of Court Day, May 26, 1861." *Maryland Historical Magazine* 56 (1961): 384–398.

Fairman, Charles. *Mr. Justice Miller and the Supreme Court, 1862–1890*. Cambridge, MA: Harvard University Press, 1939.

———. *Reconstruction and Reunion, 1864–88, Part One*. Vol. 6, *Oliver Wendell Holmes Devise History of the Supreme Court of the United States*. New York: Macmillan; London: Collier-Macmillan, 1971.

Farber, Daniel. *Lincoln's Constitution*. Chicago: University of Chicago Press, 2003.

Fehrenbacher, Don. E. *The Dred Scott Case: Its Significance in American Law and Politics*. New York: Oxford University Press, 1978.

———. "Roger B. Taney and the Sectional Crisis." *Journal of Southern History* 43 (1977): 555–566.

Fehrenbacher, Don E., and Virginia Fehrenbacher. *Recollected Words of Abraham Lincoln*. Stanford: Stanford University Press, 1996.

Field, Henry M. *The Life of David Dudley Field*. New York: Charles Scribner's Sons, 1898. Reprint, Littleton, CO: Fred B. Rothman, 1995.

Field, Stephen J. *Personal Reminiscences of Early Days in California*. Washington, DC: Printed for a few friends, 1893. Reprint, New York: Da Capo Press, 1968.

Finkelman, Paul. *Dred Scott v. Sandford: A Brief History with Documents*. Boston: Bedford/St. Martin's, 1997.

———. "'Hooted Down the Page of History': Reconsidering the Greatness of Chief Justice Taney." *Journal of Supreme Court History* 1994: 83–102.

Frank, John P. *Justice Daniel Dissenting: A Biography of Peter V. Daniel, 1784–1860*. Cambridge, MA: Harvard University Press, 1964.

———. *Lincoln as a Lawyer*. Urbana: University of Illinois Press, 1961.

———. "Peter V. Daniel." In *The Supreme Court Justices: Illustrated Biographies, 1789–1995*. Edited by Clare Cushman, 2nd ed., 136–140. Washington, DC: Congressional Quarterly, 1995.

Fried, Joseph P. "The U.S. Supreme Court during the Civil War." *Civil War Times Illustrated* 1, no. 10 (February 1963): 28–35.

Friedman, Leon. "Salmon P. Chase." In *The Justices of the United States Supreme Court, 1789–1969: Their Lives and Major Opinions*. Edited by Leon Friedman and Fred L. Israel, vol. 1, 1113–1128. New York: Chelsea House, 1969.

Friedman, Leon, and Fred L. Israel, eds. *The Justices of the United States Supreme Court, 1789–1969: Their Lives and Major Opinions*. 4 vols. New York: Chelsea House, 1969.

Gatell, Frank Otto. "James M. Wayne." In *The Justices of the United States Supreme Court, 1789–1969: Their Lives and Major Opinions*. Edited by Leon Friedman and Fred L. Israel, vol. 1, 601–611. New York: Chelsea House, 1969.

———. "John Catron." In *The Justices of the United States Supreme Court, 1789–1969: Their Lives and Major Opinions.* Edited by Leon Friedman and Fred L. Israel, vol. 1, 737–749. New York: Chelsea House, 1969.

———. "John McLean." In *The Justices of the United States Supreme Court, 1789–1969: Their Lives and Major Opinions.* Edited by Leon Friedman and Fred L. Israel, vol. 1, 535–546. New York: Chelsea House, 1969.

———. "Robert C. Grier." In *The Justices of the United States Supreme Court, 1789–1969: Their Lives and Major Opinions.* Edited by Leon Friedman and Fred L. Israel, vol. 2, 873–883. New York: Chelsea House, 1969.

———. "Roger B. Taney." In *The Justices of the United States Supreme Court, 1789–1969: Their Lives and Major Opinions.* Edited by Leon Friedman and Fred L. Israel, vol. 1, 635–655. New York: Chelsea House, 1969.

———. "Samuel Nelson." In *The Justices of the United States Supreme Court, 1789–1969: Their Lives and Major Opinions.* Edited by Leon Friedman and Fred L. Israel, vol. 2, 817–829. New York: Chelsea House, 1969.

Gillette, William. "John A. Campbell." In *The Justices of the United States Supreme Court, 1789–1969: Their Lives and Major Opinions.* Edited by Leon Friedman and Fred L. Israel, vol. 2, 927–939. New York: Chelsea House, 1969.

———. "Nathan Clifford." In *The Justices of the United States Supreme Court, 1789–1969: Their Lives and Major Opinions.* Edited by Leon Friedman and Fred L. Israel, vol. 2, 963–975. New York: Chelsea House, 1969.

———. "Noah H. Swayne." In *The Justices of the United States Supreme Court, 1789–1969: Their Lives and Major Opinions.* Edited by Leon Friedman and Fred L. Israel, vol. 2, 989–999. New York: Chelsea House, 1969.

———. "Samuel Miller." In *The Justices of the United States Supreme Court, 1789–1969: Their Lives and Major Opinions.* Edited by Leon Friedman and Fred L. Israel, vol. 2, 1011–1024. New York: Chelsea House, 1969.

Goodwin, Doris Kearns. *Team of Rivals: The Political Genius of Abraham Lincoln.* New York: Simon & Schuster, 2005.

Guelzo, Allen C. *Lincoln's Emancipation Proclamation: The End of Slavery in America.* New York: Simon & Schuster, 2004.

Hart, Albert Bushnell. *Salmon Portland Chase.* Boston: Houghton Mifflin, 1899.

Hartnett, Edward A. "The Constitutional Puzzle of Habeas Corpus." *Boston College Law Review* 46 (2005): 251–291.

Herndon, William H., and Jesse W. Weik. *Herndon's Life of Lincoln: The History and Personal Recollections of Abraham Lincoln as Originally Written by William H. Herndon and Jesse W. Weik.* Introduction and notes by Paul M. Angle. Cleveland: World Publishing Co., 1949.

Hofstadter, Richard. *The American Political Tradition and the Men Who Made It.* New York: Alfred A. Knopf, 1948.

Holzer, Harold. *Lincoln at Cooper Union: The Speech That Made Abraham Lincoln President.* New York: Simon & Schuster, 2004.

Holzer, Harold, ed. *The Lincoln-Douglas Debates: The First Complete, Unexpurgated Text.* New York: Fordham University Press, 2004.

Hopkins, V[incent] Charles. *Dred Scott's Case.* New York: Russell and Russell, 1967.

Howard, McHenry. *Recollections of a Maryland Confederate Soldier and Staff Officer under Johnston, Jackson and Lee.* Baltimore: Williams and Wilkins, 1914. Reprint, Dayton, OH: Morningside Bookshop, 1975.

Huebner, Timothy S. *The Southern Judicial Tradition: State Judges and Sectional Distinctiveness, 1790–1890.* Athens: University of Georgia Press, 1999.

———. *The Taney Court: Justices, Rulings, and Legacy.* Santa Barbara, CA: ABC-CLIO, 2003.

Hyman, Harold M. *A More Perfect Union: The Impact of the Civil War and Reconstruction on the Constitution.* New York: Alfred A. Knopf, 1973.

———. *The Reconstruction Justice of Salmon P. Chase: In Re Turner and Texas v. White.* Lawrence: University Press of Kansas, 1997.

Jackson, Jeffrey D. "The Power to Suspend Habeas Corpus: An Answer from the Arguments Surrounding *Ex Parte Merryman.*" *University of Baltimore Law Review* 34 (2004–2005): 11–54.

Jaffa, Harry V. "Abraham Lincoln." In *Encyclopedia of the American Constitution.* Edited by Leonard W. Levy, Kenneth L. Karst, and Dennis J. Mahoney. New York: Macmillan, 1986.

———. *A New Birth of Freedom: Abraham Lincoln and the Coming of the Civil War.* Lanham, MD: Rowman and Littlefield, 2000.

Julian, George. *Political Recollections, 1840 to 1872.* Chicago: Jansen, McClurg, 1884.

Kaufman, Kenneth C. *Dred Scott's Advocate: A Biography of Roswell M. Field.* Columbia: University of Missouri Press, 1996.

Kens, Paul. *Justice Stephen Field: Shaping Liberty from the Gold Rush to the Gilded Age.* Lawrence: University Press of Kansas, 1997.

King, Willard L. *Lincoln's Manager, David Davis.* Cambridge, MA: Harvard University Press, 1960.

Klaus, Samuel, ed. *The Milligan Case.* New York: Alfred A. Knopf, 1929. Reprint, New York: Da Capo Press, 1970.

Klement, Frank L. *The Copperheads in the Middle West.* Chicago: University of Chicago Press, 1960.

———. "The Indianapolis Treason Trials and *Ex Parte Milligan.*" In *American Political Trials.* Edited by Michal R. Belknap, 101–127. Westport, CT: Greenwood Press, 1981.

———. *The Limits of Dissent: Clement L. Vallandigham and the Civil War.* New York: Fordham University Press, 1998. Originally published 1970 by University Press of Kentucky.

Koenig, Louis W. "'The Most Unpopular Man in the North.'" *American Heritage* 15, no. 2 (February 1964): 12–14, 81–88.

Kohn, Alan C. "*Failing Justice: Charles Evans Whittaker of the Supreme Court*, by Craig Alan Smith." *Journal of Supreme Court History* 31 (2006): 91–96.

Kutler, Stanley I. "David Davis." In *The Justices of the United States Supreme Court, 1789–1969: Their Lives and Major Opinions*. Edited by Leon Friedman and Fred L. Israel, vol. 2, 1045–1053. New York: Chelsea House, 1969.

———. *Judicial Power and Reconstruction Politics*. Chicago: University of Chicago Press, 1968.

Lamon, Ward Hill. *The Life of Abraham Lincoln*. Boston: James R. Osgood, 1872.

———. *Recollections of Abraham Lincoln, 1847–1865*. Edited by Dorothy Lamon Teilhard. Chicago: A. C. McClurg, 1895.

Larson, Henrietta M. *Jay Cooke, Private Banker*. Cambridge, MA: Harvard University Press, 1936. Reprint, New York: Greenwood Press, 1968.

Lawrence, Alexander A. *James Moore Wayne, Southern Unionist*. Chapel Hill: University of North Carolina Press, 1943.

Lewis, Walker. *Without Fear or Favor: A Biography of Chief Justice Roger Brooke Taney*. Boston: Houghton Mifflin, 1965.

Lincoln, Abraham. *Collected Works of Abraham Lincoln*. Edited by Roy P. Basler. 9 vols. New Brunswick, NJ: Rutgers University Press, 1953–1955.

Logan, Mrs. John A. *Thirty Years in Washington: or Life and Scenes in Our National Capital*. Hartford, CT: A. D. Worthington, 1901.

Lowe, Jennifer M., ed. *The Supreme Court and the Civil War: A Special Edition of the Journal of Supreme Court History*. Washington, DC: Supreme Court Historical Society, 1996.

Lurie, Jonathan. *The Chase Court: Justices, Rulings, and Legacy*. Santa Barbara, CA: ABC-CLIO, 2004.

Madison, James. *The Debates in the Federal Convention of 1787 Which Framed the Constitution of the United States of America*. Edited by Gaillard Hunt and James Brown Scott. New York: Oxford University Press, 1920. Reprint, Westport, CT: Greenwood Press, 1970.

Marvin, William. *A Treatise on the Law of Wreck and Salvage*. Boston: Little, Brown, 1858.

McCloskey, Robert. "Stephen J. Field." In *The Justices of the United States Supreme Court, 1789–1969: Their Lives and Major Opinions*. Edited by Leon Friedman and Fred L. Israel, vol. 2, 1069–1089. New York: Chelsea House, 1969.

McGinty, Brian. "A Heap o' Trouble." *American History Illustrated* 16, no. 2 (May 1981): 34–39.

———. "War in the Court." *Civil War Times Illustrated* 19, no. 5 (August 1980): 22–25, 39–41.

McPherson, James M. *Battle Cry of Freedom: The Civil War Era*. New York: Oxford University Press, 1988.

Murray, Robert Bruce. *Legal Cases of the Civil War*. Harrisburg, PA: Stackpole Books, 2003.

Neely, Mark E., Jr. *The Fate of Liberty: Abraham Lincoln and Civil Liberties*. New York: Oxford University Press, 1991.

———. "Justice Embattled: The Lincoln Administration and the Controversy over Conscription in 1863." In *The Supreme Court and the Civil War: A Special Edition of the Journal of Supreme Court History*. Edited by Jennifer M. Lowe, 47–61. Washington, DC: Supreme Court Historical Society, 1996.

Nevins, Allan. "The Case of the Copperhead Conspirator." In *Quarrels That Have Shaped the Constitution*. Edited by John A. Garraty, 90–108. New York: Harper & Row, 1996.

Newberry, Farrar. *A Life of Mr. Garland of Arkansas: A Thesis for the Master's Degree*. N.p., privately printed, 1908.

Newmyer, R. Kent. *The Supreme Court under Marshall and Taney*. Wheeling, IL: Harlan Davidson, 1968.

Newton, Thomas Wodehouse Legh, Baron. *Lord Lyons: A Record of British Diplomacy*. Vol. 1. London: Edward Arnold, 1913.

Nicolay, John G., and John Hay. *Abraham Lincoln: A History*. 10 vols. New York: Century Co., 1890

———. "Lincoln's Inauguration." *The Century* 35 (December 1887): 265–283.

Niehoff, Leonard M. "David Davis." In *The Supreme Court Justices: Illustrated Biographies, 1789–1995*. Edited by Clare Cushman, 2nd ed., 181–185. Washington, DC: Congressional Quarterly, 1995.

Niven, John. *Salmon P. Chase: A Biography*. New York: Oxford University Press, 1995.

Niven, John, et al., eds. *The Salmon P. Chase Papers*. 5 vols. Kent, OH: Kent State University Press, 1993.

Nygaard, Richard L. "Cracking the High Court." In *Law Day Stories: An Anthology of Stories about Lawyers, Lawmakers, and the Law*, 34–37. Chicago: American Bar Association Special Committee on Youth Education for Citizenship, 1995.

Oakes, James. *The Radical and the Republican: Frederick Douglass, Abraham Lincoln, and the Triumph of Antislavery Politics*. New York: W. W. Norton, 2007.

Palmer, Ben W. *Marshall and Taney: Statesmen of the Law*. New York: Russell and Russell, 1966.

Palmer, Beverly Wilson, ed. *The Selected Letters of Charles Sumner*. Vol. 2. Boston: Northeastern University Press, 1990.

Paludan, Phillip Shaw. "Taney, Lincoln and the Constitutional Conversation." In *The Supreme Court and the Civil War: A Special Edition of the Journal of Supreme Court History*. Edited by Jennifer M. Lowe, 22–35. Washington, DC: Supreme Court Historical Society, 1996.

———. *The Presidency of Abraham Lincoln*. Lawrence: University Press of Kansas, 1994.

Pease, Theodore Calvin, and James G. Randall, eds. *The Diary of Orville Hickman Browning.* 2 vols. (Collections of the Illinois State Historical Library, vols. 20 and 22.) Springfield: Illinois State Historical Library, 1925, 1933.

Phillips, Ulrich B., ed. "The Correspondence of Robert Toombs, Alexander H. Stephens, and Howell Cobb." *Annual Report of the American Historical Association for the Year 1911.* Washington, DC: Government Printing Office, 1913.

Pierce, Edward L., ed. *Memoir and Letters of Charles Sumner.* Vol. 4. Boston: Roberts Brothers, 1893.

Pomeroy, John Norton. *Some Account of the Work of Stephen J. Field. As a Legislator, State Judge, and Judge of the Supreme Court of the United States.* New York: S. B. Smith, 1881. Reprint, Littleton, CO: Fred B. Rothman, 1986.

Porter, David. *Incidents and Anecdotes of the Civil War.* New York: D. Appleton, 1886.

Pride, David T. "Nathan Clifford." In *The Supreme Court Justices: Illustrated Biographies, 1789–1995.* Edited by Clare Cushman, 2nd ed., 166–170. Washington, DC: Congressional Quarterly, 1995.

———. "Stephen J. Field." In *The Supreme Court Justices: Illustrated Biographies, 1789–1995.* Edited by Clare Cushman, 2nd ed., 186–190. Washington, DC: Congressional Quarterly, 1995.

Proceedings of the Bench and Bar of the Supreme Court of the United States In Memoriam John Archibald Campbell. Washington, DC: Government Printing Office, 1889.

Proceedings of the Bench and Bar of the Supreme Court of the United States In Memoriam Nathan Clifford. Washington, DC: Government Printing Office, 1881.

Proceedings of the Bench and Bar of the Supreme Court of the United States on the Occasion of the Death of Benjamin R. Curtis, Formerly an Associate Justice of the Said Court, at the October Term, 1874. Washington, DC: Joseph L. Pearson, Printer, 1874.

Proceedings of the Bench and Bar of the Supreme Court of the United States on the Occasion of the Death of Roger Brooke Taney, Fifth Chief Justice of the Said Court, at the December Term, 1864. Washington, DC: McGill & Witherow, 1865.

Randall, James G. *Constitutional Problems under Lincoln.* Rev. ed. Urbana: University of Illinois Press, 1964.

———. *Lincoln the President: Midstream.* New York: Dodd, Mead, 1952.

Rehnquist, William H. *All the Laws but One: Civil Liberties in Wartime.* New York: Alfred A. Knopf, 1998.

———. *The Supreme Court.* New ed. New York: Alfred A. Knopf, 2001.

Rice, Allen Thorndike, ed. *Reminiscences of Abraham Lincoln by Distinguished Men of His Time.* New York: North American Review, 1888.

Richardson, James D. *Compilation of the Messages and Papers of the Presidents.* Vol. 7. New York: Bureau of National Literature, 1897.

Ross, Michael A. *Justice of Shattered Dreams: Samuel Freeman Miller and the Supreme*

Court during the Civil War Era. Baton Rouge: Louisiana State University Press,
 2003.

Rossiter, Clinton. *The Supreme Court and the Commander in Chief.* Ithaca: Cornell University Press, 1951.

Saunders, Robert, Jr. *John Archibald Campbell, Southern Moderate, 1811–1889.*
 Tuscaloosa: University of Alabama Press, 1997.

Schurz, Carl. *The Reminiscences of Carl Schurz.* 3 vols. New York: McClure, 1907–
 1908.

Schwartz, Bernard. *A History of the Supreme Court.* New York: Oxford University Press,
 1993.

Segal, Charles M., ed. *Conversations with Lincoln.* New York: G. P. Putnam's Sons,
 1961.

Semonche, John E. *Keeping the Faith: A Cultural History of the U.S. Supreme Court.*
 Lanham, MD: Rowman and Littlefield, 1998.

Shapiro, Samuel. *Richard Henry Dana, Jr., 1815–1882.* East Lansing: Michigan State
 University Press, 1961.

Sheads, Scott Sumpter, and Daniel Carroll Toomey. *Baltimore during the Civil War.*
 Linthicum, MD: Toomey Press, 1997.

Shurtleff, Kathleen. "Benjamin R. Curtis." In *The Supreme Court Justices: Illustrated Biographies, 1789–1995.* Edited by Clare Cushman, 2nd ed., 156–160. Washington,
 DC: Congressional Quarterly, 1995.

Siegel, Martin. *The Taney Court: 1836–1864.* Vol. 3, *The Supreme Court in American
 Life.* Millwood, NY: Associated Faculty Press, 1987.

Silver, David M. *Lincoln's Supreme Court.* Urbana: University of Illinois Press, 1956.

Simon, James F. *Lincoln and Chief Justice Taney: Slavery, Secession, and the President's
 War Powers.* New York: Simon & Schuster, 2006.

Smith, Charles W., Jr. *Roger B. Taney: Jacksonian Jurist.* Chapel Hill: University of
 North Carolina Press, 1936.

Smith, William Ernest. *The Francis Preston Blair Family in Politics.* 2 vols. New York:
 Macmillan, 1933. Reprint, New York: Da Capo Press, 1969.

Steiner, Bernard C. *Life of Roger Brooke Taney, Chief Justice of the United States Supreme
 Court.* Baltimore: Williams and Wilkins, 1922.

Steiner, Mark E. *An Honest Calling: The Law Practice of Abraham Lincoln.* DeKalb:
 Northern Illinois University Press, 2006.

Streichler, Stuart. *Justice Curtis in the Civil War Era: At the Crossroads of American
 Constitutionalism.* Charlottesville: University of Virginia Press, 2005.

*Supplement to the Congressional Globe: Containing the Proceedings of the Senate Sitting for
 the Trial of Andrew Johnson, President of the United States. Fortieth Congress, Second
 Session.* Washington: Rives and Bailey, 1868.

Strong, George Templeton. *The Diary of George Templeton Strong.* Edited by Allan

Nevins and Milton Halsey Thomas. Abridged by Thomas J. Pressly. Seattle: University of Washington Press, 1988.

Surdam, David G. "The Union Navy's Blockade Reconsidered." *Naval War College Review* 51, no. 4 (1998): 85–107.

Surrency, Erwin C. *History of the Federal Courts*. New York: Oceana Publications, 1987.

Swisher, Carl Brent. "Mr. Chief Justice Taney." In *Mr. Justice*. Edited by Allison Dunham and Philip B. Kurland. Chicago: University of Chicago Press, 1956.

———. *Roger B. Taney*. New York: Macmillan, 1935. Reprint, Hamden, CT: Archon Books, 1961.

———. *Stephen J. Field: Craftsman of the Law*. Washington, DC: Brookings Institution, 1930. Reprint, Hamden, CT: Archon Books, 1963.

———. *The Taney Period, 1836–64*. Vol. 5, *Oliver Wendell Holmes Devise History of the Supreme Court of the United States*. New York: Macmillan; London: Collier-Macmillan, 1974.

Tyler, Samuel. *Memoir of Roger Brooke Taney, LL.D., Chief Justice of the Supreme Court of the United States*. Baltimore: John Murphy, 1872. Reprint, New York: Da Capo Press, 1970.

Vladeck, Stephen I. "The Field Theory: Martial Law, the Suspension Power, and the Insurrection Act." *Temple Law Review* 80 (2007).

Vorenberg, Michael. *Final Freedom: The Civil War, the Abolition of Slavery, and the Thirteenth Amendment*. Cambridge: Cambridge University Press, 2001.

The War of the Rebellion: A Compilation of the Official Records of the Union and Confederate Armies. 70 vols. Washington, DC: Government Printing Office, 1880–1901.

Warren, Charles. *The Supreme Court in United States History*. Rev. ed., 2 vols. Boston: Little, Brown, 1926.

Weber, Jennifer L. *Copperheads: The Rise and Fall of Lincoln's Opponents in the North*. New York: Oxford University Press, 2006.

Weisenburger, Francis P. *The Life of John McLean: A Politician on the United States Supreme Court*. Columbus: Ohio State University Press, 1937. Reprint, New York: Da Capo Press, 1971.

Welles, Gideon. *Lincoln and Seward: Remarks upon the Memorial Address of Chas. Francis Adams, on the Late Wm. H. Seward*. New York: Sheldon & Company, 1874. Reprint, Freeport, NY: Books for Libraries Press, 1969.

Wheaton, Henry. *Elements of International Law*. 8th ed. Edited, with notes, by Richard Henry Dana, Jr. Boston: Little, Brown, 1866.

White, G. Edward. "Salmon Portland Chase and the Judicial Culture of the Supreme Court in the Civil War Era." In *The Supreme Court and the Civil War: A Special Edition of the Journal of Supreme Court History*. Edited by Jennifer M. Lowe, 37–45. Washington, DC: Supreme Court Historical Society, 1996.

White, Ronald C. *Lincoln's Greatest Speech: The Second Inaugural*. New York: Simon & Schuster, 2002.

Williams, Frank J. *Judging Lincoln*. Carbondale: Southern Illinois University Press, 2002.

Wilson, Douglas L. *Lincoln's Sword: The Presidency and the Power of Words*. New York: Alfred A. Knopf, 2006.

Woldman, Albert A. *Lawyer Lincoln*. New York: Carroll & Graf, 1994.

Woodward, C. Vann, ed. *Mary Chesnut's Civil War*. New Haven: Yale University Press, 1981.

Acknowledgments

Thanks to William C. (Jack) Davis of the Virginia Center for Civil War Studies, editor, prolific author, and eloquent historian of the Civil War, for recommending this book to Harvard University Press, and to Kathleen McDermott, Alexander Morgan, and Julie Ericksen Hagen, who combined to give it a good home after it arrived at Harvard. My appreciation also to Deborah Lawrence of California State University, Fullerton, and Jon Lawrence of the University of California, Irvine, who helped with my research at the Huntington Library in San Marino, and to the librarians at the Sandra Day O'Connor College of Law at Arizona State University in Tempe, the Hayden Library at ASU, the Maryland Historical Society in Baltimore, and the Library of Congress in Washington. The curator of the Supreme Court helped me gather portraits of the Supreme Court justices. Mert and Marianne Kayan of Silver Spring, Maryland, were kind hosts during two long research trips to Washington, and Jim Barnett was a never-failing source of support and encouragement.

Beyond all of this, it would be futile to name names, for many years in and out of the law have brought me in contact with countless men and women—professors, judges, fellow lawyers, and others—who have contributed to my appreciation of the Supreme Court as an indispensable institution in American life, and Abraham Lincoln as the looming presence of American history.

Index